SPANISH NOW!
VOL. 2
¡El español actual!

by

Christopher Kendris, Ph.D.

Mont Pleasant Public High School
Schenectady, New York

BARRON'S

New York • London • Toronto • Sydney

Title page photo: Man on a swing drawing by GOYA, Courtesy of The Hispanic Society of America (Museum and Library), New York, New York.

For St. Sophia Greek Orthodox Church of Albany, New York, my parish.

For my family: My lovely wife Yolanda, my two handsome sons Alex and Ted, who are gentlemen and scholars, my sweet daughter-in-law Tina Marie McMaster Kendris, my two lovable and well-behaved grandchildren Alexander Bryan and Daniel Patrick Christopher. God bless my family with love, health, happiness, and good and honorable works.

For my brother, Dr. Thomas Kendris, and for his wife Athena and their family.

For my friends since childhood, Melba Anastas Lee and her sister Bessie Anastas, and Bill Lee.

For my friends, Mary and Tom Mangus of Norfolk, Virginia, and for their son John.

With love

And to the beautiful memory of Teresa and Ronald Gilbert who were very kind to me when I first met them in Maine many years ago until they died. God bless their souls.

All inquiries should be addressed to:
Barron's Educational Series, Inc.
250 Wireless Boulevard
Hauppauge, New York 11788

Library of Congress Catalog Card No. 87-20141

International Standard Book No. 0-8120-2518-0

Library of Congress Cataloging-in-Publication Data

Kendris, Christopher.
    Spanish now! : vol. two = El español actual! / by Christopher Kendris.
      p.   cm.
    Includes index.
    ISBN 0-8120-2518-0
    1. Spanish language—Grammar—1950-
    2. Spanish language—Text-books for foreign speakers—English.
I.Title. II. Title: Español actual.
PC4112.K44 1987   87-20141
468.2'421—dc19   CIP

PRINTED IN THE UNITED STATES OF AMERICA

789   100   987654321

Table of Contents

Structures and Verbs

Note to Teachers and Students

SPANISH NOW! Vol. 2 is a work that reflects my strong desire to make the study of Spanish stimulating for the student of any age by infusing the book with life and vigor. It contains original stories (some of which are humorous), many skits, playlets, sketches, scenes and dialogues. The book is also saturated with exercises that will please the traditional and the modern teacher because the drills and exercises are imaginative, varied and entertaining.

This book also features evidence of Spanish as a living language used throughout the world. The book contains photographs of authentic documents, famous Spanish persons and places, crossword and other word games that tease the brain, simple riddles, proverbs, reproductions of masterpieces of Spanish art, and many other features not found normally in a Spanish textbook. You say that masterpieces of Spanish art belong in a museum? That they are dead? They are dead when a student is not aware of them. They are alive when a student sees them. Some masterpieces of Spanish art are in this book to educate our students so that they can become aware of such great Spanish artists as Goya, Sorolla, Murillo, Velázquez, El Greco, just to mention a few. Have you ever noticed, for example, that in the painting *The Duchess of Alba* by Goya (which is in Work Unit 10) the duchess is pointing to the floor near her feet where the artist signed his name upside-down? Take a close look at the delicate detail of her gown and the unusual expression on her face. Personally, I consider this painting the *Mona Lisa* of great Spanish art. Give me one good reason why our students should not have the chance to see Spanish art by great Spanish masters. The few included in this volume might very well inspire some of our students to appreciate Spanish art.

The stories and dialogues in this volume, for the most part, tell of the adventures of an imaginary Spanish family: Clara and Francisco Rodríguez and their two children, Juana and Pedro, and their dog, Coco. This book makes studying Spanish fun! There is something in it for every teacher and every student of Spanish.

Supplemental materials such as transparencies, cassettes, and other audiolingual software can be used advantageously because this book contains stories, dialogues, and a variety of exercises that give abundant practice in basic and intermediate reading, writing, and speaking in Spanish.

The language content in this book meets the minimum standards and sequence of a course of study in Spanish level 2 presented in curriculum guides issued, for example, by the New York State Education Department, Bureau of Secondary Curriculum Development, and those of the New York City Foreign Language Program for secondary schools.

A separate manual with answer keys to all exercises is provided for the teacher.

Special thanks go out to my friends and colleagues, Dr. Hilda Garcerán de Vall and her distinguished husband Dr. Julio Garcerán, who are both teachers of the Spanish language, and who are authors of the book *Guía del idioma español,* published by Las Americas Publishing Company. I deeply appreciate their helpful suggestions while reading the manuscript to make certain that the Spanish contained in this book is *correcto como debe ser.*

I am also grateful for the assistance provided by the Embajada de España, Oficina Cultural, Washington, D.C., for furnishing me with dates, facts, figures, and cultural information in the introduction and elsewhere in this book.

If you have any suggestions as to the improvement of this book in the next edition, please let me know by writing to the publisher. I will appreciate it.

Christopher Kendris
B.S., M.S., M.A., Ph.D.

About the Author

Dr. Christopher Kendris earned his B.S. and M.S. degrees at Columbia University where he held a New York State scholarship, and his M.A. and Ph.D. degrees at Northwestern University. He also earned two diplomas with distinction at the Université de Paris (en Sorbonne), Faculté des Lettres, Ecole Supérieure de Préparation et de Perfectionnement des Professeurs de Français à l'Etranger, and at the Institut de Phonétique (en Sorbonne), Paris. In 1986, he was one of ninety-five teachers in the U.S. who was awarded a Rockefeller Foundation Fellowship for Teachers of Foreign Languages in American High Schools. His fellowship provided for summer studies in Europe in creative ways to teach Romance Languages.

Dr. Kendris is currently teaching languages at Mont Pleasant Public High School in Schenectady, NY. He has taught foreign languages at the College of The University of Chicago as visiting summer lecturer and at Northwestern University, where he held a Teaching Assistantship in French and Tutorial Fellowships in Spanish and French for four years. He has also taught at Colby College, Duke University, Rutgers—the State University of New Jersey, and the State University of New York at Albany. He served as Chairman of the Foreign Languages Department at Farmingdale High School, Farmingdale, NY, where he was also a teacher of Spanish and French. He also worked at The Library of Congress, Washington, D.C. using his language skills.

Dr. Kendris has lived in France, Greece, and Germany and has traveled in Canada, England, Belgium, Switzerland, Italy, Spain, and Portugal.

Introduction

Reprinted with permission of United Nations

¡Hola!	¡Buenos días!	¡Hola!	¡Buenos días!	¡Hola!	¡Buenos días!
Hi!	Hello!	Hi!	Hello!	Hi!	Hello!

Did you know that there are approximately 300,000,000 Spanish-speaking people all over the world? Spanish is the official language in the following lands: Spain, Argentina, Peru, Chile, Ecuador, Bolivia, Uruguay, Paraguay, Colombia, Venezuela, Costa Rica, Honduras, Guatemala, El Salvador, Nicaragua, Mexico, Cuba, the Dominican Republic, Equatorial Guinea (a republic in West equatorial Africa, formerly known as Spanish Guinea), and the Philippines, where Spanish is one of the three official languages. According to the 1980 census, it is estimated that 11.1 million Americans use Spanish at home and about three-fourths of these Spanish-speaking Americans also speak English. **¡Totalmente formidable!**

Abbreviations Used In This Book

abs. absolute
adj. adjective
adv. adverb
art. article
aux. auxiliary (helping)
ca. circa, about, around + year
cf. compare
conj. conjunction
def. definite
dem. demonstrative
dir. direct
ed. edition
e.g. for example
etc. and so on, and so forth
excl. exclamation
f., fem. feminine
fam. familiar
ff. and the following
fut. future
i.e. that is, that is to say
imper. imperative
imperf. imperfect
indef. indefinite
indic. indicative
indir. indirect

interj. interjection
m., masc. masculine
n. noun
neg. negative
neut. neuter
num. numeral, number
obj. object
part. participle
perf. perfect
pers. person
pl. plural
pluperf. pluperfect
poss. possessive
prep. preposition
pres. present
pret. preterit
prog. progressive
pron. pronoun
refl. reflexive
rel. relative
s., sing. singular
sub. subjunctive
subj. subject
superl. superlative
v. verb
WU Work Unit

STRUCTURES AND VERBS

La familia Rodríguez: Presentación

Somos la familia Rodríguez. Somos cinco en la familia.

Me llamo Clara Rodríguez. Soy la madre. Tengo un buen esposo. Estoy contenta.

Me llamo Francisco Rodríguez. Soy el padre. Tengo una buena esposa. Estoy contento.

5

Me llamo Juana Rodríguez. Soy la hija. Tengo un buen hermano. Estoy contenta.

Me llamo Pedro Rodríguez. Soy el hijo. Tengo una buena hermana. Estoy contento.

Me llamo Coco. Soy el perrito. Tengo una buena familia. Estoy contento.

10

VOCABULARIO: Consult the vocabulary section in the back pages.

PRESENTE DE INDICATIVO		PRESENTE DE INDICATIVO	
ser (to be)		estar (to be)	
Singular		Singular	
yo	**soy**	yo	**estoy**
tú	**eres**	tú	**estás**
Ud. (él, ella)	**es**	Ud. (él, ella)	**está**
Plural		Plural	
nosotros (-as)	**somos**	nosotros (-as)	**estamos**
vosotros (-as)	**sois**	vosotros (-as)	**estáis**
Uds. (ellos, ellas)	**son**	Uds. (ellos, ellas)	**están**

EJERCICIOS

I. Conteste las siguientes preguntas con oraciones completas según la presentación de esta lección.

1. ¿Cómo se llama la madre? _____

2. ¿Cómo se llama el padre? _____

3. ¿Cómo se llama la hija? _____

4. ¿Cómo se llama el hijo? _____

5. ¿Cómo se llama el perrito? _____

II. Complete las siguientes oraciones según la presentación de esta lección.

1. Clara Rodríguez es _____; está _____

2. Francisco Rodríguez es _____; está _____

3. Juana Rodríguez es _____; está _____

4. Pedro Rodríguez es _____; está _____

5. Coco es _____; está _____

III. Escriba las seis formas del verbo **ser** en el presente de indicativo _____

_____

IV. Escriba las seis formas del verbo **estar** en el presente de indicativo _____

_____

3

REVIEW EXERCISES SPANISH LEVEL 1

I. Conteste las siguientes preguntas con oraciones completas.

Modelo: ¿Cómo se llama usted?   **Respuesta:** Me llamo Carlos Santiago.

1. ¿Cómo se llama usted? _____

2. ¿Cuántos años tiene usted? _____

3. ¿En qué ciudad vive usted? ¿Cuál es la dirección? _____

_____

4. ¿Cuántos días hay en el mes de enero? _____

5. Mencione dos cosas que usted tiene en el bolsillo en este momento. _____

_____

II. Escriba oraciones completas empleando los siguientes modismos.

1. tener hambre: _____

2. tener sed: _____

3. tener prisa: _____

4. tener frío: _____

5. tener calor: _____

III. Escriba oraciones completas empleando los siguientes modismos.

1. hacer un viaje: _____

2. hacer una pregunta: _____

3. estar bien: _____

4. estar de acuerdo: _____

5. ir de compras: _____

Estructuras de la lengua

SER AND ESTAR

These two verbs mean *to be* but note the differences in use:

Generally speaking, use **ser** when you want to express *to be.*

Use **estar** when *to be* is used in the following ways:

(a) Health: **¿Cómo está Ud.?** / How are you?

> **Estoy bien** / I am well.
> **Estoy enfermo (enferma)** / I am sick.

(b) Location: persons, places, things

> (1) **Estoy en la sala de clase** / I am in the classroom.
> (2) **La escuela está lejos** / The school is far.
> (3) **Barcelona está en España** / Barcelona is (located) in Spain.
> (4) **Los libros están en la mesa** / The books are on the table.

(c) State or condition that may change: persons

> (1) **Estoy contento (contenta)** / I am happy.
> (2) **Los alumnos están cansados (Las alumnas están cansadas)** / The students are tired.
> (3) **María está triste hoy** / Mary is sad today.
> (4) **Estoy listo (lista)** / I am ready.
> (5) **Estoy pálido (pálida)** / I am pale.
> (6) **Estoy ocupado (ocupada)** / I am busy.
> (7) **Estoy seguro (segura)** / I am sure.
> (8) **Este hombre está vivo** / This man is alive.
> (9) **Ese hombre está muerto** / That man is dead.
> (10) **Este hombre está borracho** / This man is drunk.

(d) State or condition that may change: things and places

> (1) **La ventana está abierta** / The window is open.
> (2) **La taza está llena** / The cup is full.
> (3) **El té está caliente** / The tea is hot.
> (4) **La limonada está fría** / The lemonade is cold.
> (5) **La biblioteca está cerrada los domingos** / The library is closed on Sundays.

(e) To form the progressive present of a verb, use the present tense of **estar** + the present participle of the main verb:

> **Estoy estudiando en mi cuarto y no puedo salir esta noche** / I am studying in my room and I cannot go out tonight.

(f) To form the progressive past of a verb, use the imperfect tense of **estar** + the present participle of the main verb:

> **Mi hermano estaba leyendo cuando (yo) entré en el cuarto** / My brother was reading when I entered (came into) the room.

5

Dos diferencias

Dibujo 1

Dibujo 2

Entre estos dos dibujos existen dos diferencias. ¿Cuáles son?
There are two differences in these two drawings. What are they?

    Modelo: En oraciones completas, escriba las dos diferencias entre los dos dibujos. *(In complete sentences, write the two differences between the two drawings.)*

    Solución: 1. En el primer dibujo, la ventana está abierta. En el segundo dibujo, la ventana está cerrada. *(In the first drawing, the window is open. In the second drawing, the window is closed.)*

                2. En el primer dibujo, el té (el café) está caliente. En el segundo dibujo, el té (el café) está frío (o: no está caliente). *(In the first drawing, the tea (coffee) is hot. In the second drawing, the tea (the coffee) is cold (or: is not hot.)*

EJERCICIOS

I. En oraciones completas escriba las dos diferencias entre los dos dibujos.

Dos diferencias

Dibujo 1

Dibujo 2

Entre estos dos dibujos existen dos diferencias. ¿Cuáles son?

Solución: 1. _____

_____

_____

2. _____

_____

_____

II. En oraciones completas, escriba las cuatro diferencias entre los dos dibujos.

Cuatro diferencias

Dibujo 1

Dibujo 2

Entre estos dos dibujos existen cuatro diferencias. ¿Cuáles son?

Solución: 1. _____

2. _____

3. _____

4. _____

ARTICLES

Definite article

There are four forms of the definite article (the) in Spanish. They are as follows:

	Singular	Plural
Masculine	**el**	**los**
Feminine	**la**	**las**

EXAMPLES:
> **el libro** (the book); **los libros** (the books)
> **la pluma** (the pen); **las plumas** (the pens)

A definite article agrees in gender and number with the noun it modifies.

If a noun is masculine singular, you must use the masculine singular form of *the*, which is **el.** If a noun is masculine plural, you must use the masculine plural form of *the*, which is **los.** If a noun is feminine singular, you must use the feminine singular form of *the*, which is **la.** If a noun is feminine plural, you must use the feminine plural form of *the*, which is **las.**

How do you know if a noun is masculine or feminine? See farther on in the beginning of the topic **Nouns.**

If a feminine singular noun begins with stressed **a** or **ha**, use **el**, not **la.** This is done in order to avoid slurring the **a** in **la** with the stressed **a** or **ha** at the beginning of the noun that follows. Actually, that is what happened; the two vowel sounds **a** were not pronounced distinctly because they were slurred and **el** replaced **la.** For example, **hambre** (hunger) is a feminine noun but in the singular it is stated as **el hambre.** NOTE: **Tengo mucha hambre.** And NOTE:

> **el agua** / the water; but **las aguas** / the waters
> **el hacha** / the axe; but **las hachas** / the axes

However, if the def. art. is in front of an adj. that precedes the noun, this is not observed: **la alta montaña** / the high (tall) mountain, **la árida llanura** / the arid (dry) prairie.

Contraction of the definite article el

When the preposition **a** or **de** is in front of the definite article **el,** it contracts as follows:

> **a** + **el** changes to **al**
> **de** + **el** changes to **del**

EXAMPLES:
> **Voy al parque** / I am going to the park.
> **Vengo del parque** / I am coming from the park.

But if the def. art. **el** is part of a denomination or title of a work, there is no contraction: **Los cuadros de El Greco.**

The definite article is used:

(a) In front of each noun even if there is more than one noun stated, as in a series, which is not always done in English: **Tengo el libro, el cuaderno, y la pluma** / I have the book, notebook, and pen.

(b) With a noun when you make a general statement: **Me gusta el café** / I like coffee; **La leche es buena para la salud** / Milk is good for health.

(c) With a noun of weight or measure: **un dólar la libra; un peso la libra** / one dollar a pound (per pound).

9

LAS CAMPOCOMIDAS
rápidas·nutritivas·deliciosas

Salchichón Gran Serrano

Chopped Pork

Salchichón Catedral

Lunch

Jamón Cocido Extra

Chorizo Pamplona

Salami

Reprinted with permission of LECTURAS (Ediciones HYMSA), Barcelona

(d) In front of a noun indicating a profession, rank, title followed by the name of the person: **El profesor Gómez es inteligente** / Professor Gómez is intelligent; **La señora García es muy amable** / Mrs. García is very nice; **El doctor Torres está enfermo** / Dr. Torres is sick.

But in direct address (when talking directly to the person and you mention the rank, profession, *etc.*), do not use the definite article: **Buenas noches, señor Gómez** / Good evening, Mr. Gómez.

(e) With the name of a language: **Estudio el español** / I study Spanish.

For examples of when you do not use the definite article with the name of a language, see **(b)** in the list "The definite article is not used," which follows.

(f) With the name of a subject matter: **Estudio la historia** / I study history.

(g) With the days of the week, when in English we use *on:* **Voy al cine el sábado** / I am going to the movies on Saturday.

(h) With parts of the body or articles of clothing, especially if the possessor is clearly stated: **Me pongo el sombrero** / I put on my hat; **Me lavo la cara todas las mañanas** / I wash my face every morning.

(i) With common expressions, for example: **a la escuela** / to school; **en la iglesia** / in church; **en la clase** / in class; **la semana pasada** / last week; **la semana próxima** / next week.

(j) With the seasons of the year: **en la primavera** / in spring; **en el verano** / in summer; **en el otoño** / in autumn; **en el invierno** / in winter.

(k) To show possession with the preposition **de** + a common noun: **el libro del alumno** / the pupil's book; **los libros de los alumnos** / the pupils' books; **los niños de las mujeres** / the women's children.

Note that when a proper noun is used, the definite article is not needed with **de** to show possession: **el libro de Juan** / John's book; **el libro de María** / Mary's book; **los libros de Juan y de María** / John's and Mary's books.

(l) With names of some cities, countries and continents: **la Argentina, el Brasil, el Canadá, los Estados Unidos, la Habana, la América del Norte, la América Central, la América del Sur.**

(m) With a proper noun modified by an adjective: **el pequeño José** / Little Joseph.

(n) With a noun in apposition with a pronoun: **Nosotros los norteamericanos** / We North Americans.

(o) With an infinitive used as a noun, especially when it begins a sentence: **El estudiar es bueno** / Studying is good. There are some exceptions: **Ver es creer** / Seeing is believing; and other proverbs. But you do not normally use the definite article with an infinitive if it does not begin a sentence: **Es bueno estudiar** / It is good to study. This is a general rule.

(p) When telling time: **Es la una** / It is one o'clock; **Son las dos** / It is two o'clock.

The definite article is not used:

(a) In direct address with the rank, profession, title of the person to whom you are talking or writing: **Buenos días, señora Molina** / Good morning, Mrs. Molina.

(b) After the verb **hablar** when the name of a language is right after a form of **hablar**: **Hablo español** / I speak Spanish.

(c) After the prepositions **en** and **de** with the name of a language or a subject matter: **Estoy escribiendo en inglés** / I am writing in English; **La señora Johnson es profesora de inglés** / Mrs. Johnson is a teacher of English; **El señor Gómez es profesor de historia** / Mr. Gómez is a teacher of history.

(d) With a proper noun to show possession when using **de: los libros de Marta** / Martha's books.

(e) With an infinitive if the infinitive does not begin the sentence: **Es bueno trabajar** / It is good to work. **Me gusta viajar** / I like to travel. This is a general rule.

(f) With a noun in apposition with a noun: **Madrid, capital de España, es una ciudad interesante** / Madrid, capital of Spain, is an interesting city.

(g) With a numeral that denotes the order of succession of a monarch: **Carlos V (Quinto)** / Charles the Fifth.

(h) With names of some countries and continents: **España** / Spain; **Francia** / France; **México** / Mexico; **Europa** / Europe; **Asia** / Asia; **África** / Africa.

EJERCICIOS

I. Discriminación de los sonidos. Su profesor de español va a pronunciar una sola palabra, sea la de la letra A, sea la de la letra B. Puntee A o B para indicar que su profesor de español ha pronunciado la palabra de la letra A o la palabra de la letra B.

> **Modelo:** ☉ A. hoy
> ☐ B. hay

He punteado la letra A porque creo que mi profesor de español ha pronunciado la palabra de la letra A.

1. ☐ A. pero   3. ☐ A. cuando
   ☐ B. perro   ☐ B. cuanto

2. ☐ A. porque   4. ☐ A. hacia
   ☐ B. ¿por qué?   ☐ B. hacía

II. Varias palabras en una sola. Utilizando las letras en la palabra **ADVENIR,** ¿cuántas palabras puede usted escribir? Escriba diez palabras, por lo menos.

> ADVENIR

1. _____   3. _____   5. _____   7. _____   9. _____

2. _____   4. _____   6. _____   8. _____   10. _____

III. Varias palabras en una sola. Utilizando las letras en la palabra **ESPAÑA,** ¿cuántas palabras puede usted escribir? Escriba cuatro palabras, por lo menos.

> ESPAÑA

1. _____   3. _____

2. _____   4. _____

IV. LETRA RELOJ. Tres palabras se esconden en este reloj: Una palabra de las doce a las cuatro, una palabra de las cuatro a las seis y, por fin, una palabra de las siete a las once.

La misma letra puede emplearse en la palabra que sigue. Este reloj no tiene agujas. ¡Es un reloj de palabras! Use la forma de ser o estar en el presente de indicativo.

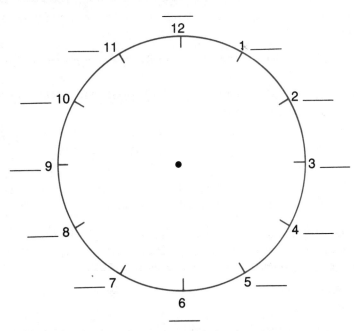

De las doce a las cuatro: Nosotros _____ la familia Rodríguez.

De las cuatro a las seis: Yo _____ el hijo.

De las siete a las once: Yo _____ contento.

The neuter article lo

The neuter article **lo** has idiomatic uses, generally speaking.
It is used:

(a) With a masculine singular form of an adjective that is used as a noun: **lo bueno** / the good; **lo malo** / the bad; **lo simpático** / what(ever) is kind.

(b) With a past participle: **lo dicho y lo escrito** / what has been said and what has been written.

(c) With an adjective or adverb + **que,** meaning *how:* **Veo lo fácil que es** / I see how easy it is.

Indefinite article

In Spanish, there are four forms of the indefinite article (a, an, some, a few). They are as follows:

	Singular	Plural
Masculine	**un**	**unos**
Feminine	**una**	**unas**

EXAMPLES:

> **un libro** (a book); **unos libros** (some books, a few books)
> **una naranja** (an orange); **unas naranjas** (some oranges, a few oranges)

An indefinite article agrees in gender and number with the noun it modifies.

If a noun is masculine singular, you must use the masculine singular form of *a, an* which is **un.** If a noun is masculine plural, you must use the masculine plural form of *some, a few* which is **unos.**

If a noun is feminine singular, you must use the feminine singular form of *a, an* which is **una.** If a noun is feminine plural, you must use the feminine plural form of *some, a few* which is **unas.**

How do you know if a noun is masculine or feminine? See farther on in the beginning of the topic **Nouns.**

The plural of the indefinite article indicates an indefinite number: **unas treinta personas** / some thirty persons.

The indefinite article is used:

(a) When you want to say *a* or *an.* It is also used as a numeral to mean *one:* **un libro** / a book or one book; **una pluma** / a pen or one pen. If you want to make it clear that you mean *one,* you may use **solamente** *(only)* in front of **un** or **una: Tengo solamente un libro** / I have (only) one book.

(b) With a modified noun of nationality, profession, rank, or religion: **El doctor Gómez es un médico excelente** / Dr. Gómez is an excellent doctor.

(c) In front of each noun in a series, which we do not always do in English: **Tengo un libro, un cuaderno y una pluma** / I have a book, notebook, and pen. This use is the same for the definite article in a series of nouns.

(d) In the plural when an indefinite number is indicated: **Tengo unos dólares** / I have some (a few) dollars.

The indefinite article is not used:

(a) With **cien** and **mil: cien libros** / a (one) hundred books; **mil dólares** / a (one) thousand dollars.

(b) **cierto, cierta** and **tal: cierto lugar** / a certain place; **cierta persona** / a certain person; **tal hombre** / such a man; **tal caso** / such a case

(c) With **otro, otra: otro libro** / another book; **otra pluma** / another pen.

(d) With an unmodified noun of nationality, profession, rank, or religion: **Mi hijo es dentista** / My son is a dentist; **Soy mexicano** / I am Mexican; **Es profesora** / She is a teacher. However, when the subject is qualified, the indefinite article is used.

(e) When you use **Qué** in an exclamation: **¡Qué hombre!** / What a man! **¡Qué lástima!** / What a pity!

(f) With some negations, particularly with the verb **tener,** or in an interrogative statement before an unmodified noun object: **¿Tiene Ud. libro?** / Do you have a book? **No tengo libro** / I don't have a book.

(g) With a noun in apposition: **Martí, gran político y más grande poeta . . .** / Martí, a great politician and greatest poet . . .

NOUNS

A noun is a word that refers to a person (**Roberto, Elena, el muchacho, la muchacha**), a thing (**el libro, la pluma**), a place (**la casa, la escuela, el parque**), a quality (**la excelencia, la honra**).

In Spanish, a noun is either masculine or feminine. When you learn a noun in Spanish, you must learn it with the article, for example: **el libro, la pluma; el muchacho, la muchacha; el hombre, la mujer.**

A noun that refers to a male person or animal is masculine in gender, naturally: **el hombre, el toro, el tío, el padre.** A noun that refers to a female person or animal is feminine in gender, naturally: **la mujer, la chica, la tía, la vaca, la madre.** This is easy to understand. What is not so easy to understand for us English-speaking persons is that a noun referring to a thing, a place, or a quality also has a gender. You must learn the gender of a noun when you learn the word by using the article with it.

14   Generally speaking, a noun that ends in **o** is masculine: **el libro.**

Generally speaking, a noun that ends in **a** is feminine; also a noun that ends in **ción, sión, dad, tad, tud, umbre: la casa, la lección, la ilusión, la ciudad, la dificultad, la nacionalidad, la solicitud, la costumbre.**

Generally speaking, a noun that ends in **nte** refers to a person and the gender is masculine or feminine, depending on whether it refers to a male or female person:

el estudiante / la estudiante; el presidente / la presidente

Generally speaking, it is difficult to tell the gender of a noun that ends in **e.** Some are feminine, some are masculine. You must learn the gender of the noun when you learn the word with the definite or indefinite article.

MASCULINE	FEMININE
el aire / air	**la calle** / street
el arte / art	**la clase** / class
el baile / dance	**la fe** / faith
el bosque / forest	**la fuente** / fountain
el coche / car	**la gente** / people
el parque / park	**la leche** / milk

EJERCICIOS

I. **El aspecto común.** ¿Cuál es el aspecto común de estos objetos? Escriba su contestación con una frase.

Modelo:

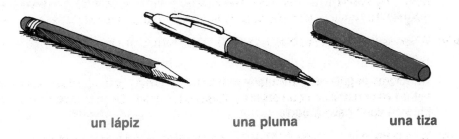

un lápiz   una pluma   una tiza

Respuesta: Son cosas para escribir.

1. **El aspecto común.** ¿Cuál es el aspecto común de estos dibujos? Escriba su contestación con una frase.

Respuesta: _____

2. El aspecto común. ¿Cuál es el aspecto común de estos dibujos? Escriba su contestación con una frase.

Respuesta: _____

II. **Varias palabras en una sola.** Utilizando las letras en la palabra **LÁSTIMA** ¿cuántas palabras puede usted escribir? Escriba seis palabras, por lo menos.

┌─────────────┐
│ **LÁSTIMA** │
└─────────────┘

1. _____   3. _____   5. _____

2. _____   4. _____   6. _____

Irregular gender of nouns

Feminine nouns that end in **o.** Three common ones are:

la mano / hand; **la radio** (**la radio** is the radiotelephonic broadcast that we listen to; **el radio** is the object, the apparatus) / radio; **la foto** / photo (actually, this word is a shortened form of **la fotografía**)

Masculine nouns that end in **a.** Four common ones are:

el día / day; **el clima** / climate; **el drama** / drama; **el mapa** / map

Nouns that end in **ista**

These nouns are generally masculine or feminine, depending on whether they refer to male or female persons:

el dentista, la dentista / dentist; **el novelista, la novelista** / novelist

Plural of nouns

To form the plural of a noun that ends in a vowel, add **s:**

**el chico / los chicos; la chica / las chicas; el libro / los libros
la dentista / las dentistas; el coche / los coches; la clase / las clases**

To form the plural of a noun that ends in a consonant, add **es:**

el profesor / los profesores; la flor / las flores; la ciudad / las ciudades

A noun that ends in **z** changes **z** to **c** before adding **es:**

el lápiz / los lápices; la luz / las luces

Sometimes a masculine plural noun refers to both male and female persons:

los padres / the parents, the mother and father
los tíos / the aunt and uncle, the aunts and uncles
los niños / the children, the little boy and little girl, the little boys and little girls
los hijos / the children, the son and daughter, the sons and daughters

Generally, a noun that ends in **ión** drops the accent mark in the plural. The accent mark is not needed in the plural because the stress naturally falls on the syllable that contained the accent mark in the singular. This happens because another syllable is added when the noun is made plural: **la lección / las lecciones; la ilusión / las ilusiones**

Generally, a noun that ends in **és** drops the accent mark in the plural. The accent mark is not needed in the plural because the stress naturally falls on the syllable that contained the accent mark in the singular. This happens because another syllable is added when the noun is made plural: **el francés** / the Frenchman; **los franceses** / the Frenchmen

Sometimes the accent mark is kept in the plural in order to keep the stress where it is in the singular. This generally happens when there are two vowels together and one of them is strong and the other weak: **el país / los países**

Some nouns have a plural ending but they are regarded as singular because they are compound nouns; that is to say, the single word is made of two words which combine into one: **el tocadiscos** / the record player; **los tocadiscos** / the record players; **el paraguas** / the umbrella; **los paraguas** / the umbrellas; **el abrelatas** / the can opener; **los abrelatas** / the can openers; **el sacapuntas** / the pencil sharpener.

Generally speaking, a noun that ends in **s** in the singular with no stress on that final syllable remains the same in the plural: **el lunes / los lunes; el martes / los martes**

Generally speaking, a noun that ends in **s** in the singular with the stress on that syllable (usually it is a word of one syllable) requires the addition of **es** to form the plural: **el mes / los meses**

Some nouns that contain no accent mark in the singular require an accent mark in the plural in order to preserve the stress where it fell naturally in the singular: **el joven** / the young man; **los jóvenes** / the young men

Nouns that change meaning according to gender

Some nouns have one meaning when masculine and another meaning when feminine. Here are two common examples:

NOUN	MASCULINE GENDER MEANING	FEMININE GENDER MEANING
capital	capital (money)	capital (city)
cura	priest	cure

Nouns used as adjectives

It is common in English to use a noun as an adjective: *a history class, a silk tie, a gold watch.* When this is done in Spanish, the preposition **de** is usually placed in front of the noun that is used as an adjective and both are placed after the noun that is being described:

una clase de historia / a history class (a class of history); **una corbata de seda** / a silk tie (a tie of silk); **un reloj de oro** / a gold watch (a watch of gold)

Also note that the preposition **para** *(for)* is used in order to indicate that something is intended for something: **una taza para café** / a coffee cup (a cup for coffee). However, if the cup is filled with coffee, we say in Spanish: **una taza de café** / a cup of coffee

Nouns ending in ito or illo

Generally speaking, the ending **ito** or **illo** can be added to a noun to form the diminutive form of a noun. This makes the noun take on the meaning of little or small in size:

un vaso / a glass (drinking); **un vasito** / a little drinking glass; **una casa** / a house; **una casita** / a little house; **un cigarro** / a cigar; **un cigarillo** / a cigarette

To form the diminutive in Spanish, ordinarily drop the final vowel of the noun and add **ito** or **illo**: **una casa** / **una casita.** If the final letter of the noun is a consonant, merely add **ito** or **illo**: **papel** / paper; **papelito** *or* **papelillo** / small bit of paper

At other times, these diminutive endings give a favorable quality to the noun, even a term of endearment:

una chica / a girl; **una chiquita** / a cute little girl. Here, note that before dropping the final vowel **a** to add **ita,** you must change **c** to **q** in order to preserve the hard sound of *K* in **chica; un perro** / a dog; **un perrito** / a darling little dog; **una abuela** / a grandmother; **abuelita** / "dear old granny"

In English, we do something similar to this: drop / droplet; doll / dolly *or* dollie; pig / piggy *or* piggie or piglet; bath / bathinette; book / booklet; John / Johnny; Ann / Annie.

EJERCICIOS

I. Escriba la forma correcta del presente de indicativo de los verbos SER o ESTAR. Estudie la presentación de la familia Rodríguez y las reglas antes de comenzar.

1. ¿Cómo está Ud.?— ¿Yo? _____ bien, gracias.

2. Hoy, (yo) _____ enfermo.

3. La escuela _____ lejos.

4. (Yo) _____ el pàdre. Me llamo Francisco Rodríguez.

5. Barcelona _____ en España.

6. (Yo) _____ la madre. Me llamo Clara Rodríguez. _____ contenta.

7. Juana, ¿por qué _____ (tú) pálida hoy?

8. La ventana _____ abierta.

9. (Nosotros) _____ la familia Rodríguez.

10. El café _____ caliente.

II. En las siguientes oraciones escriba la forma correcta del artículo determinado (definite article) **el, la, los, las** si es necesario. Antes de comenzar, estudie las reglas de esta lección.

1. Tengo _____ libro, _____ cuaderno y _____ pluma.

2. Me gusta _____ café pero _____ leche es buena para _____ salud.

3. Esto cuesta un dólar _____ libra.

4. ¿Por qué está ausente _____ profesor Gómez?

5. Buenas noches, _____ señor Rodríguez.

6. ¿Qué lengua extranjera estudia Ud.?— ¿Yo? Estudio _____ español.

7. Me lavo _____ cara todas las mañanas.

8. ¿Dónde están _____ libros de _____ alumnos?

9. ¿Qué hora es? ¿Es _____ una?—No es _____ una. Son _____ dos.

10. ¿Habla Ud. _____ español?— ¿Yo? Sí, hablo _____ español.

11. ¿Dónde están _____ alumnas? ¿Están en _____ clase?

12. En _____ verano, me gusta nadar en _____ piscina.

13. ¿Dónde están _____ cuadernos de _____ alumnas?

14. ¿Qué lengua hablan en _____ Brasil? ¿Y en _____ Habana? ¿Y en _____ Estados

Unidos?

15. Nosotros _____ norteamericanos tenemos muchos amigos de habla española.

16. Madrid, _____ capital de España, es una ciudad interesante.

17. ¿En qué lengua escribe Ud.?— ¿Yo? Escribo en _____ español.

18. Hace mucho frío aquí en _____ invierno y en _____ primavera hace fresco.

19. ¿Estudia Ud. _____ historia?— ¿Yo? Sí, estudio _____ historia y me gusta mucho.

20. ¿Dónde está _____ doctor Torres?

III. En las siguientes oraciones escriba la forma correcta del artículo indeterminado (indefinite article) **un, una, unos, unas** si es necesario. Antes de comenzar, estudie las reglas de esta lección.

1. En esta clase hay _____ veinte personas.

2. Tengo solamente _____ libro y _____ pluma.

3. Este señor es _____ médico. Es _____ médico excelente.

4. Tengo _____ cuaderno, _____ naranjas y _____ dólares.

5. El hijo del señor Robles es _____ dentista.

6. ¿Es _____ profesora la señora García?

7. Sí, la señora García es _____ profesora excelente.

8. ¿Es Ud. _____ norteamericano?— Sí, soy _____ mexicano.

9. El señor López es muy inteligente. ¡Qué _____ hombre!

10. Necesito _____ otro libro y _____ otra pluma.

IV. Escriba la forma correcta del artículo determinado (definite article) **el, la, los, las.** Antes de comenzar, estudie las reglas de esta lección.

1. _____ hombre	5. _____ vaca	9. _____ ciudad
2. _____ mujer	6. _____ tío	10. _____ coches
3. _____ padre	7. _____ toro	11. _____ fuentes
4. _____ madre	8. _____ presentación	12. _____ bailes

V. Escriba el plural de las siguientes palabras.

1. el chico _____
2. la chica _____
3. el dentista _____
4. la dentista _____
5. el coche _____

6. el profesor _____
7. la profesora _____
8. la flor _____
9. la ciudad _____
10. el lápiz _____

VI. Escriba el plural de las siguientes palabras.

1. la luz _____
2. la lección _____
3. la ilusión _____
4. el francés _____
5. el país _____

6. el tocadiscos _____
7. el paraguas _____
8. el abrelatas _____
9. el sacapuntas _____
10. el lunes _____

VII. Escriba el singular de las siguientes palabras.

1. los países _____
2. las luces _____
3. los lápices _____
4. las flores _____
5. los paraguas _____

6. los martes _____
7. los meses _____
8. los lunes _____
9. los jóvenes _____
10. los tocadiscos _____

VIII. Traduzca las siguientes expresiones.

1. a history class _____
2. a silk tie _____
3. a gold watch _____

4. a coffee cup _____
5. a cup of coffee _____
6. a Spanish class _____

IX. Traduzca las siguientes palabras.

1. a drinking glass; a little drinking glass _____

2. a girl; a cute little girl _____

3. a dog; a darling little dog _____

4. a house; a little house _____

X. Dictado. Escriba las frases que su profesor de español va a pronunciar.

1. _____

2. _____

3. _____

XI. HUMOR. La adivinanza para hoy. *(The riddle for today.)*
¿Qué hay en el medio de Barcelona?

Solución: _____

XII. La palabra española "la ropa" no significa en inglés "rope" sino "clothes, clothing."

la ropa / clothes, clothing
la cuerda / rope, cord
La ropa está suspendida en la cuerda. The clothes are hanging on the line.

| Mnemonic tip | **Cuerda** = cord, rope. The letters **crd** are in **cuerda** and in cord. |

¿Cuántos ejemplos puede Ud. decir y escribir?

XIII. En español hay muchas palabras que se escriben y se pronuncian idénticamente, pero tienen distinto significado.

Por ejemplo:
sobre *n.m.* envelope
sobre *prep.* on, upon
El sobre está sobre la mesa. The envelope is on the table.

¿Cuántos ejemplos puede Ud. decir y escribir?

XIV. Complete este crucigrama.

VERTICALES

1. Mi lápiz no tiene punta. Necesito un _____.

2. Una casa pequeña es una _____.

5. No hay bastante _____ para leer.

6. Mi hermano está estudiando en _____ cuarto y yo estoy estudiando en el mío.

HORIZONTALES

3. Cuando está lloviendo, tomo mi par_____.

4. Voy _____ parque.

5. Me gustan _____ flores.

7. Necesito una _____ para café.

8. Mi madre _____ mi padre son amables.

9. Mi hermano tiene una corbata de _____.

XV. ¿Cuántas palabras españolas puede Ud. hallar en el vocablo NOMBRES? Encuentre quince por lo menos. Usted puede utilizar las letras en cualquier orden y añadir signos de acento o tilde, si es necesario, para formar nuevas palabras. Por ejemplo: sé, señor.

NOMBRES

1. _____   4. _____   7. _____   10. _____   13. _____

2. _____   5. _____   8. _____   11. _____   14. _____

3. _____   6. _____   9. _____   12. _____   15. _____

The Virgin with Saint Inés and Saint Tecla *by EL GRECO (1541–1614)*
Courtesy of The National Gallery of Art, Washington, D.C.

A Girl and Her Duenna *by Bartolomé Esteban MURILLO (1617–1682)*
Courtesy of The National Gallery of Art, Washington, D. C.

*Have you ever looked out your window to see
what's going on in the streets?*

Juana está en la ventana con su madre

Todas las noches Juana trabaja, aprende y escribe sus lecciones después de cenar.
Pero esta noche Juana está en la ventana con su madre. Las dos miran lo que pasa en la
calle. Es una noche de fiesta en las calles para celebrar el dos de mayo, la guerra de Independencia de España que duró cinco años, de 1808 hasta 1813. Hay un desfile magnífico, y
hay música. Hay mucha gente en la calle, por ejemplo, muchachas y mujeres hermosas y   5
lindas; hay, también, muchachos y hombres guapos. Juana está loca de curiosidad. Todo el
mundo camina, canta, baila, come y bebe.

En la calle, debajo de la ventana, un soldado guapo habla con Juana. El soldado
pregunta:

—¿Quiere Ud. bajar y bailar y cantar conmigo?   10

Juana responde:

—En otra ocasión. Todas las noches trabajo, aprendo y escribo mis lecciones.

Juana sonríe y la madre de Juana ríe.

Antes de cerrar la ventana, Juana guiña el ojo y se ríe sin motivo.

VOCABULARIO: Consult the vocabulary section in the back pages.

EJERCICIOS

I. Conteste las siguientes preguntas con oraciones completas.

1. ¿Dónde está Juana? _____

2. ¿Dónde está la madre de Juana? _____

3. ¿Qué hace Juana todas las noches? _____

4. ¿Qué miran Juana y su madre? _____

5. ¿Qué celebra la gente? _____

6. ¿Qué hay en la calle? _____

7. ¿Qué hace todo el mundo? _____

8. ¿Quién está debajo de la ventana? _____

9. ¿Qué pregunta el soldado a Juana? _____

10. ¿Qué responde Juana y qué hace antes de cerrar la ventana? _____

II. ¿Sí o No?

1. Todas las mañanas Juana trabaja, aprende y escribe sus lecciones. _____

2. Esta noche Juana está en la ventana con su hermana. _____

3. En la calle, hay un desfile magnífico, hay música y mucha gente. _____

4. En la calle, debajo de la ventana, un soldado habla con otro soldado. _____

5. Juana baila con el soldado guapo y los dos cantan, comen y beben. _____

III. Acróstico. Complete cada palabra en español según la lectura.

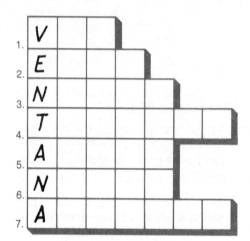

1. Otra _____.

2. Juana _____ en la ventana.

3. Esta _____ Juana está en la ventana.

4. Hay, _____, muchachos y hòmbres guapos.

5. _____ de cerrar la ventana, Juana guiña el ojo.

6. Es una _____ de fiesta.

7. Juana trabaja, _____ y escribe sus lecciones.

Estructuras de la lengua

A. Introduction

A verb is a word that expresses an action *(to work)* or a state of being *(to think)*. Tense means time. Spanish and English verb tenses are divided into three main groups of time: past, present, and future. A verb tense shows if an action took place (past), is taking place (present), or will take place (future). Here, we will review the present indicative tense.

Spanish verbs are divided into three main conjugations (types) according to the infinitive ending, which can be either **—ar, —er, —ir.** You might say that these endings mean *to* in English: **trabajar** *(to work),* **aprender** *(to learn),* **escribir** *(to write).* In this unit, we will review all three types in the present indicative.

You must memorize the personal endings for each of the **—ar, —er, —ir** infinitive types. You must also memorize the personal subject pronouns in Spanish because each one must agree with its own personal ending on the verb. These are all given in dark letters in the chart on the next page.

	—AR type	—ER type	—IR type
Infinitives ———→	**trabajar** *to work*	**aprender** *to learn*	**escribir** *to write*
	I work; do work; am working.	I learn; do learn; am learning.	I write; do write; am writing.
Singular 1. **Yo**	trabaj**o**	aprend**o**	escrib**o**
2. **Tú** *You* (fam.)	trabaj**as**	aprend**es**	escrib**es**
3. **Él** *He;* **Ella** *She*	trabaj**a**	aprend**e**	escrib**e**
Ud. *You* (formal)			
Plural 1. **Nosotros-as** *We*	trabaj**amos**	aprend**emos**	escrib**imos**
2. **Vosotros-as**	trabaj**áis**	aprend**éis**	escrib**ís**
You (fam.)			
3. **Ellos-as** *They*	trabaj**an**	aprend**en**	escrib**en**
Uds. *You* (formal)			

Rules and observations

1. To form the present tense of a regular verb ending in **—ar,** drop the **—ar.** What remains is called the *stem.* Add to the stem the personal endings shown in the above chart. They are: **-o, -as, -a; -amos, -áis, -an.** Note that the characteristic vowel in this set of endings is the letter **a,** except for the first person singular, which is **o.** This is the first conjugation type.

2. To form the present tense of a regular verb ending in **—er,** drop the **—er.** What remains is called the *stem.* Add to the stem the personal endings shown in the above chart. They are: **-o, -es, -e; -emos, -éis, -en.** Note that the characteristic vowel in this set of endings is the letter **e,** except for the first person singular, which is **o.** This is the second conjugation type.

3. To form the present tense of a regular verb ending in **—ir,** drop the **—ir.** What remains is called the *stem.* Add to the stem the personal endings shown in the above chart. They are: **-o, -es, -e; -imos, -ís, -en.** Note that these endings are exactly the same as those for the **—er** type verbs explained in par. 2 above, except for the first and second persons plural which are **-imos** and **-ís.**

4. Also note the three possible translations into English for Spanish verbs in the present indicative tense, as shown on the above chart.

B. Some common regular verbs of the first conjugation type: **—AR**

acabar to finish, to end, to complete
aceptar to accept
acompañar to accompany
acusar to accuse
admirar to admire
adoptar to adopt
adorar to adore, to worship
alumbrar to illuminate, to light, to enlighten
amar to love
andar to walk
anunciar to announce

apreciar to appreciate
articular to articulate, to pronounce distinctly
atacar to attack
ayudar to help, to aid, to assist
bailar to dance
bajar to go down
borrar to erase
botar to fling, to cast (away), to throw (away), to launch
buscar to look for, to search
cambiar to change

caminar to walk, to move along
cantar to sing
celebrar to celebrate
cenar to have dinner (supper)
cepillar to brush
cocinar to cook
colocar to put, to place
completar to complete
comprar to buy, to purchase
contestar to answer, to reply
cortar to cut, to cut off, to cut out

cruzar to cross
charlar to chat, to prattle
chistar to mumble, to mutter
declarar to declare
dejar to let, to permit, to allow, to leave (something behind you)
denunciar to denounce
descansar to rest
desear to desire, to want
dibujar to design, to draw, to sketch
dudar to doubt
echar to cast, to fling, to hurl, to pitch, to throw
emplear to employ, to use
enojar to anger, to annoy, to vex
enseñar to teach, to show, to point out
entrar to enter, to go in, to come in
escuchar to listen (to)
esperar to expect, to hope, to wait (for)
estimar to estimate, to esteem, to respect, to value
estudiar to study
explicar to explain
expresar to express
faltar to be lacking, to be wanting, to lack, to miss, to need
formar to form, to shape
fumar to smoke
ganar to earn, to gain, to win
gastar to spend (money), to wear out, to waste
gozar to enjoy

gritar to shout, to scream, to shriek, to cry out
habitar to inhabit, to dwell, to live, to reside
hablar to talk, to speak
hallar to find, to come across
indicar to indicate, to point out
invitar to invite
lavar to wash (something or someone)
levantar to raise (something or someone)
llegar to arrive
llenar to fill
llevar to carry (away), to take (away), to wear
llorar to weep, to cry, to whine
marchar to march, to walk, to function (machine), to run (machine)
matar to kill
mirar to look (at), to watch
nadar to swim
necesitar to need
ocupar to occupy
olvidar to forget
osar to dare, to venture
pagar to pay
parar to stop (someone or something)
pasar to pass (by), to happen, to spend (time)
perdonar to pardon, to forgive, to excuse
pintar to paint
practicar to practice
preguntar to ask, to inquire, to question

preparar to prepare
presentar to present, to display, to show, to introduce
prestar to lend
principiar to begin, to start
proclamar to proclaim, to promulgate
pronunciar to pronounce
quedar to remain
quemar to burn, to fire
regalar to give as a present, to make a present of, to give as a gift
regresar to return, to go back, to regress
reparar to repair, to mend, to notice, to observe
sacar to take out (something), to get
saltar to jump, to leap, to hop, to spring
saludar to greet, to salute
secar to dry, to wipe dry
separar to separate, to detach, to sort, to set apart
telefonear to telephone
terminar to end, to terminate, to finish
tocar to play (musical instrument), to knock (on the door)
tomar to take
trabajar to work
tratar to try, to treat a subject
usar to use, to employ, to wear
viajar to travel
visitar to visit

C. Some common regular verbs of the second conjugation type: —ER

aprender to learn
beber to drink
comer to eat
comprender to understand
correr to run, to race, to flow
creer to believe

deber to owe, must, ought
depender to depend
leer to read
responder to answer, to respond, to reply
romper to break, to shatter

tañer to pluck, to play (a stringed musical instrument)
temer to fear, to dread
vender to sell

D. Some common regular verbs of the third conjugation type: —IR

abrir to open
admitir to admit
añadir to add
asistir to attend
cubrir to cover
cumplir to fulfill, to keep (a

promise), to reach one's birthday (use with **años**)
decidir to decide
describir to describe, to sketch, to delineate
descubrir to discover

discutir to discuss
escribir to write
gruñir to grumble, to grunt, to growl, to creak
insistir to insist, to persist
omitir to omit

partir to leave, to depart, to divide, to split

permitir to permit, to admit, to allow, to grant

prohibir to prohibit, to forbid

pulir to polish

recibir to receive

remitir to remit, to forward, to transmit

subir to go up

sufrir to suffer, to endure, to bear up, to undergo

unir to unite, to connect, to join, to bind, to attach

vivir to live

Personal pronouns

Subject Pronouns

Singular
1. **yo** / I
2. **tú** / you *(familiar)*
3. **usted** / you *(polite)*
   él / he, it
   ella / she, it

Plural
1. **nosotros (nosotras)** / we
2. **vosotros (vosotras)** / you *(fam.)*
3. **ustedes** / you *(polite)*
   ellos / they
   ellas / they

Examples

Yo hablo.
Tú hablas.
Usted habla.
Él habla.
Ella habla.

Nosotros hablamos
Vosotros habláis.
Ustedes hablan.
Ellos hablan.
Ellas hablan.

As you can see in the examples given here, a subject pronoun is ordinarily placed in front of the main verb.

In Spanish, subject pronouns are not used at all times. The ending of the verb tells you if the subject is 1st, 2nd, or 3rd person in the singular or plural. Of course, in the 3rd person sing. and pl. there is more than one possible subject with the same ending on the verb form. In that case, if there is any doubt as to what the subject is, it is mentioned for the sake of clarity. At other times, subject pronouns in Spanish are used when you want to be emphatic, to make a contrast between this person and that person, or out of simple courtesy. You must be certain to know the endings of the verb forms in all the tenses (see the entry **Verbs** in the Index) in the three persons of the singular and of the plural so that you can figure out the subject if it is not clearly stated. In addition to pronouns as subjects, nouns are also used as subjects. Any noun—whether common (**el hombre, la mujer, el cielo, la silla,** *etc.*) or proper (**María, Juan y Elena, los Estados Unidos,** *etc.*) are always 3rd person, either singular or plural.

Generally speaking, in some Latin American countries **ustedes** (3rd pers., pl.) is used in place of **vosotros** or **vosotras** (2nd pers., pl.).

E. Interrogative word order

1. Generally speaking, the subject is placed after the verb when asking a question.

2. An inverted question mark is placed at the beginning of a written question so that the reader knows that a question is about to be asked. A question mark at the end of the question is required, as in English.

EXAMPLES:

Declarative statement	Interrogative statement
(a) **Juana está en la ventana.**	**¿Está Juana en la ventana?**
(b) **Ud. quiere bailar y cantar.**	**¿Quiere Ud. bailar y cantar?**

29

EJERCICIOS

I. Cambie las siguientes oraciones sustituyendo las palabras *en letras cursivas* por un pronombre personal.

Modelo: *Juana y su madre* están en la ventana.   **Ellas** están en la ventana.

A. Verbos con la terminación **—AR**

1. *Juana* trabaja mucho. _____

2. *El soldado* baila bien. _____

3. *La señora* Rodríguez canta bien. _____

4. *Juana y Pedro* estudian las lecciones. _____

5. *María y yo* preparamos la lección. _____

B. Verbos con la terminación **—ER**

1. *Juana y María* aprenden mucho en la escuela. _____

2. *Pablo y Pedro* beben leche todos los días. _____

3. *Cristóbal, Juan y yo* comemos juntos. _____

4. *Los alumnos y las alumnas* comprenden la lección. _____

5. *El niño* teme la oscuridad. _____

C. Verbos con la terminación **—IR**

1. *El profesor* abre la ventana. _____

2. *Las alumnas* reciben buenas notas. _____

3. *María y José* parten hoy. _____

4. *Ud. y Ricardo* escriben las oraciones. _____

5. *Ud., Juan y Cristóbal* viven en la misma casa. _____

II. Cambie las siguientes oraciones sustituyendo el pronombre personal como sujeto entre paréntesis en lugar de las palabras *en letras cursivas*. Cambie el verbo en la forma necesaria.

Modelo: *Juana* aprende la lección.   (Yo) **Yo aprendo** la lección.

A. *La señora López* anda despacio.

1. (Yo) _____   6. (Nosotros) _____

2. (Tú) _____   7. (Vosotros) _____

3. (Ud.) _____   8. (Uds.) _____

4. (Él) _____   9. (Ellos) _____

5. (Ella) _____   10. (Ellas) _____

B. *Juanita* responde bien.

1. (Yo) _____   6. (Ud. y yo) _____

2. (Uds.) _____   7. (Él) _____

3. (Tú) _____   8. (Ellas) _____

4. (Ella y él) _____   9. (Tú y yo) _____

5. (Ud.) _____   10. (Uds. y ellos) _____

C. *Carlos y yo* escribimos la lección.

1. (Ud.) _____   6. (Tú) _____

2. (Yo) _____   7. (Ella) _____

3. (Uds.) _____   8. (Él) _____

4. (Nosotros) _____   9. (Vosotros) _____

5. (Ellos) _____   10. (Ellas) _____

III. Conteste las siguientes preguntas en forma afirmativa con oraciones completas. En la respuesta (a) use la palabra **Sí.** En la respuesta (b) use la palabra **también** según los modelos.

Modelos: a. **¿Canta Ud. bien?**
               b. **¿Y Uds.?**

Escriba: a. **Sí, yo canto bien.**
               b. **Nosotros cantamos bien, también.**

A. Verbos con la terminación **—AR**

1. a. ¿Baila Ud. todas las noches? _____

   b. ¿Y Juana? _____

2. a. ¿Borra la profesora la palabra en la pizarra? _____

   b. ¿Y los otros alumnos? _____

3. a. ¿Trabaja María en la clase de español? _____

   b. ¿Y Carlos y Juan? _____

4. a. ¿Tocas tú el piano? _____

   b. ¿Y las muchachas? _____

5. a. ¿Llora la niña? _____

   b. ¿Y los niños? _____

6. a. ¿Espera Juanita el autobús? _____

   b. ¿Y sus amigos? _____

B. Verbos con la terminación —**ER**

   1. a. ¿Aprende Ud. el español? _____

      b. ¿Y los otros alumnos? _____

   2. a. ¿Beben leche los niños? _____

      b. ¿Y Andrés? _____

   3. a. ¿Come la familia a las ocho? _____

      b. ¿Y Ud.? _____

   4. a. ¿Comprende Ud. el español? _____

      b. ¿Y ellos? _____

   5. a. ¿Lee María el cuento? _____

      b. ¿Y Uds.? _____

C. Verbos con la terminación —**IR**

   1. a. ¿Abre el profesor la puerta? _____

      b. ¿Y tú? _____

   2. a. ¿Recibe José buenas notas? _____

      b. ¿Y Cristóbal? _____

   3. a. ¿Sonríe el profesor de vez en cuando? _____

      b. ¿Y los otros profesores? _____

   4. a. ¿Escribe Ud. cartas? _____

      b. ¿Y nosotros? _____

   5. a. ¿Vivimos en la misma casa? _____

      b. ¿Y Miguel y María? _____

IV. Conteste que sí a las siguientes preguntas en oraciones completas, según el modelo.

   Modelo: **¿Toma Ud. leche en el café?**   **Sí, tomo leche en el café.**

     1. ¿Trabaja Ud. todos los días? _____

     2. ¿Viaja el señor Pérez de vez en cuando? _____

     3. ¿Usa Ud. guantes en el invierno? _____

     4. ¿Leen los alumnos mucho? _____

32   5. ¿Vende la casa la familia Rodríguez? _____

6. ¿Corre Ud. a la clase de español? _____

7. ¿Vivimos Juan y yo en la misma casa? _____

8. ¿Reciben Carlos y Carlota buenas notas? _____

9. ¿Admite Ud. siempre la verdad? _____

10. ¿Habla Ud. español en la clase de español? _____

V. Componga oraciones en el presente de indicativo empleando los siguientes verbos.

1. hablar _____

2. comer _____

3. recibir _____

VI. Dictado. Escriba las frases que su profesor de español va a pronunciar.

1. _____

2. _____

3. _____

Romina y Albano pasean entre los árboles con su hija.

El dúo musical con sus dos hijos, Ylenia y Yari. Los cuatro forman una familia muy unida.

ROMINA Y ALBANO
celebran sus 14 años de casados en S'Agaró

Romina y Albano, en compañía de sus dos hijos, Ylenia y Yari, han celebrado sus catorce años de vida en común en la Gavina, de S'Agaró, de una forma sencilla, como viene siendo habitual en ellos. El matrimonio está en España para realizar las habituales galas por todo el país. Al preguntarles sobre los regalos de aniversario, nos contesta de manera decidida: «Nosotros procuramos mantener un buen equilibrio familiar, cuesta lo suyo, pero hoy por hoy lo vamos consiguiendo. Nuestra vida está hecha de pequeños detalles cotidianos. Cada día celebramos el hecho de estar juntos. Por esto, al llegar a los catorce años, no hacemos una gran fiesta social, porque en las fiestas sociales todo es superficial. Nuestro mejor regalo es estar juntos y divertirnos».

Albano afirmó que esto no quería decir que no se hicieran nunca obsequios: «Romina y yo nos regalamos cosas, y a los chicos, pero lo hacemos cuando menos lo esperamos... A nosotros nos gusta sorprendernos todos los días.

VII. Complete la siguiente oración con tantos nombres como Ud. pueda decir y escribir.
Modelo

Yo deseo
- un vaso de leche / a glass of milk
- una cereza / a cherry
- dinero / money
- un vaso de agua / a glass of water
- tener amigos / to have friends

- música / music
- paz / peace
- felicidad / happiness
- la verdad / the truth

VIII. En español hay muchas palabras que se escriben y se pronuncian idénticamente, pero tienen distinto significado.

Por ejemplo:

cocina *n.f.* kitchen
cocina *3rd pers., sing., pres. indic. of* **cocinar** / to cook

El cocinero cocina en la cocina. The cook is cooking in the kitchen.

presente de indicativo

cocinar / to cook

yo	cocino	nosotros	cocinamos
tú	cocinas	vosotros	cocináis
Ud.		Uds.	
él	**cocina**	ellos	cocinan
ella		ellas	

¿Cuántos ejemplos puede Ud. decir, escribir y dibujar?

IX. En español hay muchas palabras que se escriben y se pronuncian idénticamente, pero un signo de acento es necesario para notar su diferente significado.

Por ejemplo:

el *def. art., masc., sing.* / the
él *subj. pron., masc., sing.* / he; *also obj. of a prep.* / him (**para él** / for him)

Yo compro el billete para él y tú compras el billete para ella. I'm buying the ticket for him and you're buying the ticket for her.

¿Cuántos ejemplos puede Ud. decir y escribir?

X. Otro ejemplo:

¿A ti te gusta el té? / Do you like tea?

XI. En español hay muchas palabras que se escriben y se pronuncian idénticamente, pero tienen distinto significado.

Por ejemplo:

deber *n.m.* duty, obligation
deber *v.* to owe, ought to, should, must
Deber un deber es natural. To owe an obligation is natural.
Debe de ser tarde. Debo ir. It must be late. I have to go.

Mnemonic tip	**Deber** contains *deb* and so does *debt*.

presente de indicativo

deber

yo	debo	nosotros	debemos
tú	debes	vosotros	debéis
Ud.		Uds.	
él	debe	ellos	deben
ella		ellas	

¿Cuántos ejemplos puede Ud. decir y escribir?

La señora Rodríguez está buscando en el guardarropa, Juana está buscando en el tocador y Pedro está buscando debajo de la cama.

Have you ever looked high and low for some-thing you lost?

¿Dónde está mi sombrero?

El señor Rodríguez está buscando su sombrero. La señora Rodríguez está buscando el sombrero en el guardarropa. Juana está buscando en el tocador y Pedro está buscando debajo de la cama.

El señor Rodríguez:	¿Dónde está mi sombrero?	
Juana:	Ahora estoy buscando en el tocador, papá.	5
Pedro:	Y ahora yo estoy buscando debajo de la cama. Estamos buscando en todas partes, papá.	
La señora Rodríguez:	Yo estoy buscando, también, Francisco. Estoy buscando en el guardarropa. ¡Oh! Estoy buscando tu sombrero por todas partes.	
El señor Rodríguez:	Ahora estoy buscando debajo de la silla. Vamos a buscar en la cocina, en la sala, en el cuarto de baño, en el sótano, debajo de la cama, debajo del tocador, en el guardarropa, en el garaje. ¡Por todas partes!	10
Juana:	¡Mira! ¡Mira, papá! ¡Coco se está comiendo tu sombrero! ¡Está debajo del tocador!	15
El señor Rodríguez:	¡Oh! ¡No! ¡Dios mío!	
	(El señor Rodríguez sale del dormitorio.)	
La señora Rodríguez:	¿Adónde vas, Francisco?	
El señor Rodríguez:	Voy al centro para comprar otro sombrero. ¡Caramba!	
La señora Rodríguez:	¡Espera! ¡Espera, Francisco! Voy contigo. Quiero comprar una falda.	20

VOCABULARIO: Consult the vocabulary section in the back pages.

EJERCICIOS

I. Seleccione la respuesta correcta conforme al significado de la lectura en esta lección.

1. El señor Rodríguez está buscando (a) en el tocador (b) debajo de la cama (c) su sombrero (d) en el guardarropa _____

2. Juana está buscando (a) debajo de la cama (b) en la sala (c) debajo del tocador (d) en el tocador _____

3. Pedro está buscando (a) debajo de la silla (b) en el garaje (c) en el cuarto de baño (d) debajo de la cama _____

4. El sombrero está (a) en el tocador (b) debajo del tocador (c) debajo de la cama (d) en la cocina _____

5. El perrito está comiendo el sombrero debajo (a) de la cama (b) de la silla (c) del guardarropa (d) del tocador _____

II. Responda en español en frases completas.

  Modelo: **¿Quién está buscando debajo de la cama?**
  Respuesta: **Pedro está buscando debajo de la cama.**

1. ¿Quién está buscando en el tocador? _____

2. ¿Quién está buscando en el guardarropa? _____

3. ¿Quién está buscando debajo de la silla? _____

III. Acróstico. Complete cada palabra en español.

1. cellar

2. other, *m.s.*

3. Look!

4. bath

5. to receive

6. to wait (for)

7. to answer

8. eye

Estructuras de la lengua

Verbs irregular in the present indicative, including stem-changing verbs and orthographical changing verbs

  NOTE that the first three forms up to the semicolon are the 1st, 2nd, and 3rd persons of the singular; the three verb forms under those are the 1st, 2nd, and 3rd persons of the plural. The subject pronouns are not given in order to emphasize the verb forms.

acordar / to agree (upon)
  acuerdo, acuerdas, acuerda;
  acordamos, acordáis, acuerdan

  This is a stem-changing verb. The **o** in the stem changes to **ue** when stressed.

acordarse / to remember
  me acuerdo, te acuerdas, se acuerda;
  nos acordamos, os acordáis, se acuerdan

  This is a stem-changing verb. The **o** in the stem changes to **ue** when stressed.

acostarse / to go to bed, to lie down
  me acuesto, te acuestas, se acuesta;
  nos acostamos, os acostáis, se acuestan

  This is a stem-changing verb. The **o** in the stem changes to **ue** when stressed.

almorzar / to lunch, to have lunch
  almuerzo, almuerzas, almuerza;
  almorzamos, almorzáis, almuerzan

  This is a stem-changing verb. The **o** in the stem changes to **ue** when stressed.

aparecer / to appear, to show up
aparezco, apareces, aparece;
aparecemos, aparecéis, aparecen

This —**cer** verb changes only in the 1st person singular where the **c** changes to **zc.**

caber / to fit, to be contained
quepo, cabes, cabe;
cabemos, cabéis, caben

Irregular in the 1st pers. sing. only in this tense.

caer / to fall
caigo, caes, cae;
caemos, caéis, caen

Irregular in the 1st pers. sing. only in this tense. Pres. part. is **cayendo.**

cerrar / to close
cierro, cierras, cierra;
cerramos, cerráis, cierran

A stem-changing verb. The **e** in the stem changes to **ie** when stressed.

cocer / to cook
cuezo, cueces, cuece;
cocemos, cocéis; cuecen

A stem-changing and orthographical changing verb. The **o** in the stem changes to **ue** when stressed. Also, this —**cer** verb changes **c** to **z** in front of **o** or **a.**

coger / to seize, to grasp, to grab, to catch
cojo, coges, coge;
cogemos, cogéis, cogen

An orthographical changing verb. This —**ger** verb changes **g** to **j** in front of **o** or **a.**

colgar / to hang
cuelgo, cuelgas, cuelga;
colgamos, colgáis, cuelgan

A stem-changing verb. The **o** in the stem changes to **ue** when stressed.

comenzar / to begin, to start, to commence
comienzo, comienzas, comienza;
comenzamos, comenzáis, comienzan

A stem-changing verb. The **e** in the stem changes to **ie** when stressed.

conducir / to conduct, to lead, to drive

conduzco, conduces, conduce;
conducimos, conducís, conducen

This —**cir** verb changes only in the 1st pers. sing. of this tense where the **c** changes to **zc.**

confesar / to confess
confieso, confiesas, confiesa;
confesamos, confesáis, confiesan

A stem-changing verb. The **e** in the stem changes to **ie** when stressed.

conocer / to know, to be acquainted with
conozco, conoces, conoce;
conocemos, conocéis, conocen

An orthographical changing verb. This —**cer** verb changes **c** to **zc** only in the 1st pers. sing. of this tense.

construir / to construct, to build
construyo, construyes, construye;
construimos, construís, construyen

This —**uir** verb requires the insertion of **y** in front of the regular present tense endings **o, es, e,** and **en.** Pres. part. is **construyendo.**

contar / to count, to relate
cuento, cuentas, cuenta;
contamos, contáis, cuentan

A stem-changing verb. The **o** in the stem changes to **ue** when stressed.

contener / to contain, to hold
contengo, contienes, contiene;
contenemos, contenéis, contienen

A stem-changing verb and an irregular form in the 1st pers. sing. of this tense. The **e** in the stem changes to **ie** when stressed.

continuar / to continue
continúo, continúas, continúa;
continuamos, continuáis, continúan

This —**uar** verb is a stem-changing verb. The **u** in the stem changes to **ú** when stressed.

corregir / to correct
corrijo, corriges, corrige;
corregimos, corregís, corrigen

An orthographical and stem-changing verb. The **g** changes to **j** in front of **o** or **a** in order to keep its original sound of *h,* as in the English word *hello.* Also, **e** in stem changes to **i** when stressed. Pres. part. is **corrigiendo.**

costar / to cost
cue**sta;
cue**stan

An impersonal verb used in the 3rd pers. sing. and plural. A stem-changing verb. The **o** in the stem changes to **ue** because of stress.

dar / to give
doy, das, da;
damos, **dais,** dan

An irregular form in the 1st pers. sing. and no accent mark is needed in the 2nd pers. plural.

decir / to say, to tell
digo, dices, dice;
decimos, decís, **dicen**

An irregular form in the 1st pers. sing. Also, the **e** in the stem changes to **i** when stressed. Pres. part. is **diciendo.**

defender / to defend
def**iendo, defiendes, defiende;**
defendemos, defendéis, def**ienden**

A stem-changing verb. The **e** in the stem changes to **ie** when stressed.

desaparecer / to disappear
desaparez**co, desapareces, desaparece;**
desaparecemos, desaparecéis, desaparecen

This —**cer** verb changes only in the 1st pers. sing. where **c** changes to **zc.**

despedir / to dismiss
despido, despides, despide;
despedimos, despedís, despiden

A stem-changing verb. The **e** in the stem changes to **i** when stressed. Pres. part. is **despidiendo.**

despedirse (de) / to say good-bye (to), to take leave (of)
me despido, te despides, se despide;
nos despedimos, os despedís, se despiden

A stem-changing verb. The **e** in the stem changes to **i** when stressed. Pres. part. is **despidiéndose.**

despertarse / to awaken, to wake up (oneself)
me desp**ierto, te despiertas, se despierta;**
nos despertamos, os despertáis, se desp**iertan**

A stem-changing verb. The **e** in the stem changes to **ie** when stressed.

destruir / to destroy
destru**yo, destruyes, destruye;**
destruimos, destruís, destru**yen**

This —**uir** verb requires the insertion of **y** in front of the regular present tense endings **o, es, e,** and **en.** Pres. part. is **destruyendo.**

detener / to detain, to stop (someone or something)
deten**go, detienes, detiene;**
detenemos, detenéis, det**ienen**

An irregular form in the 1st pers. sing. Also, the **e** in the stem changes to **ie** when stressed in the forms noted.

devolver / to return (something), to give back (something)
devu**elvo, devuelves, devuelve;**
devolvemos, devolvéis, devu**elven**

A stem-changing verb. The **o** in the stem changes to **ue** when stressed.

dirigir / to direct
diri**jo, diriges, dirige;**
dirigimos, dirigís, dirigen

An orthographical changing verb. The **g** changes to **j** in front of **o** or **a** in order to keep its original sound of *h,* as in the English word *hello.*

divertirse / to have a good time, to enjoy oneself
me div**ierto, te diviertes, se divierte;**
nos divertimos, os divertís, se div**ierten**

A stem-changing verb. The **e** in the stem changes to **ie** when stressed. Pres. part. is **divirtiéndose.**

doler / to ache, to pain, to hurt, to cause grief, to cause regret
du**elo, dueles, duele;**
dolemos, doléis, du**elen**

A stem-changing verb. The **o** in the stem changes to **ue** when stressed.

dormir / to sleep
  d**ue**rmo, d**ue**rmes, d**ue**rme;
  dormimos, dormís, d**ue**rmen

  A stem-changing verb. The **o** in the stem changes to **ue** when stressed. Pres. part. is **durmiendo.**

dormirse / to fall asleep
  me d**ue**rmo, te d**ue**rmes, se d**ue**rme;
  nos dormimos, os dormís, se d**ue**rmen

  A stem-changing verb. The **o** in the stem changes to **ue** when stressed. Pres. part. is **durmiéndose.**

elegir / to elect
  el**ij**o, el**i**ges, el**i**ge;
  elegimos, elegís, el**i**gen

  An orthographical and stem-changing verb. The **g** changes to **j** in front of **o** or **a** in order to keep its original sound of *h,* as in the English word *hello.* Also, the second **e** in the stem changes to **i** when stressed. Pres. part. is **eligiendo.**

empezar / to begin, to start
  emp**ie**zo, emp**ie**zas, emp**ie**za;
  empezamos, empezáis, emp**ie**zan

  A stem-changing verb. The second **e** in the stem changes to **ie** when stressed.

encontrar / to meet, to encounter, to find
  enc**ue**ntro, enc**ue**ntras, enc**ue**ntra;
  encontramos, encontráis, enc**ue**ntran

  An orthographical changing verb. The **o** in the stem changes to **ue** when stressed.

entender / to understand
  ent**ie**ndo, ent**ie**ndes, ent**ie**nde;
  entendemos, entendéis, ent**ie**nden

  A stem-changing verb. The second **e** in the stem changes to **ie** when stressed.

enviar / to send
  env**í**o, env**í**as, env**í**a;
  enviamos, enviáis, env**í**an

  This —**iar** verb changes **i** to **í** in the stem when stressed.

escoger / to choose, to select
  esco**j**o, esco**g**es, esco**g**e;
  escogemos, escogéis, escogen

An orthographical changing verb. This —**ger** verb changes **g** to **j** in front of **o** or **a.**

estar / to be
  estoy, estás, está;
  estamos, estáis, están

freír / to fry
  fr**í**o, fr**í**es, fr**í**e;
  fre**í**mos, freís, fr**í**en
  Pres. part. is **friendo.**

gemir / to groan, to moan
  g**i**mo, g**i**mes, g**i**me;
  gemimos, gemís, g**i**men

  A stem-changing verb. The **e** in the stem changes to **i** when stressed. Pres. part. is **gimiendo.**

guiar / to guide, to drive, to lead
  gu**í**o, gu**í**as, gu**í**a;
  guiamos, guiáis, gu**í**an

  This —**iar** verb changes **i** in the stem to **í** when stressed.

haber / to have (as an auxiliary or helping verb)
  he, has, ha;
  hemos, habéis, han

hacer / to do, to make
  ha**go,** haces, hace;
  hacemos, hacéis, hacen
  Irregular form only in the 1st pers. sing. in this tense, as noted.

helar / to freeze
  h**ie**la OR está helando (in the present progressive form)
  This impersonal verb, referring to the weather, is used in the 3rd pers. The **e** in the stem changes to **ie** because it is stressed. The present progressive form may be used also when referring to weather conditions in the present, as noted here.

huir / to flee, to escape, to run away, to slip away
  hu**y**o, hu**y**es, hu**y**e;
  huimos, huís, hu**y**en

  This —**uir** verb requires the insertion of **y** in front of the regular present tense endings **o, es, e,** and **en.** Pres. part. is **huyendo.**

ir / to go
  voy, vas, va;
  vamos, vais, van
  Pres. part. is **yendo.**

VIVA CON SUS HIJOS LA FANTASTICA AVENTURA
DE UN VIAJE A DISNEYWORLD

Descubra también que los Barquillos Cuétara "una auténtica gozada" como dicen sus hijos. Cuatro "frescos" sabores para elegir: Fres-N. Fres-Coco, Fres-Lemón y Demecao.

Los Barquillos Cuétara son ligeros y gustan a todos siempre y en cualquier momento y ni usted misma podrá resistir la fresca y deliciosa tentación de su sabor, si los mete en el frigorífico este verano.

Participe en el Concurso y podrá vivir con sus hijos la aventura, fantástica pero real, de un viaje a Disneyworld, al que Cuétara tiene el gusto de invitarle.

BASES DEL CONCURSO

Presentaciones:
FRES-COCO: Paquete aluminio 175 grs. y Estuches familiares ½ Kg., 1 Kg. y 1.5 Kg
FRES-NATA: Paquete aluminio 175 grs. y Estuche familiar ½ Kg
FRES-LEMON: Paquete aluminio 175 grs. y Estuche familiar ½ Kg
DEMECAO: Paquete aluminio 175 grs. y Estuches familiares ½ Kg. y 1 Kg

irse / to go away
me voy, te vas, se va;
nos vamos, os vais, se van

Pres. part. is **yéndose.**

jugar / to play
ju**e**go, ju**e**gas, ju**e**ga;
jugamos, jugáis, ju**e**gan

A stem-changing verb because **u** in the stem changes to **ue** when stressed.

llover / to rain
ll**ue**ve OR está lloviendo (in the present progressive form)

This impersonal verb, referring to the weather, is used in the 3rd pers. The **o** in the stem changes to **ue** because it is stressed. The present progressive form may be used also when referring to weather conditions in the present, as noted here.

mentir / to lie, to tell a lie
mi**e**nto, mi**e**ntes, mi**e**nte;
mentimos, mentís, mi**e**nten

A stem-changing verb because **e** in the stem changes to **ie** when stressed. Pres. part. is **mintiendo.**

morir / to die
m**ue**ro, m**ue**res, m**ue**re;
morimos, morís, m**ue**ren

A stem-changing verb because **o** in the stem changes to **ue** when stressed. Pres. part. is **muriendo.**

mostrar / to show, to point out
m**ue**stro, m**ue**stras, m**ue**stra;
mostramos, mostráis, m**ue**stran

A stem-changing verb because **o** in the stem changes to **ue** when stressed.

nacer / to be born
na**zc**o, naces, nace;
nacemos, nacéis, nacen

This —**cer** verb changes only in the 1st pers. sing. where **c** changes to **zc.**

negar / to deny
ni**e**go, ni**e**gas, ni**e**ga;
negamos, negáis, ni**e**gan

A stem-changing verb because **e** in the stem changes to **ie** when stressed.

nevar / to snow
ni**e**va OR está nevando (in the present progressive form)

This impersonal verb, referring to the weather, is used in the 3rd pers. The **e** in the stem changes to **ie** because it is stressed. The present progressive form may be used also when referring to weather conditions in the present, as noted here.

obedecer / to obey
obede**zc**o, obedeces, obedece;
obedecemos, obedecéis, obedecen

An orthographical changing verb. This —**cer** verb changes **c** to **zc** only in the 1st pers. sing. of this tense.

obtener / to obtain, to get
obten**go**, obti**e**nes, obti**e**ne;
obtenemos, obtenéis, obti**e**nen

The 1st pers. sing. form is irregular. As a stem-changing verb, the **e** in the stem changes to **ie** when stressed.

ofrecer / to offer
ofre**zc**o, ofreces, ofrece;
ofrecemos, ofrecéis, ofrecen

An orthographical changing verb. This —**cer** verb changes **c** to **zc** only in the 1st pers. sing. of this tense.

oír / to hear
oigo, oyes, oye;
oímos, oís, oyen

An irregular verb. Pres. part. is **oyendo.**

oler / to smell
huelo, hueles, huele;
olemos, oléis, **huelen**

An orthographical and stem-changing verb because **o** in the stem changes to **ue** when stressed and *h* is added as noted. Pres. part. is regular: **oliendo.**

pedir / to ask for, to request
pido, pides, pide;
pedimos, pedís, piden

A stem-changing verb because **e** in the stem changes to **i** when stressed. Pres. part. is **pidiendo.**

pensar / to think
pienso, piensas, piensa;
pensamos, pensáis, piensan

A stem-changing verb because **e** in the stem changes to **ie** when stressed.

perder / to lose
pierdo, pierdes, pierde;
perdemos, perdéis, pierden

A stem-changing verb because **e** in the stem changes to **ie** when stressed.

poder / to be able, can
puedo, puedes, puede;
podemos, podéis, pueden

A stem-changing verb because **o** in the stem changes to **ue** when stressed. Pres. part. is **pudiendo.**

poner / to put, to place
pongo, pones, pone;
ponemos, ponéis, ponen

Irregular in the 1st pers. sing. only of this tense.

preferir / to prefer
prefiero, prefieres, prefiere;
preferimos, preferís, prefieren

A stem-changing verb because the second **e** in the stem changes to **ie** when stressed. Pres. part. is **prefiriendo.**

probar / to prove, to test, to try
pruebo, pruebas, prueba;
probamos, probáis, prueban

A stem-changing verb because **o** in the stem changes to **ue** when stressed.

producir / to produce
produzco, produces, produce;
producimos, producís, producen

This —**cir** verb changes **c** to **zc** only in the 1st pers. sing. of this tense.

proteger / to protect
protejo, proteges, protege;
protegemos, protegéis, protegen

An orthographical changing verb because this —**ger** verb changes **g** to **j** in front of **o** or **a.**

querer / to want, to wish
quiero, quieres, quiere;
queremos, queréis, quieren

A stem-changing verb because **e** in the stem changes to **ie** when stressed.

recoger / to pick, to pick up, to gather
recojo, recoges, recoge;
recogemos, recogéis, recogen

An orthographical changing verb because this —**ger** verb changes **g** to **j** in front of **o** or **a.**

recomendar / to recommend, to advise, to commend
recomiendo, recomiendas, recomienda;
recomendamos, recomendáis, recomiendan

A stem-changing verb because **e** in the stem changes to **ie** when stressed.

recordar / to remember
recuerdo, recuerdas, recuerda;
recordamos, recordáis, recuerdan

A stem-changing verb because **o** in the stem changes to **ue** when stressed.

referir / to refer
refiero, refieres, refiere;
referimos, referís, refieren

A stem-changing verb because the second **e** in the stem changes to **ie** when stressed. Pres. part. is **refiriendo.**

reír / to laugh
río, ríes, ríe;
reímos, reís, ríen

The pres. part. is also irregular: **riendo.**

reñir / to scold, to quarrel, to argue
riño, riñes, riñe;
reñimos, reñís, riñen

A stem-changing verb because **e** in the stem changes to **i** when stressed. Past part. is also irregular: **riñendo.**

repetir / to repeat
repito, repites, repite;
repetimos, repetís, repiten

A stem-changing verb because the second **e** in the stem changes to **i** when stressed. Pres. part. is also irregular: **repitiendo.**

resfriarse / to catch cold
me resfrío, te resfrías, se resfría;
nos resfriamos, os resfriáis, se
resfrían

This —**iar** verb changes **i** to **í** when stressed.

resolver / to resolve, to solve (a problem)
resuelvo, resuelves, resuelve;
resolvemos, resolvéis, resuelven

A stem-changing verb because **o** in the stem changes to **ue** when stressed.

reunir / to gather, to join, to unite
reúno, reúnes, reúne;
reunimos, reunís, reúnen

The **u** in the stem changes to **ú** when stressed.

rogar / to beg, to request
ruego, ruegas, ruega;
rogamos, rogáis, ruegan

A stem-changing verb because **o** in the stem changes to **ue** when stressed.

saber / to know, to know how
sé, sabes, sabe;
sabemos, sabéis, saben

Irregular only in the 1st pers. sing. of this tense.

salir / to go out
salgo, sales, sale;
salimos, salís, salen

Irregular only in the 1st pers. sing. of this tense.

seguir / to follow, to pursue, to continue
sigo, sigues, sigue;
seguimos, seguís, siguen

An orthographical changing verb because **u** in the stem drops only in the 1st pers. sing. of this tense. Also, a stem-changing verb because **e** in the stem changes to **i** when stressed. Pres. part. is also irregular: **siguiendo.**

sentarse / to sit down
me siento, te sientas, se sienta;
nos sentamos, os sentáis, se sientan

A stem-changing verb because **e** in the stem changes to **ie** when stressed.

sentir / to feel sorry, to regret, to feel, to experience, to sense
siento, sientes, siente;
sentimos, sentís, sienten

A stem-changing verb because **e** in the stem changes to **ie** when stressed. Pres. part. is also irregular: **sintiendo.**

sentirse / to feel (well, sick)
me siento, te sientes, se siente;
nos sentimos, os sentís, se sienten

A stem-changing verb because **e** in the stem changes to **ie** when stressed. Pres. part. is also irregular: **sintiéndose.**

ser / to be
soy, eres, es;
somos, sois, son

Pres. part. is **siendo.**

servir / to serve
sirvo, sirves, sirve;
servimos, servís, sirven

A stem-changing verb because **e** in the stem changes to **i** when stressed. Pres. part. is also irregular: **sirviendo.**

soler / to be in the habit of, to be accustomed to, to have the custom of
suelo, sueles, suele;
solemos, soléis, suelen

A stem-changing verb because **o** in the stem changes to **ue** when stressed. This verb is generally used in this tense, in the imperfect indicative, and in the present subjunctive. It is followed by an inf.: **Suelo lavarme las manos antes de comer** / I am in the habit of washing my hands before eating.

sonar / to ring, to sound
sueno, suenas, suena;
sonamos, sonáis, suenan

A stem-changing verb because **o** in the stem changes to **ue** when stressed.

soñar / to dream
sueño, sueñas, sueña;
soñamos, soñáis, sueñan

A stem-changing verb because **o** in the stem changes to **ue** when stressed.

45

sonreír / to smile
sonrío, sonríes, sonríe;
sonreímos, sonreís, sonríen

The pres. part. is also irregular:
sonriendo

suponer / to suppose, to assume
supongo, supones, supone;
suponemos, suponéis, suponen

Irregular in the 1st pers. sing. only of
this tense.

sustituir / to substitute
sustitu**y**o, sustitu**y**es, sustitu**y**e;
sustituimos, sustituís, sustitu**y**en

This **—uir** verb requires the insertion of **y** in front of the regular
present tense endings **o, es, e,** and
en. Pres. part. is also irregular:
sustituyendo.

tener / to have, to hold
tengo, tienes, **tie**ne;
tenemos, tenéis; **tie**nen

An irregular form in the 1st pers.
sing. of this tense. Also, **e** in the
stem changes to **ie** when stressed.

traducir / to translate
tradu**zc**o, traduces, traduce;
traducimos, traducís, traducen

An orthographical changing verb
because this **—cer** verb changes **c**
to **zc** only in the 1st pers. sing. of this
tense.

traer / to bring
traigo, traes, trae;
traemos, traéis, traen

Irregular in the 1st pers. sing. only of
this tense. Also, the pres. part. is
irregular: **trayendo.**

tronar / to thunder
tru**e**na OR está tronando (in the
present progressive form)

This impersonal verb, referring to
the weather, is used in the 3rd pers.
The **o** in the stem changes to **ue**
because it is stressed. The present
progressive form may be used also
when referring to weather conditions in the present, as noted here.

valer / to be worth, to be worthy
valgo, vales, vale;
valemos, valéis, valen

Irregular only in the 1st pers. sing. of
this tense.

vencer / to conquer, to overcome
ven**z**o, vences, vence;
vencemos, vencéis, vencen

An orthographical changing verb
because **c** changes to **z** in front of **o**
or **a.**

venir / to come
vengo, vienes, **vie**ne;
venimos, venís, **vie**nen

The pres. part. is also irregular:
viniendo.

ver / to see
veo, ves, ve;
vemos, veis, ven

vestir / to clothe, to dress
v**i**sto, v**i**stes, v**i**ste;
vestimos, vestís, v**i**sten

A stem-changing verb because **e** in
the stem changes to **i** when
stressed. Pres. part. is also irregular: **vistiendo.**

vestirse / to dress oneself, to get
dressed
me v**i**sto, te v**i**stes, se v**i**ste;
nos vestimos, os vestís, se v**i**sten

A stem-changing verb because **e**
in the stem changes to **i** when
stressed. Pres. part. is also irregular: **vistiéndose.**

volar / to fly
v**ue**lo, v**ue**las, v**ue**la;
volamos, voláis, v**ue**lan

A stem-changing verb because **o** in
the stem changes to **ue** when
stressed.

volver / to return
v**ue**lvo, v**ue**lves, v**ue**lve;
volvemos, volvéis, v**ue**lven

A stem-changing verb because **o** in
the stem changes to **ue** when
stressed.

EJERCICIOS

I. Cambie el verbo del infinitivo al presente de indicativo.

    Modelo: **estar**   Yo _____ en la clase de español.

          Escriba: Yo estoy en la clase de español.

  1. volver: ¿A qué hora _____ Juana?

  2. acordarse: Yo _____ de usted.

  3. acostarse: María, ¿a qué hora te _____ todas las noches?

  4. almorzar: Todas las mañanas yo _____ a las siete.

  5. cerrar: Antes de comenzar la lección, el profesor _____ la puerta.

  6. conocer: Yo _____ bien esta ciudad.

  7. contar: Los alumnos _____ de uno a mil.

  8. costar: ¿Cuánto _____ este libro?

  9. dar: Todos los días yo _____ gracias a Dios.

10. decir: Siempre yo _____ la verdad. ¿Y Ud.?

II. Complete las oraciones a continuación. Escriba en cada oración el presente de indicativo de los verbos escritos abajo. Use cada verbo solamente una vez.

    Modelo: **dormir**   Cada noche (yo) _____ ocho horas.

                  Cada noche (yo) duermo ocho horas.

dormir	**hacer**	**morir**	**perder**	**preferir**
empezar	**ir**	**oír**	**poder**	**querer**
estar	**jugar**	**pensar**	**poner**	**ser**

  1. Yo duermo ocho horas cada noche. ¿Y Ud.? ¿Cuántas horas _____ usted cada noche?

  2. ¿A qué hora _____ la clase de español?

  3. Tu haces lo mejor posible y yo _____ lo mejor posible.

  4. Ud. está aquí y yo _____ aquí también.

  5. Tú vas al cine esta tarde y yo _____ al teatro.

  6. La señora Sánchez es muy vieja. Está gravemente enferma y _____.

  7. Alberto juega al tenis y yo _____ al béisbol.

  8. ¿Oye Ud. el ruido, señor?—Sí, yo _____ el ruido.

  9. Algunas veces yo pierdo el tiempo. ¿Y Ud.? ¿Por qué _____ Ud. el tiempo?

47

10. Yo pienso en las vacaciones de Navidad. ¿En qué _____ Ud.?

11. ¿ _____ tú hacer esto?—Sí, yo _____ hacer eso.

12. ¿Qué _____ Ud. hacer esta tarde? ¿Ir al cine o ir a la biblioteca?

13. Cuando vuelvo a casa, siempre _____ mis libros sobre la mesa en la cocina.

14. ¿Quiere Ud. ir al cine conmigo?—Sí, yo _____ ir al cine con usted.

15. La señora Sánchez _____ muy vieja. Está gravemente enferma y muere.

III. Conteste las siguientes preguntas en el afirmativo en el presente de indicativo con oraciones completas. En la oración (a) use la palabra **Sí.** En la oración (b) use la palabra **también** según los modelos.

Modelos: a. ¿Sabe Ud. la lección para hoy?   a. Sí, yo sé la lección para hoy.
           b. ¿Y los otros alumnos?   b. Los otros alumnos saben la
                                                    lección para hoy, también.

1. a. ¿Sabe Ud. qué hora es? _____

   b. ¿Y los otros alumnos? _____

2. a. ¿Sale Ud. de la escuela a las tres y media? _____

   b. ¿Y los profesores? _____

3. a. ¿Se sienta Ud. en esta silla? _____

   b. ¿Y Juana? _____

4. a. ¿Eres tú un buen alumno? _____

   b. ¿Y María? _____

5. a. ¿Sonríe Ud. de vez en cuando? _____

   b. ¿Y Pedro y Juana? _____

6. a. ¿Tiene Ud. dinero en el bolsillo? _____

   b. ¿Y el señor Rodríguez? _____

7. a. ¿Trae Ud. el libro de español a clase? _____

   b. ¿Y los otros alumnos? _____

8. a. ¿Viene Ud. a la fiesta esta noche? _____

b. ¿Y nosotros? _____

9. a. ¿Ve Ud. el aeroplano en el cielo? _____

   b. ¿Y el niño? _____

10. a. ¿Vuela el pájaro en el cielo? _____

   b. ¿Y los otros pájaros? _____

IV. En español hay muchas palabras que se escriben y se pronuncian idénticamente, pero un signo de acento es necesario para distinguir su significado.

Por ejemplo:

Yo sé / I know   **se** / *reflex. pron.* / oneself, himself, herself, yourself, yourselves, themselves

Yo sé que su amigo se llama José. I know that your friend's name is José.

presente de indicativo

saber / to know

yo	sé	nosotros	sabemos
tú	sabes	vosotros	sabéis
Ud.		Uds.	
él	sabe	ellos	saben
ella		ellas	

Mnemonic tip

Saber is to know something, to know a fact.
Conocer is to know in the sense of to be acquainted with a person, a place, a thing.

Yo sé que tú conoces a José, mi mejor amigo.
I know that you know José, my best friend.

¿Cuántos ejemplos puede Ud. decir y escribir?
¿Puede Ud. dar un "mnemonic tip"?

V. En español hay muchas palabras que se escriben y se pronuncian idénticamente, pero un signo de acento es necesario para distinguir su significado.

Por ejemplo:

de *prep.* of, from   **Dé al señor la taza grande de la cocina.** Give to the gentleman the big cup from the kitchen.

dé *3rd person, singular (Ud.), Imperative* (Command) of **dar** / to give

dar / to give

presente de indicativo

yo	doy	nosotros	damos
tú	das	vosotros	dais
Ud.		Uds.	
él	da	ellos	dan
ella		ellas	

Imperativo

(yo)	—	(nosotros)	demos
(tú)	da; no des	(vosotros)	dad; no deis
(Ud.)	**dé**	(Uds.)	den

¿Cuántos ejemplos puede Ud. decir y escribir?

The Present Participle (participio) and the Present Progressive Tense

Present participle: A present participle is a verb form which, in English, ends in *-ing;* for example, *singing, eating, receiving.* In Spanish, a present participle is regularly formed as follows:

drop the **ar** of an **-ar** ending verb, like **cantar,** and add **-ando: cantando** / singing
drop the **er** of an **-er** ending verb, like **comer,** and add **-iendo: comiendo** / eating
drop the **ir** of an **-ir** ending verb, like **recibir,** and add **-iendo: recibiendo** / receiving

In English, a gerund also ends in *-ing* but there is a distinct difference in use between a gerund and a present participle in English. In brief, it is this: In English, when a present participle is used as a noun it is called a gerund; for example: *Reading is good.* As a present participle in English: The boy fell asleep *while reading.*

In the first example *(Reading is good), reading* is a gerund because it is the subject of the verb *is.* In Spanish, however, we must not use the present participle form as a noun to serve as a subject; we must use the infinitive form of the verb in Spanish: **Leer es bueno.**

Common irregular present participles are as follows. You ought to know them so that you may be able to recognize them if they are on the next standardized test in Spanish that you take.

INFINITIVE	PRESENT PARTICIPLE
caer / to fall	**cayendo** / falling
conseguir / to attain, to achieve	**consiguiendo** / attaining, achieving
construir / to construct	**construyendo** / constructing
corregir / to correct	**corrigiendo** / correcting
creer / to believe	**creyendo** / believing
decir / to say, to tell	**diciendo** / saying, telling
despedirse / to say good-bye	**despidiéndose** / saying good-bye
destruir / to destroy	**destruyendo** / destroying
divertirse / to enjoy oneself	**divirtiéndose** / enjoying oneself
dormir / to sleep	**durmiendo** / sleeping
huir / to flee	**huyendo** / fleeing
ir / to go	**yendo** / going
leer / to read	**leyendo** / reading
mentir / to lie (tell a falsehood)	**mintiendo** / lying
morir / to die	**muriendo** / dying
oír / to hear	**oyendo** / hearing
pedir / to ask (for), to request	**pidiendo** / asking (for), requesting
poder / to be able	**pudiendo** / being able
reír / to laugh	**riendo** / laughing
repetir / to repeat	**repitiendo** / repeating
seguir / to follow	**siguiendo** / following
sentir / to feel	**sintiendo** / feeling
servir / to serve	**sirviendo** / serving
traer / to bring	**trayendo** / bringing
venir / to come	**viniendo** / coming
vestir / to dress	**vistiendo** / dressing

The present participle is needed to form the present progressive tense by using **estar** in the present indicative tense plus the present participle of the main verb you are using; *e.g.,* **Estoy hablando** (I am talking), *i.e.,* I am (in the act of) talking (right now).

EJERCICIOS

I. Cambie el verbo del presente de indicativo al presente progresivo.

    Modelo: Hablo. ⟶ Estoy hablando.

1. Trabajo. _____	13. Escribo. _____
2. Ando. _____	14. Remito. _____
3. Bailo. _____	15. Subo. _____
4. Busco. _____	16. Vivo. _____
5. Contesto. _____	17. Caigo. _____
6. Aprendo. _____	18. Digo. _____
7. Bebo. _____	19. Duermo. _____
8. Como. _____	20. Voy. _____
9. Leo. _____	21. Oigo. _____
10. Vendo. _____	22. Traigo. _____
11. Corro. _____	23. Vengo. _____
12. Abro. _____	24. Sirvo. _____

II. Cambie el verbo del presente progresivo al presente de indicativo.

    Modelo: Estoy hablando ⟶ Hablo.

1. Estoy trabajando. _____	8. Estoy andando. _____
2. Estamos bailando. _____	9. Están comiendo. _____
3. Ud. está buscando. _____	10. Uds. están contestando. _____
4. Ella está aprendiendo. _____	11. Él está oyendo. _____
5. Juana está trayendo. _____	12. Pedro está diciendo. _____
6. Estoy sirviendo. _____	13. Tú estás corriendo. _____
7. Estamos bebiendo. _____	14. Estoy cayendo. _____

III. Dictado. Escriba las oraciones que su profesor de español va a leer.

1. _____

2. _____

3. _____

IV. **¿Qué puede Ud. lanzar?** / What can you throw?

Escriba una lista de cosas que Ud. puede lanzar.

Por ejemplo:

Puedo lanzar una pelota / I can throw a ball.
Puedo lanzar una moneda / I can throw a coin.
    un lápiz / a pencil
    una pluma / a pen
    un libro / a book
    un cuaderno / a notebook
    un huevo / an egg
    un ladrillo / a brick

¿Cuántos ejemplos puede Ud. decir y escribir?

presente de indicativo

poder / to be able, can

yo	puedo	nosotros	podemos
tú	puedes	vosotros	podéis
Ud.		Uds.	
él	puede	ellos	pueden
ella		ellas	

V. **¿Qué puede Ud. mirar?** / What can you look at?

Escriba una lista de cosas que Ud. puede mirar.

Por ejemplo:

Puedo mirar la televisión / I can look at (watch) television.
Puedo mirar el cielo / I can look at the sky.
    el pájaro en la jaula / the bird in the cage
    las estrellas / the stars
    la luna / the moon

¿Cuántos ejemplos puede Ud. decir y escribir?

INDEFINITE AND NEGATIVE WORDS COMMONLY USED

algo / something, anything (with **sin,** use **nada; sin nada** / without anything)

alguien / anybody, anyone, someone, somebody (with **sin,** use **nadie; sin nadie** / without any-one)

alguno, alguna, algunos, algunas / some, any

jamás / ever, never, not ever

nada / nothing (**sin nada** / without anything); after **sin, nada** is used instead of **algo; Ella no quiere nada** / She does not want anything.

nadie / nobody, no one, not anyone, not anybody (**sin nadie** / without anybody); after **sin, nadie** is used instead of **alguien**

ni / neither, nor

ni . . . ni / neither . . . nor

ni siquiera / not even

ninguno, ninguna / no one, none, not any, not anybody

nunca / never, not ever, ever

o / or

o . . . o / either . . . or

siempre / always

también / also, too

tampoco / neither; **ni yo tampoco** / nor I either

unos cuantos, unas cuantas / a few, some, several

EJERCICIOS

I. Una la palabra en español con su equivalente en inglés.

1. **algo** _____ always

2. **alguien** _____ not even

3. **alguno** _____ never

4. **jamás** _____ something

5. **nada** _____ nothing

6. **nadie** _____ someone

7. **ni** _____ some, any

8. **ni siquiera** _____ nobody, no one

9. **nunca** _____ neither, nor

10. **siempre** _____ ever

II. Traduzca.

1. something _____

2. a few, some, several _____

3. ever _____

4. never _____

5. either . . . or _____

6. neither . . . nor _____

7. not even _____

8. no one, nobody _____

9. somebody, someone _____

10. without anything _____

The Adoration of the Magi (ca. 1655-1660) by Bartolomé Esteban MURILLO (1617-1682)
Courtesy of The Toledo Museum of Art, Toledo, Ohio.

The Agony in the Garden (1590s) by EL GRECO (1541–1614)
Courtesy of The Toledo Museum of Art, Toledo, Ohio

La señora Rodríguez levanta la mano para espantar las moscas.

Have you ever been at a public auction?
Let's see what happens to
Señora Rodríguez.

¡Vete! ¡Vete!

La señora Rodríguez y su esposo salen de casa para ir a una venta pública. A la señora Rodríguez le gustan mucho las ventas públicas. Quiere comprar una pequeña mesa redonda para el vestíbulo de la casa.

Los señores Rodríguez llegan y entran en la sala de ventas. Oyen la voz del subastador que está hablando a un grupo de personas.   5

El subastador: Señoras y señores, ¡Atención! ¡Por favor!
(Los señores Rodríguez se sientan en la quinta fila cerca de la puerta.)

El subastador: Tengo aquí, señoras y señores, un sillón muy hermoso. ¿Quién ofrece cincuenta pesetas?
(El señor Rodríguez está hablando a su esposa en voz baja:—Todo es muy elegante aquí.   10
Muy elegante.)
(La señora Rodríguez responde en voz baja:—Sí, querido mío, pero a mí no me gustan todas estas moscas en esta sala. ¡Y el sillón es muy feo!)

El subastador: ¡Muchas gracias, señor! ¡Tengo cincuenta pesetas por este sillón tan hermoso! ¿Quién ofrece sesenta pesetas? . . . Sesenta pesetas no es mucho   15
dinero por este sillón muy hermoso. ¿Quién ofrece sesenta pesetas?
(La señora Rodríguez dice a su esposo en voz baja:—¡Las moscas en esta sala son terribles!)

El subastador: ¡Muchas gracias, señora! ¡Muchas gracias! Tengo sesenta pesetas de la dama en la primera fila. ¿Quién ofrece setenta pesetas?   20
(La señora Rodríguez pregunta a su esposo en voz baja:—Francisco, ¿quién es la dama en la primera fila que ofrece sesenta pesetas por el sillón monstruoso? ¡Está loca!)

(El señor Rodríguez responde:—Yo no sé, querida mía.)

El subastador: ¡Muchas gracias, señora! ¡Muchas gracias! ¡Tengo una oferta de setenta pesetas! . . . ¡Muchas gracias, señor! Tengo una oferta de ochenta pesetas.   25
¿Quién ofrece noventa pesetas? . . . ¿Muchas gracias, señora! Tengo una oferta de noventa pesetas de la dama allá en la tercera fila. ¿Quién ofrece cien pesetas? ¿Cien pesetas? ¿Cien pesetas? ¿Quién ofrece cien pesetas?
(La señora Rodríguez levanta la mano para espantar las moscas— ¡Oh! ¡Estas moscas!)   30

El subastador: ¡Muchas gracias, señora! ¡Tengo cien pesetas de la dama en la quinta fila cerca de la puerta! ¡Tengo cien pesetas! ¿Quién ofrece más? ¡¿Nadie?! ¡Es la última oferta! Una vez, dos veces, tres veces. ¡Se terminó! ¡Vendido a la graciosa dama que está con su esposo en la quinta fila cerca de la puerta! Ud. puede pagar al cajero, por favor, señora.   35
(Todo el mundo mira para ver quién es la señora. ¡Es la señora Rodríguez!)

La señora Rodríguez: ¿Quién? ¿Yo?

EJERCICIOS

I. Seleccione la respuesta correcta según la lectura de esta lección.

1. La señora Rodríguez y su esposo (a) llegan (b) pueden (c) se sientan (d) salen de casa para ir a una venta pública. _____

2. A la señora Rodríguez le gustan mucho (a) las pequeñas mesas redondas (b) los vestíbulos (c) los sillones (d) las ventas públicas. _____

3. Los señores Rodríguez oyen la voz (a) de la dama en la primera fila (b) de la dama en la tercera fila (c) del cajero (d) del subastador. _____

4. La señora Rodríguez piensa que el sillón es muy (a) fea (b) feo (c) hermoso (d) hermosa. _____

5. La dama en la tercera fila ofrece (a) sesenta (b) setenta (c) ochenta (d) noventa pesetas. _____

6. La dama que ofrece sesenta pesetas está en la (a) primera (b) segunda (c) tercera (d) quinta fila. _____

7. La señora Rodríguez levanta la mano para (a) ofrecer cien pesetas (b) responder (c) contestar (d) espantar las moscas. _____

8. Los señores Rodríguez están sentados en la quinta fila cerca (a) de la ventana (b) de la puerta (c) del sillón (d) de la pequeña mesa redonda. _____

9. La persona que está hablando a un grupo de personas es (a) la señora Rodríguez (b) el señor Rodríguez (c) la dama en la primera fila (d) el subastador. _____

10. La señora Rodríguez quiere comprar (a) un sillón (b) un vestíbulo (c) una silla (d) una pequeña mesa redonda. _____

II. Acróstico. Complete este acróstico en español.

1. is **hablando**
2. to sit down
3. door
4. there
5. nobody
6. third, *m.s.*
7. attention
8. round, *m.s.*

III. Escriba frases con el vocabulario a continuación. Consulte la lectura de esta lección.

1. el cajero _____

2. cien pesetas _____

3. espantar _____

4. está hablando _____

5. feo _____

6. loco _____

7. mosca _____

8. primer _____

9. tercer _____

10. todo el mundo _____

Estructuras de la lengua

NEGATION OF VERB FORMS

(a) To make a verb form negative, place **no** in front of the verb form:

Yo comprendo.   **Yo no comprendo.**   **Estoy leyendo.**   **¿Trabaja Ud.?**
I understand.   *I do not understand.*   **No estoy leyendo.**   **¿No trabaja Ud.?**

(b) To make an infinitive negative, place **no** in front of it:

No entrar.   **No fumar.**   **No estacionar.**   **Prefiero no escuchar.**
Do not enter.   *Do not smoke.*   *Do not park.*   *I prefer not to listen.*
  or   or
No smoking.   *No parking.*

(c) To make a verb form negative when there is a direct object pronoun, place **no** in front of the direct object pronoun:

No lo creo.   **No lo sé.**   **No la conozco.**
I don't believe it.   *I don't know it.*   *I don't know her.*

(d) To make a verb form negative when there is an indirect object pronoun, place **no** in front of the indirect object pronoun:

No le hablo a él.   **Pablo no me habla.**   **Juan no le habla a ella.**
I don't talk to him.   *Paul does not talk to me.*   *John does not talk to her.*

(e) To make a verb form negative when the verb is reflexive, place **no** in front of the reflexive pronoun:

Tú no te lavas.   **No me siento aquí.**   **No me llamo Juan.**
You do not wash yourself.   *I am not sitting here.*   *My name is not John.*

(f) To make a verb form negative when the verb is in the imperative, place **no** in front of the verb form:

¡No hable Ud.!   **¡No me escriba (Ud.)!**   **¡No entres (tú)!**
Do not talk!   *Do not write to me!*   *Do not enter!*

(g) With some negations, particularly with the verb **tener,** or in an interrogative statement before an unmodified noun object, the indefinite article is not ordinarily used:

¿Tiene Ud. libro?—No, señor, no tengo libro.
Do you have a book? — No, sir, I do not have a book.

NUMBERS

Cardinal numbers: zero to one hundred million

0	cero	62	sesenta y dos, *etc.*
1	uno, una	**70**	**setenta**
2	dos	71	setenta y uno, setenta y una
3	tres	72	setenta y dos, *etc.*
4	cuatro	**80**	**ochenta**
5	cinco	81	ochenta y uno, ochenta y una
6	seis	82	ochenta y dos, *etc.*
7	siete	**90**	**noventa**
8	ocho	91	noventa y uno, noventa y una
9	nueve	92	noventa y dos, *etc.*
10	**diez**	**100**	**ciento (cien)**
11	once	101	ciento uno, ciento una
12	doce	102	ciento dos, *etc.*
13	trece	**200**	**doscientos, doscientas**
14	catorce	300	trescientos, trescientas
15	quince	400	cuatrocientos, cuatrocientas
16	**dieciséis**	500	quinientos, quinientas
17	**diecisiete**	600	seiscientos, seiscientas
18	**dieciocho**	700	setecientos, setecientas
19	**diecinueve**	800	ochocientos, ochocientas
20	**veinte**	900	novecientos, novecientas
21	**veintiuno**	**1,000**	**mil**
22	**veintidós**	2,000	dos mil
23	**veintitrés**	3,000	tres mil, *etc.*
24	**veinticuatro**	100,000	cien mil
25	**veinticinco**	200,000	doscientos mil, doscientas mil
26	**veintiséis**	300,000	trescientos mil, trescientas mil, *etc.*
27	**veintisiete**	**1,000,000**	**un millón (de + noun)**
28	**veintiocho**	2,000,000	dos millones (de + noun)
29	**veintinueve**	3,000,000	tres millones (de + noun), *etc.*
30	**treinta**	100,000,000	cien millones (de + noun)
31	treinta y uno, treinta y una		
32	treinta y dos, *etc.*		
40	**cuarenta**		

Approximate numbers

unos veinte libros / about (some) twenty books
unas treinta personas / about (some) thirty persons

41	cuarenta y uno, cuarenta y una
42	cuarenta y dos, *etc.*
50	**cincuenta**
51	cincuenta y uno, cincuenta y
52	una
60	cincuenta y dos, *etc.*
61	**sesenta**
	sesenta y uno, sesenta y una

Simple arithmetical expressions

dos **y** dos son cuatro	$2 + 2 = 4$
diez **menos** cinco son cinco	$10 - 5 = 5$
tres **por** cinco son quince	$3 \times 5 = 15$
diez **dividido por** dos son cinco	$10 \div 2 = 5$

Ordinal numbers: first to tenth

primero, primer, primera	first	1st
segundo, segunda	second	2nd
tercero, tercer, tercera	third	3rd
cuarto, cuarta	fourth	4th
quinto, quinta	fifth	5th
sexto, sexta	sixth	6th
séptimo, séptima	seventh	7th
octavo, octava	eighth	8th
noveno, novena	ninth	9th
décimo, décima	tenth	10th

NOTE that beyond 10th the cardinal numbers are used instead of the ordinal numbers, but when there is a noun involved, the cardinal number is placed after the noun: **el día 15** (**el día quince** / the fifteenth day).

NOTE also that in titles of monarchs, *etc.* the definite article is not used between the person's name and the number, but it is in English: **Alfonso XIII (Alfonso Trece** / Alfonso the Thirteenth).

AND NOTE that **noveno** (9th) changes to **nono** in such titles: **Luis IX (Luis Nono** / Louis the Ninth).

EJERCICIOS

I. Escriba la palabra que corresponde a los números según el modelo.

Modelo: $3 + 3 = 6$ **Tres y tres son seis.**

1. $8 + 7 = 15$ _____

2. $15 - 7 = 8$ _____

3. $6 \times 8 = 48$ _____

4. $21 \div 7 = 3$ _____

II. Dé la palabra en español. Escriba el nombre de los números a continuación.

1. 0 _____	6. 16 _____	11. 40 _____
2. 4 _____	7. 20 _____	12. 50 _____
3. 6 _____	8. 22 _____	13. 60 _____
4. 7 _____	9. 30 _____	14. 70 _____
5. 15 _____	10. 32 _____	15. 80 _____

61

III. Traduzca al español.

1. Do not talk! (Use **Ud.**) _____

2. Do not write to me! (Use **Ud.**) _____

3. Do not enter! (Use **Tú**) _____

4. I do not understand. _____

5. Don't you have a book? (Use **Ud.**) _____

6. I prefer not to listen. _____

7. They prefer not to work. _____

8. Mary doesn't talk to me. _____

9. Jane doesn't talk to her. _____

10. I don't know it. _____

IV. Dictado. Escriba las oraciones que su profesor de español va a leer.

1. _____

2. _____

3. _____

V. La palabra misteriosa. Usando el vocabulario dado más abajo, busque las palabras españolas en el árbol. Las palabras están escritas horizontalmente, verticalmente, y a la inversa. Raye las palabras encontradas. Ponga en orden las siete letras que quedan para hallar la palabra misteriosa.

Feliz / Happy   **regalo** / gift   **nieve** / snow
Navidad / Christmas   **amor** / love   **luz** / light

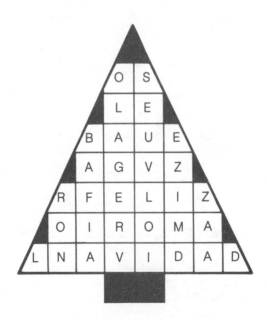

VI. Complete este crucigrama.

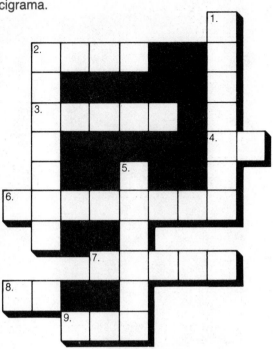

HORIZONTALES: 2. Una persona duerme sobre una _____. 3. Sinónimo de **esposa.** 4. Forma del verbo **ser,** tercera persona, singular, en el presente de indicativo. 6. Gerundio de **hablar.** 7. Una persona se sienta en una _____. 8. Forma del verbo **saber,** primera persona, singular, en el presente de indicativo. 9. Contrario de **hermoso.**

VERTICALES: 1. Contrario de **último.** 2. Sinónimo de **andar.** 5. Sinónimo de **esposo.**

Madrid. Monumento a Goya.
Reprinted with permission of Oficina Nacional Española de Turismo, Paris.

Doña Teresa Sureda *by Francisco José de GOYA y Lucientes (1746–1828)*
Courtesy of The National Gallery of Art, Washington, D.C.

¡Qué almuerzo!

In this scene, Clara and Francisco Rodríguez are with their friends María and José Sánchez. The Sánchez family lives in Puerto Rico but at present they are visiting their friends who now live in New York City. They are all with their children in Central Park to celebrate the 4th of July.

¡Viva el cuatro de julio!

Clara Rodríguez:	¿Vengan, todos, vengan! Vamos a sentarnos en la hierba ahora. Vamos a comenzar con los bocadillos de carne. Juana, ¿tienes los bocadillos?
Juana:	¿Los bocadillos? ¿Qué bocadillos? No tengo los bocadillos. Tengo solamente los pasteles.
Clara Rodríguez:	¿No tienes los bocadillos de carne? Bueno, bueno . . . Pedro, tú tienes los bocadillos, de seguro.
Pedro:	No, mamá, no los tengo. Tengo solamente los bizcochos.
Clara Rodríguez:	Francisco, querido mío, tú tienes, seguramente, el rosbif, las chuletas de ternera, la carne de cerdo, el jamón, y el pollo.
Francisco Rodríguez:	No, querida mía, no los tengo. Tengo solamente tres cubos de helado.
Clara Rodríguez:	María, tú tienes, seguramente, los bocadillos de carne, el rosbif, las chuletas de ternera, la carne de cerdo, el jamón, y el pollo.
María Sánchez:	No, amiga mía. Tengo solamente bizcochos, pasteles, y postres.
Clara Rodríguez:	José, tú tienes, de seguro, las salchichas y los salchichones.
José Sánchez:	No, amiga mía. Tengo solamente bizcochos, pasteles y postres. Tengo también una botella de agua mineral. El agua mineral es buena para la salud.
Clara Rodríguez:	¡Qué almuerzo!
Los niños:	¡Qué fortuna! ¡Nosotros los niños preferimos los postres!
Clara Rodríguez:	Pues, amigos míos, ¡vamos a comer los bizcochos, los pasteles, y el helado!

5

10

15

20

VOCABULARIO: Consult the vocabulary section in the back pages.

EJERCICIOS

I. Seleccione la respuesta correcta según la lectura de esta lección.

1. Las ocho personas en esta escena van a tomar el almuerzo   (a) en casa   (b) en Puerto Rico   (c) en la hierba   (d) en el comedor   _____

2. María y José Sánchez son   (a) de Puerto Rico   (b) de Nueva York   (c) de España   (d) de México   _____

67

3. El rosbif y el jamón son   (a) deliciosos   (b) carnes   (c) sabrosos   (d) abun-
dantes   _____

4. Para el almuerzo hay solamente   (a) carne   (b) bocadillos   (c) chuletas de ternera   (d) pasteles y helado   _____

5. Las ocho personas en esta escena van a comer   (a) salchichas   (b) salchichones   (c) bocadillos   (d) pasteles y helado   _____

II. ¿Sí o No?

1. Francisco es el esposo de Clara Rodríguez.   _____

2. María es la esposa de José Sánchez.   _____

3. El Central Park es un parque en Puerto Rico.   _____

4. El pastel es un postre.   _____

5. El helado es una especie de carne.   _____

III. Complete este crucigrama.

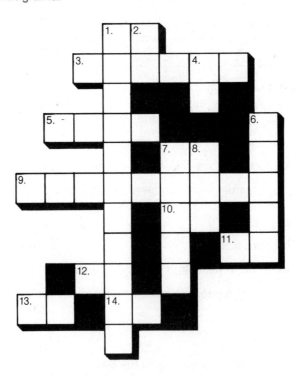

HORIZONTALES: **1.** Forma reflexiva del pronombre personal, tercera persona, s. y pl.   **3.** Sustantivo del verbo *helar.*   **5.** Líquido transparente.   **7.** Adjetivo posesivo, segunda persona, singular.   **9.** Nada más, únicamente.   **10.** Contrario de *sí.*   **11.** Complemento indirecto (indirect
object pron.).   **12.** Una preposición que se puede usar aquí en lugar de *sobre.*   **13.** Complemento directo (direct object pron., f.s.).   **14.** Forma reflexiva del pronombre personal, segunda persona, s.

VERTICALES: **1.** Sinónimo de *de seguro.*   **2.** Artículo determinado, m.s.   **4.** Preposición.   **6.** Forma del verbo *tener,* pres. indic., tercera persona, s.   **7.** Forma del verbo *tener,* pres.
indic., primera persona, s.   **8.** Número cardinal.

IV. Acróstico. Complete las palabras en español.

1. biscuit

2. eye

3. meat

4. to attack

5. surely

6. incredible

7. language

8. lesson

9. eighty

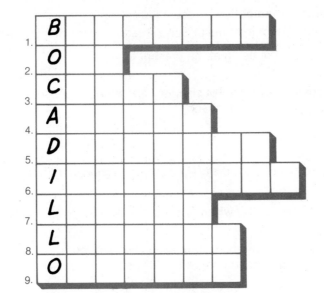

V. LETRA RELOJ. Cuatro palabras se esconden en este reloj: Una palabra de las doce a las tres, una palabra de las tres a las seis, una palabra de las seis a las nueve y, por fin, una palabra de las nueve a las doce.

La misma letra es común a la palabra que sigue.

Este reloj no tiene agujas. ¡Es un reloj de palabras!

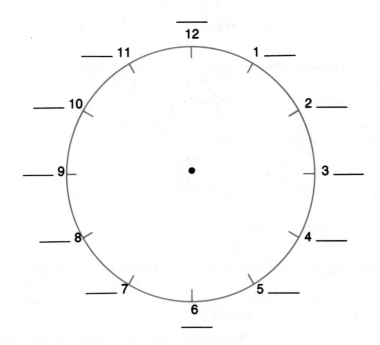

De las doce a las tres es un sinónimo del nombre **trabajo.**
De las tres a las seis es el antónimo de **nada.**
De las seis a las nueve es un animal, en el plural.
De las nueve a las doce es un sinónimo de **supremo.**

Estructuras de la lengua

Tense No. 1: Presente de indicativo (Present indicative)

This tense is used most of the time in Spanish and English. It indicates:

(a) An action or a state of being at the present time.

> EXAMPLES:
>
> 1. **Hablo** español / *I speak* Spanish, or *I am speaking* Spanish, or *I do speak* Spanish.
> 2. **Creo en** Dios / *I believe* in God.

(b) Habitual action.

> EXAMPLE:
>
> **Voy** a la biblioteca todos los días / *I go* to the library every day, or *I do go* to the library every day.

(c) A general truth, something which is permanently true.

> EXAMPLES:
>
> 1. Seis menos dos **son** cuatro / Six minus two *are* four.
> 2. El ejercicio **hace** maestro al novicio / Practice *makes* perfect.

(d) Vividness when talking or writing about past events.

> EXAMPLE:
>
> El asesino **se pone** pálido. **Tiene** miedo. **Sale** de la casa y **corre** a lo largo del río / The murderer *turns* pale. *He is* afraid. *He goes out* of the house and *runs* along the river.

(e) A near future.

> EXAMPLES:
>
> Mi hermano **llega** mañana / My brother *arrives* tomorrow.
> ¿**Escuchamos** un disco ahora? / Shall we listen to a record now?

(f) An action or state of being that occurred in the past and *continues up to the present.* In Spanish this is an idiomatic use of the *Present tense* of a verb with **hace,** which is also in the *Present.*

> EXAMPLE:
>
> **Hace** tres horas que **miro** la televisión / *I have been watching* television for three hours.

(g) The meaning of *almost* or *nearly* when used with **por poco.**

> EXAMPLE:
>
> Por poco me **matan** / They almost *killed* me.

This tense is regularly formed as follows:

Drop the **—ar** ending of an infinitive, like **hablar,** and add the following endings: **o, as, a; amos, áis, an**
> You then get: **hablo, hablas, habla;**
> **hablamos, habláis, hablan**

Drop the **—er** ending of an infinitive, like **beber,** and add the following endings: **o, es, e; emos, éis, en**
> You then get: **bebo, bebes, bebe;**
> **bebemos, bebéis, beben**

Drop the **—ir** ending of an infinitive, like **recibir,** and add the following endings: **o, es, e; imos, ís, en**
> You then get: **recibo, recibes, recibe;**
> **recibimos, recibís, reciben**

NOTE: For verbs irregular in the present indicative, see Work Unit 3.

¿CUÁNTO TIEMPO HACE QUE + PRESENT TENSE . . . ?

(a) Use this formula when you want to ask *How long* + *the present perfect tense* in English:

¿Cuánto tiempo hace que Ud. estudia español? / How long have you been studying Spanish?

¿Cuánto tiempo hace que Ud. espera el autobús? / How long have you been waiting for the bus?

(b) When this formula is used, you generally expect the person to tell you how long a time it has been, *e.g.,* one year, two months, a few minutes.

(c) This is used when the action began at some time in the past and continues up to the present moment. That is why you must use the present tense of the verb—the action of studying, waiting, *etc.* is still going on at the present.

HACE + LENGTH OF TIME + QUE + PRESENT TENSE

(a) This formula is the usual answer to the question above.

(b) Since the question is asked in terms of *how long,* the usual answer is in terms of time: a year, two years, a few days, months, minutes, *etc.:*

Hace tres años que estudio español / I have been studying Spanish for three years.

Hace veinte minutos que espero el autobús / I have been waiting for the bus for twenty minutes.

(c) The same formula is used if you want to ask *how many weeks, how many months, how many minutes,* etc.:

¿Cuántos años hace que Ud. estudia español? / How many years have you been studying Spanish?

¿Cuántas horas hace que Ud. mira la televisión? / How many hours have you been watching television?

¿DESDE CUÁNDO + PRESENT TENSE . . . ?

This is another way of asking *How long (since when)* + *the present perfect tense* in English, as given above.

¿Desde cuándo estudia Ud. español? / How long have you been studying Spanish?

PRESENT TENSE + DESDE HACE + LENGTH OF TIME

This formula is the usual answer to the previous question.

Estudio español desde hace tres años / I have been studying Spanish for three years.

ACABAR DE + INF.

The Spanish idiomatic expression **acabar de + inf.** is expressed in English as *to have just* + past participle.

In the present indicative:

María acaba de llegar / Mary has just arrived.
Acabo de comer / I have just eaten.
Acabamos de terminar la lección / We have just finished the lesson.

NOTE: When you use **acabar** in the present tense, it indicates that the action of the main verb (+ inf.) has just occurred now in the present. In English, we express this by using *have just* + the past participle of the main verb: **Acabo de llegar** / I have just arrived.

71

EJERCICIOS

I. Escriba el número y la persona de los siguientes verbos que están en el presente de indicativo.

    Modelo: estudio   **Escriba:** singular, primera persona

1. hablo _____
2. voy _____
3. trabajamos _____
4. escriben _____
5. aprende _____
6. amo _____
7. andamos _____
8. vivimos _____
9. quepo _____
10. cierro _____

11. digo _____
12. sé _____
13. pongo _____
14. cuelgo _____
15. doy _____
16. cuesta _____
17. dais _____
18. soy _____
19. eres _____
20. son _____

II. Escriba el infinitivo de los siguientes verbos que están en el presente de indicativo.

    Modelo: voy   **Escriba:** ir

1. vamos _____
2. doy _____
3. acuerdo _____
4. almuerzo _____
5. cierran _____
6. quepo _____
7. cuezo _____
8. conozco _____
9. das _____
10. digo _____

11. duermen _____
12. estoy _____
13. fríe _____
14. he _____
15. hago _____
16. vamos _____
17. muere _____
18. nieva _____
19. pienso _____
20. pueden _____

III. Escriba la forma femenina de los siguientes sustantivos.

    Modelo: esposo   **Escriba:** esposa

1. hombre _____
2. muchacho _____
3. hermano _____

4. tío _____
5. chico _____
6. padre _____

7. abuelo _____   9. profesor _____

8. dentista _____   10. amigo _____

IV. Escriba la forma femenina de los siguientes adjetivos.

   Modelo: hermoso   **Escriba:** hermosa

1. bello _____   6. viejos _____

2. feo _____   7. interesantes _____

3. elegante _____   8. inglés _____

4. pequeño _____   9. blanco _____

5. pocos _____   10. inteligente _____

V. Componga frases con el vocabulario de esta lección.

   Modelo: bocadillos   **Escriba:** Juana, ¿tienes los bocadillos?

1. las salchichas _____

2. los bizcochos _____

3. el helado _____

4. fortuna _____

5. la carne _____

VI. Cambie el infinitivo del verbo al presente de indicativo.

   Modelo: Yo no los *tener.*   **Escriba:** Yo no los tengo.

1. Yo no *saber* la lección. _____

2. Yo no *decir* la respuesta. _____

3. Nosotros *poder* escribir la lección. _____

4. ¿Qué *querer* Ud. hacer? _____

5. Yo *salir* de la escuela a las tres. _____

6. Estos libros *ser* excelentes. _____

7. María, ¿cuántos años *tener* tú? _____

8. Nosotros los estudiantes *ser* serios. _____

   _____

9. Yo *venir* a tu casa todos los días. Y María, ¿cuándo *venir* ella? _____

   _____

10. Yo *ver* la escuela. Y usted, ¿*ver* la casa? _____

VII. Responda en español en frases completas.

    Modelo: ¿Adónde va Ud. esta tarde?   **Escriba:** Esta tarde voy a la playa.

1. ¿En qué cuarto de su casa mira Ud. la televisión? _____

_____

2. ¿En qué mes del año comienzan las vacaciones de verano? _____

_____

3. ¿En qué ciudad vive Ud.? _____

4. ¿Qué hace Ud. los sábados? _____

5. ¿Cuántos años tiene Ud.? ¿Y su madre? _____

VIII. Responda en español en frases completas.

    Modelo: ¿Cuántos años hace que Ud. estudia español?
    Escriba: Hace dos años que estudio español.

1. ¿Cuántos minutos hace que Ud. espera el autobús? _____

_____

2. ¿Cuánto tiempo hace que Ud. lee este libro? _____

_____

3. ¿Cuántas horas hace que Ud. mira la televisión? _____

_____

4. ¿Cuántos años hace que Ud. estudia español? _____

_____

5. ¿Desde cuándo estudia Ud. español? _____

_____

IX. Traduzca.

1. Mary has just arrived. _____

2. I have just eaten. _____

3. We have just finished the lesson. _____

4. I have just spoken. _____

5. I have just written a letter. _____

X. Varias palabras en una sola. Utilizando las letras en la palabra **AFORTUNADAMENTE,** ¿cuántas palabras puede usted escribir? Escriba diez palabras, por lo menos.

> **AFORTUNADAMENTE**

1. _____   3. _____   5. _____   7. _____   9. _____

2. _____   4. _____   6. _____   8. _____   10. _____

XI. Humor. La adivinanza para hoy. *(The riddle for today.)*

1. ¿Qué hay en el medio de Sevilla?

Solución: _____

Return from Egypt *by Francisco de ZURBARÁN*
Courtesy of The Toledo Museum of Art, Toledo, Ohio

75

The Return of the Prodigal Son *by Bartolomé Esteban MURILLO (1617–1682)*
Courtesy of The National Gallery of Art, Washington, D.C.

*Have you or any of your friends ever thought
of leaving home? Of running away? Read
what happens to Pablo in the following story,
which is based on the parable of the prodigal
son.*

Un padre y sus dos hijos

Un padre tenía dos hijos que se llamaban Andrés y Pablo. Andrés tenía veinte años y Pablo tenía dieciocho.

Un día, Pablo, el más joven, le dijo a su padre:

—Padre, dame, por favor, la tierra de tu propiedad que me pertenece. Quiero partir para buscar mi libertad y para divertirme. Para hacer esto, necesito dinero. No me gusta vivir en este pequeño pueblo porque no estoy contento aquí. Quiero ir a Nueva York donde hay muchas diversiones y mucho que hacer. 5

El padre no sabía que hacer. Pensó en la petición de su hijo y después de algunos días, vendió la mitad de su tierra y le dio el dinero a su hijo. La otra mitad era la herencia para Andrés, el hijo mayor, la cual recibiría a la muerte del padre. 10

Pablo tomó el dinero, que era una gran fortuna, y fue a Nueva York. En aquella ciudad se divertía todas las noches hasta la madrugada en las tabernas gastando mucho dinero. Todos los días iba al cine, al teatro y a otros espectáculos divertidos con sus nuevos amigos. A las muchachas les daba regalos, dulces, y flores. Durante el día, dormía y durante la noche se divertía. Estaba muy contento. 15

Después de dos años, cuando Pablo había gastado toda la fortuna que su padre le había dado, no tenía nada que comer. Pidió dinero a sus amigos y a sus amigas pero no le dieron nada, diciendo que no tenían bastante dinero.

Pablo fue a buscar trabajo para ganarse la vida, pero no halló nada.

Pablo se puso a pensar. Se dijo: No tengo más dinero. He gastado toda la fortuna que mi 20 padre me dio como herencia. No tengo dinero para pagar la habitación donde vivo. Tengo mucha hambre y no tengo nada que comer. Regresaré a la casa de mi padre porque él me ama.

Regresó a la casa de su padre. Pablo estaba sucio y los vestidos que llevaba también estaban sucios y rasgados. Cuando su padre lo vio llegar a la puerta de su casa, lo reconoció 25 inmediatamente, a pesar de su apariencia diferente. El padre corrió al encuentro de su hijo, lo recibió con abrazos y besos paternales.

De rodillas, Pablo le dijo a su padre:

—Padre mío, perdóname. He sido tonto, he hecho tantas cosas tontas, gasté todo el dinero que tú me diste, no pude hallar trabajo para vivir, no tenía nada que comer. Mis amigos 30 nuevos no me dieron ninguna ayuda. Padre, no merezco llamarme tu hijo. Perdóname, padre mío. ¿Puedes aceptarme en tu casa?

El padre respondió:

—Hijo mío, mi casa es tu casa. Todo lo que tengo es tuyo. Tú eres mi hijo. Por supuesto, te acepto. Entra en tu casa. Tú te habías perdido y yo te he encontrado. 35

Entretanto, Andrés, el hijo mayor, regresó a casa por la noche después de haber trabajado en los campos de su padre todo el día. Cuando vio a su hermano que había regresado, se enojó al ver que el padre había recibido a su hermano depravado en la casa. Dijo a su padre:

—Padre mío, ¿cómo puedes aceptar a tu hijo menor después de malgastar tu dinero y 40 después de perder dos años de su vida no haciendo más que divertirse? Este hermano ingrato no merece llamarse tu hijo y no merece llamarse mi hermano.

El padre le contestó:

—Hijo mío, tu hermano se había perdido, estaba muerto y ahora vive. Pablo se ha encontrado y nosotros lo hemos encontrado también. Entra y vamos a comer los tres juntos. 45 Ahora estamos contentos, gracias a Dios.

VOCABULARIO: Consult the vocabulary section in the back pages.

EJERCICIOS

I. Seleccione la respuesta correcta conforme al significado de la lectura en esta lección.

1. ¿Cuántos hijos tenía el padre?
   (a) cinco   (b) cuatro   (c) tres   (d) dos   _____

2. ¿Cuántos años tenía Andrés?
   (a) diecisiete   (b) dieciocho   (c) diecinueve   (d) veinte   _____

3. ¿Cuántos años tenía Pablo?
   (a) diecisiete   (b) dieciocho   (c) diecinueve   (d) veinte   _____

4. Pablo quiere partir para
   (a) trabajar y ganar dinero   (b) buscar su libertad y para divertirse   (c) pedir
   dinero a sus amigos   (d) dar regalos, dulces y flores a las muchachas   _____

5. Después de haber gastado toda la fortuna, Pablo no tenía nada que
   (a) aceptar   (b) amar   (c) decir   (d) comer   _____

II. ¿Sí o No?

1. El padre vendió la mitad de su tierra y le dio el dinero a Pablo.   _____

2. En Nueva York Pablo halló trabajo.   _____

3. Pablo iba con frecuencia a la escuela.   _____

4. Pablo quiere ir a Nueva York para divertirse.   _____

5. Después de dos años, Pablo no tenía dinero para pagar la habitación donde vivía. _____

6. Al regresar a su casa, Pablo estaba sucio y los vestidos que llevaba también estaban sucios y rasgados.   _____

7. Cuando el padre vio a Pablo llegar a la puerta de su casa, no lo reconoció.   _____

8. Andrés estaba muy contento al ver a su hermano después de dos años.   _____

9. Andrés cree que su hermano es ingrato.   _____

10. El padre, Andrés y Pablo van a comer los tres juntos, y ahora están contentos. _____

III. Sopa de letras (Alphabet soup). Busque cuatro sinónimos del adjetivo *contento*. Los cuatro sinónimos pueden aparecer de derecha a izquierda, de izquierda a derecha, de abajo arriba y viceversa, y en diagonal.

G	A	C	S	E	X
C	O	N	A	N	O
I	Z	P	T	C	D
F	E	L	I	Z	A
K	L	Á	S	A	T
O	Q	C	F	N	N
R	I	I	E	T	A
J	M	D	C	O	C
N	P	O	H	P	N
D	E	L	O	X	E

Estructuras de la lengua

Tense No. 2: Imperfecto de indicativo (Imperfect indicative)

This is a past tense. Imperfect suggests incomplete. The imperfect tense expresses an action or a state of being that was continuous in the past and its completion is not indicated. This tense is used, therefore, to express:

(a) An action that was going on in the past at the same time as another action.

EXAMPLE:

Mi hermano **leía** y mi padre **hablaba** / My brother *was reading* and my father *was talking*.

(b) An action that was going on in the past when another action occurred.

EXAMPLE:

Mi hermana **cantaba** cuando yo entré / My sister *was singing* when I came in.

(c) An action that a person did habitually in the past.

EXAMPLES:

1. Cuando **estábamos** en Nueva York, **íbamos** al cine todos los sábados / When *we were* in New York, *we went* to the movies every Saturday; When *we were* in New York, *we used to go* to the movies every Saturday.
2. Cuando **vivíamos** en California, **íbamos** a la playa todos los días / When *we used to live* in California, *we would go* to the beach every day.

NOTE: In this last example, *we would go* looks like the Conditional, but it is not. It is the imperfect tense in this sentence because habitual action in the past is expressed.

(d) A description of a mental, emotional, or physical condition in the past.

EXAMPLES:

1. (mental condition) **Quería** ir al cine / *I wanted* to go to the movies.
   Common verbs in this use are **creer, desear, pensar, poder, preferir, querer, saber, sentir.**
2. (emotional condition) **Estaba** contento de verle / *I was* happy to see him.
3. (physical condition) Mi madre **era** hermosa cuando **era** pequeña / My mother *was* beautiful when she *was* young.

(e) The time of day in the past.

EXAMPLES:

1. ¿Qué hora **era?** / What time *was* it?
2. **Eran** las tres / *It was* three o'clock.

The Infanta María Theresa *by Diego Rodríguez de Silva y VELÁZQUEZ*
Courtesy, Museum of Fine Arts, Boston.

(f) An action or state of being that occurred in the past and *lasted for a certain length of time* prior to another past action. In English it is usually translated as a Pluperfect tense and is formed with *had been* plus the present participle of the verb you are using. It is like the special use of the **Presente de indicativo** except that the action or state of being no longer exists at present. This is an idiomatic use of the *Imperfect tense* of a verb with **hacía**, which is also in the *Imperfect*.

EXAMPLE:

Hacía tres horas que **miraba** la televisión cuando mi hermano entró / *I had been watching television for three hours when my brother came in.*

(g) An indirect quotation in the past.

EXAMPLE:

Present: Dice que **quiere** venir a mi casa / He says *he wants* to come to my house.
Past: Dijo que **quería** venir a mi casa / He said *he wanted* to come to my house.

This tense is regularly formed as follows:

Drop the —**ar** ending of an infinitive, like **hablar,** and add the following endings: **aba, abas, aba; ábamos, abais, aban**

You then get: **hablaba, hablabas, hablaba;**
 hablábamos, hablabais, hablaban

The usual equivalent in English is: I was talking OR I used to talk OR I talked; you were talking OR you used to talk OR you talked, *etc.*

Drop the —**er** ending of an infinitive, like **beber,** or the —**ir** ending of an infinitive, like **recibir,** and add the following endings: **ía, ías, ía; íamos, íais, ían**

You then get: **bebía, bebías, bebía;**
 bebíamos, bebíais, bebían

 recibía, recibías, recibía;
 recibíamos, recibíais, recibían

The usual equivalent in English is: I was drinking OR I used to drink OR I drank; you were drinking OR you used to drink OR you drank, *etc;* I was receiving OR I used to receive OR I received; you were receiving OR you used to receive OR you received, *etc.*

Verbs irregular in the imperfect indicative

ir / to go **iba, jbas, iba;** (I was going, I used to go, *etc.*)
 íbamos, ibais, iban

ser / to be **era, eras, era;** (I was, I used to be, *etc.*)
 éramos, erais, eran

ver / to see **veía, veías, veía;** (I was seeing, I used to see, *etc.*)
 veíamos, veíais, veían

EJERCICIOS

I. Cambie los verbos de las siguientes frases al **imperfecto de indicativo.**

 Modelo: Mi hermana lee un buen libro. **Escriba:** Mi hermana leía un buen libro.

1. José habla español. _____

2. Yo hablo español e inglés. _____

3. Nosotros trabajamos todos los días. _____

4. Tomo crema con el café. _____

5. Juanita bebe leche todas las mañanas. _____

6. Para el desayuno bebo café con leche. _____

7. Mis padres siempre reciben cartas en el correo. _____

_____

8. Vivimos en esta casa. _____

9. Voy al cine los sábados. _____

10. ¿Qué hora es? _____

11. Son las tres. _____

12. Veo a mi amiga todas las noches. _____

13. Vemos muchas películas en español. _____

14. La casa es blanca. _____

OPTIONAL EXERCISES II to VII:

II. Escriba las seis formas del verbo **hablar** en el imperfecto de indicativo.

_____

III. Escriba las seis formas del verbo **beber** en el imperfecto de indicativo.

_____

IV. Escriba las seis formas del verbo **recibir** en el imperfecto de indicativo.

_____

V. Escriba las seis formas del verbo **ir** en el imperfecto de indicativo.

_____

VI. Escriba las seis formas del verbo **ser** en el imperfecto de indicativo.

_____

VII. Escriba las seis formas del verbo **ver** en el imperfecto de indicativo.

_____

VIII. Escriba respuestas afirmativas según los modelos.

> **Modelos:** a. ¿Cantaba Ud. ayer?   a. Sí, yo cantaba ayer.
> b. ¿Y los alumnos?   b. Los alumnos cantaban ayer, también.

A. Verbos con la terminación —AR

1. a. ¿Y Bailaba Ud. todas las noches? _____

   b. ¿Y Juanita? _____

2. a. ¿Borraba la profesora las palabras en la pizarra? _____

_____

   b. ¿Y los alumnos? _____

3. a. ¿Trabajaba Carlos en la clase de español? _____

_____

   b. ¿Y Roberto y Juana? _____

4. a. ¿Tocabas tú el piano? _____

   b. ¿Y las muchachas? _____

5. a. ¿Lloraba el niño? _____

   b. ¿Y Uds.? _____

6. a. ¿Esperaba Elena el tren? _____

   b. ¿Y tú? _____

B. Verbos con la terminación —**ER**

1. a. ¿Aprendía Ud. el francés? _____

   b. ¿Y los otros alumnos? _____

2. a. ¿Bebían leche los niños? _____

   b. ¿Y las mujeres? _____

3. a. ¿Comía la familia a las siete? _____

   b. ¿Y María y José Sánchez? _____

4. a. ¿Leía Isabel el cuento? _____

   b. ¿Y nosotros? _____

5. a. ¿Recibía Ud. regalos? _____

   b. ¿Y las chicas? _____

C. Verbos con la terminación —**IR**

1. a. ¿Abría la profesora la ventana? _____

   b. ¿Y Uds.? _____

2. a. ¿Recibía Juan buenas notas? _____

   b. ¿Y Cristóbal? _____

3. a. ¿Escribías tú cartas a Roberto y a Adolfo? _____

   b. ¿Y tu hermano? _____

4. a. ¿Vivía Ud. aquí en esta casa? _____

   b. ¿Y María y Elena? _____

5. a. ¿Cubría Ud. la mesa? _____

   b. ¿Y Alicia y Claudia? _____

D. Verbos irregulares en el imperfecto de indicativo.

1. a. ¿Iba Ud. al centro ayer? _____

   b. ¿Y Berta? _____

2. a. ¿Era verde la casa? _____

   b. ¿Y el garaje? _____

3. a. ¿Veías a Daniel por la tarde? _____

   b. ¿Y Ud. y Cristina? _____

IX. Componga preguntas en el imperfecto de indicativo empleando los siguientes verbos.

1. hablar   ¿ _____

2. comer   ¿ _____

3. escribir   ¿ _____

4. ir   ¿ _____

5. ser   ¿ _____

The Present Participle and Past Progressive Tense

Review the present participle and the present progressive tense in Work Unit 3.

The past progressive tense is formed by using **estar** in the imperfect indicative plus the present participle of the main verb you are using; e.g., **Estaba hablando** (I was talking, i.e., I was [in the act of] talking (then, at some point in the past).

The progressive forms (present and past) are generally used when you want to emphasize what you are saying or what you were saying; if you don't want to do that, then just use the simple present or the imperfect indicative, e.g., say **Hablo,** rather than **Estoy hablando;** or **Hablaba,** rather than **Estaba hablando.**

In brief, the present progressive is used to describe with intensification what is happening or going on at present. The past progressive is used to describe with intensification what was happening, what was going on at some point in the past.

Instead of using **estar** to form these two progressive tenses, sometimes **ir** is used: **Va hablando** / He (she) keeps right on talking; **Iba hablando** / He (she) kept right on talking. Note that they do not have the exact meaning as **Está hablando** and **Estaba hablando.**

Estar (to be) en el imperfecto de indicativo

Singular   Plural

yo	**estaba**	nosotros (-as)	**estábamos**
tú	**estabas**	vosotros (-as)	**estabais**
Ud. (él, ella)	**estaba**	Uds. (ellos, ellas)	**estaban**

EJERCICIOS

I. Cambie el verbo del presente progresivo al pasado progresivo.

Modelo: Estoy hablando. ⟶ Estaba hablando.

1. Estoy cantando. _____

2. Estás trabajando. _____

3. Está aprendiendo. _____

4. Estamos leyendo. _____

5. Estáis riendo. _____

6. Están trayendo. _____

7. Estoy diciendo. _____

8. Estamos durmiendo. _____

9. Están oyendo. _____

10. Estás repitiendo. _____

II. HUMOR. La adivinanza para hoy.

¿Qué tiene patas y brazos pero no tiene manos?

Respuesta: _____

Use of **acabar de** in the imperfecto de indicativo

The Spanish idiomatic expression **acabar de + inf.** is expressed in English as *to have just +* past participle. This is a very common expression which you surely will find on any standardized test in Spanish.

In the imperfecto de indicativo:

María acababa de llegar / Mary had just arrived.
Acababa de comer / I had just eaten.
Acabábamos de terminar la lección / We had just finished the lesson.

NOTE: When you use **acabar** in the imperfect indicative, it indicates that the action of the main verb (+ inf.) had occurred at some time in the past when another action occurred in the past. In English, we express this by using *had just +* the past participle of the main verb: **Acabábamos de entrar en la casa cuando el teléfono sonó** / We had just entered the house when the telephone rang.

When **acabar** is used in the imperfect indicative + the inf. of the main verb being expressed, the verb in the other clause is usually in the preterit tense. The preterit is tense no. 3 of the 7 simple tenses and it is introduced in the following lesson, Work Unit 7.

EJERCICIOS

I. Traduzca.

1. Mary had just arrived. _____

2. I had just eaten. _____

3. We had just finished the lesson. _____

4. I had just left. _____

5. I had just written a letter. _____

II. Dictado. Escriba las frases que su profesor de español va a pronunciar.

1. _____

2. _____

3. _____

¿CUÁNTO TIEMPO HACÍA QUE + IMPERFECT TENSE . . . ?

(a) If the action of the verb began in the past and ended in the past, use the imperfect tense.

(b) This formula is equivalent to the English: *How long + past perfect tense:*
   ¿Cuánto tiempo hacía que Ud. hablaba cuando entré en la sala de clase? / How long had you been talking when I entered into the classroom?

HACÍA + LENGTH OF TIME + QUE + IMPERFECT TENSE

(a) This formula is the usual answer to the question as stated above.

(b) The imperfect tense of the verb is used here because the action began in the past and ended in the past; it is not going on at the present moment.

   Hacía una hora que yo hablaba cuando Ud. entró en la sala de clase / I had been talking for one hour when you entered the classroom.

¿DESDE CUÁNDO + IMPERFECT TENSE . . . ?

This is another way of asking the question stated above.

   ¿Desde cuándo hablaba Ud. cuando yo entré en la sala de clase? / How long had you been talking when I entered into the classroom?

IMPERFECT TENSE + DESDE HACÍA + LENGTH OF TIME

This is another way of answering the question stated above.

   (Yo) hablaba desde hacía una hora cuando Ud. entró en la sala de clase / I had been talking for one hour when you entered into the classroom.

Hacer (to do, to make) en el imperfecto de indicativo

Singular		Plural	
yo	**hacía**	nosotros (-as)	**hacíamos**
tú	**hacías**	vosotros (-as)	**hacíais**
Ud. (él, ella)	**hacía**	Uds. (ellos, ellas)	**hacían**

EJERCICIOS

I. Traduzca al inglés.

1. ¿Cuánto tiempo hacía que Ud. hablaba cuando yo entré en la sala de clase?

2. Hacía una hora que yo hablaba cuando Ud. entró en la sala de clase. _____

_____

3. ¿Desde cuándo hablaba Ud. cuando yo entré en la sala de clase? _____

_____

II. Responda en español en frases completas.

Modelo: ¿Cuánto tiempo hacía que Ud. miraba la televisión cuando yo entré?

Escriba: Hacía una hora que yo miraba la televisión cuando Ud. entró.

1. ¿Cuánto tiempo hacía que Ud. hablaba con Elena cuando María entró? _____

_____

2. ¿Cuántos minutos hacía que Ud. esperaba el autobús cuando llegó? _____

_____

3. ¿Cuántos años hacía que Ud. vivía en Puerto Rico cuando Ud. partió para Nueva York? __

_____

4. ¿Desde cuándo leía Ud. este libro cuando Ud. salió para ir al cine? _____

_____

III. **Discriminación de los sonidos.** Su profesor de español va a pronunciar una sola palabra, sea la de la letra A, sea la de la letra B. Escoja la palabra que su profesor pronuncia escribiendo la letra en la línea.

Modelo: A. pero
B. perro ___B___

He escrito la letra B en la línea porque mi profesor de español ha pronunciado la palabra de la letra B.

1. A. lápiz

   B. lápices_____

2. A. donde

   B. ¿dónde?_____

3. A. huevo

   B. nuevo_____

4. A. cuando

   B. ¿cuándo?_____

5. A. hoja

   B. hogar_____

6. A. tras

   B. tres_____

IV. Uno por tres. Ponga en las casillas una palabra que, con la palabra ya inscrita, permitirá formar otra palabra. La tercera palabra—que será el resultado de la palabra ya inscrita y de la palabra que usted va a escribir—figura en la lectura de esta lección.

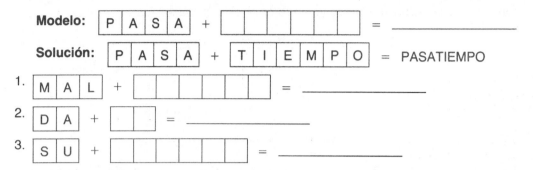

Modelo: | P | A | S | A | + | | | | | | | = _____

Solución: | P | A | S | A | + | T | I | E | M | P | O | = PASATIEMPO

1. | M | A | L | + | | | | | | | = _____

2. | D | A | + | | | = _____

3. | S | U | + | | | | | | | = _____

ADJECTIVES

Definition: An adjective is a word that describes a noun or pronoun in some way.

Agreement: An adjective agrees in gender and number with the noun or pronoun it describes. **Gender** means masculine, feminine, or neuter. **Number** means singular or plural.

Descriptive adjectives

A descriptive adjective is a word that describes a noun or pronoun: **casa blanca, chicas bonitas, chicos altos**; Ella es **bonita.**

Limiting adjectives

A limiting adjective limits the number of the noun: **una casa, un libro, algunos muchachos, muchas veces, dos libros, pocos amigos.**

Gender

An adjective that ends in **o** in the masculine singular changes **o** to **a** to form the feminine: **rojo / roja, pequeño / pequeña**

An adjective that expresses a person's nationality, which ends in a consonant, requires the addition of **a** to form the feminine singular: **Juan es español / María es española; Pierre Cardin es francés / Simone Signoret es francesa; El señor Armstrong es inglés / La señora Smith es inglesa.** Note that the accent mark on **francés** and **inglés** drops in the feminine because the stress falls naturally on the vowel **e.**

An adjective that ends in **e** generally does not change to form the feminine: **un muchacho inteligente / una muchacha inteligente.**

An adjective that ends in a consonant generally does not change to form the feminine: **una pregunta difícil / un libro difícil; un chico feliz / una chica feliz**—except for an adjective of nationality and adjectives that end in **-án, -ón, -ín, -or** (**trabajador / trabajadora,** industrious).

Position

Normally, a descriptive adjective is placed after the noun it describes: **una casa amarilla; un libro interesante.**

Two descriptive adjectives, **bueno** and **malo,** are sometimes placed in front of the noun. When placed in front of a masculine singular noun, the **o** drops: **un buen amigo; un mal alumno.**

A limiting adjective is generally placed in front of the noun: **algunos estudiantes; mucho dinero; muchos libros; cada año; tres horas; pocos alumnos; varias cosas.**

In an interrogative sentence, the predicate adjective precedes the subject when it is a noun: **¿Es bonita María? ¿Es inteligente la profesora?**

Some adjectives have a different meaning depending on their position:

> **un nuevo sombrero** / a new (different, another) hat
> **un sombrero nuevo** / a new (brand new) hat

un gran hombre / a great man
un hombre grande / a large, big man

una gran mujer / a great woman
una mujer grande / a large, big woman

la pobre niña / the poor girl (unfortunate, unlucky)
la niña pobre / the poor girl (poor, not rich)

As nouns

At times an adjective is used as a noun if it is preceded by an article or a demonstrative adjective: **el viejo** / the old man; **aquel viejo** / that old man; **la joven** / the young lady; **estos jóvenes** / these young men; **este ciego** / this blind man.

Shortened forms (apocopation of adjectives)

Certain masculine singular adjectives drop the final **o** when in front of a masculine singular noun:

alguno: algún día	primero: el primer año
bueno: un buen amigo	tercero: el tercer mes
malo: mal tiempo	uno: un dólar
ninguno: ningún libro	

NOTE that when **alguno** and **ninguno** are shortened, an accent mark is required on the **u.**

Santo shortens to **San** before a masculine singular saint: **San Francisco, San José;** but remains **Santo** in front of **Do-** or **To-: Santo Domingo, Santo Tomás.**

Grande shortens to **gran** when in front of any singular noun, whether masc. or fem.: **un gran hombre** / a great (famous) man; **una gran mujer** / a great (famous) woman.

Ciento shortens to **cien** when in front of any plural noun, whether masc. or fem.: **cien libros** / one (a) hundred books; **cien sillas** / one (a) hundred chairs.

Ciento shortens to **cien** when in front of a number greater than itself: **cien mil** / one hundred thousand; **cien millones** / one hundred million.

Ciento remains **ciento** when combined with any other number which is smaller than itself: **ciento tres dólares.**

NOTE that in English we say *one* hundred or *a* hundred, but in Spanish no word is used in front of **ciento** or **cien** to express *one* or *a*; it is merely **ciento** or **cien.** For an explanation of when to use **ciento** or **cien,** see above.

Cualquiera and **cualesquiera** lose the final **a** in front of a noun: **cualquier hombre, cualquier día,** but if after the noun, the final **a** remains: **un libro cualquiera.**

Plural of adjectives

Like nouns, to form the plural of an adjective, add **s** if the adj. ends in a vowel: **blanco / blancos; blanca / blancas.**

If an adj. ends in a consonant, add **es** to form the plural: **español / españoles; difícil / difíciles.**

NOTE that the accent on **difícil** remains in the plural in order to keep the stress there: **difíciles.**

Some adjectives drop the accent mark in the plural because it is not needed to indicate the stress. The stress falls naturally on the same vowel in the plural: **cortés / corteses; alemán / alemanes.**

Some adjectives add the accent mark in the plural because the stress needs to be kept on the vowel that was stressed in the singular where no accent mark was needed. In the singular, the stress falls naturally on that vowel: **joven / jóvenes.**

An adjective that ends in **z** changes **z** to **c** and adds **es** to form the plural: **feliz / felices.** Here, there is no need to add an accent mark because the stress falls naturally on the vowel **i,** as it does in the singular.

If an adjective describes or modifies two or more nouns that are all masculine, naturally the masculine plural is used: **Roberto y Felipe están cansados.**

If an adjective describes or modifies two or more nouns that are all feminine, naturally the feminine plural is used: **Elena y Marta están cansadas.**

If an adjective describes or modifies two or more nouns of different genders, the masculine plural is used: **Pablo y Juanita están cansados; María, Elena, Marta, y Roberto están cansados.**

Comparatives and Superlatives

Comparatives

Of equality: **tan . . . como** (as . . . as)
   María es tan alta como Elena / Mary is as tall as Helen.

Of a lesser degree: **menos . . . que** (less . . . than)
   María es menos alta que Anita / Mary is less tall than Anita.

Of a higher degree: **más . . . que** (more . . . than)
   María es más alta que Isabel / Mary is taller than Elizabeth.

Superlatives

To express the superlative degree, use the comparative forms given above with the appropriate definite article:

With a proper noun: **Anita es la más alta** / Anita is the tallest.
   Roberto es el más alto / Robert is the tallest.
   Anita y Roberto son los más altos / Anita and Robert are the tallest.
   Marta y María son las más inteligentes / Martha and Mary are the most intelligent.

With a common noun: **La muchacha más alta de la clase es Anita** / The tallest girl in the class is Anita.
   El muchacho más alto de la clase es Roberto / The tallest boy in the class is Robert.

NOTE that after a superlative in Spanish, *in* is expressed by **de**, not **en**.

When two or more superlative adjectives describe the same noun, **más** or **menos** is used only once in front of the first adjective: **Aquella mujer es la más pobre y vieja.**

Absolute superlative: adjectives ending in **-ísimo, -ísima, -ísimos, -ísimas**

To express an adj. in a very high degree, drop the final vowel (if there is one) and add the appropriate ending among the following, depending on the correct agreement: **-ísimo, -ísima, -ísimos, -ísimas: María está contentísima** / Mary is very (extremely) happy; **Los muchachos están contentísimos.** These forms may be used instead of **muy** + adj. (**muy contenta** / **muy contentos**); **una casa grandísima** / **una casa muy grande.**

Never use **muy** in front of **mucho.** Say: **muchísimo. Muchísimas gracias** / many thanks; thank you very, very much.

Irregular comparatives and superlatives

ADJECTIVE	COMPARATIVE	SUPERLATIVE
bueno (good)	**mejor** (better)	**el mejor** (best)
malo (bad)	**peor** (worse)	**el peor** (worst)
grande (large)	**más grande** (larger)	**el más grande** (largest)
	mayor (greater, older)	**el mayor** (greatest, oldest)
pequeño (small)	**más pequeño** (smaller)	**el más pequeño** (smallest)
	menor (smaller, younger)	**el menor** (smallest, youngest)

NOTE, of course, that you must be careful to make the correct agreement in gender and number.

NOTE also that in English, the superlative is sometimes expressed with the definite article *the* and sometimes it is not.

Más que (more than) or **menos que** (less than) becomes **más de, menos de** + a number:

El Señor Gómez tiene más de cincuenta años.
Mi hermano tiene más de cien dólares.
> BUT: **No tengo más que dos dólares** / I have only two dollars.
> In this example, the meaning is *only,* expressed by **no** in front of the verb; in this case, you must keep **que** to express *only.*

Tanto, tanta, tantos, tantas + noun + **como:** as much (as many) . . . as

Tengo tanto dinero como usted / I have as much money as you.
Tengo tantos libros como usted / I have as many books as you.
Tengo tanta paciencia como usted / I have as much patience as you.
Tengo tantas plumas como usted / I have as many pens as you.

Demonstrative adjectives

A demonstrative adjective is used to point out someone or something. Like other adjectives, a demonstrative adjective agrees in gender and number with the noun it modifies. The demonstrative adjectives are:

ENGLISH MEANING	MASCULINE	FEMININE
this *(here)*	**este libro**	**esta pluma**
these *(here)*	**estos libros**	**estas plumas**
that *(there)*	**ese libro**	**esa pluma**
those *(there)*	**esos libros**	**esas plumas**
that *(farther away or out of sight)*	**aquel libro**	**aquella pluma**
those *(farther away or out of sight)*	**aquellos libros**	**aquellas plumas**

If there is more than one noun, a demonstrative adjective is ordinarily used in front of each noun: **este hombre y esta mujer** / this man and (this) woman.

The demonstrative adjectives are used to form the demonstrative pronouns.

Possessive adjectives

A possessive adjective is a word that shows possession and it agrees in gender and number with the noun, not with the possessor. A short form of a possessive adjective is placed in front of the noun. If there is more than one noun stated, a possessive adjective is needed in front of each noun: **mi madre y mi padre** / my mother and (my) father.

There are two forms for the possessive adjectives: the short form and the long form. **The short form is placed in front of the noun.** The short forms are:

ENGLISH MEANING	BEFORE A SINGULAR NOUN	BEFORE A PLURAL NOUN
1. my	**mi amigo, mi amiga**	**mis amigos, mis amigas**
2. your	**tu amigo, tu amiga**	**tus amigos, tus amigas**
3. your, his, her, its	**su amigo, su amiga**	**sus amigos, sus amigas**
1. our	**nuestro amigo** **nuestra amiga**	**nuestros amigos** **nuestras amigas**
2. your	**vuestro amigo** **vuestra amiga**	**vuestros amigos** **vuestras amigas**
3. your, their	**su amigo, su amiga**	**sus amigos, sus amigas**

In order to clarify the meanings of **su** or **sus,** when there might be ambiguity, do the following: Replace **su** or **sus** with the definite article + the noun and add **de Ud., de él, de ella, de Uds., de ellos, de ellas:**

> **su libro** OR **el libro de Ud., el libro de él, el libro de ella; el libro de Uds., el libro de ellos, el libro de ellas**

> **sus libros** OR **los libros de Ud., los libros de él, los libros de ella; los libros de Uds., los libros de ellos, los libros de ellas**

The long form is placed after the noun. The long forms are:

ENGLISH MEANING	AFTER A SINGULAR NOUN	AFTER A PLURAL NOUN
1. my; (of) mine	**mío, mía**	**míos, mías**
2. your; (of) yours	**tuyo, tuya**	**tuyos, tuyas**
3. your, his, her, its; (of yours, of his, of hers, of its)	**suyo, suya**	**suyos, suyas**
1. our; (of) ours	**nuestro, nuestra**	**nuestros, nuestras**
2. your; (of) yours	**vuestro, vuestra**	**vuestros, vuestras**
3. your, their; (of yours, of theirs)	**suyo, suya**	**suyos, suyas**

EXAMPLES: **amigo mío** / my friend; **un amigo mío** / a friend of mine

The long forms are used primarily:

(a) In direct address, that is to say, when you are talking directly to someone or when writing a letter to someone:

> **¡Hola, amigo mío! ¿Qué tal?** / Hello, my friend! How are things? **Queridos amigos míos** / My dear friends

(b) When you want to express *of mine, of yours, of his, of hers,* etc.

(c) With the verb **ser: Estos libros son míos** / These books are mine.

(d) In the expression: **¡Dios mío!** / My heavens! My God!

In order to clarify the meanings of **suyo, suya, suyos, suyas** (since they are third person singular or plural), do the same as for **su** and **sus: dos amigos suyos** can be clarified as **dos amigos de Ud., dos amigos de él, dos amigos de ella, dos amigos de Uds., dos amigos de ellos, dos amigos de ellas** / two friends of yours, of his, of hers, *etc.*

The long forms of the possessive adjectives are used to serve as possessive pronouns.

A possessive adjective is ordinarily not used when referring to an article of clothing being worn or to parts of the body, particularly when a reflexive verb is used: **Me lavo las manos antes de comer** / I wash my hands before eating.

Two or more descriptive adjectives

Two or more descriptive adjectives of equal importance are placed after the noun. If there are two, they are joined by **y** (or **e**). If there are more than two, the last two are connected by **y** (or **e**):

un hombre alto y guapo / a tall, handsome man

una mujer alta, hermosa e inteligente / a tall, beautiful and intelligent woman

Cuanto más (menos) . . . tanto más (menos) / the more (the less) . . . the more (less)

A proportion or ratio is expressed by **cuanto más (menos) . . . tanto más (menos)** / the more (the less) . . . the more (less):

Cuanto más dinero tengo, tanto más necesito / The more money I have, the more I need.

Cuanto menos dinero tengo, tanto menos necesito / The less money I have the less I need.

Comparison between two clauses

(a) Use **de lo que** to express *than* when comparing two clauses with different verbs if an adjective or adverb is the comparison:

Esta frase es más fácil de lo que Ud. cree / This sentence is easier than you think.

Paula trabaja mejor de lo que Ud. cree / Paula works better than you think.

(b) Use the appropriate form of **de lo que, de los que, de la que, de las que** when comparing two clauses with the same verbs if a noun is the comparison:

Tengo más dinero de lo que Ud. tiene / I have more money than you have.

María tiene más libros de los que Ud. tiene / Mary has more books than you have.

Roberto tiene más amigas de las que tiene Juan / Robert has more girl friends than John has.

EJERCICIOS

I. Traduzca.

1. a white house _____

2. pretty girls _____

3. many times _____

4. two books _____

5. few friends _____

6. an intelligent girl _____

7. an intelligent boy _____

8. a difficult question _____

9. a difficult book _____

10. a happy girl _____

II. Escriba el femenino de los siguientes adjetivos.

Modelos: blanco ⟶ blanca
rojos ⟶ rojas

1. amarillo _____

2. interesante _____

3. poco _____

4. muchos _____

5. varios _____

6. cada _____

7. algunos _____

8. inteligente _____

9. bonito _____

10. pobre _____

III. Traduzca al español.

1. a new (different, another) hat _____

2. a new (brand new) hat _____

3. a great man _____

4. a large, big man _____

5. a great woman _____

6. a large, big woman _____

7. the poor girl (unfortunate, unlucky) _____

8. the poor girl (poor, not rich) _____

IV. Traduzca al español.

1. the old man _____ 4. the young man _____

2. that old man _____ 5. these young men _____

3. the young lady _____ 6. this blind man _____

V. Traduzca al español.

1. some day _____ 4. not any (not one) book _____

2. a good friend *(m.)* _____ 5. the first year _____

3. bad weather _____ 6. the third month _____

VI. Traduzca al español.

1. a great (famous) man _____ 4. one hundred chairs _____

2. a great (famous) woman _____ 5. one hundred thousand _____

3. one hundred books _____ 6. one hundred million _____

VII. Cambie los siguientes adjetivos al plural.

    Modelo: difícil   difíciles

1. español _____ 4. joven _____

2. cortés _____ 5. feliz _____

3. alemán _____ 6. cansado _____

VIII. Traduzca al inglés.

1. María es tan alta como Elena. _____

2. Carlota es menos alta que Anita. _____

3. Ana es más alta que Isabel. _____

4. Anita es la más alta. _____

5. Roberto es el más alto. _____

6. Anita y Roberto son los más altos. _____

7. Marta y María son las más inteligentes. _____

8. La muchacha más alta de la clase es Anita. _____

_____

9. El muchacho más alto de la clase es Roberto. _____

_____

10. Aquella mujer es la más pobre y vieja. _____

IX. Escriba el superlativo absoluto de los siguientes adjetivos.

    Modelos: **contento** ⟶ **contentísimo**
                   grande   ⟶ **grandísimo, grandísima**

1. contentos _____   4. estudioso _____

2. mucho _____   5. hermosa _____

3. bueno _____   6. grande _____

X. Escriba la forma correcta del adjetivo demostrativo según el modelo a continuación.

    Modelos: libro   ⟶ este libro
                  pluma   esta pluma
                  chicos   estos chicos
                  escuelas estas escuelas

1. pluma _____   6. hombre _____

2. escuelas _____   7. mujer _____

3. lápiz _____   8. lápices _____

4. cuaderno _____   9. libros _____

5. muchacha _____   10. lección _____

XI. Escriba la forma correcta del adjetivo demostrativo según el modelo a continuación.

    Modelos: libro   ⟶ ese libro
                  pluma   esa pluma
                  chicos   esos chicos
                  escuelas esas escuelas

1. pluma _____   6. hombre _____

2. escuelas _____   7. mujer _____

3. lápiz _____   8. lápices _____

4. cuaderno _____   9. libros _____

5. muchacha _____   10. lección _____

XII. Escriba la forma correcta del adjetivo demostrativo según el modelo a continuación.

Modelos: libro ⟶ aquel libro
pluma   aquella pluma
chicos   aquellos chicos
escuelas   aquellas escuelas

1. pluma _____

2. escuelas _____

3. lápiz _____

4. cuaderno _____

5. muchacha _____

6. hombre _____

7. mujer _____

8. lápices _____

9. libros _____

10. lección _____

XIII. Traduzca al español.

1. my friend *(m.)* _____

2. your friend *(f.) (2nd pers., s.)* _____

3. your book *(3rd pers., s.)* _____

4. my notebooks _____

5. your pencils *(2nd pers., s.)* _____

6. his car _____

7. her cars _____

8. our house _____

9. their tickets _____

10. your money *(2nd pers., pl.)* _____

XIV. Traduzca al español.

1. My dear friends *(m.)*, how are you today? _____

2. Hello, my friend *(f.)*! How are things? _____

3. These books are mine. _____

4. My God! _____

5. Mrs. Rodríguez is a tall, beautiful and intelligent woman. _____

_____

6. Mr. Rodríguez is a tall, handsome man. _____

7. This sentence is easier than you think. _____

8. Mary has more books than you have. _____

9. Robert has more girl friends than John has. _____

10. Isabel has more boy friends than Mary has. _____

_____

XV. Sopa de letras (Alphabet soup). Busque cuatro sinónimos del adjetivo *delicado.* Los cuatro sinónimos pueden aparecer de derecha a izquierda, de izquierda a derecha, de abajo arriba y viceversa, y en diagonal.

O	Z	I	M	R	E	F	N	E
E	N	F	E	M	I	O	T	K
Z	Y	X	C	A	S	L	W	M
G	I	H	J	D	L	I	S	O
M	P	O	N	É	R	G	V	N
S	U	T	V	B	P	Á	R	J
F	D	E	T	I	E	R	N	O
D	G	E	C	L	B	F	Q	A

XVI. ¿Qué tiene Ud. en la mano?

Respuesta: _____

XVII. ¿Cuántos alumnos hay en esta clase?

Respuesta: _____

XVIII. Ponga las siguientes letras en orden para hallar adjetivos españoles.

1. I O B T A N _____

2. R E D A N G _____

3. Q E Ñ U E P O _____

4. N E G I L T T I N E E _____

5. X R E A T Ñ A _____

XIX. ¿Cuántas palabras españolas puede Ud. hallar en la palabra ADJETIVOS? Halle veinte y una palabras, por lo menos. Usted puede añadir signos de acento o tilde, si es necesario, para formar nuevas palabras. Por ejemplo: tío, adiós.

$$\boxed{\text{A D J E T I V O S}}$$

1. ____	4. ____	7. ____	10. ____	13. ____	16. ____	19. ____
2. ____	5. ____	8. ____	11. ____	14. ____	17. ____	20. ____
3. ____	6. ____	9. ____	12. ____	15. ____	18. ____	21. ____

XX. Describa a una muchacha con tantos adjetivos como Ud. pueda decir y escribir.

EJEMPLO:

Teresa es . . .

inteligente	**alta**
bonita	**americana**
bella	**española**
activa	**mexicana**

¿Cuántos adjetivos puede Ud. decir y escribir?

How many more can you add to these? Remember that your adjectives are describing a girl.

XXI. En español hay muchas palabras que se escriben y se pronuncian idénticamente, pero tienen un significado diferente. Se distinguen por el acento ortográfico.

Por ejemplo:

tu *possessive adjective, familiar, 2nd pers., sing.* / your
tú *subject pronoun, 2nd person, sing.*
¿Tú tienes tu libro? / You have your book?

¿Cuántos ejemplos puede Ud. decir y escribir?

Mnemonic tip	**Este, estos, esta, estas** have the t's; **Ese, esos, esa, esas** DON'T.

¿Puede Ud. dar un "mnemonic tip"?

The Annunciation *by EL GRECO (1541–1614)*
Courtesy of The Toledo Museum of Art, Toledo, Ohio

¡Oh, señor! ¡Su autógrafo, por favor! Aquí tiene Ud. mi programa y mi pluma.

Have you ever asked someone for an auto-
graph? That's what Juana Rodríguez did
while she was at the theater in Seville during
intermission.

El autógrafo especial

Anoche, la familia Rodríguez fue al teatro. Vieron el drama *El Burlador de Sevilla,* una de las mejores comedias de Tirso de Molina. Salieron de la casa a las siete y media, y llegaron al teatro a las ocho. Entraron en el teatro y se sentaron en sus asientos a las ocho y cuarto. El espectáculo comenzó a las ocho y media.

Durante el entreacto, la señora Rodríguez fue a hablar con algunas damas. El señor   5
Rodríguez fue a tomar un café; Pedro, el hijo, fue a comprar chocolate y Juana, la hija, fue a beber jugo de naranja.

La señora Rodríguez habló con las damas y, después, regresó a su asiento. El señor Rodríguez tomó su café y regresó a su asiento también. Pedro comió su chocolate y regresó a su asiento. Juana bebió su jugo de naranja, pero antes de regresar a su asiento, vio a un   10
hombre y ella le dijo:

—¡Oh! ¡Señor! ¡Usted es el gran actor Juan Robles!
—Pero . . . , señorita . . . , respondió el señor.
—¡Oh! ¡Señor! ¡Su autógrafo, por favor! Aquí tiene mi programa y
mi pluma. Escriba su autógrafo en mi programa, por favor, dijo Juana.   15

—Pero . . . , pero . . . ,—dijo el señor.
—Usted es muy modesto—dijo Juana.
—Pero . . . , No soy modesto, señorita . . . Pero si Ud. insiste . . . Aquí tiene usted mi autógrafo—dijo el señor.
—Muchas gracias, señor. Muchas gracias—dijo Juana.   20

Juana regresó a su asiento.

La pieza se terminó, y todo el mundo salió del teatro.
Afuera, Juana anunció:
—¡Miren! ¡Miren mi programa! ¡Tengo el autógrafo de Juan Robles!
—¿Juan Robles? ¿De veras? ¡Increíble!—dijo la madre.   25

Juana dio el programa a su madre, y ésta leyó: "No soy Juan Robles. Me llamo José Blanco".

—¡No es posible! ¡Oh! ¡He hecho una tontería!—exclamó Juana.
—No es una tontería. Tú tienes el autógrafo de José Blanco. Todo el mundo no tiene el autógrafo de José Blanco en su programa—, respondió Pedro.   30
—¿Quién es José Blanco?—preguntó el padre.
—Es una persona como tú y yo—, contestó la madre—. ¡Ahora tenemos un autógrafo especial!
Y rieron a carcajadas.

VOCABULARIO: Consult the vocabulary section in the back pages.

EJERCICIOS

I. Seleccione la respuesta correcta conforme al significado de la lectura en esta lección.

1. Anoche, la familia Rodríguez fue (a) al cine (b) al teatro (c) a la iglesia (d) a la biblioteca _____

2. Vieron el drama *El Burlador de Sevilla,* una de las mejores comedias de (a) Bartolomé Esteban Murillo (b) Francisco de Goya (c) El Greco (d) Tirso de Molina _____

3. Salieron de la casa a las siete y media y llegaron al teatro (a) a las ocho (b) a las ocho y cuarto (c) a las ocho y media (d) a las nueve _____

4. Entraron en el teatro y se sentaron en sus asientos (a) a las ocho (b) a las ocho y cuarto (c) a las ocho y media (d) a las nueve menos quince _____

5. Durante el entreacto, la señora Rodríguez fue a hablar con (a) Pedro (b) algunos señores (c) Juana (d) algunas damas _____

6. Durante el entreacto, el señor Rodríguez fue (a) a tomar un café (b) a hablar con algunos señores (c) a comprar chocolate (d) a beber jugo de naranja _____

7. Durante el entreacto, Pedro fue (a) a comprar chocolate (b) a beber jugo de naranja (c) a tomar un café (d) a hablar con las chicas bonitas _____

8. Durante el entreacto, Juana fue (a) a hablar con algunos muchachos (b) a comprar chocolate (c) a beber jugo de naranja (d) a hablar con algunas damas _____

9. Antes de regresar a su asiento, Juana vio a (a) una amiga (b) un amigo (c) unos amigos (d) un hombre _____

10. Juana recibió el autógrafo especial de (a) un gran actor (b) una persona común y corriente (c) Juan Robles (d) un amigo suyo _____

II. Seleccione la forma correcta del verbo en el **pretérito.**

1. La señora Rodríguez _____ con algunas damas.
   (a) habla (b) está hablando (c) hablaba (d) habló _____

2. El señor Rodríguez _____ su café.
   (a) toma (b) está tomando (c) tomó (d) tomaba _____

3. La señora Rodríguez _____ a su asiento.
   (a) regresa (b) está regresando (c) regresaba (d) regresó _____

4. Pedro _____ su chocolate.
   (a) comió (b) come (c) comía (d) está comiendo _____

5. Juana _____ su jugo de naranja.
   (a) bebe (b) bebió (c) bebía (d) está bebiendo _____

III. Sopa de letras (Alphabet soup). Halle las palabras en español por las palabras en inglés. Las palabras pueden aparecer de derecha a izquierda, de izquierda a derecha, de abajo arriba y viceversa, y en diagonal.

1. stupid, foolish, dumb thing
2. everybody
3. really
4. play (theater)
5. better
6. orange (fruit)
7. to laugh
8. He took.
9. She drank.
10. He ate.

T	O	D	O	E	L	M	U	N	D	O
O	A	E	B	D	C	E	Ó	M	O	T
N	F	V	H	N	A	R	A	N	J	A
T	C	E	P	R	Q	A	E	V	A	U
E	O	R	O	J	E	M	X	Í	P	Z
R	M	A	C	B	E	D	G	H	R	O
Í	I	S	B	E	B	I	Ó	C	U	A
A	Ó	F	P	I	E	Z	A	T	E	O

IV. HUMOR. La adivinanza para hoy.

¿Qué hay en el medio de Sevilla?

Solución: _____

V. ¿Cuál es la palabra más larga de la lengua española?

Respuesta: _____

VI. Varias palabras en una sola. Utilizando las letras en la palabra ARGENTINA, ¿cuántas palabras puede usted escribir? Escriba cinco palabras, por lo menos.

ARGENTINA

1. _____   3. _____   5. _____

2. _____   4. _____

VII. Discriminación de los sonidos. Su profesor de español va a pronunciar una sola palabra, sea la letra A, sea la letra B. Escoja la palabra que su profesor pronuncia y escriba la letra en la línea.

1. A. lama
   B. llama _____

2. A. hambre
   B. hombre _____

3. A. hallado
   B. helado _____

4. A. amo
   B. amó _____

Estructuras de la lengua

Tense No. 3: Pretérito (Preterit)
   This tense expresses an action that was completed at some time in the past.

   EXAMPLES:
   1. Mi padre **llegó** ayer / My father *arrived* yesterday; My father *did arrive* yesterday.
   2. María **fue** a la iglesia esta mañana / Mary *went* to church this morning; Mary *did go* to church this morning.
   3. ¿Qué **pasó**? What *happened*? *What did happen?*

4. **Tomé** el desayuno a las siete / I *had* breakfast at seven o'clock. I *did have* breakfast at seven o'clock.

5. **Salí** de casa, **tomé** el autobús y **llegué** a la escuela a las ocho / I *left* the house, I *took* the bus and I *arrived* at school at eight o'clock.

In Spanish, some verbs that express a mental state have a different meaning when used in the Preterit.

EXAMPLES:

1. La **conocí** la semana pasada en el baile / I *met* her last week at the dance. (**Conocer,** which means *to know* or *be acquainted with,* means *met,* that is, introduced to for the first time, in the Preterit.)

2. **Pude** hacerlo / I *succeeded* in doing it. (**Poder,** which means *to be able,* means *succeeded* in the Preterit.)

3. **No pude** hacerlo / I *failed* to do it. (**Poder,** when used in the negative in the Preterit, means *failed* or *did not succeed.*)

4. **Quise** llamarlo / I *tried* to call you. (**Querer,** which means *to wish* or *want,* means *tried* in the Preterit.)

5. **No quise** hacerlo / I *refused* to do it. (**Querer,** when used in the negative in the Preterit, means *refused.*)

6. **Supe** la verdad / I *found out* the truth. (**Saber,** which means *to know,* means *found out* in the Preterit.)

7. **Tuve** una carta de mi amigo Roberto / I *received* a letter from my friend Robert. (**Tener,** which means *to have,* means *received* in the Preterit.)

This tense is regularly formed as follows:

Drop the —**ar** ending of an infinitive, like **hablar,** and add the following endings: **é, aste, ó; amos, asteis, aron**

You then get: **hablé, hablaste, habló;**
  hablamos, hablasteis, hablaron

The usual equivalent in English is: I talked OR I did talk, you talked OR you did talk, *etc.* OR I spoke OR I did speak; you spoke OR you did speak, *etc.*

Drop the —**er** ending of an infinitive, like **beber,** or the —**ir** ending of an infinitive, like **recibir,** and add the following endings: **í, iste, ió; imos, isteis, ieron**

You then get: **bebí, bebiste, bebió;**
  bebimos, bebisteis, bebieron

  recibí, recibiste, recibió;
  recibimos, recibisteis, recibieron

The usual equivalent in English is: I drank OR I did drink; you drank OR you did drink, *etc.;* I received OR I did receive, *etc.*

Verbs irregular in the preterit, including stem-changing verbs and orthographical changing verbs

NOTE that the first three forms up to the semicolon are the 1st, 2nd, and 3rd persons of the singular; the three verb forms under those are the 1st, 2nd, and 3rd persons of the plural. The subject pronouns are not given in order to emphasize the verb forms.

acercarse / to approach, to draw near
  me acerqué, te acercaste, se acercó;
  nos acercamos, os acercasteis, se acercaron

An orthographical changing verb because **c** changes to **qu** in front of **é** in the 1st pers. sing. of this tense.

advertir / to notify, to warn, to give notice, to give warning
  advertí, advertiste, advirtió;
  advertimos, advertisteis, advirtieron

A stem-changing verb because **e** in the stem changes to **i** in the 3rd pers. sing. and plural of this tense.

alcanzar / to reach, to overtake
alcancé, alcanzaste, alcanzó;
alcanzamos, alcanzasteis, alcanzaron

An orthographical changing verb because **z** changes to **c** in front of **é** in the 1st pers. sing. of this tense.

almorzar / to have lunch, to each lunch
almorcé, almorzaste, almorzó;
almorzamos, almorzasteis, almorzaron

An orthographical changing verb because **z** changes to **c** in front of **é** in the 1st pers. sing. of this tense.

alzar / to heave, to lift, to pick up, to raise (prices)
alcé, alzaste, alzó;
alzamos, alzasteis, alzaron

An orthographical changing verb because **z** changes to **c** in front of **é** in the 1st pers. sing. of this tense.

andar / to walk
anduve, anduviste, anduvo;
anduvimos, anduvisteis, anduvieron

apagar / to extinguish
apagué, apagaste, apagó;
apagamos, apagasteis, apagaron

An orthographical changing verb because **g** changes to **gu** in front of **é** in the 1st pers. sing. of this tense.

aplicar / to apply
apliqué, aplicaste, aplicó;
aplicamos, aplicasteis, aplicaron

An orthographical changing verb because **c** changes to **qu** in front of **é** in the 1st pers. sing. of this tense.

arrancar / to pull out, to uproot
arranqué, arrancaste, arrancó;
arrancamos, arrancasteis, arrancaron

An orthographical changing verb because **c** changes to **qu** in front of **é** in the 1st pers. sing. of this tense.

atacar / to attack
ataqué, atacaste, atacó;
atacamos, atacasteis, atacaron

An orthographical changing verb because **c** changes to **qu** in front of **é** in the 1st pers. sing. of this tense.

atraer / to attract, to allure, to charm
atraje, atrajiste, atrajo;
atrajimos, atrajisteis, atrajeron

avanzar / to advance
avancé, avanzaste, avanzó;
avanzamos, avanzasteis, avanzaron

An orthographical changing verb because **z** changes to **c** in front of **é** in the 1st pers. sing. of this tense.

averiguar / to find out, to inquire, to investigate
averigüé, averiguaste, averiguó;
averiguamos, averiguasteis, averiguaron

An orthographical changing verb because **u** changes to **ü** in front of **é** in the 1st pers. sing. of this tense. The two dots over the **ü** are called dieresis or diaeresis; in Spanish, they are called *diéresis*. They indicate that each of the two vowels (**üé**) has a separate and distinct pronunciation. The dieresis mark is used in **averigüé** to tell you that **güé** should be pronounced as *gway*, not *gay*. Why? In order to preserve the *gw* sound in the infinitive.

bendecir / to bless
bendije, bendijiste, bendijo;
bendijimos, bendijisteis, bendijeron

buscar / to look for, to search, to seek
busqué, buscaste, buscó;
buscamos, buscasteis, buscaron

An orthographical changing verb because **c** changes to **qu** in front of **é** in the 1st pers. sing. of this tense.

caber / to fit, to be contained
cupe, cupiste, cupo;
cupimos, cupisteis, cupieron

caer / to fall
caí, caíste, cayó;
caímos, caísteis, cayeron

An orthographical changing verb because **i** in **ió** of the 3rd pers. sing. ending changes to **y** and i in **ieron** of the 3rd pers. plural ending changes to **y**. The reason for this spelling change is the strong vowel **a** right in front of those two endings.

ALSO NOTE that i in **iste** changes to **í** in the 2nd pers. sing. and i in **isteis** changes to **í** in the 2nd pers. plural because of the strong vowel **a** in front of those two endings. The same thing happens in **caímos.**

colgar / to hang
colgué, colgaste, colgó;
colgamos, colgasteis, colgaron

An orthographical changing verb because **g** changes to **gu** in front of **é** in the 1st pers. sing. of this tense.

105

colocar / to place, to put
coloqué, colocaste, colocó;
colocamos, colocasteis, colocaron

An orthographical changing verb because **c** changes to **qu** in front of **é** in the 1st pers. sing. of this tense.

comenzar / to begin, to commence, to start
comencé, comenzaste, comenzó;
comenzamos, comenzasteis, comenzaron

An orthographical changing verb because **z** changes to **c** in front of **é** in the 1st pers. sing. of this tense.

componer / to compose
compuse, compusiste, compuso;
compusimos, compusisteis, compusieron

comunicar / to communicate
comuniqué, comunicaste, comunicó;
comunicamos, comunicasteis, comunicaron

An orthographical changing verb because **c** changes to **que** in front of **é** in the 1st pers. sing. of this tense.

conducir / to conduct, to lead, to drive
conduje, condujiste, condujo;
condujimos, condujisteis, condujeron

conseguir / to get, to obtain, to attain, to succeed in
conseguí, conseguiste, consiguió;
conseguimos, conseguisteis, consiguieron

A stem-changing verb because **e** in the stem changes to **i** in the 3rd pers. sing. and pl. of this tense. Pres. part. is **consiguiendo.**

construir / to construct, to build
construí, construiste, construyó;
construimos, construisteis, construyeron

This **—uir** verb changes **i** to **y** in the 3rd pers. sing. and pl. of this tense.

contener / to contain, to hold
contuve, contuviste, contuvo;
contuvimos, contuvisteis, contuvieron

contradecir / to contradict
contradije, contradijiste, contradijo;
contradijimos, contradijisteis, contradijeron

contribuir / to contribute
contribuí, contribuiste, contribuyó;
contribuimos, contribuisteis, contribuyeron

This **—uir** verb changes **i** to **y** in the 3rd pers. sing. and pl. of this tense.

convenir / to agree
convine, conviniste, convino;

convinimos, convinisteis, convinieron

Pres. part. is also irregular: **conviniendo.**

convertir / to convert
convertí, convertiste, convirtió;
convertimos, convertisteis, convirtieron

A stem-changing verb because **e** in the stem changes to **i** in the 3rd pers. sing. and pl. of this tense. Pres. part. is also irregular: **convirtiendo.**

corregir / to correct
corregí, corregiste, corrigió;
corregimos, corregisteis, corrigieron

A stem-changing verb because **e** in the stem changes to **i** in the 3rd pers. sing. and pl. of this tense. Pres. part. is also irregular: **corrigiendo.**

creer / to believe
creí, creíste, creyó;
creímos, creísteis, creyeron

An orthographical changing verb because **i** in **ió** of the 3rd pers. sing. ending changes to **y** and i in **ieron** of the 3rd pers. plural ending changes to **y**. Also note that i in **iste** changes to **í** in the 2nd pers. sing. and i in **isteis** changes to **í** in the 2nd pers. pl. because of the strong vowel **e** in front of those two endings. The same thing happens in **creímos.**

cruzar / to cross
crucé, cruzaste, cruzó;
cruzamos, cruzasteis, cruzaron

An orthographical changing verb because **z** changes to **c** in front of **é** in the 1st pers. sing. of this tense.

dar / to give
di, diste, dio;
dimos, disteis, dieron

decir / to say, to tell
dije, dijiste, dijo;
dijimos, dijisteis, dijeron

dedicar / to dedicate, to devote
dediqué, dedicaste, dedicó;
dedicamos, dedicasteis, dedicaron

An orthographical changing verb because **c** changes to **qu** in front of **é** in the 1st pers. sing. of this tense.

despedir / to dismiss
despedí, despediste, despidió;
despedimos, despedisteis, despidieron

A stem-changing verb because **e** in the stem changes to **i** in the 3rd pers. sing. and pl. of this tense. Pres. part. is **despidiendo.**

despedirse (de) / to say good-bye (to), to take leave (of)
me despedí, te despediste, se despidió;
nos despedimos, os despedisteis, se despidieron

A stem-changing verb because **e** in the stem changes to **i** in the 3rd pers. sing. and pl. of this tense. Pres. part. is **despidiéndose.**

destruir / to destroy
destruí, destruiste, destruyó;
destruimos, destruisteis, destruyeron

This —**uir** verb changes **i** to **y** in the 3rd pers. sing. and pl. of this tense.

desvestirse / to undress, to get undressed
me desvestí, te desvestiste, se desvistió;
nos desvestimos, os desvestisteis, se desvistieron

A stem-changing verb because **e** in the stem changes to **i** in the 3rd pers. sing. and pl. of this tense. Pres. part. is **desvistiéndose.**

detener / to detain, to stop (someone or something)
detuve, detuviste, detuvo;
detuvimos, detuvisteis, detuvieron

detenerse / to stop (oneself or itself)
me detuve, te detuviste, se detuvo;
nos detuvimos, os detuvisteis, se detuvieron

divertirse / to have a good time, to enjoy oneself
me divertí, te divertiste, se divirtió;
nos divertimos, os divertisteis, se divirtieron

A stem-changing verb because **e** in the stem changes to **i** in the 3rd pers. sing. and pl. of this tense. Pres. part. is **divirtiéndose.**

dormir / to sleep
dormí, dormiste, durmió;
dormimos, dormisteis, durmieron

A stem-changing verb because **o** in the stem changes to **u** in the 3rd pers. sing. and pl. of this tense. Pres. part. is **durmiendo.**

dormirse / to fall asleep
me dormí, te dormiste, se durmió;
nos dormimos, os dormisteis, se durmieron

A stem-changing verb because **o** in the stem changes to **u** in the 3rd pers. sing. and pl. of this tense. Pres. part. is **durmiéndose.**

elegir / to elect
elegí, elegiste, eligió;
elegimos, elegisteis, eligieron

A stem-changing verb because **e** in the stem changes to **i** in the 3rd pers. sing. and pl. of this tense. Pres. part. is **eligiendo.**

empezar / to begin, to start
empecé, empezaste, empezó;
empezamos, empezasteis, empezaron

An orthographical changing verb because **z** changes to **c** in front of **é** in the 1st pers. sing. of this tense.

encargar / to entrust, to put in charge
encargué, encargaste, encargó;
encargamos, encargasteis, encargaron

An orthographical changing verb because **g** changes to **gu** in front of **é** in the 1st pers. sing. of this tense.

entregar / to surrender, to give up, to hand over, to deliver
entregué, entregaste, entregó;
entregamos, entregasteis, entregaron

An orthographical changing verb because **g** changes to **gu** in front of **é** in the 1st pers. sing. of this tense.

equivocarse / to be mistaken
me equivoqué, te equivocaste, se equivocó;
nos equivocamos, os equivocasteis, se equivocaron

An orthographical changing verb because **c** changes to **qu** in front of **é** in the 1st pers. sing. of this tense.

estar / to be
estuve, estuviste, estuvo;
estuvimos, estuvisteis, estuvieron

explicar / to explain
expliqué, explicaste, explicó;
explicamos, explicasteis, explicaron

An orthographical changing verb because **c** changes to **qu** in front of **é** in the 1st pers. sing. of this tense.

gemir / to groan, to moan
gemí, gemiste, gimió;
gemimos, gemisteis, gimieron

A stem-changing verb because **e** in the stem changes to **i** in the 3rd pers. sing. and pl of this tense. Pres. part. is **gimiendo.**

gozar / to enjoy
gocé, gozaste, gozó;
gozamos, gozasteis, gozaron

An orthographical changing verb because **z** changes to **c** in front of **é** in the 1st pers. sing. of this tense.

gruñir / to grumble, to grunt, to growl, to creak (as doors, hinges, *etc.*)
gruñí, gruñiste, gruñó;
gruñimos, gruñisteis, gruñeron

This —**ñir** verb drops **i** in the ending **ió** in the 3rd pers. sing. and drops **i** in the ending **ieron** in the 3rd pers. pl. because **ñ** is in front of those two endings. The sound of **ieron** is still the same without **i** because of the sound of **ñ**. Pres. part. is **gruñendo**.

haber / to have (as an auxiliary or helping verb)
hube, hubiste, hubo;
hubimos, hubisteis, hubieron

hacer / to do, to make
hice, hiciste, hizo;
hicimos, hicisteis, hicieron

herir / to harm, to hurt, to wound
herí, heriste, hirió;
herimos, heristeis, hirieron

A stem-changing verb because **e** changes to **i** in the stem in the 3rd pers. sing. and pl. of this tense. Pres. part. is **hiriendo**.

huir / to flee, to escape, to run away, to slip away
huí, huiste, huyó;
huimos, huisteis, huyeron

This —**uir** verb changes **i** to **y** in the 3rd pers. sing. and pl. of this tense. Pres. part. is **huyendo**.

imponer / to impose
impuse, impusiste, impuso;
impusimos, impusisteis, impusieron

incluir / to enclose, to include
incluí, incluiste, incluyó;
incluimos, incluisteis, incluyeron

This —**uir** verb changes **i** to **y** in the 3rd pers. sing. and pl. of this tense. Pres. part. is **incluyendo**.

indicar / to indicate
indiqué, indicaste, indicó;
indicamos, indicasteis, indicaron

An orthographical changing verb because **c** changes to **qu** in front of **é** in the 1st pers. sing. of this tense.

inducir / to induce, to influence, to persuade
induje, indujiste, indujo;
indujimos, indujisteis, indujeron

influir / to influence
influí, influiste, influyó;
influimos, influisteis, influyeron

This —**uir** verb changes **i** to **y** in the 3rd pers. sing. and pl. of this tense. Pres. part. is **influyendo**.

introducir / to introduce
introduje, introdujiste, introdujo; introdujimos, introdujisteis, introdujeron

ir / to go
fui, fuiste, fue;
fuimos, fuisteis, fueron
NOTE that these forms are the same for **ser** in the preterit.

irse / to go away
me fui, te fuiste, se fue;
nos fuimos, os fuisteis, se fueron

jugar / to play (game or sport)
jugué, jugaste, jugó;
jugamos, jugasteis, jugaron

An orthographical changing verb because **g** changes to **gu** in front of **é** in the 1st pers. sing. of this tense.

lanzar / to throw, to hurl, to fling, to launch
lancé, lanzaste, lanzó;
lanzamos, lanzasteis, lanzaron

An orthographical changing verb because **z** changes to **c** in front of **é** in the 1st pers. sing. of this tense.

leer / to read
leí, leíste, leyó;
leímos, leísteis, leyeron

An orthographical changing verb because **i** in **ió** of the 3rd pers. sing. ending changes to **y** and **i** in **ieron** of the 3rd pers. plural ending changes to **y**. Also note that **i** in **iste** changes to **í** in the 2nd pers. sing. and **i** in **isteis** changes to **í** in the 2nd pers. pl. because of the strong vowel **e** in front of those two endings. The same thing happens in **leímos**. Remember that the regular endings in the preterit of an —**er** and —**ir** verb are: **í, iste, ió; imos, isteis, ieron.**

llegar / to arrive
llegué, llegaste, llegó;
llegamos, llegasteis, llegaron

An orthographical changing verb because **g** changes to **gu** in front of **é** in the 1st pers. sing. of this tense.

marcar / to mark
marqué, marcaste, marcó;
marcamos, marcasteis, marcaron

An orthographical changing verb because **c** changes to **qu** in front of **é** in the 1st pers. sing. of this tense.

mentir / to lie, to tell a lie
mentí, mentiste, mintió;
mentimos, mentisteis, mintieron

A stem-changing verb because **e** in the stem changes to **i** in the 3rd pers. sing. and pl. of this tense. Pres. part. is **mintiendo.**

morir / to die
morí, moriste, murió;
morimos, moristeis, murieron

A stem-changing verb because **o** in the stem changes to **u** in the 3rd pers. sing. and pl. of this tense. Pres. part. is **muriendo.**

negar / to deny
negué, negaste, negó;
negamos, negasteis, negaron

An orthographical changing verb because **g** changes to **gu** in front of **é** in the 1st pers. sing. of this tense.

obligar / to obligate, to compel
obligué, obligaste, obligó;
obligamos, obligasteis, obligaron

An orthographical changing verb because **g** changes to **gu** in front of **é** in the 1st pers. sing. of this tense.

obtener / to obtain, to get
obtuve, obtuviste, obtuvo;
obtuvimos, obtuvisteis, obtuvieron

oír / to hear (sometimes can mean to understand)
oí, oíste, oyó;
oímos, oísteis, oyeron

An orthographical changing verb because **i** in **ió** of the 3rd pers. sing. ending and **i** in **ieron** of the 3rd pers. plural ending both change to **y.**

ALSO NOTE that **iste** changes to **íste, imos** to **ímos,** and **isteis** to **ísteis** because of the strong vowel **o** in front of those endings. Remember that the regular endings in the preterit of an —**er** and —**ir** verb are: **í, iste, ió; imos, isteis, ieron.**

oponer / to oppose
opuse, opusiste, opuso;
opusimos, opusisteis, opusieron

pagar / to pay
pagué, pagaste, pagó;
pagamos, pagasteis, pagaron

An orthographical changing verb because **g** changes to **gu** in front of **é** in the 1st pers. sing. of this tense.

pedir / to ask for, to request
pedí, pediste, pidió;
pedimos, pedisteis, pidieron

A stem-changing verb because **e** in the stem changes to **i** in the 3rd pers. sing. and pl. of this tense. Pres. part. is **pidiendo.**

pescar / to fish
pesqué, pescaste, pescó;
pescamos, pescasteis, pescaron

An orthographical changing verb because **c** changes to **qu** in front of **é** in the 1st pers. sing. of this tense.

poder / to be able, can
pude, pudiste, pudo;
pudimos, pudisteis, pudieron

poner / to put, to place
puse, pusiste, puso;
pusimos, pusisteis, pusieron

ponerse / to put on, to become (pale, angry, etc.), to set (of the sun)
me puse, te pusiste, se puso;
nos pusimos, os pusisteis, se pusieron

poseer / to possess, to own
poseí, poseíste, poseyó;
poseímos, poseísteis, poseyeron

An orthographical changing verb because **i** in **ió** of the 3rd pers. sing. ending and **i** in **ieron** of the 3rd pers. plural ending both change to **y.**

ALSO NOTE that **iste** changes to **íste, imos** to **ímos,** and **isteis** to **ísteis** because of the strong vowel **e** in front of those endings. Remember that the regular endings in the preterit of an —**er** and —**ir** verb are: **í, iste, ió; imos, isteis, ieron.**

predecir / to predict, to forecast, to foretell
predije, predijiste, predijo;
predijimos, predijisteis, predijeron

preferir / to prefer
preferí, preferiste, prefirió;
preferimos, preferisteis, prefirieron

A stem-changing verb because **e** in the stem changes to **i** in the 3rd pers. sing. and pl. of this tense. Pres. part. is **prefiriendo.**

producir / to produce
produje, produjiste, produjo;
produjimos, produjisteis, produjeron

proponer / to propose
propuse, propusiste, propuso;
propusimos, propusisteis, propusieron

publicar / to publish
publiqué, publicaste, publicó;
publicamos, publicasteis, publicaron

An orthographical changing verb because **c** changes to **qu** in front of **é** in the 1st pers. sing. of this tense.

querer / to want, to wish
quise, quisiste, quiso;
quisimos, quisisteis, quisieron

realizar / to realize, to carry out, to fulfill
realicé, realizaste, realizó;
realizamos, realizasteis, realizaron

An orthographical changing verb because **z** changes to **c** in front of **é** in the 1st pers. sing. of this tense.

referir / to refer
referí, referiste, refirió;
referimos, referisteis, refirieron

A stem-changing verb because **e** in the stem changes to **i** in the 3rd pers. sing. and pl. of this tense. Pres. part. is **refiriendo**.

reír / to laugh
reí, reíste, rió;
reímos, reísteis, rieron

Pres. part. is **riendo**.

repetir / to repeat
repetí, repetiste, repitió;
repetimos, repetisteis, repitieron

A stem-changing verb because **e** in the stem changes to **i** in the 3rd pers. sing. and pl. of this tense. Pres. part. is **repitiendo**.

replicar / to reply
repliqué, replicaste, replicó;
replicamos, replicasteis, replicaron

An orthographical changing verb because **c** changes to **qu** in front of **é** in the 1st pers. sing. of this tense.

rezar / to pray
recé, rezaste, rezó;
rezamos, rezasteis, rezaron

An orthographical changing verb because **z** changes to **c** in front of **é** in the 1st pers. sing. of this tense.

rogar / to beg, to request
rogué, rogaste, rogó;
rogamos, rogasteis, rogaron

An orthographical changing verb because **g** changes to **gu** in front of **é** in the 1st pers. sing. of this tense.

saber / to know, to know how
supe, supiste, supo;
supimos, supisteis, supieron

sacar / to take out
saqué, sacaste, sacó;
sacamos, sacasteis, sacaron

An orthographical changing verb because **c** changes to **qu** in front of **é** in the 1st pers. sing. of this tense.

secar / to dry, to wipe dry
sequé, secaste, secó;
secamos, secasteis, secaron

An orthographical changing verb because **c** changes to **qu** in front of **é** in the 1st pers. sing. of this tense.

seguir / to follow, to pursue, to continue
seguí, seguiste, siguió;
seguimos, seguisteis, siguieron

A stem-changing verb because **e** in the stem changes to **i** in the 3rd pers. sing. and pl. of this tense. Pres. part. is **siguiendo**.

sentir / to feel sorry, to regret, to feel, to experience, to sense
sentí, sentiste, sintió;
sentimos, sentisteis, sintieron

A stem-changing verb because **e** in the stem changes to **i** in the 3rd pers. sing. and pl. of this tense. Pres. part. is **sintiendo**.

ser / to be
fui, fuiste, fue;
fuimos, fuisteis, fueron

NOTE that these forms are the same for **ir** in the preterit.

servir / to serve
serví, serviste, sirvió;
servimos, servisteis, sirvieron

A stem-changing verb because **e** in the stem changes to **i** in the 3rd pers. sing. and pl. of this tense. Pres. part. is **sirviendo**.

significar / to mean, to signify
signifiqué, significaste, significó;
significamos, significasteis, significaron

An orthographical changing verb because **c** changes to **qu** in front of **é** in the 1st pers. sing. of this tense.

sonreír / to smile
sonreí, sonreíste, sonrió;
sonreímos, sonreísteis, sonrieron

Pres. part. is **sonriendo**.

suplicar / to supplicate, to beseech, to entreat, to beg
supliqué, suplicaste, suplicó;
suplicamos, suplicasteis, suplicaron

An orthographical changing verb because **c** changes to **qu** in front of **é** in the 1st pers. sing. of this tense.

suponer / to suppose
supuse, supusiste, supuso;
supusimos, supusisteis, supusieron

tener / to have, to hold
tuve, tuviste, tuvo;
tuvimos, tuvisteis, tuvieron

tocar / to touch, to play (music or a musical instrument)
toqué, tocaste, tocó;
tocamos, tocasteis, tocaron

An orthographical changing verb because **c** changes to **qu** in front of **é** in the 1st pers. sing. of this tense.

traducir / to translate
traduje, tradujiste, tradujo;
tradujimos, tradujisteis, tradujeron

traer / to bring
traje, trajiste, trajo;

trajimos, trajisteis, trajeron
Pres. part. is **trayendo.**

tropezar / to stumble
tropecé, tropezaste, tropezó;
tropezamos, tropezasteis, tropezaron

An orthographical changing verb because **z** changes to **c** in front of **é** in the 1st pers. sing. of this tense.

venir / to come
vine, viniste, vino;
vinimos, vinisteis, vinieron

ver / to see
vi, viste, vio;
vimos, visteis, vieron

vestir / to dress, to clothe (someone)
vestí, vestiste, vistió;
vestimos, vestisteis, vistieron

A stem-changing verb because **e** in the stem changes to **i** in the 3rd pers. sing. and pl. of this tense. Pres. part. is **vistiendo.**

vestirse / to dress, to clothe (oneself)
me vestí, te vestiste, se vistió;
nos vestimos, os vestisteis, se vistieron

A stem-changing verb because **e** in the stem changes to **i** in the 3rd pers. sing. and pl. of this tense. Pres. part. is **vistiéndose.**

EJERCICIOS

I. Seleccione la forma correcta del verbo en el **pretérito.**

1. Antes de regresar a su asiento, Juana _____ a un hombre.
   (a) ve   (b) está viendo   (c) veía   (d) vio

   _____

2. Cuando Juana vio al hombre, ella le _____ "Buenos días".
   (a) dice   (b) está diciendo   (c) decía   (d) dijo

   _____

3. El hombre _____ su autógrafo en el programa que Juana tenía a la mano.
   (a) escribió   (b) escribe   (c) está escribiendo   (d) escribía

   _____

4. Juana le _____ al hombre su programa y su pluma para escribir su autógrafo.
   (a) da   (b) dio   (c) está dando   (d) daba

   _____

5. Cuando la pieza se terminó, todo el mundo _____ del teatro.
   (a) salió   (b) sale   (c) está saliendo   (d) salía

   _____

6. Afuera, Juana   (a) anuncia   (b) anunció   (c) está anunciando   (d) anunciaba
   las   noticias.

   _____

7. Juana dio el programa a su madre y ésta   (a) lee   (b) leyó   (c) leía   (d) está
   leyendo   los anuncios.

   _____

8. Pedro _____ que todo el mundo no tiene el autógrafo de José Blanco.
   (a) dijo   (b) dije   (c) dice   (d) está diciendo

   _____   **111**

9. Juana _____ una tontería.   (a) hace   (b) hizo   (c) está haciendo   (d) hacía   _____

10. Juana _____ que hizo una tontería.   (a) exclamó   (b) exclama   (c) exclamaba
(d) está exclamando   _____

II. Cambie el verbo entre paréntesis al **pretérito.**

Modelo: Ayer, yo (ver) a mis amigos en el centro. _____vi_____

1. ¿Qué (ver) Ud. en la televisión ayer por la noche?   _____

2. El año pasado Miguel (ir) a Puerto Rico.   _____

3. Ayer, después de la comida, mi hermana (servir) el café.   _____

4. Esta mañana una persona (tocar) a la puerta.   _____

5. ¿Quién (traer) este pastel?   _____

6. Ayer yo (tener) una carta de mi amigo Roberto que vive en España.   _____

7. La semana pasada yo (conocer) a Juana en el baile.   _____

8. Yo (poder) hacerlo.   _____

9. Yo (querer) llamar a mi amiga Carlota.   _____

10. Juana no (querer) ir a casa de Elena.   _____

III. Escriba las seis formas de cada verbo en el **pretérito.**

Modelo: ser _____fui, fuiste, fue; fuimos, fuisteis, fueron_____

1. ser _____

2. tener _____

3. traer _____

4. venir _____

5. preferir _____

6. querer _____

7. reír _____

8. saber _____

9. sacar _____

10. morir _____

IV. Seleccione el verbo en el imperfecto de indicativo o en el pretérito, según convenga. Estudie otra vez el imperfecto de indicativo en el Work Unit 6.

Modelo: Mi hermano _____ un libro y mi padre hablaba cuando yo entré.
(a) leía   (b) leyó   _____a_____

1. Mi hermana _____ cuando yo llamé. (a) cantó (b) cantaba _____

2. Cuando _____ en Nueva York, íbamos al cine todos los días. (a) estábamos
   (b) estuvimos _____

3. Mi padre _____ ayer. (a) llegaba (b) llegó _____

4. Cuando _____ en California, íbamos a la playa todos los días. (a) vivíamos
   (b) vivimos _____

5. Esta mañana María _____ a la iglesia. (a) iba (b) fue _____

6. Mi madre _____ hermosa cuando era pequeña. (a) era (b) fue _____

7. ¿Qué hora _____ cuando Ud. llegó? (a) era (b) fue _____

8. ¿Qué _____? (a) pasó (b) pasaba _____

9. ¿Qué hora era? _____ las tres. (a) Eran (b) Fueron _____

10. Hacía tres horas que yo _____ la televisión cuando mi madre llamó. (a) miré
    (b) miraba _____

11. Salí de casa, _____ el autobús y llegué a la escuela a las ocho. (a) tomaba
    (b) tomé _____

12. Esta mañana yo _____ el desayuno a las siete. (a) tomé (b) tomaba _____

13. Juana _____ contentísima de ver a su amiga Carlota. (a) estuvo (b) estaba _____

V. Conteste las siguientes preguntas en el afirmativo con oraciones completas. En la oración (a)
use la palabra **Sí.** En la oración (b) use la palabra **también** según los modelos.

Modelos: **a. ¿Abrió Ud. la ventana?**   **a. Sí, (yo) abrí la ventana.**
             b. ¿Y su madre?   **b. Mi madre abrió la ventana, también.**

1. a. ¿Escribió Ud. una carta? _____

    b. ¿Y Carlos? _____

2. a. ¿Oyó Ud. el ruido? _____

    b. ¿Y los alumnos? _____

3. a. ¿Oyeron la música los estudiantes? _____

    b. ¿Y usted? _____

4. a. ¿Pagó Ud. la cuenta? _____

    b. ¿Y Casandra y Claudio? _____

5. a. ¿Pidió Ud. dinero a su padre ayer? _____

    b. ¿Y su hermano? _____

6. a. ¿Pescaron los muchachos en este lago? _____

   b. ¿Y ustedes? _____

7. a. ¿Pudo Ud. abrir la ventana? _____

   b. ¿Y la profesora? _____

8. a. ¿Puso Ud. el dinero en el bolsillo? _____

   b. ¿Y el señor Rodríguez? _____

9. a. ¿Hizo Ud. muchas cosas ayer? _____

   b. ¿Y Daniel y David? _____

10. a. ¿Fue la señora Rodríguez al teatro el sábado pasado? _____

    b. ¿Y ustedes? _____

VI. **Juego de palabras.** Complete las palabras verticalmente en español por las palabras en inglés. Todas las palabras son formas de verbos en el **pretérito.**

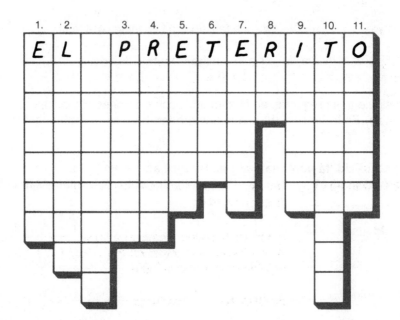

1. I studied.	4. He repeated.	7. He elected.	10. I telephoned.
2. They called.	5. I began.	8. I laughed.	11. They dared.
3. We paid.	6. I brought.	9. I invited.	

VII. ¿Qué instrumento musical toca Ud?

   Respuesta: _____

VIII. ¿Qué mira Ud?

Respuesta: _____

IX. A veces, si Ud. pronuncia incorrectamente una palabra española, es posible que Ud. pronuncie otra palabra que existe en la lengua. Esto puede ser desconcertante.

EJEMPLO:

hablo / I speak, am speaking, do speak   (1st pers., sing., present indicative
         I talk, am talking, do talk   of **hablar**)

habló / He (She) spoke.   (3rd pers., sing., preterit of **hablar**)
         He (She) talked.

Mnemonic tip

In **hablo,** the stress is on A.
In **habló,** the stress is on O
because there is an accent mark
on O.

hablar / to speak, to talk
present indicative   preterit

yo **hablo**	nosotros hablamos	yo hablé	nosotros hablamos
tú hablas	vosotros habláis	tú hablaste	vosotros hablasteis
Ud. ⎫ él ⎬habla ella ⎭	Uds. ⎫ ellos ⎬hablan ellas ⎭	Ud. ⎫ él ⎬**habló** ella ⎭	Uds. ⎫ ellos ⎬hablaron ellas ⎭

¿Cuántos ejemplos puede Ud. decir y escribir?

Mnemonic tip

The general rule for stress in pronouncing a Spanish word is:

If a word in Spanish ends in a vowel, n or s, stress (raise your voice) on the vowel in the syllable next to the last one:

muCHAcha   esTAban   reGAlos

If a word ends in a letter other than a vowel, n or s, stress the last syllable:

feLIZ   abandoNAR   reLOJ

X. LETRA RELOJ. Cuatro palabras se esconden en este reloj: una palabra de las doce a las tres, una palabra de las tres a las seis, una palabra de las seis a las nueve y, por fin, una palabra de las nueve a las doce.

La misma letra es común a la palabra que sigue.

Este reloj no tiene agujas. ¡Es un reloj de palabras!

115

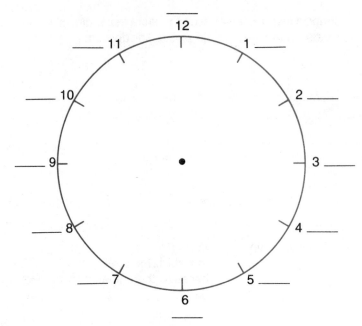

De las doce a las tres es un sinónimo de **años.**

De las tres a las seis es un sinónimo de **mujer.**

De las seis a las nueve es un sinónimo de **pájaros.**

De las nueve a las doce es la tercera persona, singular, presente de indicativo del verbo **salir.**

XI. Las palabras escondidas. En la rejilla, busque las palabras en español por las palabras en inglés de la lista que figuran a continuación.

Las palabras están inscritas en todas las direcciones: de abajo arriba, de arriba abajo, de derecha a izquierda, de izquierda a derecha, al derecho y al revés, y en diagonal.

La misma letra puede ser común a varias palabras.

A	L	Á	M	P	A	R	A	A
B	D	C	E	U	I	O	E	U
A	M	P	L	E	L	A	M	A
V	N	E	H	R	V	E	S	L
P	U	C	E	T	R	E	O	F
L	O	P	C	A	M	A	S	O
C	M	E	A	S	A	N	E	M
A	M	C	S	A	S	A	C	B
A	R	T	U	P	I	T	I	R
A	I	E	O	U	L	N	P	A
L	F	A	M	B	L	E	Á	F
C	A	A	S	S	A	V	L	O

door
houses
car
pencils
beds
chair
window
table
lamp
carpet

ADVERBS

Definition: An adverb is a word that modifies a verb, an adjective or another adverb.

Regular formation: An adverb is regularly formed by adding the ending **mente** to the fem. sing. form of an adj.:

>**lento, lenta / lentamente:** slow / slowly; **rápido, rápida / rápidamente:** rapid / rapidly

If the form of the adj. is the same for the fem. sing. and masc. sing. **(fácil, feliz)**, add **mente** to that form.

>**fácil** (easy) / **fácilmente** (easily)
>**feliz** (happy) / **felizmente** (happily)

NOTE that an accent mark on an adjective remains when changed to an adverb. And note that the Spanish ending **mente** is equivalent to the ending **-ly** in English.

An adverb remains invariable; that is to say, it does not agree in gender and number and therefore does not change in form.

There are many adverbs that do not end in **mente**. Some common ones are:

abajo / below	**bien** / well	**hoy** / today	**siempre** / always	**aquí** / here
arriba / above	**mal** / badly	**mañana** / tomorrow	**nunca** / never	**allí** / there

The adverbial ending **ísimo**

Never use **muy** in front of **mucho**. Say **muchísimo: Elena trabaja muchísimo** / Helen works a great deal; Helen works very, very much.

Regular comparison of adverbs

>**María corre tan rápidamente como Elena** / Mary runs as rapidly as Helen.

>**María corre menos rápidamente que Anita** / Mary runs less rapidly than Anita.

>**María corre más rápidamente que Isabel** / Mary runs more rapidly than Elizabeth.

Irregular comparative adverbs

>**mucho, poco** / much, little: **Roberto trabaja mucho; Felipe trabaja poco.**

>**bien, mal** / well, badly: **Juan trabaja bien; Lucas trabaja mal.**

>**más, menos** / more, less: **Carlota trabaja más que Casandra; Elena trabaja menos que Marta.**

>**mejor, peor** / better, worse: **Paula trabaja mejor que Anita; Isabel trabaja peor que Elena.**

Con, sin + noun

At times, an adverb can be formed by using the prep. **con** (with) or **sin** (without) + a noun.

>**con cuidado** / carefully   **con dificultad** / with difficulty
>**sin cuidado** / carelessly   **sin dificultad** / without difficulty

The adverb **recientemente** (recently) becomes **recién** before a past participle: **los recién llegados** / the ones recently arrived; the recently arrived (ones)

Interrogative adverbs

Some common interrogative adverbs are: **¿cómo?** / how? **¿cuándo?** / when? **¿por qué?** / why? **¿para qué?** / why? **¿dónde?** / where? **¿adónde?** / where to? (to where)?

Adverbs replaced by adjectives

An adverb may sometimes be replaced by an adjective whose agreement is with the subject, especially if the verb is one of motion:

Las muchachas van y vienen silenciosas / The girls come and go silently.

EJERCICIOS

I. Forme adverbios de los siguientes adjetivos.

Modelo: lento→lentamente

1. rápido_____
2. fácil_____
3. alegre_____

4. absoluto_____
5. feliz_____
6. cierto_____

II. Escriba seis adverbios que no terminan en **-mente.**

1. _____
2. _____
3. _____

4. _____
5. _____
6. _____

III. Traduzca al español.

1. Cristina runs as rapidly as Helen. _____

2. Claudia runs less rapidly than Anita. _____

3. David runs more rapidly than Enrique. _____

4. Roberto works a lot; Felipe works a little. _____

5. Juana works well; Lucas works badly. _____

6. Carlota works more than Casandra. _____

7. Elena works less than Marta. _____

8. Paula works better than Dora. _____

9. Isabel works worse than Elisa. _____

10. Michael talks carelessly and he does not study well. _____

IV. Conteste las siguientes preguntas en el afirmativo con oraciones completas. En la oración (a) use la palabra **Sí.** En la oración (b) use la palabra **también,** según los modelos.

Modelos: a. ¿Trabaja Ud. con cuidado?   Escriba: **a. Sí, trabajo con cuidado.**
b. ¿Y Emilia?   **b. Emilia trabaja con cuidado, también.**

1. a. ¿Estudia Ud. sin cuidado? _____

   b. ¿Y los otros alumnos? _____

2. a. ¿Lee Emilio con dificultad? _____

   b. ¿Y tú? _____

3. a. ¿Estudió Ud. la lección sin dificultad? _____

   b. ¿Y Uds.? _____

4. a. ¿Escribiste la carta con cuidado? _____

   b. ¿Y Edita? _____

5. a. ¿Corre María tan rápidamente como Elena? _____

   b. ¿Y ustedes? _____

6. a. ¿Habla Ricardo menos rápidamente que Ramón? _____

   b. ¿Y Rebeca y Tomás? _____

7. a. ¿Escribe Samuel más rápidamente que Sara? _____

   b. ¿Y ellos? _____

8. a. ¿Duerme Susana más que Teresa? _____

   b. ¿Y los niños? _____

9. a. ¿Van y vienen silenciosas Eva y María? _____

   b. ¿Y Roberto y Carlos? _____

10. a. ¿Trabaja Elena muchísimo? _____

    b. ¿Y todos los alumnos en la clase de español? _____

V. Varias palabras en una sola. Utilizando las letras en la palabra **COLOMBIA,** ¿cuántas palabras puede usted escribir? Escriba seis palabras, por lo menos.

COLOMBIA

1. _____   4. _____

2. _____   5. _____

3. _____   6. _____

VI. Jeroglífico. Rellene las casillas a continuación con las letras de la palabra que describe el dibujo.

Para hallar la solución de este jeroglífico, rellene las casillas del modo siguiente: en la casilla 1, escriba la primera letra de la persona en el primer dibujo; en la casilla 2, escriba la segunda letra de la persona en el segundo dibujo; en la casilla 3, escriba la tercera letra del objeto en el tercer dibujo; en la casilla 4, escriba la letra A.

119

Después de haber rellenado las cuatro casillas de la solución de aquel modo, usted encontrará el nombre de un gran pintor español.

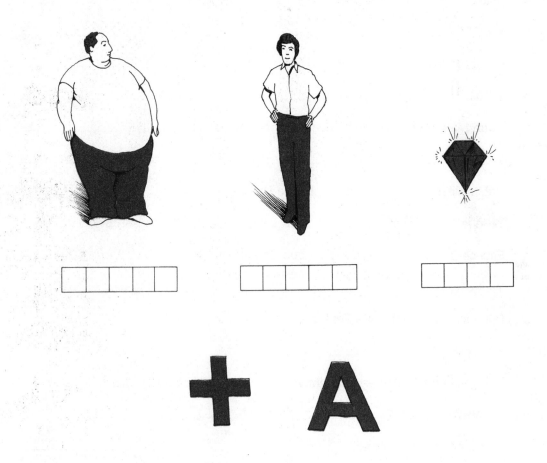

Solución: ☐☐☐☐

VII. Algunos alumnos confunden las palabras **mujer** y **mejor.**

la mujer / the woman
   mejor *adj., adv.* / better

Esta mujer trabaja mejor que ésa. This woman works better than that one.

Mnemonic tip	**Mejor** contains **e** after the first letter and so does *better.* ¿Qué palabras españolas confunde usted? ¿Puede Ud. dar un "mnemonic tip"?

Mnemonic tip	Exception to the general rule of stress in pronouncing a Spanish word: If it is customary to stress a syllable other than the one next to the last syllable when the word ends in a vowel, *n* or *s,* you must write an accent mark on the vowel in the syllable that is stressed to tell the reader to stress that syllable: **pretérito.**

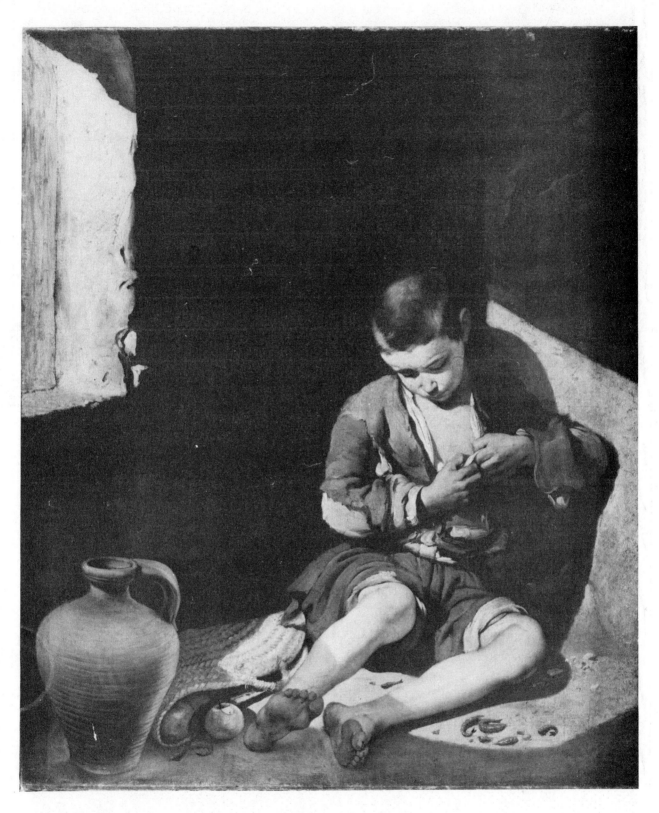

Niño espulgándose *by Bartolomé Esteban MURILLO (1617-1682)*
Reprinted with permission of La Réunion des Musées Nationaux, Paris.

Los signos del zodiaco.

*Let's see what Pedro's horoscope reveals for
today. What does yours say?*

Zodiaco

Pedro está leyendo el periódico en la cocina. Lee la página que contiene el horóscopo.

I **Aries** (Aries)
21 marzo–20 abril

Ud. será rico (rica) en diez años.

II **Tauro** (Taurus)
21 abril–21 mayo   5

A la edad de noventa años, Ud. tendrá mucha paciencia. Hoy
Ud. recibirá una carta interesante.

III **Géminis** (Gemini)
22 mayo–21 junio

Una persona rica querrá casarse con usted en el porvenir.   10
Tenga paciencia.

IV **Cáncer** (Cancer)
22 junio–23 julio

Hoy usted encontrará obstáculos peligrosos en su vida.

V **Leo** (Leo)   15
24 julio–23 agosto

Alguien que está enamorado de usted le dará muchos regalos para su
cumpleaños. Escríbale una carta.

VI **Virgo** (Virgo)
24 agosto–23 septiembre   20

Alguien le regalará a usted un automóvil magnífico.

VII **Libra** (Libra)
24 septiembre–23 octubre

¡Qué fortuna! Ud. verá un gran cambio en su vida personal.

VIII **Escorpión** (Scorpio)   25
24 octubre–22 noviembre

Ud. hará un viaje a un país extranjero.

IX **Sagitario** (Sagittarius)
23 noviembre–21 diciembre

Hoy Ud. hablará con una mujer preciosa.   30

X   **Capricornio** (Capricorn)
22 diciembre–20 enero

No salga de casa hoy. Quédese en casa. Hay peligro
en las calles.

XI   **Acuario** (Aquarius)   35
21 enero–19 febrero

Ud. recibirá una invitación muy agradable.

XII   **Piscis** (Pisces)
20 febrero–20 marzo

Hoy una persona muy simpática vendrá a su casa.   40

El teléfono suena. He aquí la conversación entre Pedro y su amiga Lola:

Lola: ¿Pedro? ¿Qué tal?

Pedro: Así, así. ¿Y tú?

Lola: Muy bien, gracias. Escucha, Pedro. Habrá una tertulia en mi casa esta noche. Bailaremos y cantaremos. Mi madre preparará pasteles deliciosos. Nos divertiremos   45
mucho. Enrique vendrá; así como Pablo, Roberto, Ramón, Susana, tu hermana
Juana, Queta, Luisa y muchos otros amigos. ¿Quieres venir también?

Pedro: Espera un momento, Lola. Yo no leí mi horóscopo hoy. Voy a leerlo en el periódico.
Un momento, por favor, Lola.

Pedro lee el horóscopo en el periódico. Lee su signo del Zodiaco, Capricornio.   50
Entonces continúa su conversación por teléfono con Lola.

Pedro: Lola, mi horóscopo dice: "No salga de casa hoy. Quédese en casa. Hay peligro en
las calles."

Lola: ¿Eres supersticioso, Pedro? ¿Estás loco?

Pedro: No soy supersticioso y no estoy loco. Escucha, Lola. Iré a tu casa, de todos   55
modos.
    Más tarde, Pedro sale de casa para ir a la tertulia en casa de Lola. Cuando Pedro cruza la calle,

ve que un camión grande viene a toda velocidad hacia él. Pedro _____

_____

_____

(NOTE TO THE STUDENT: WRITE YOUR OWN ENDING TO THIS STORY IN ONE OR TWO SENTENCES, IN SPANISH,
OF COURSE!)

VOCABULARIO: Consult the vocabulary section in the back pages.

EJERCICIOS

I. Seleccione la respuesta correcta conforme al significado de la lectura en esta lección.

1. Pedro está leyendo el periódico en   (a) el cuarto de baño   (b) la sala   (c) su
dormitorio   (d) la cocina   _____

2. Pedro lee la página que contiene   (a) las noticias internacionales   (b) los deportes   (c) las noticias de empleos   (d) el horóscopo   _____

3. La declaración que *Ud. será rico (rica) en diez años* se halla en el signo del Zodiaco   (a) Tauro   (b) Géminis   (c) Aries   (d) Libra   _____

4. La persona que telefona a Pedro es   (a) Roberto   (b) Ramón   (c) Queta   (d) Lola   _____

5. Lola quiere invitar a Pedro a venir a su casa porque habrá   (a) una discusión sobre temas políticos   (b) una tertulia   (c) una discusión sobre el horóscopo en el periódico   (d) una conferencia   _____

6. La persona que preparará pasteles deliciosos será   (a) la madre de Pedro   (b) la madre de Lola   (c) Lola   (d) Juana, la hermana de Pedro   _____

7. En casa de Lola, todos bailarán y   (a) estudiarán   (b) llorarán   (c) cantarán   (d) dormirán   _____

8. La declaración que *Ud. hará un viaje a un país extranjero* se halla en el signo del Zodiaco   (a) Aries   (b) Leo   (c) Virgo   (d) Escorpión   _____

9. Al principio, Pedro no acepta la invitación de Lola porque el horóscopo dice que es necesario   (a) hacer un viaje   (b) leer el periódico   (c) quedarse en casa a causa del peligro en las calles   (d) preparar pasteles deliciosos   _____

10. Más tarde, Pedro sale de casa para   (a) ver un gran camión en la calle   (b) comprar un periódico   (c) leer su horóscopo en la biblioteca   (d) ir a la tertulia en casa de Lola   _____

II. ¿Sí o No?

1. Pedro está leyendo un libro en la cocina.   _____

2. Pedro lee la página que contiene las noticias internacionales.   _____

3. Pedro habla por teléfono con Lola.   _____

4. Al principio, Lola piensa que Pedro es supersticioso.   _____

5. Al fin, Pedro acepta la invitación de Lola.   _____

III. Ordene las palabras hasta formar una oración con sentido.

1. leyendo / está / Pedro / la cocina / en / el periódico. _____

_____

2. será / Ud. / años / en / diez / rico. _____

_____

3. hará / Ud. / viaje / un / a / país / un / extranjero. _____

_____

4. hablará / Ud. / una amiga / con / preciosa. _____

_____

5. recibirá / Ud. / carta / una / hoy / de / amigo / un / amable. _____

_____

IV. Varias palabras en una sola. Utilizando las letras en la palabra **VENEZUELA,** ¿cuántas palabras puede usted escribir? Escriba ocho palabras, por lo menos.

VENEZUELA

1. _____   3. _____   5. _____   7. _____

2. _____   4. _____   6. _____   8. _____

V. Palabras en bloque. Junte las palabras en bloque, dos por dos, para formar cuatro otras.

CON	POR	PARA	EN
QUE	TENER	DA	CERRAR

Solución: 1. _____   3. _____

2. _____   4. _____

Estructuras de la lengua

Tense No. 4: Futuro (Future)

In Spanish and English, the future tense is used to express an action or a state of being that will take place at some time in the future.

EXAMPLES:

1. Lo **haré** / I *shall do* it; I *will do* it.
2. **Iremos** al campo la semana que viene / We *shall go* to the country next week; We *will go* to the country next week.

Also, in Spanish the future tense is used to indicate:

(a) Conjecture regarding the present.

EXAMPLES:

1. ¿Qué hora **será**? / I *wonder* what time it is.
2. ¿Quién **será**? / Who *can that be?* I *wonder who that is.*

(b) Probability regarding the present.

EXAMPLES:

1. **Serán** las cinco / It *is probably* five o'clock; It *must be* five o'clock.
2. **Tendrá** muchos amigos / He *probably has* many friends; He *must have* many friends.
3. María **estará** enferma / Mary *is probably* sick; Mary *must be* sick.

(c) An indirect quotation.

EXAMPLE: María dice que **vendrá** mañana / Mary says that she *will come* tomorrow.

Finally, remember that the future is never used in Spanish after *si* when *si* means *if*.

This tense is regularly formed as follows:

Add the following endings to the whole infinitive: **é, ás, á; emos, éis, án**

NOTE that these future endings happen to be related to the endings of **haber** in the present indicative: **he, has, ha; hemos, habéis, han.** ALSO NOTE the accent marks on the future endings, except for **emos.**

You then get: **hablaré, hablarás, hablará;**
hablaremos, hablaréis, hablarán

beberé, beberás, beberá;
beberemos, beberéis, beberán

recibiré, recibirás, recibirá;
recibiremos, recibiréis, recibirán

The usual equivalent in English is: I shall talk OR I will talk, you will talk, *etc.;* I shall drink OR I will drink, you will drink, *etc.;* I shall receive OR I will receive, you will receive, *etc.*

Verbs irregular in the future

caber / to fit, to be contained
cabré, cabrás, cabrá;
cabremos, cabréis, cabrán

The **e** of the inf. ending drops.

decir / to say, to tell
diré, dirás, dirá;
diremos, diréis, dirán

The **e** and **c** of the inf. drop.

haber / to have (as an auxiliary or helping verb)
habré, habrás, habrá;
habremos, habréis, habrán

The **e** of the inf. ending drops.

hacer / to do, to make
haré, harás, hará;
haremos, haréis, harán

The **c** and **e** of the inf. drop.

poder / to be able, can
podré, podrás, podrá;
podremos, podréis, podrán

The **e** of the inf. ending drops.

poner / to put, to place
pondré, pondrás, pondrá;
pondremos, pondréis, pondrán

The **e** of the inf. ending drops and **d** is added.

querer / to want, to wish
querré, querrás, querrá;
querremos, querréis, querrán

The **e** of the inf. ending drops and you are left with two **r**'s.

saber / to know, to know how
sabré, sabrás, sabrá;
sabremos, sabréis, sabrán

The **e** of the inf. ending drops.

salir / to go out
saldré, saldrás, saldrá;
saldremos, saldréis, saldrán

The **i** of the inf. ending drops and **d** is added.

tener / to have, to hold
tendré, tendrás, tendrá;
tendremos, tendréis, tendrán

The **e** of the inf. ending drops and **d** is added.

valer / to be worth, to be worthy
valdré, valdrás, valdrá;
valdremos, valdréis, valdrán

The **e** of the inf. ending drops and **d** is added.

venir / to come
vendré, vendrás, vendrá;
vendremos, vendréis, vendrán

The **i** of the inf. ending drops and **d** is added.

EJERCICIOS

I. Seleccione la forma correcta del verbo en el **futuro.**

1. La semana que viene _____ al campo.
   (a) vamos   (b) fuimos   (c) íbamos   (d) iremos _____

2. ¿Cuándo _____ Ud. un viaje a España?
   (a) hace   (b) hacía   (c) hizo   (d) hará _____

3. Marta dice que _____ mañana.
   (a) viene   (b) venía   (c) vendrá   (d) vino _____

4. ¿Cuando lo hará Ud.? Lo _____ en algunos días.
   (a) hago   (b) hice   (c) estoy haciendo   (d) haré _____

5. Pedro, ¿_____ (tú) la lección para mañana?
   (a) sabes   (b) sabrás   (c) sabías   (d) supiste _____

OPTIONAL EXERCISE FOR ENRICHMENT

II. Escriba las seis formas de cada verbo en el **futuro.**

   Modelo: caber   **cabré, cabrás, cabrá; cabremos, cabréis, cabrán**

   1. decir _____

   2. haber _____

   3. hacer _____

   4. poder _____

   5. poner _____

   6. querer _____

   7. saber _____

   8. salir _____

   9. tener _____

   10. valer _____

   11. venir _____

   12. hablar _____

   13. aprender _____

   14. vivir _____

III. Conteste las siguientes preguntas en el afirmativo con oraciones completas. En la oración (a) use la palabra **Sí.** En la oración (b) use la palabra **también** según los modelos.

Modelos: a. ¿Cantará Ud. en el baile esta noche?

a. Sí, cantaré en el baile esta noche.

b. ¿Y las otras personas?

b. Las otras personas, también, cantarán en el baile esta noche.

1. a. ¿Hablarán los alumnos a la profesora de español? _____

_____

b. ¿Y tú? _____

2. a. ¿Aprenderás la lección de español para mañana? _____

_____

b. ¿Y Esteban? _____

3. a. ¿Escribirán Uds. las cartas a sus amigos? _____

_____

b. ¿Y Edmundo y Emilio? _____

4. a. ¿Escucharéis (vosotros) la música esta noche? _____

b. ¿Y Elisa y Ud.? _____

5. a. ¿Beberás la leche? _____

b. ¿Y Arturo? _____

IV. Conteste las siguientes preguntas en el negativo con oraciones completas. En la oración (**a**) use la palabra **No.** En la oración (b) use la palabra **tampoco** según los modelos:

Modelos: a. ¿Vendrá Ud. a mi casa esta tarde?

a. No. No vendré a su casa esta tarde.

b. ¿Y Uds.?

b. No. No vendremos a su casa esta tarde tampoco.

1. a. ¿Saldrá Ud. de casa esta noche? _____

_____

b. ¿Y sus padres? _____

_____

2. a. ¿Dirás mentiras? _____

b. ¿Y tu hermanito? _____

3. a. ¿Harán sus amigos un viaje a Francia? _____

b. ¿Y Ud. y Enrique? _____

129

4. a. ¿Irán los señores Rodríguez al restaurante? _____

_____

b. ¿Y los señores Sánchez? _____

_____

5. a. ¿Cabrán estas cosas en la caja? _____

b. ¿Y este vaso? _____

V. Ordene las palabras en las cajas para formar una oración con sentido.

Modelo:

los señores Rodríguez	al restaurante	irán

Escriba: Los señores Rodríguez irán al restaurante.

1.

las cartas	Uds.	sus amigos	a	escribirán

_____

2.

mi padre	hoy	me dará	dinero	mucho

_____

3.

mi madre	saldrá	no	hoy	de casa

_____

VI. En español hay muchas palabras que se escriben y se pronuncian idénticamente, pero un signo de acento es necessario para distinguir su significado.

Por ejemplo:
    si *conj.* if   **Sí. Si Pablo viene, le hablaré.**
    sí *adv.* yes   Yes. If Paul comes, I will talk to him.

    ¿Cuántos ejemplos puede Ud. decir y escribir?

REFLEXIVE VERBS

Reflexive pronouns	**Examples**

Singular
1. **me** / myself   **Me lavo** / I wash myself.
2. **te** / yourself   **Te lavas** / You wash yourself.
3. **se** / yourself, himself, **Ud. se lava** / You wash yourself; **Pablo se**
        herself, itself   **lava** / Paul washes himself, *etc.*

Plural

1. **nos** / ourselves	**Nosotros (-as) nos lavamos.**
2. **os** / yourselves	**Vosotros (-as) os laváis.**
3. **se** / yourselves, themselves	**Uds. se lavan** / You wash yourselves; **Ellos (Ellas) se lavan** / They wash themselves.

A reflexive verb contains a reflexive pronoun, and the action of the verb falls on the subject and its reflexive pronoun either directly or indirectly. For that reason the reflexive pronoun must agree with the subject: **yo me . . . , tú te . . . , Ud. se . . . , él se . . . , ella se . . . , nosotros nos . . . , vosotros os . . . , Uds. se . . . , ellos se . . . , ellas se . . . .**

A reflexive pronoun is ordinarily placed in front of the verb form, as you can see in the examples.

To make these sentences negative, place **no** in front of the reflexive pronoun: **Yo no me lavo, Tú no te lavas, Ud. no se lava,** *etc.*

NOTE that **me, te, nos, os** are not only reflexive pronouns but they are also direct object pronouns and indirect object pronouns.

A reflexive verb in Spanish is not always reflexive in English, for example:

Spanish	English
levantarse	to get up
sentarse	to sit down

There are some reflexive verbs in Spanish that are also reflexive in English, for example:

Spanish	English
bañarse	to bathe oneself
lavarse	to wash oneself

The following reflexive pronouns are also used as reciprocal pronouns, meaning "each other" or "to each other": **se, nos, os.** Examples:

Ayer por la noche, María y yo nos vimos en el cine / Yesterday evening, Mary and I saw each other at the movies.

Roberto y Teresa se escriben todos los días / Robert and Teresa write to each other every day.

If the meaning of these three reflexive pronouns (**se, nos, os**) is not clear when they are used in a reciprocal meaning, any of the following may be added accordingly to express the idea of "each other" or "to each other": **uno a otro, una a otra, unos a otros,** *etc.*

Some common reflexive verbs

abstenerse   to abstain
aburrirse   to be bored, to grow tired, to grow weary
acercarse (qu)   (a + obj.)   to approach, to draw near
acordarse (ue)   (de + obj.)   to remember
acostarse (ue)   to go to bed, to lie down
adelantarse a   to go forward, to go ahead, to move ahead, to take the lead
afeitarse   to shave oneself
alegrarse (de)   to be glad, to rejoice
apresurarse   to hasten, to hurry, to rush
asustarse   to be frightened, to be scared
bañarse   to bathe oneself, to take a bath
burlarse de   to make fun of, to poke fun at, to ridicule
callarse   to be silent, to keep quiet
cansarse   to become tired, to become weary, to get tired
casarse con   to get married, to marry
cuidarse   to take care of oneself
dedicarse (qu)   to devote oneself

desayunar (se)   to breakfast, to have breakfast (may be reflexive or not)
despedirse (i)   to take leave of, to say good-bye to
despertarse (ie)   to wake (oneself) up
desvestirse (i)   to undress oneself, to get undressed
detenerse   to stop (oneself)
disculparse   to apologize, to excuse (oneself)
divertirse (ie, i)   to have a good time, to enjoy oneself
ducharse   to take a shower, to shower oneself
enfadarse   to become angry
enfermarse   to get sick, to fall sick, to become ill
enojarse   to become angry, to get angry, to get cross
equivocarse (qu)   to be mistaken
hacerse   to become
informarse   to inform oneself, to find out
interesarse en   to be interested (in)
irse   to go away
lavarse   to wash oneself
levantarse   to get up, to rise
limpiarse   to clean oneself
llamarse   to be called, to be named
marcharse   to go away, to leave
mirarse   to look at oneself, to look at each other **(uno a otro; unos a otros)**
mojarse   to get wet, to wet oneself
ocultarse   to hide oneself
pararse   to stop (oneself)
parecerse (zc)   to resemble each other, to look alike
pasearse   to take a walk, to parade
peinarse   to comb one's hair
pintarse   to make up (one's face)
ponerse   to put (clothing), to become, to set (of sun)
preocuparse   to be concerned, to worry, to be worried
prepararse   to be prepared, to get ready, to prepare oneself
protegerse (j)   to protect oneself
quedarse   to remain, to stay
quitarse   to take off (clothing), to remove oneself, to withdraw
reírse   to laugh
secarse (qu)   to dry oneself
sentarse (ie)   to sit down
sentirse (ie, i)   to feel (well, ill)
vestirse (i)   to dress oneself, to get dressed

EJERCICIOS

OPTIONAL EXERCISES FOR ENRICHMENT

I. Escriba las seis formas del verbo **lavarse** en el presente de indicativo.

_____

II. Escriba las seis formas del verbo **bañarse** en el presente de indicativo.

_____

III. Escriba las seis formas del verbo **lavarse** en el futuro.

IV. Escriba las seis formas del verbo **bañarse** en el futuro.

_____

V. Traduzca al español.

1. Yesterday evening, Mary and I saw each other at the movies. _____

_____

2. Robert and Teresa write to each other every day. _____

_____

3. I wash myself every morning before leaving for school. _____

_____

4. Do you wash yourself every evening before going to bed? _____

_____

5. Robert does not wash himself every day. _____

VI. Conteste las preguntas siguientes en el afirmativo con oraciones completas. En la oración (a) use la palabra **Sí.** En la oración (b) use la palabra **también** según los modelos.

Modelos: a. **¿Se lava Ud. todos los días?**   a. **Sí, me lavo todos los días.**
b. **¿Y María y José?**   b. **María y José se lavan, también, todos los días.**

1. a. ¿Se lavan Uds. todas las noches? _____

_____

b. ¿Y tú? _____

_____

2. a. ¿Se baña Ud. todas las mañanas? _____

_____

b. ¿Y los otros miembros de su familia? _____

_____

3. a. ¿Te lavarás antes de comer? _____

_____

b. ¿Y sus amigos? _____

_____

4. a. ¿Se acuerda Ud. que hoy es mi aniversario? _____

_____

b. ¿Y Carolina y Carlota? _____

_____

5. a. ¿Se acostará Ud. a las diez? _____

_____

b. ¿Y ustedes? _____

_____

VII. Conteste las siguientes preguntas. Son preguntas personales.

Modelo: ¿A qué hora se acuesta Ud. todas las noches?
Escriba: Todas las noches me acuesto a las once.

1. ¿A qué hora se levanta Ud. todas las mañanas? _____

_____

2. ¿A qué hora se levantará Ud. mañana? _____

_____

3. ¿A qué hora se acostó Ud. anoche? _____

_____

4. ¿Se afeita su padre todas las mañanas? _____

_____

5. ¿Se alegra Ud. cuando recibe buenas notas? _____

_____

6. ¿Se alegró Ud. ayer cuando recibió buenas notas en español? _____

_____

7. ¿Se bañó su hermanito ayer por la noche? _____

_____

8. ¿Se burla Ud. de un alumno cuando no sabe la lección? _____

_____

9. ¿A qué hora se despierta Ud. por la mañana? _____

_____

10. ¿A qué hora se despertó Ud. esta mañana? _____

_____

11. ¿A qué hora se despertará Ud. mañana? _____

_____

12. ¿Se divertirán sus amigos en el baile esta noche? _____

_____

13. ¿Se quedará Ud. en casa hoy? _____

_____

14. ¿Se secarán los niños después de bañarse? _____

_____

15. ¿Y usted? ¿Se secará Ud. después de bañarse? _____

_____

VIII. **Dictado.** Escriba las oraciones que su profesor de español va a leer.

1. _____

2. _____

3. _____

PRONOUNS

Definition: A pronoun is a word that takes the place of a noun; for example, in English there are these common pronouns: I, you, he, she, it, we, they, me, him, her, us, them—to mention a few.

Pronouns are divided into certain types: personal, prepositional, relative, interrogative, demonstrative, possessive, indefinite and negative.

A personal pronoun is used as the subject of a verb, direct or indirect object of a verb or verb form, as a reflexive pronoun object, and as object of a preposition.

Correct use of pronouns in Spanish is not easy—nor in English, for that matter. For example, in English, you can often hear people using pronouns incorrectly: "between you and *I*" ought to be stated as "between you and *me*"; "if you have any questions, see *myself*" ought to be stated as "if you have any questions, see *me*"; "*Who* did you see?" ought to be stated as "*Whom* did you see?" And there are many more incorrect uses of pronouns in English.

Personal pronouns

Subject pronouns	Examples
Singular	
1. **yo** / I	**Yo** hablo.
2. **tú** / you (familiar)	**Tú** hablas.
3. **usted** / you (polite)	**Usted** habla.
él / he, it	**Él** habla.
ella / she, it	**Ella** habla.
Plural	
1. **nosotros (nosotras)** / we	**Nosotros** hablamos.
2. **vosotros (vosotras)** / you (fam.)	**Vosotros** habláis.
3. **ustedes** / you (polite)	**Ustedes** hablan.
ellos / they	**Ellos** hablan.
ellas / they	**Ellas** hablan.

135

As you can see in the examples given here, a subject pronoun is ordinarily placed in front of the main verb.

In Spanish, subject pronouns are not used at all times. The ending of the verb tells you if the subject is 1st, 2nd, or 3rd person in the singular or plural. Of course, in the 3rd person sing. and pl. there is more than one possible subject with the same ending on the verb form. In that case, if there is any doubt as to what the subject is, it is mentioned for the sake of clarity. At other times, subject pronouns in Spanish are used when you want to be emphatic, to make a contrast between this person and that person, or out of simple courtesy. You must be certain to know the endings of the verb forms in all the tenses (see the entry **Verbs** in the Index) in the three persons of the singular and of the plural so that you can figure out the subject if it is not clearly stated. In addition to pronouns as subjects, nouns are also used as subjects. Any noun—whether common (**el hombre, la mujer, el cielo, la silla,** *etc.*) or proper (**María, Juan y Elena, los Estados Unidos,** *etc.*) are always 3rd person, either singular or plural.

Generally speaking, in some Latin American countries **ustedes** (3rd pers., pl.) is used in place of **vosotros** or **vosotras** (2nd pers., pl.)

Direct object pronouns	Examples
Singular	
1. **me** / me	**María me ha visto** / Mary has seen me.
2. **te** / you *(fam.)*	**María te había visto** / Mary had seen you.
3. **le, la** / you	**María le (la) ve** / Mary sees you.
le / him; **lo** / him, it	**María le (lo) ve** / Mary sees him (it).
la / her, it	**María la ve** / Mary sees her (it).
Plural	
1. **nos** / us	**María nos había visto** / Mary had seen us.
2. **os** / you *(fam.)*	**María os ha visto** / Mary has seen you.
3. **los, las** / you	**María los (las) ve** / Mary sees you.
los / them	**María los ve** / Mary sees them.
las / them	**María las ve** / Mary sees them.

In Latin American countries, **lo** is generally used instead of **le** to mean *him*. You can tell from the context of what is written or said if **lo** means *him* or *it* (masc.). NOTE that the plural of **le** as direct object pronoun is **los.**

NOTE that in the 3rd pers., plural, the direct objects **los** (masc.) and **las** (fem.) refer to people and things.

ALSO NOTE that in the 3rd pers. singular, the direct object pronoun **le** is masc. and **la** is fem. and both mean *you.* You can tell from the context of what is written or said if **le** means *you* (masc. sing.) or if it means *him.*

Here is a summing up of the various meanings of the direct object pronouns **le, lo, la, los, las:**

le: him, you *(masc.)*
lo: him, it *(masc.)*
la: her, you *(fem.),* it *(fem.)*
los: you *(masc. pl.),* them *(people or things, masc., pl.)*
las: you *(fem. pl.),* them *(people or things, fem., pl.)*

As you can see in the examples given, a direct object pronoun ordinarily is placed in front of the main verb.

There is also the neuter **lo** direct object pronoun. It does not refer to any particular noun that is f. or m.; that is why it has no gender and is called *neuter.* It usually refers to an idea or a statement:

¿Está Ud. enfermo? / Are you sick? **Sí, lo estoy** / Yes, I am.
¿Son amigos? / Are they friends? **Sí, lo son** / Yes, they are.

Of course, your reply could be **Sí, estoy enfermo** and **Sí, son amigos.** But because your verb is a form of **estar** or **ser,** you do not have to repeat what was mentioned; neuter **lo** takes its place as a direct object pronoun. This neuter **lo** direct object pronoun is also used with other verbs, *e.g.,* **pedir, preguntar** and **parecer:**

María parece contenta / Mary seems happy. **Sí, lo parece** / Yes, she does (Yes, she does seem *so*).

To make the above object pronouns negative, place **no** in front of the direct object pronouns: **María no me ve,** *etc.* To make the other examples negative place **no** in front of the verb.

Indirect object pronouns	Examples
Singular	
1. **me** / to me	**Pablo me ha hablado** / Paul has talked to me.
2. **te** / to you *(fam.)*	**Pablo te habla** / Paul talks to you.
3. **le** / to you, to him, to her, to it	**Pablo le habla** / Paul talks to you (to him, to her, to it).
Plural	
1. **nos** / to us	**Pablo nos ha hablado** / Paul has talked to us.
2. **os** / to you *(fam.)*	**Pablo os habla** / Paul talks to you.
3. **les** / to you, to them	**Pablo les habla** / Paul talks to you (to them).

To make these sentences negative, place **no** in front of the indirect object pronouns: **Pablo no me habla** / Paul does not talk to me.

NOTE that **me, te, nos, os** are direct object pronouns and indirect object pronouns.

NOTE that **le** as an indirect object pronoun has more than one meaning. If there is any doubt as to the meaning, merely add after the verb any of the following accordingly to clarify the meaning: **a Ud., a él, a ella: Pablo le habla a usted** / Paul is talking to you.

NOTE that **les** has more than one meaning. If there is any doubt as to the meaning, merely add after the verb any of the following, accordingly: **a Uds., a ellos, a ellas: Pablo no les habla a ellos** / Paul is not talking to them.

As you can see in the examples given, an indirect object pronoun ordinarily is placed in front of the main verb.

An indirect object pronoun is needed when you use a verb that indicates a person is being deprived of something, *e.g.,* to steal something *from* someone, to take something *off* or *from* someone, to buy something from someone, and actions of this sort. The reason why an indirect object pronoun is needed is that you are dealing with the preposition **a** + **noun** or **pronoun** and it must be accounted for. Examples:

Los ladrones le robaron todo el dinero a él / The robbers stole all the money from him.
La madre le quitó al niño el sombrero / The mother took off the child's hat.
Les compré mi automóvil a ellos / I bought my car from them.

The indirect object pronouns are used with the verb **gustar** and with the following verbs: **bastar, faltar** or **hacer falta, sobrar, quedarle (a uno), tocarle (a uno), placer, parecer.**

EXAMPLES:

A Ricardo le gusta el helado / Richard likes ice cream (*i.e.,* Ice cream is pleasing to him, to Richard.)

A Juan le bastan cien dólares / One hundred dollars are enough for John.

A los muchachos les faltan cinco dólares / The boys need five dollars (*i.e.,* Five dollars are lacking to them, to the boys). OR: **A la mujer le hacen falta cinco dólares** / The woman needs five dollars (*i.e.,* Five dollars are lacking to her, to the woman).

To put it simply, the indirect object pronoun is needed in the examples given above because some kind of action is being done *to* someone.

137

EJERCICIOS

I. Cambie las siguientes frases usando el pronombre que convenga por el complemento directo, según los modelos.

Modelos: **María vio a Elena.**   Escriba: **María la vio.**
Pepe leyó el libro.   **Pepe lo leyó.**

1. José vio a Margarita. _____

2. Pablo verá a Paula mañana. _____

3. Los alumnos miraban la pizarra. _____

4. La profesora leía la página. _____

5. El profesor escribió la oración. _____

6. La alumna leyó el libro. _____

7. Juana comió el pastel. _____

8. Esteban bebió la leche. _____

9. El vendedor vendió las bicicletas. _____

10. La señora Rodríguez compró los zapatos. _____

11. El presidente anunció las noticias. _____

12. Los profesores corrigieron los temas. _____

13. Los alumnos vieron a los profesores. _____

14. La profesora abrió las ventanas. _____

15. Los alumnos cerraron los libros. _____

II. Cambie las siguientes frases usando el pronombre que convenga por el complemento indirecto, según los modelos.

Modelos: **Ricardo habla a Florencia.**
Miguel no dice la verdad a su padre.

Escriba: **Ricardo le habla.**
Miguel no le dice la verdad.

1. Mañana Pablo hablará a la profesora. _____

2. Pedro dirá la verdad a su madre. _____

3. María dará los chocolates a sus amigas. _____

4. Los señores Rodríguez dieron un regalo a Juana y a Pedro. _____

_____

5. La profesora de español dará buenas notas a los alumnos. _____

_____

III. Conteste las siguientes preguntas en el afirmativo según el modelo.

Modelo: ¿Me dará Ud. mi libro?   Escriba: Sí, le daré su libro.

1. ¿Me dirá Ud. la verdad? _____

2. ¿Os habla Pablo a vosotros? _____

3. ¿Le dio María a usted el dinero? _____

4. ¿Les habla Alicia a ustedes? _____

5. ¿Les dio Ricardo a ellos el chocolate? _____

6. ¿A Ricardo le gusta el helado? _____

7. ¿A Juan le bastan cien dólares? _____

8. ¿A los muchachos les faltan cinco dólares? _____

   _____

9. ¿A la mujer le hacen falta diez pesetas? _____

   _____

10. ¿Le robaron los ladrones todo el dinero a él? _____

   _____

PROPER NAMES OF BOYS AND GIRLS IN SPANISH AND ENGLISH

	Girls		Boys
Spanish	English	Spanish	English
Adela	Adele	**Abrahán**	Abraham
Ágata	Agatha	**Adán**	Adam
Alejandra	Alexandra	**Adolfo**	Adolph
Alejandrina	Alexandrina	**Alano**	Alan, Allen
Alicia	Alice	**Alberto**	Albert
Amada	Amy	**Alejandro**	Alexander
Amelia	Amelie	**Alfonso**	Alphonso
Ana	Anne, Anna, Hannah	**Alfredo**	Alfred
Bárbara	Barbara	**Aluino**	Alwin
Beatriz	Beatrice	**Andrés**	Andrew
Berta	Bertha	**Antonio**	Anthony
Brígida	Bridget	**Arturo**	Arthur
Carlota	Charlotte	**Atanasio**	Athanasios
Carolina	Caroline	**Bartolomé**	Bartholomew
Casandra	Cassandra	**Basilio**	Basil
Catarina	Catherine	**Beltrán**	Bertram
Clara	Clare, Clara	**Bernardo**	Bernard
Claudia	Claudia	**Carlos**	Charles
Constanza	Constance	**Claudio**	Claude

PROPER NAMES OF BOYS AND GIRLS IN SPANISH AND ENGLISH

Girls		Boys	
Spanish	English	Spanish	English
Cristina	Christine	**Clemente**	Clement
Dolores	Dolores	**Constantino**	Constantine
Dora	Dora, Doris	**Cristián**	Christian
Dorotea	Dorothy	**Cristóbal**	Christopher
Edita	Edith	**Daniel**	Daniel
Elena	Ellen, Helen	**Darío**	Darius
Elisa	Eliza	**David**	David
Ema	Emma	**Diego**	James
Emilia	Emily	**Dionisio**	Dennis
Engracia	Grace	**Domingo**	Dominic
Enriqueta	Harriet, Henrietta	**Edmundo**	Edmund
Ester	Esther	**Eduardo**	Edward
Eugenia	Eugenia	**Eliseo**	Ellis, Elisha
Eva	Eve	**Emilio**	Emil
Florencia	Florence	**Enrique**	Henry
Francisca	Frances	**Ernesto**	Ernest
Gabriela	Gabrielle	**Esteban**	Stephen, Steven
Genoveva	Genevieve	**Eugenio**	Eugene
Gerarda	Geraldine	**Federico**	Frederick
Gertrudis	Gertrude	**Francisco**	Francis
Hilda	Hilda	**Geofredo**	Geoffrey
Inés	Agnez, Inez	**Gerardo**	Gerald, Gerard
Irene	Irene	**Gilberto**	Gilbert
Isabel	Elizabeth	**Gregorio**	Gregory
Josefa	Josephine	**Gualtero**	Walter
Juana	Jane	**Guillermo**	William
Judit	Judith	**Herberto**	Herbert
Julia	Julia, Juliet	**Hugo**	Hugh
Lola	Lola, Dolores	**Hunfredo**	Humphrey
Lolita	Lolita, Dolores	**Isidoro**	Isidor
Lucía	Lucy	**Jacobo**	Jacob
Luisa	Louise, Louisa	**Jaime**	James
Manola	Emma	**Javier**	Xavier
Manuela	Emma	**Jerónimo**	Jerome
Margarita	Margaret, Margery	**Jesús**	Jesus
María	Mary	**Jonatán**	Jonathan
Mariana	Marian	**Jorge**	George
Marta	Martha	**José**	Joseph
Matilde	Mathilda	**Juan**	John
Paula	Paula	**Julián**	Julian
Paulina	Pauline	**Julio**	Julius
Queta	Harriet, Henrietta	**Justino**	Justin
Rebeca	Rebecca	**León**	Leo, Leon
Rosa	Rose	**Leonardo**	Leonard
Rosalía	Rosalie	**Lorenzo**	Lawrence
Sara	Sarah	**Luis**	Louis, Lewis
Sofía	Sophia, Sophie	**Manuel**	Manuel, Emmanuel
Susana	Susan, Suzanne	**Marcelo**	Marcel
Teodora	Theodora	**Marcos**	Mark
Teresa	Theresa	**Mateo**	Matthew

Still Life *by Juan VAN DER HAMEN Y LEÓN (1596–1631)*
Courtesy of The National Gallery of Art, Washington, D.C.

El pelo está corto y se mueve con gracia
en el viento. Este corte es revuelto.
Es el modelo A.

Este corte es serio y sencillo. Es la
moderación elegante. Es el modelo C.

En este modelo, el pelo, ya sea seco
o mojado, se repone con los dedos.
Este corte es realmente revuelto.
Es el modelo B.

Este corte sencillo y serio es clásico.
Es el modelo D.

*Have you ever wanted to change the style of
your hair for some special reason? Let's see
what happens to Juana and Pedro.*

En la peluquería para señoras y señores

Hoy, Juana se va a la peluquería. Le gustaría tener un corte de pelo porque esta noche se va al baile con Carlos, uno de sus amigos. Tiene cita en la peluquería a las cuatro y media de la tarde.

Pedro está con Juana. Le gustaría también tener un nuevo corte de pelo ya que va al mismo baile con Lolita, una de sus amigas. 5

Aquí están entrando en la peluquería.

JUANA	Buenas tardes.
PEDRO	Buenas tardes.
EL PELUQUERO	Buenas tardes, Juana. Buenas tardes, Pedro. Ustedes han llegado a las cuatro en punto. Juana, siéntese aquí. Una de mis peluqueras, que se 10 llama Nina, va a encargarse de usted. Pedro, siéntese allí. Voy a encargarme de usted.
JUANA	De acuerdo, gracias.
PEDRO	De acuerdo, gracias.
EL PELUQUERO	Bueno, Pedro, voy a empezar con un champú, como siempre, ¿no? 15
PEDRO	Sí, eso es. Empiece con un champú, como siempre, por favor.
LA PELUQUERA	Bueno, Juana, voy a empezar con un champú, como siempre, ¿no?
JUANA	Sí, eso es. Empiece con un champú, como siempre, por favor.
LA PELUQUERA	¿Le gustaría más un corte de pelo revuelto o serio?
JUANA	Me parece que prefiero un corte de pelo revuelto . . . no . . . no revuelto . . . 20 Hágame un corte de pelo serio y sencillo . . . no . . . No estoy segura. No puedo elegir entre un corte de pelo revuelto y un corte serio y sencillo. ¿Qué opina usted?
LA PELUQUERA	Voy a enseñarle dos cortes de pelo revueltos para darle una idea.
	¿Le gusta este corte? 25

El pelo está corto y se mueve con gracia en el viento. Este corte es revuelto. Es el modelo A.

¿O le gusta más éste?

En este modelo, el pelo, ya sea seco o mojado, se repone con los dedos.

Este corte es realmente revuelto. Es el modelo B.   30

JUANA   Oh, yo no sé. Me gustan estos dos cortes revueltos. Me parece que prefiero el modelo A . . . No . . . Me gusta más el modelo B. Oh, yo no sé. Enséñeme un corte serio y sencillo.

LA PELUQUERA   De acuerdo. Voy a enseñarle dos cortes de pelo serios y sencillos.

¿Le gusta éste?   35

Este corte es serio y sencillo. Es la moderación elegante. Es el modelo C.

¿O tal vez éste?

Este corte sencillo y serio es clásico. Es el modelo D.

JUANA   Bueno, he tomado una decisión. Hágame un corte serio y sencillo tal como en el modelo C. Me comportaré bien esta noche después del baile con Carlos.   40

LA PELUQUERA   Muy bien. Ahora empiezo.

EL PELUQUERO   Y usted, Pedro ¿qué tipo de corte le gustaría? Se le voy a enseñar dos. ¿Cuál le gusta más? Este es el modelo A.

¿Le gusta éste?

Este corte es corto y neto, con los cabellos al cepillo suave por encima. Es el
modelo A.   45

¿O más bien éste?

De perfíl, el pelo está pegado hacia atrás. Le cortaré un mechón desordenado
que recaerá sobre la frente. Esto le dará una nota de natural. Es el modelo B.

¿O tal vez preferiría usted un corte realmente revuelto? ¿Como éste? Es un
verdadero revoltijo. Es el modelo C.   50

Entonces, Pedro, ¿usted ha elegido?

PEDRO   Sí, he elegido. Hágame un corte tal como en el modelo B. Este es muy serio. No
               me gusta en absoluto el corte revuelto del modelo C.

Una hora después, Juana y Pedro se marchan de la peluquería y los dos están muy felices y
contentos de sus nuevos cortes de pelo. Ahora están listos para el baile de esta noche. Juana se 55
comportará bien y Pedro también porque tienen cortes de pelo serios y sencillos.

¿Y usted? Si usted es una joven, ¿qué tipo de corte le gusta? ¿El modelo A, B, C o D? Si usted
es un joven, ¿le gusta más el modelo A o B? ¿O tal vez el C?

Tome una decisión pronto. El peluquero está esperando.

VOCABULARIO: Consult the vocabulary section in the back pages.

EJERCICIOS

I. Conteste las siguientes preguntas con frases completas.

1. ¿Adónde va Juana hoy? _____

_____

2. ¿Por qué ella quiere tener un corte de pelo deslumbrante? _____

_____

3. ¿A qué hora Juana tiene cita en la peluquería? _____

_____

4. ¿Quién va a la peluquería con Juana? _____

_____

5. ¿Por qué Pedro quiere tener un nuevo corte? _____

_____

6. ¿Cuántos modelos de cortes enseña la peluquera a Juana? _____

_____

7. ¿Juana ha elegido un corte serio y sencillo? ¿O un corte revuelto? _____

_____

8. ¿Cuántos modelos de cortes enseña el peluquero a Pedro? _____

_____

9. ¿Pedro ha elegido un corte serio y sencillo? ¿O un corte revuelto? _____

_____

10. ¿Y ustedes? ¿Cuál de estos modelos les gusta más? ¿Por qué? _____

_____

_____

II. Discriminación de los sonidos. Su profesor de español va a pronunciar una sola palabra, sea la de la letra A, sea la de la letra B. Puntee A o B para indicar que su profesor de español ha pronunciado la palabra de la letra A o la palabra de la letra B.

Modelo:　　◉ A. hoy

☐ B. hay

He punteado la letra A porque creo que mi profesor de español ha pronunciado la palabra de la letra A.

1. ☐ A. gustará
   ☐ B. gustaría

2. ☐ A. amigos
   ☐ B. amigas

3. ☐ A. cuatro
   ☐ B. cuarto

4. ☐ A. pero
   ☐ B. perro

III. Uno por tres. Ponga en las casillas una palabra que—con la palabra ya inscrita—permitirá formar otra palabra. La tercera palabra (que será el resultado de la palabra ya inscrita y de la palabra que usted va a escribir) figura en la lectura de esta lección.

Modelo: | R | E | P | R | E | S | E | N | T | A | + | ☐ | ☐ | ☐ | = _____

Solución: representados | D | O | S | = representados

1. | P | O | R | + | ☐ | ☐ | ☐ | = _____

2. | H | A | G | A | + | ☐ | ☐ | = _____

3. | D | E | + | ☐ | ☐ | ☐ | = _____

IV. Las palabras escondidas. En la rejilla, busque las palabras en español por las palabras en inglés en la lista a continuación. Cuando las haya encontrado, ráyelas. Las palabras escondidas están en la lectura de esta lección.

En la rejilla, las palabras están escritas en todas las direcciones: de abajo arriba, de arriba abajo, de derecha a izquierda, de izquierda a derecha, al derecho y al revés, y en diagonal. Anote que la misma letra puede ser común a varias palabras.

hair
hairstylist, *fem.*
dance, *n.*
haircut
fingers
afternoon
appointment
okay
shampoo
always

O	D	R	E	U	C	A	E	D	A
D	E	A	C	E	O	R	D	T	S
C	C	H	P	O	R	O	I	D	I
A	H	E	E	L	T	C	I	E	E
B	A	I	L	E	E	E	O	D	M
P	M	L	U	P	D	D	L	O	P
S	P	I	Q	M	E	P	R	S	R
A	Ú	H	U	O	P	R	A	A	E
B	A	I	E	L	E	D	E	D	T
A	C	U	R	D	L	O	C	I	T
P	L	E	A	O	O	C	O	R	E

147

V. Sopa de letras (Alphabet soup). Busque cinco sinónimos del sustantivo *gusto.* Los cinco sinónimos pueden aparecer de derecha a izquierda, de izquierda a derecha, de abajo arriba y viceversa, y en diagonal.

G	G	T	S	O	L	R
S	C	E	D	M	E	A
A	P	Q	R	C	T	S
T	A	L	A	G	I	R
I	O	L	I	B	Ú	J
S	P	L	A	E	R	U
F	S	S	A	T	I	S
A	L	E	G	R	Í	A
C	L	I	E	N	T	I
C	A	M	O	P	I	R
I	N	A	L	E	S	O
Ó	M	U	N	O	E	F
N	A	T	U	V	I	U
L	O	V	E	M	E	E

Estructuras de la lengua

Tense No. 5: Potencial simple (Conditional)

The Conditional is used in Spanish and in English to express:

(a) An action that you *would do* if something else were possible.

EXAMPLE:

Iría a España si tuviera dinero / *I would go* to Spain if I had money.

(b) A conditional desire. This is a conditional of courtesy.

EXAMPLE:

Me **gustaría** tomar una limonada / *I would like (I should like)* to have a lemonade . . . (if you are willing to let me have it).

(c) An indirect quotation.

EXAMPLES:

María *dijo* que **vendría** mañana / Mary *said* that she *would come* tomorrow.
María *decía* que **vendría** mañana / Mary *was saying* that she *would come tomorrow.*
María *había dicho* que **vendría** mañana / Mary *had said* that she *would come* tomorrow.

(d) Conjecture regarding the past.

EXAMPLE:

¿Quién **sería?** / *I wonder who that was.*

(e) Probability regarding the past.

EXAMPLE:

Serían las cinco cuando salieron / *It was probably* five o'clock when they went out.

This tense is regularly formed as follows:

Add the following endings to the whole infinitive: **ía, ías, ía; íamos, íais, ían**

NOTE that these conditional endings are the same endings of the imperfect indicative for **—er** and **—ir** verbs.

You then get: **hablaría, hablarías, hablaría; hablaríamos, hablaríais, hablarían**

bebería, beberías, bebería; beberíamos, beberíais, beberían

recibiría, recibirías, recibiría; recibiríamos, recibiríais, recibirían

The usual translation in English is: I would talk, you would talk, *etc.;* I would drink, you would drink, *etc.;* I would receive, you would receive, *etc.*

Verbs irregular in the conditional

caber / to fit, to be contained
cabría, cabrías, cabría; cabríamos, cabríais, cabrían

The **e** of the inf. ending drops.

decir / to say, to tell
diría, dirías, diría; diríamos, diríais, dirían

The **e** and **c** of the inf. drop.

haber / to have (as an auxiliary or helping verb)
habría, habrías, habría; habríamos, habríais, habrían

The **e** of the inf. ending drops.

hacer / to do, to make
haría, harías, haría; haríamos, haríais, harían

The **c** and **e** of the inf. drop.

poder / to be able, can
podría, podrías, podría; podríamos, podríais, podrían

The **e** of the inf. ending drops.

poner / to put, to place
pondría, pondrías, pondría; pondríamos, pondríais, pondrían

The **e** of the inf. ending drops and **d** is added.

querer / to want, to wish
querría, querrías, querría; querríamos, querríais, querrían

The **e** of the inf. ending drops and you are left with two **r**'s.

saber / to know, to know how
sabría, sabrías, sabría; sabríamos, sabríais, sabrían

The **e** of the inf. ending drops.

salir / to go out
saldría, saldrías, saldría; saldríamos, saldríais, saldrían

The **i** of the inf. ending drops and **d** is added.

tener / to have, to hold
tendría, tendrías, tendría; tendríamos, tendríais, tendrían

The **e** of the inf. ending drops and **d** is added.

valer / to be worth, to be worthy
valdría, valdrías, valdría; valdríamos, valdríais, valdrían

The **e** of the inf. ending drops and **d** is added.

venir / to come
vendría, vendrías, vendría; vendríamos, vendríais, vendrían

The **i** of the inf. ending drops and **d** is added.

EJERCICIOS

I. Traduzca al español.

1. I would go to Spain if I had money. _____

_____

2. I would like to have a lemonade. _____

_____

3. Mary said that she would come tomorrow. _____

_____

4. Mary was saying that she would come tomorrow. _____

_____

5. Mary had said that she would come tomorrow. _____

_____

6. I wonder who that was at the door. _____

_____

7. It was probably five o'clock when they went out. _____

_____

8. I would like to have a haircut. _____

_____

9. Would you like a simple haircut or a "wild, crazy" **(revuelto)** haircut? _____

_____

_____

10. It would be a great honor for me. _____

OPTIONAL EXERCISES FOR ENRICHMENT: Ex. II, III, IV, V

II. Escriba las seis formas del verbo **hablar** en el potencial.

_____

III. Escriba las seis formas del verbo **beber** en el potencial.

_____

IV. Escriba las seis formas del verbo **recibir** en el potencial.

_____

V. Escriba las seis formas de cada verbo en el potencial.

    Modelo: caber   **cabría, cabrías, cabría; cabríamos, cabríais, cabrían**

    1. decir _____

    2. haber _____

3. hacer _____

4. poder _____

5. poner _____

6. querer _____

7. saber _____

8. salir _____

9. tener _____

10. valer _____

11. venir _____

12. trabajar _____

13. aprender _____

VI. Cambie el verbo al **potencial**.

Modelo: ¿Le hablará Ud. a José?　　Escriba: ¿Le hablaría Ud. a José?

1. ¿Beberás (tú) la leche? _____

2. ¿Recibirán los niños los juguetes? _____

3. ¿Trabajarán Uds. esta noche? _____

4. ¿Cabrá el vaso en esta caja? _____

5. ¿Dirá el alumno la verdad? _____

6. ¿Hará Ud. un viaje al Canadá? _____

7. ¿Irá Ud. a Inglaterra? _____

8. ¿Podrás venir a mi casa? _____

9. ¿Sabrán los estudiantes la lección? _____

10. ¿Saldremos a las nueve? _____

INTRODUCTION TO SIMPLE LETTER WRITING

The date

Examples of acceptable forms are as follows.

4 de diciembre de 1988　　**Diciembre 4, 1988**
el 4 de diciembre de 1988　**Diciembre 4 de 1988**

Note that the month is not usually capitalized. However, it is capitalized when it is the first word of the date statement. In Spanish newspapers, magazines and business letters, you will find the month sometimes capitalized, sometimes not.

Abbreviations of titles in front of the name of the person to whom the letter is addressed.

Sr. for señor   **Sra.** for señora   **Srta.** for señorita   **Dr.** or **D.** for Doctor

Salutations

Examples of acceptable salutations are as follows.

Estimado señor:	**Estimable señor:**
Estimado señor Blanco:	**Estimable señor García:**
Estimada señora:	**Estimable señora:**
Estimada señora Sánchez:	**Estimable señora Rodríguez:**
Distinguido señor:	**Distinguida señora:**
Señores:	**Muy estimados señores:**
Muy estimables señores:	**Muy señores nuestros:**
Estimados señores:	**Muy estimado señor López:**

Phrases commonly used

Acuso recibo de . . . I acknowledge receipt of . . .
Sírvanse (Sírvase) enviarme . . . Please send me . . .
Estoy interesado en . . . I am interested in . . .
En espera de . . . Hoping for . . . Waiting for . . .
Tengo el gusto de informar . . . I have the pleasure of informing . . .
Me es grato informar . . . I am happy to inform . . .
Doy a usted las gracias por . . . I thank you for . . .
Mucho apreciaría . . . I would very much appreciate . . .
En contestación a . . . In reply to . . .
Con referencia a . . . With reference to . . .
Gracias por . . . Thank you for . . .

Closing line

Examples of acceptable complimentary closing statements are as follows.

Atentamente,	**Cordialmente,**
Muy atentamente,	**Sinceramente,**

EJERCICIOS

I. Traduzca esta carta al español.

January 1, 1988

Mr. Juan López, Director
Compañía Bicicletas Para Todos
Avenida Mucho Macho 123
San Juan, Puerto Rico

Dear Mr. López:

Please send me some pictures of all the bicycles that you sell. I would very much appreciate a prompt reply.

Thank you for your kindness.

(Here, write a complimentary closing)

(Here, write your name
and address.)

_____

_____

_____

_____

_____

II. Write a letter in Spanish to a friend. It must contain at least five sentences. In Work Unit 8, you will find a list of names of boys and girls in Spanish with English equivalents. Tell the boy or girl that (1) your birthday is next Saturday, (2) you would like him or her to come to your party at your house, (3) everyone will have a lot of fun, (4) many friends will be there, and (5) you would like to know if he or she can come. Don't forget to write the date on your letter, a salutation, a complimentary closing, and write your name, in Spanish, of course!

_____

_____

_____

_____

_____

_____

_____

_____

_____

_____

_____

_____

_____

_____

_____

_____

_____

_____

III. Write another letter in Spanish. Write about anything. This is free composition. Be sure to write at least five sentences. Remember that a sentence must contain a verb form. Suggested topics: a movie you saw or you are going to see, a party you went to or will go to, how you spent last weekend or how you will spend this coming weekend, a vacation you took or plan to take, something about yourself or about your best friend.

IV. OPTIONAL EXERCISE. Your teacher may give you other topics to write about in other short letters. Or, you may write another letter on any topic.

PRONOUNS (Continuation from Work Unit 8)

Prepositional pronouns

Pronouns that are used as objects of prepositions are called prepositional pronouns or disjunctive pronouns. They are as follows:

Singular

1. **para mí** / for me, for myself

2. **para ti** / for you, for yourself

3. **para usted (Ud.)** / for you
   para él / for him, for it
   para ella / for her, for it

Plural

1. **para nosotros (nosotras)** / for us, for ourselves

2. **para vosotros (vosotras)** / for you, for yourselves

3. **para ustedes (Uds.)** / for you
   para ellos / for them
   para ellas / for them

Also note the following:

3. **para sí** / for yourself, for himself, for herself, for itself

3. **para sí** / for yourselves, for themselves

NOTE the following exceptions with the prepositions **con, entre,** and **menos:**

conmigo / with me
contigo / with you *(fam.)*
consigo / with yourself, with yourselves, with himself, with herself, with themselves
entre tú y yo / between you and me
menos yo / except me

Position of object pronouns

You surely must review pronouns and their positions. You can expect to find them in short sentences and in reading passages on any standardized test in Spanish because they are used very commonly in the Spanish language. In the reading passages, you will have to recognize their meaning according to their position with regard to a verb form. In sentences, sometimes short or long, you will probably have to choose the correct pronoun to fit in the blank space.

In the sections above, I reviewed for you single object pronouns and their position. In this section, there is a summary review of the position of a single object pronoun and a review of double object pronouns and their position with regard to a verb or verb form. By double object pronouns is meant one direct object pronoun and one indirect object pronoun. Which one comes first and where do you put them?

Position of a single object pronoun: a summary

Review the normal position of a single object pronoun as given above in the examples when dealing with a simple tense or a compound tense.

Attach the single object pronoun to an infinitive: **Juan quiere escribirlo** / John wants to write it.

OR

If the main verb is **poder, querer, saber, ir a,** you may place the object pronoun in front of the main verb:

Juan lo quiere escribir / John wants to write it; **¿Puedo levantarme?** or **¿Me puedo levantar?** / May I get up?

Attach the single object pronoun to a present participle: **Juan está escribiéndolo** / John is writing it.

NOTE that when you attach an object pronoun to a present participle, you must add an accent mark on the vowel that was stressed in the present participle before the object pronoun was attached. The accent mark is needed to keep the stress where it originally was.

OR

If the main verb is a progressive form with **estar** or another auxiliary, you may place the object pronoun in front of the main verb:

Juan lo está escribiendo / John is writing it.

When you are dealing with a verb form in the affirmative imperative (command), you must attach the single object pronoun to the verb form and add an accent mark on the vowel that was stressed in the verb form before the single object pronoun was added. The accent mark is needed to keep the stress where it originally was:

¡Hábleme Ud., por favor! / Talk to me, please!

When you are dealing with a verb form in the negative imperative (command), you must place the object pronoun in front of the verb form, where it normally goes:

¡No me hable Ud., por favor! / Do not talk to me, please!

Position of double object pronouns: a summary

An indirect object pronoun is always placed in front of a direct object pronoun. They are never separated from each other.

With a verb in a simple tense or in a compound tense in the affirmative or negative:

The indirect object pronoun is placed in front of the direct object pronoun and both are placed in front of the verb form:

Juan me lo da / John is giving it to me.
Juan te la daba / John was giving it to you.
Juan nos los dio / John gave them to us.
Juan os las dará / John will give them to you.

María no me lo ha dado / Mary has not given it to me.
María no te la había dado / Mary had not given it to you.
María no nos los habrá dado / Mary will not have given them to us.
María no os las habría dado / Mary would not have given them to you.

With a verb in a simple tense or in a compound tense in the interrogative:

The indirect object pronoun still remains in front of the direct object pronoun and both still remain in front of the verb form. The subject (whether a noun or pronoun) is placed after the verb form:

¿Nos la dio Juan? / Did John give it to us?
¿Te lo ha dado Juan? / Has John given it to you?

With a verb in the affirmative imperative (command):

The object pronouns are still in the same order (indirect object + direct object) but they are attached to the verb form and an accent mark is added on the vowel that was stressed in the verb form before the two object pronouns were added. The accent mark is needed to keep the stress where it originally was:

¡Dígamelo Ud., por favor! / Tell it to me, please!

With a verb in the negative imperative (command):

The position of **no** and the two object pronouns is still the same as usual, in front of the verb form:

¡No me lo diga Ud., por favor! / Don't tell it to me, please!

When dealing with an infinitive, attach both object pronouns (indirect, direct) to the infinitive:

Juan quiere dármelo / John wants to give it to me.
Juan no quiere dármelo / John does not want to give it to me.

OR

If the main verb is **poder, querer, saber, ir a,** you may place the two object pronouns in front of the main verb:

Juan me lo quiere dar / John wants to give it to me.
Juan no me lo quiere dar / John does not want to give it to me.

When dealing with a present participle, attach both object pronouns (indirect, direct) to the present participle:

Juan está escribiéndomelo / John is writing it to me.

Juan no está escribiéndomelo / John is not writing it to me.

OR

If the main verb is a progressive form with **estar** or another auxiliary, you may place the two object pronouns (indirect, direct) in front of the main verb:

Juan me lo está escribiendo / John is writing it to me.
Juan no me lo está escribiendo / John is not writing it to me.

Juana me lo estaba escribiendo / Jane was writing it to me.

When an indirect object pronoun and a direct object pronoun are both 3rd person, either singular or plural or both singular or both plural, the indirect object pronoun (**le** or **les**) changes to **se** because it cannot stand as **le** or **les** in front of a direct object pronoun beginning with the letter "l". Review the direct object pronouns, 3rd person sing. and plural. Also, review the indirect object pronouns, 3rd person sing. and plural.

Juan se lo da / John is giving it to you (to him, to her, to it, to you *plural,* to them).

¡Dígaselo Ud.! / Tell it to him!
¡No se lo diga Ud.! / Don't tell it to him!

Juan quiere dárselo.
Juan se lo quiere dar. } John wants to give it to her.

Juan está escribiéndoselo.
Juan se lo está escribiendo. } John is writing it to them.

Since the form **se** can have more than one meaning (to him, to her, to them, *etc.*), in addition to the fact that it looks exactly like the reflexive pronoun **se,** any doubt as to its meaning can be clarified merely by adding any of the following accordingly: **a Ud., a él, a ella, a Uds., a ellos, a ellas.**

If you are dealing with a reflexive pronoun, it is normally placed in front of an object pronoun:

Yo me lo puse / I put it on (me, on myself).

Demonstrative pronouns

Demonstrative pronouns are formed from the demonstrative adjectives. To form a demonstrative pronoun write an accent mark on the stressed vowel of a demonstrative adjective.

A demonstrative pronoun is used to take the place of a noun. It agrees in gender and number with the noun it replaces. The demonstrative pronouns are:

MASCULINE	FEMININE	NEUTER	ENGLISH MEANING	
éste	ésta	esto	this one *(here)*	
éstos	éstas		these *(here)*	
ése	ésa	eso	that one *(there)*	
ésos	ésas		those *(there)*	
aquél	aquélla	aquello	that one	{ *(farther away or*
aquéllos	aquéllas		those	*out of sight)*

EXAMPLES
Me gustan este cuadro y ése / I like this picture and that one.
Me gustan estos guantes y aquéllos / I like these gloves and those.
Esta falda y ésa son bonitas / This skirt and that one are pretty.
Estas camisas y aquéllas son hermosas / These shirts and those are beautiful.

NOTE that the neuter forms do not have an accent mark. They are not used when you are referring to a particular noun. They are used when referring to an idea, a statement, a situation, a clause, a phrase. Never use the neuter pronouns to refer to a person. Examples:

¿Qué es esto? / What is this?
¿Qué es eso? / What is that?
¿Qué es aquello? / What is that (way over there)?

Eso es fácil de hacer / That is easy to do.
Es fácil hacer eso / It is easy to do that.
Eso es / That's right.

Juan no estudia, y esto me inquieta / John does not study and this worries me.

NOTE also that the English term *the latter* is expressed in Spanish as **éste, ésta, éstos,** or **éstas;** and *the former* is expressed in Spanish as **aquél, aquélla, aquéllos, aquéllas**—depending on the gender and number of the noun referred to.

AND NOTE that in English the order is generally "the former . . . the latter"—in other words, "the one that was mentioned first . . . the one that was mentioned last." In Spanish, however, the stated order is the opposite: "the latter . . . the former"—in other words, "the one that was just mentioned last . . . the one that was mentioned first:"

Roberto y Antonio son inteligentes; éste (meaning Antonio) **es alto y aquél es pequeño** / Robert and Anthony are intelligent; the former (meaning Roberto) is short and the latter is tall.

The pronouns **el de, la de, los de, las de; el que, la que, los que, las que**
These pronouns are used in place of nouns.

EXAMPLES:

mi hermano y el (*hermano*) **de mi amigo** / my brother and my friend's (the one of my friend *or* that of my friend)
mi hermana y la (*hermana*) **de mi amigo** / my sister and my friend's (the one of my friend *or* that of my friend)
mis hermanos y los (*hermanos*) **del muchacho** / my brothers and the boy's (the ones of the boy *or* those of the boy)
mis hermanas y las (*hermanas*) **de la muchacha** / my sisters and the girl's (the ones of the girl *or* those of the girl)
El (*muchacho*) **que baila con María es mi hermano** / The one who (The boy who) is dancing with Mary is my brother.
La (*muchacha*) **que baila con Roberto es mi hermana** / The one who (The girl who) is dancing with Robert is my sister.
Los (*muchachos*) **que bailan son mis amigos** / The ones who (The boys who) are dancing are my friends.
Las (*muchachas*) **que bailan son mis amigas** / The ones who (The girls who) are dancing are my friends.

EJERCICIOS

OPTIONAL EXERCISE FOR ENRICHMENT

I. Escriba, en inglés, una definición breve de los varios tipos de pronombres siguientes. Estudie la sección de pronombres en el Work Unit 8 y en esta lección. Dé también ejemplos.

1. Personal pronoun **(pronombre personal)** _____

_____

_____

2. Direct object pronoun **(pronombre de complemento directo)** _____

_____

_____

_____

3. Indirect object pronoun **(pronombre de complemento indirecto)** _____

_____

_____

_____

4. Prepositional pronoun **(pronombre preposicional)** _____

_____

_____

_____

5. Demonstrative pronoun **(pronombre demostrativo)** _____

_____

_____

_____

II. Complete este crucigrama.

HORIZONTALES: **1.** Pronombre demostrativo, f., s. **2.** Pronombre personal como sujeto, primera persona, s. **5.** Pronombre complemento indirecto, tercera persona, pl. **6.** Pronombre reflexivo, tercera persona, s. y pl. **7.** Adjetivo posesivo, segunda persona, s. **8.** Pronombre complemento directo e indirecto, primera persona, s. **10.** Pronombre complemento directo, tercera persona, s., m.

VERTICALES: **3.** Pronombre personal como sujeto, tercera persona, s. **4.** Pronombre complemento directo, tercera persona, s., f. **5.** Pronombre complemento indirecto, tercera persona, s. **9.** Pronombre personal como sujeto, tercera persona, s., m.

III. Traduzca al español.

1. This book is for me. _____

2. This pencil is for you *(2nd pers., s.)* _____

3. These notebooks are for us. _____

4. These chocolates are for you *(3rd pers., s.)* _____

_____

5. Those letters (over there) are for them *(m.)* _____

6. John is going to the movies with me. _____

_____

7. Can I go to the movies with you? *(2nd pers., s.)* _____

_____

_____

8. There is a problem between you and me. _____

_____

_____

9. Everyone is going to the theater except me. _____

_____

_____

10. Robert took the cake with him (himself). _____

_____

IV. Traduzca al español las palabras inglesas. Escriba la oración enteramente en español, según el modelo.

Modelo: **Juan quiere escribir** (it, *m.*)
Escriba: **Juan quiere escribirlo.**

1. Daniel querría comprar (it, *f.*) _____

2. Dora desea leer (them, *m.*). _____

3. Ernesto está escribiendo (them, *f.*) _____

4. Juan (it, *m.*) está leyendo. _____

5. Pablo está leyendo (it, *m.*) _____

6. Hable (me) Ud., por favor. _____

161

7. Juan (it, *m.,* to me) da. _____

8. Roberto (it, *f.,* to you, *2nd pers., s.*) daba. _____

9. Diego (them, *m.,* to us) dio ayer. _____

10. Carolina (them, *f.,* to you, *2nd pers., pl.*) dará. _____

V. Conteste las siguientes preguntas afirmativamente, según el modelo.

   Modelo: **¿Nos la dio Juan?**   **Escriba:** **Sí, Juan nos la dio.**

1. ¿Te lo dio Juan? _____

2. ¿Estás escribiéndola? _____

3. ¿Está Ud. leyéndolo? _____

VI. Reemplace los complementos directos por los pronombres que correspondan.

   Modelo: **¿Está Ud. escribiendo la carta?**
   Escriba: **¿Está Ud. escribiéndola?**

1. ¿Está Ud. leyendo los libros? _____

2. ¿Quiere Ud. comer el pastel? _____

3. ¡Dígame la verdad, por favor! _____

4. ¡No me diga la verdad! _____

5. Juan quiere darme el dinero. _____

6. Esteban hizo la lección. _____

7. El señor Rodríguez bebió el vino. _____

8. Pedro comió las salchichas. _____

9. Las muchachas compraron las bicicletas. _____

10. La vendedora vendió todos los chocolates. _____

VII. Reemplace los complementos indirectos por los pronombres que correspondan.

   Modelo: **Juana está hablando a Francisca.**
   Escriba: **Juana está hablándole.**

1. Rafael no dijo la verdad a su padre. _____

2. Eugenia dio los pasteles a sus amigos. _____

3. Los alumnos dieron un regalo a la profesora de español. _____

4. Los estudiantes escribieron una carta al profesor de español. _____

_____

5. Ester envió un paquete a sus padres. _____

VIII. Reemplace los complementos indirectos y directos por los pronombres que correspondan.

    Modelo: Juan da el libro al profesor.   **Escriba:** **Juan se lo da.**

1. ¡Diga la verdad al padre! _____

2. ¡No diga una mentira a la madre! _____

3. Cristóbal quiere dar el regalo a Clara. _____

_____

4. Juan está escribiendo una carta a sus amigos. _____

_____

5. María está dando el chocolate al niño. _____

_____

IX. Reemplace los adjetivos demostrativos y los nombres por los pronombres demostrativos que convengan, según el modelo.

    Modelo: Me gusta este libro.   **Escriba: Me gusta éste.**

1. Me gusta este cuaderno. _____

2. Estoy leyendo esta carta. _____

3. Estamos comiendo estos pasteles. _____

4. María escribió estas oraciones. _____

5. Querría comprar ese vaso. _____

6. Pedro comprará esa corbata. _____

7. El vendedor va a mostrarnos esos zapatos. _____

_____

8. La vendedora quiere mostrarme esas faldas. _____

_____

9. Mi hermanito quiere comprar aquel juguete. _____

_____

10. Mi padre va a comprar aquella bicicleta. _____

_____

X. Traduzca al español.

1. What is this? _____

2. What is that? _____

3. What is that (way over there)? _____

4. That is easy to do. _____

5. It is easy to do that. _____

6. That's right. _____

7. John does not study and this worries me. _____

_____

8. Robert and Anthony are intelligent; the former is short and the latter is tall. _____

_____

9. I like this picture and that one. _____

_____

10. I like these gloves and those. _____

_____

XI. Una las expresiones en inglés con su traducción en español.

_____ my brother and my friend's   1. mis hermanas y las de la muchacha

_____ my sister and my friend's   2. mis hermanos y los del muchacho

_____ my brothers and the boy's   3. mi hermana y la de mi amigo

_____ my sisters and the girl's   4. mi hermano y el de mi amigo

XII. Una las oraciones en inglés con su traducción en español.

_____ The one who (The boy who) is
dancing with Mary is my brother.

1. Las (muchachas) que bailan
son mis amigas.

_____ The one who (The girl who) is
dancing with Robert is my sister.

2. Los (muchachos) que bailan
son mis amigos.

_____ The ones who (The boys who) are
dancing are my friends.

3. El (muchacho) que baila con
María es mi hermano.

_____ The ones who (The girls who) are
dancing are my friends.

4. La (muchacha) que baila con
Roberto es mi hermana.

Santa Lucía *by Francisco de ZURBARÁN (1598–1664)*
Courtesy of The National Gallery of Art, Washington, D.C.

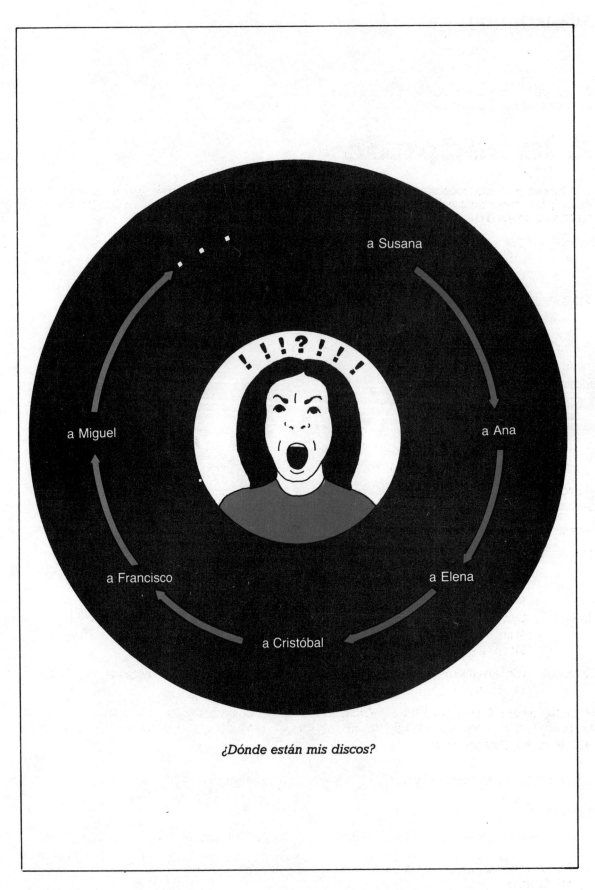

¿Dónde están mis discos?

¿Los discos? ¿Qué discos? No los tengo, Juana. Se los di a Ana. Pídeselos a ella.

*Round and round the records go and where
do they end up? ¿Quién sabe?*

A la redonda

Juana prestó sus discos a su amiga Susana en septiembre. Hoy es el primero de diciembre.
Juana quiere recobrar sus discos para escucharlos durante los días festivos de Navidad. Ella va
a ver a su amiga Susana y le dice:

Juana: Susana, yo te presté mis discos en el mes de septiembre, y hoy es el primero de
              diciembre. Quiero escucharlos durante los días festivos de Navidad. ¿Quieres   5
              devolvérmelos, por favor?

Susana: No los tengo, Juana. Se los di a Ana.* Puedes ir a verla. Pídeselos a ella.

(Juana va a ver a Ana.)

Juana: Ana, yo le presté mis discos a Susana y ella me dijo que tú los tienes ahora. Le di
              mis discos a ella en el mes de septiembre.   10

Ana: No los tengo, Juana. Se los presté a Elena. Puedes ir a verla. Se los di a ella.
              Pídeselos a ella.

(Juana va a ver a Elena.)

Juana: Elena, ¿tienes mis discos? Los tienes, yo lo sé. Se los presté a Susana. Susana
              se los dio a Ana, y Ana me dijo que tú los tienes ahora.   15

Elena: ¡Oh! ¡Los discos! ¿Qué discos? ¿Los discos de Victoria de Los Angeles? ¿de
              Plácido Domingo? ¿de Lily Pons? ¿de Judy Garland? ¿de Barry Manilow?

Juana: ¡Sí! ¡Sí! ¡Eso es!

Elena: No. No los tengo. Se los di a Cristóbal. Puedes ir a verlo. Se los di a él. Pídeselos a
              él.   20

(Juana va a ver a Cristóbal.)

Juana: Cristóbal, yo presté mis discos a Susana en septiembre, y hoy es el primero de
              diciembre. Susana me dijo que se los dio a Ana. Ana me dijo que se los dio a
              Elena. Elena me dijo que tú los tienes. Devuélvemelos, por favor.

Cristóbal: ¡Oh! Los discos. Se los di a Francisco, y Francisco se los dio a Miguel, y Miguel se   25
              los dio a . . .

*NOTE: **Se los di a Ana** / *I gave them to Anna.* When the dir. obj. pronouns **lo, la, los, las**—all in the
3rd pers., s. or pl.—are preceded by the indir. obj. pronouns **le** or **les**, both in the 3rd pers., s. or pl.
also, **le** or **les** changes to **se.**

VOCABULARIO: Consult the vocabulary section in the back pages.

EJERCICIOS

I. Seleccione la respuesta correcta conforme al significado de la lectura en esta lección.

1. La persona que prestó los discos a Ana es   (a) Juana   (b) Susana   (c) Elena
   (d) Cristóbal   _____

2. Juana prestó sus discos en   (a) la primavera   (b) el invierno   (c) el otoño
   (d) el verano   _____   **167**

3. Juana pide a Susana que ésta se los   (a) escuche   (b) preste   (c) devuelva
   (d) tenga   _____

4. Susana dio los discos a   (a) Miguel   (b) Cristóbal   (c) Elena   (d) Ana   _____

5. Elena dice a Juana que ésta puede ir a ver a   (a) Francisco   (b) Miguel
   (c) Cristóbal   (d) Ramón   _____

II. **Acróstico.** Complete este acróstico en español.

1. to return
   something
   to someone
   or to some
   place

2. Imperf.
   indic. of
   ir, 1st &
   3rd pers.,
   s.

3. ind. obj.
   pron. in
   front of
   lo, la,
   los or
   las

4. box

5. Pres. indic.
   of **oír,** 1st
   pers., s.

6. I gave them (m.)
   to her.

```
      D □ □ □ □ □ □
1.
      I □ □
2.
      S □ □
3.
      C □ □ □
4.
      O □ □
5.
      S □ □ □ □
6.
```

III. Ordene las palabras para hallar una oración significativa.

Modelo: Juana / discos / sus / prestó / Susana / a / amiga / su
Escriba: **Juana prestó sus discos a su amiga Susana.**

1. quiere / Juana / discos / sus / recobrar

   _____

2. ver / a / va / Juana / Ana / a

   _____

3. verlo / ir / puedes / a

   _____

4. los / se / a / presté / Cristóbal

   _____

5. dijo / me / Susana / que / dio / los / se / a / Ana

IV. Use las siguientes palabras en oraciones completas y luego traduzca las oraciones al inglés. Consulte el diálogo de esta lección.

1. se los: _____

 Traducción al inglés: _____

2. presté: _____

 Traducción al inglés: _____

3. escucharlos: _____

 Traducción al inglés: _____

4. va a ver: _____

 Traducción al inglés: _____

5. di: _____

 Traducción al inglés: _____

Estructuras de la lengua

Tense No. 6: Presente de subjuntivo (Present subjunctive)

The subjunctive mood is used in Spanish much more than in English. In Spanish the present subjunctive is used:

(a) To express a command in the **usted** or **ustedes** form, either in the affirmative or negative.

EXAMPLES:
1. **Siéntese** Ud. / *Sit down.*
2. **No se siente** Ud. / *Don't sit down.*
3. **Cierren** Uds. la puerta / *Close* the door.
4. **No cierren** Uds. la puerta / *Don't close* the door.
5. **Dígame** Ud. la verdad / *Tell me* the truth.

(b) To express a negative command in the familiar form **(tú).**

EXAMPLES:
1. **No te sientes** / *Don't sit down.*
2. **No entres** / *Don't come in.*
3. **No duermas** / *Don't sleep.*
4. **No lo hagas** / *Don't do it.*

(c) To express a negative command in the second person plural **(vosotros).**

EXAMPLES:
1. **No os sentéis** / *Don't sit down.*
2. **No entréis** / *Don't come in.*
3. **No durmáis** / *Don't sleep.*
4. **No lo hagáis** / *Don't do it.*

(d) To express a command in the first person plural, either in the affirmative or negative **(nosotros).**

EXAMPLES:
1. **Sentémonos** / *Let's sit down.*
2. **No entremos** / *Let's not go in.*

(e) After a verb that expresses some kind of wish, insistence, preference, suggestion, or request.

EXAMPLES:

1. *Quiero* que María lo **haga** / I want Mary to do it.

NOTE: In this example, English uses the infinitive form, *to do.* In Spanish, however, a new clause is needed introduced by *que* because there is a new subject, María. The present subjunctive of *hacer* is used (**haga**) because the main verb is *Quiero,* which indicates a wish. If there were no change in subject, Spanish would use the infinitive form, as we do in English, for example, **Quiero hacerlo** / *I want to do it.*

2. *Insisto* en que María lo **haga** / I insist that Mary *do* it.
3. *Prefiero* que María lo **haga** / I prefer that Mary *do* it.
4. *Pido* que María lo **haga** / I ask that Mary *do* it.

NOTE: In examples 2, 3, and 4 here, English also uses the subjunctive form *do.* Not so in example no. 1, however.

(f) After a verb that expresses doubt, fear, joy, hope, sorrow, or some other emotion. Notice in the following examples, however, that the subjunctive is not used in English.

EXAMPLES:

1. *Dudo* que María lo **haga** / I doubt that Mary is *doing* it; I doubt that Mary *will do* it.
2. *No creo* que María **venga** / I don't believe (I doubt) that Mary *is coming;* I don't believe (I doubt) that Mary *will come.*
3. *Temo* que María **esté** enferma / I fear that Mary *is* ill.
4. *Me alegro* de que **venga** María / I'm glad that Mary is *coming;* I'm glad that Mary *will come.*
5. *Espero* que María no **esté** enferma / I hope that Mary *is* not ill.

(g) After certain impersonal expressions that show necessity, doubt, regret, importance, urgency, or possibility. Notice, however, that the subjunctive is not used in English in all of the following examples.

EXAMPLES:

1. *Es necesario que* María lo **haga** / It is necessary for Mary to do it; It is necessary that Mary *do* it.
2. *No es cierto que* María **venga** / It is doubtful (not certain) that Mary *is coming;* It is doubtful (not certain) that Mary *will come.*
3. *Es lástima que* María **no venga** / It's too bad (a pity) that Mary *isn't coming.*
4. *Es importante que* María **venga** / It is important for Mary to come; It is important that Mary *come.*
5. *Es preciso que* María **venga** / It is necessary for Mary to come; It is necessary that Mary *come.*
6. *Es urgente que* María **venga** / It is urgent for Mary to come; It is urgent that Mary *come.*

(h) After certain conjunctions of time, such as **antes (de) que, cuando, en cuanto, después (de) que, hasta que, mientras,** and the like. The subjunctive form of the verb is used when introduced by any of these time conjunctions if the time referred to is either indefinite or is expected to take place in the future. However, if the action was completed in the past, the indicative mood is used.

EXAMPLES:

1. Le hablaré a María cuando **venga** / I shall talk to Mary when she *comes.*
2. Vámonos antes (de) que **llueva** / Let's go before *it rains.*
3. En cuanto la **vea** yo, le hablaré / As soon as *I see* her, I shall talk to her.
4. Me quedo aquí hasta que **vuelva** / I'm staying here until *he returns.*

NOTE: In the above examples, the subjunctive is not used in English.

(i) After certain conjunctions that express a condition, negation, purpose, such as, **a menos que, con tal que, para que, a fin de que, sin que, en caso (de) que,** and the like. Notice, however, that the subjunctive is not used in English in the following examples.

EXAMPLES:

    1. Démelo con tal que **sea** bueno / Give it to me provided that *it is* good.

    2. Me voy a menos que **venga** / I'm leaving unless *he comes*.

(j) After certain adverbs, such as, **acaso, quizá,** and **tal vez.**

EXAMPLE:

    Acaso **venga** mañana / Perhaps *he will come* tomorrow; Perhaps *he is coming* tomorrow.

(k) After **aunque** if the action has not yet occurred.

EXAMPLE:

    Aunque María **venga** esta noche, no me quedo / Although Mary *may come* tonight, I'm not staying; Although Mary *is coming* tonight, I'm not staying.

(l) In an adjectival clause if the antecedent is something or someone that is indefinite, negative, vague, or nonexistent.

EXAMPLES:

    1. Busco un libro que **sea** interesante / I'm looking for a book that *is* interesting.

NOTE: In this example, *que* (which is the relative pronoun) refers to *un libro* (which is the antecedent). Since *un libro* is indefinite, the verb in the following clause must be in the subjunctive **(sea).** Notice, however, that the subjunctive is not used in English.

    2. ¿Hay alguien aquí que **hable** francés? / Is there anyone here who *speaks* French?

NOTE: In this example, *que* (which is the relative pronoun) refers to *alguien* (which is the antecedent). Since *alguien* is indefinite and somewhat vague—we do not know who this anyone might be—the verb in the following clause must be in the subjunctive **(hable).** Notice, however, that the subjunctive is not used in English.

    3. No hay nadie que **pueda** hacerlo / There is no one who *can* do it.

NOTE: In this example, *que* (which is the relative pronoun) refers to *nadie* (which is the antecedent). Since *nadie* is nonexistent, the verb in the following clause must be in the subjunctive **(pueda).** Notice, however, that the subjunctive is not used in English.

(m) After **por más que** or **por mucho que.**

EXAMPLES:

    1. **Por más que hable usted,** no quiero escuchar / *No matter how much you talk,* I don't want to listen.

    2. **Por mucho que se alegre,** no me importa / *No matter how glad he is,* I don't care.

(n) After the expression **ojalá (que),** which expresses a great desire. This interjection means *would to God!* or *may God grant!* . . . It is derived from the Arabic, **ya Allah!** / (Oh, God!)

EXAMPLE:

    ¡**Ojalá que vengan** mañana! / *Would to God that they come* tomorrow! *May God grant that they come* tomorrow! *How I wish that they would come* tomorrow! *If only they would come* tomorrow!

Finally, remember that the present subjunctive is never used in Spanish after *si* when *si* means *if.*

The present subjunctive of regular verbs and many irregular verbs is normally formed as follows:

Go to the present indicative, 1st pers. sing., of the verb you have in mind, drop the ending **o,** and

for an **—ar** ending type, add: **e, es, e; emos, éis, en**

for an **—er** or **—ir** ending type, add: **a, as, a; amos, áis, an**

As you can see, the characteristic vowel in the present subjunctive endings for an **—ar** type verb is **e** in the six persons.

As you can see, the characteristic vowel in the present subjunctive endings for an **—er** or **—ir** type verb is **a** in the six persons.

You then get, for example: **hable, hables, hable;**
hablemos, habléis, hablen

beba, bebas, beba;
bebamos, bebáis, beban

reciba, recibas, reciba;
recibamos, recibáis, reciban

The usual equivalent in English is: (that I) talk OR (that I) may talk, (that you) talk OR (that you) may talk, (that he/she) talk OR (that he/she) may talk, *etc.*; (that I) drink OR (that I) may drink, (that you) drink OR (that you) may drink, (that he/she) drink OR (that he/she) may drink, *etc.*; (that I) receive OR (that I) may receive, (that you) receive OR (that you) may receive, (that he/she) receive OR (that he/she) may receive, *etc.*

Verbs irregular in the present subjunctive commonly used

The following verbs are irregular because if you go to the present indicative, 1 st pers. sing. of these verbs, you will find a form which you cannot work with according to the process of forming the present subjunctive normally, as explained above.

dar / to give
dé, des, dé;
demos, deis, den

ir / to go
vaya, vayas, vaya;
vayamos, vayáis, vayan

estar / to be
esté, estés, esté;
estemos, estéis, estén

saber / to know, to know how
sepa, sepas, sepa;
sepamos, sepáis, sepan

haber / to have (as an auxiliary or helping verb)
haya, hayas, haya;
hayamos, hayáis, hayan

ser / to be
sea, seas, sea;
seamos, seáis, sean

Other verbs irregular in the present subjunctive

Stem-changing verbs in the present indicative have the same stem changes in the present subjunctive, generally speaking. If you go to the present indicative, 1st pers. sing. of those verbs, you will find the stem change there. Drop the ending **o** and add the appropriate endings of the present subjunctive. For example, to form the present subjunctive of **pensar**, go to the 1st pers. sing. of the present indicative and there you will find **pienso**. Drop the ending **o** and add: **e, es, e; emos, éis, en.** The verbs irregular in the present indicative, including stem-changing and ortho-graphical changing verbs, are given to you alphabetically.

Orthographical changing verbs (those that change in spelling), which end in **car, gar,** and **zar** in the infinitive form, have the same spelling changes in the present subjunctive as they do in the 1st pers. sing. of the preterit. Just drop the accent mark on **é** and you have the form of the present subjunctive, generally speaking.

EXAMPLE:

Preterit, 1st pers. sing.	Present subjunctive
abracé (abra**zar**)	**abrace, abraces, abrace; abracemos, abracéis, abracen**
busqué (bus**car**)	**busque, busques, busque; busquemos, busquéis, busquen**
pagué (pa**gar**)	**pague, pagues, pague; paguemos, paguéis, paguen**

However, there are some verbs of the type that end in **car, gar,** and **zar** which are stem-changing when stressed and the process described above will not work for them. For example:

Take **almorzar.** If you go to the preterit, 1st pers. sing., you will find **almorcé.** If you drop the accent mark on **é,** you are left with **almorce,** which is not the correct form in the present subjunctive. The **o** in the stem is stressed and it changes to **ue;** the forms in the present subjunctive for this verb contain the stem change, which is found in the present indicative. The forms of **almorzar** in the present subjunctive, therefore, are: **almuerce, almuerces, almuerce; almorcemos, almorcéis, almuercen.**

Finally, remember that there is really no easy perfect system of arriving at verb forms no matter what process is used because there is usually some exception—even if only one exception. The best thing for you to do is to be sure you know the regular forms in all the tenses and the irregular forms that are commonly used. All those that you need to know and to recognize are given to you in these sections on Spanish verbs.

EJERCICIOS

I. Traduzca las palabras inglesas al español y escriba las oraciones enteramente en español.

1. *Sit down* **(Ud.),** *please.* _____

2. *Don't sit down* **(Ud.)** _____

3. *Close* **(Uds.)** las ventanas. _____

4. *Don't close* **(Ud.)** la puerta. _____

5. *Tell me* **(Ud.)** la verdad. _____

II. Dé la forma negativa de las siguientes oraciones.

Modelo: ¡Levántate!   **Escriba: ¡No te levantes!**

1. ¡Lávate!_____   4. ¡Duerme!_____

2. ¡Siéntate!_____   5. ¡Hazlo!_____

3. ¡Entra!_____   6. ¡Acuéstate!_____

III. Dé la forma negativa de las siguientes oraciones.

Modelo: ¡Levántese!   **Escriba: ¡No se levante!**

1. ¡Lávese!_____   4. ¡Siéntese!_____

2. ¡Levántese!_____   5. ¡Entre!_____

3. ¡Duerma!_____   6. ¡Hágalo!_____

173

IV. Dé la forma afirmativa de las siguientes oraciones.

Modelo: ¡No os sentéis!   **Escriba: ¡Sentaos!**

1. ¡No entréis! _____   4. ¡No os levantéis! _____

2. ¡No durmáis! _____   5. ¡No os lavéis! _____

3. ¡No lo hagáis! _____   6. ¡No os acostéis! _____

V. Traduzca al inglés.

1. Sentémonos. _____   4. Acostémonos _____

2. Lavémonos _____   5. Divirtámonos _____

3. Levantémonos _____   6. Vámonos _____

VI. Cambie el verbo entre paréntesis al presente de subjuntivo.

Modelo: Quiero que María lo (hacer).   **Escriba: Quiero que María lo haga.**

1. Quiero que José lo (hacer). _____

2. Insisto en que Gabriela la (escribir). _____

3. Prefiero que Juan me (amar). _____

4. Deseo que mis amigos me (amar). _____

5. Pido que Pedro me (responder). _____

6. Dudo que Miguel me (olvidar). _____

7. No creo que María (venir). _____

8. Temo que Arturo (estar) enfermo. _____

9. Me alegro de que (trabajar) María. _____

10. Espero que Edmundo no (estar) enfermo. _____

11. Es necesario que usted (estudiar). _____

12. No es cierto que Pablo (llegar). _____

13. Es lástima que ustedes no (poder) leer. _____

_____

14. Es importante que tú (leer). _____

15. Es preciso que nosotros (partir). _____

OPTIONAL EXERCISES FOR ENRICHMENT

VII. Escriba las seis formas de los siguientes verbos en el presente de subjuntivo, según el modelo.

Modelo: hablar   Escriba: hable, hables, hable; hablemos, habléis, hablen

1. trabajar: _____

2. beber: _____

3. recibir: _____

VIII. Escriba las seis formas de los siguientes verbos en el presente de subjuntivo.

1. dar: _____

2. estar: _____

3. haber: _____

4. ir: _____

5. saber: _____

6. decir: _____

7. pensar: _____

8. buscar: _____

9. pagar: _____

10. almorzar: _____

SUBJUNCTIVE

The subjunctive is not a tense; it is a mood or mode. Usually, when we speak in Spanish or English, we use the indicative mood. We use the subjunctive mood in Spanish for certain reasons. The following are the principal reasons.

After certain conjunctions

When the following conjunctions introduce a new clause, the verb in that new clause is in the subjunctive mood:

a fin de que / so that, in order that
a menos que / unless
a no ser que / unless
antes que *or* **antes de que** / before
como si / as if
con tal que *or* **con tal de que** / provided that
en caso que *or* **en caso de que** / in case, in case that, supposing that
para que / in order that, so that
sin que / without

EXAMPLES:

Se lo explico a ustedes a fin de que puedan comprenderlo / I am explaining it to you so that (in order that) you may be able to understand it.

Saldré a las tres y media a menos que esté lloviendo / I will go out at three thirty unless it is raining.

When the following conjunctions introduce a new clause, the verb in that new clause is sometimes in the indicative mood, sometimes in the subjunctive mood. Use the subjunctive mood if what is being expressed indicates some sort of anxious anticipation, doubt, indefiniteness, vagueness, or uncertainty. If these are not implied and if the action was completed in the past, use the indicative mood:

a pesar de que / in spite of the fact that
así que / as soon as, after
aunque / although, even if, even though
cuando / when
de manera que / so that, so as
de modo que / so that, in such a way that
después que *or* **después de que** / after
en cuanto / as soon as
hasta que / until
luego que / as soon as, after
mientras / while, as long as
siempre que / whenever, provided that
tan pronto como / as soon as

EXAMPLES:

> **Le daré el dinero a Roberto cuando me lo pida** / I shall give the money to Robert when he asks me for it. (**Pida** is in the subjunctive mood because some doubt or uncertainty is suggested and Robert may not ask for it.)

BUT: **Se lo di a Roberto cuando me lo pidió** / I gave it to Robert when he asked me for it. (No subjunctive of **pedir** here because he actually did ask me for it.)

> **Esperaré hasta que llegue el autobús** / I shall wait until the bus arrives. (**Llegue** is in the subjunctive mood here because some doubt or uncertainty is suggested and the bus may never arrive.)

BUT: **Esperé hasta que llegó el autobús** / I waited until the bus arrived. (No subjunctive of **llegar** here because the bus actually did arrive.)

> **Trabajaré hasta que Ud. venga** / I shall work until you come. (**Venga** is used here because some doubt or uncertainty is suggested and **Ud.** may never come.)

BUT: **Trabajé hasta que Ud. vino** / I worked until you came. (No subjunctive of **venir** here because **Ud.** actually did come.)

After certain adverbs

acaso
quizá *or* **quizás** } perhaps, maybe
tal vez

Tal vez hayan perdido / Perhaps they have lost. (Subjunctive is used here because some degree of uncertainty or pessimism is implied.)

Tal vez han ganado / Perhaps they have won. (No subjunctive is used here because some degree of certainty or optimism is implied.)

Por + adj. or **adv. + que** / however, no matter how

> **Por (más) interesante que sea, no quiero ver esa película** / No matter how interesting it may be, I do not want to see that film.

> **Por bien que juegue Roberto, no quiero jugar con él** / However well (No matter how well) Robert plays, I do not want to play with him.

After certain indefinite expressions

> **cualquier, cualquiera, cualesquier, cualesquiera** / whatever, whichever, any (the final **a** drops in **cualquiera** and **cualesquiera** when the word is in front of a noun)
> **cuandoquiera** / whenever
> **dondequiera** / wherever; **adondequiera** / to wherever
> **quienquiera, quienesquiera** / whoever

EXAMPLES:

> **No abriré la puerta, quienquiera que sea** / I will not open the door, whoever it may be.

> **Dondequiera que Ud. esté, escríbame** / Wherever you may be, write to me.

> **Adondequiera que Ud. vaya, dígamelo** / Wherever you may go, tell me.

After an indefinite or negative antecedent

See Work Unit 10 for a definition of an antecedent with examples. Remember to use the Index for references to explanations and examples located in different parts of this book.

The reason the subjunctive is needed after an indefinite or negative antecedent is that the person or thing desired may possibly not exist; or, if it does exist, you may never find it.

EXAMPLES:

> **Busco un libro que sea interesante** / I am looking for a book which is interesting.
> BUT: **Tengo un libro que es interesante** / I have a book which is interesting.

> **¿Conoce Ud. a alguien que tenga paciencia?** / Do you know someone who has patience?
> BUT: **Conozco a alguien que tiene paciencia** / I know someone who has patience.

> **No encontré a nadie que supiera la respuesta** / I did not find anyone who knew the answer.

> **No encuentro a nadie que sepa la respuesta** / I do not find anyone who knows the answer.
> BUT: **Encontré a alguien que sabe la respuesta** / I found someone who knows the answer.

> **No puedo encontrar a nadie que pueda prestarme dinero** / I can't meet (find) anyone who can lend me money.
> BUT: **Conozco a alguien que puede prestarme dinero** / I know somebody who can lend me money.
> AND: **Encontré a alguien que puede prestarme dinero** / I met (found) someone who can lend me money.

After ¡Que . . . !

In order to express indirectly a wish, an order, a command in the 3rd person singular or plural, you may use the exclamatory **¡Que . . . !** alone to introduce the subjunctive clause. The words generally understood to be omitted are: **Quiero que . . .** or **Deje que . . .**, which mean **I want . . .** or **Let . . .** Examples:

> **¡Que lo haga Jorge!** / Let George do it! (In other words, the complete statement would be: **¡Deje que lo haga Jorge!** or **¡Quiero que lo haga Jorge!** / I want George to do it!

> **¡Que entre!** / Let him enter! or I want him to enter! (**¡Quiero que entre!**)

After ¡Ojalá que . . . !

The exclamatory expression **Ojalá** is of Arabic origin meaning "Oh, God!" Examples:

> **¡Ojalá que vengan!** / If only they would come! (Would that they come! Oh, God, let them come!)

¡Ojalá que lleguen! / If only they would arrive! (Would that they arrive! Oh, God, let them arrive!)

After certain impersonal expressions

Generally speaking, the following impersonal expressions require the subjunctive form of the verb in the clause that follows.

Basta que . . . / It is enough that . . . ; It is sufficient that . . .
Conviene que . . . / It is fitting that . . . ; It is proper that . . .
Importa que . . . / It is important that . . .
Más vale que . . . / It is better that . . .
Es aconsejable que . . . / It is advisable that . . .
Es bueno que . . . / It is good that . . .
Es importante que . . . / It is important that . . .
Es imposible que . . . / It is impossible that . . .
Es lástima que . . . / It is a pity that . . .
Es malo que . . . / It is bad that . . .
Es mejor que . . . / It is better that . . .
Es menester que . . . / It is necessary that . . .
Es necesario que . . . / It is necessary that . . .
Es posible que . . . / It is possible that . . .
Es preciso que . . . / It is necessary that . . .
Es probable que . . . / It is probable that . . .
Es raro que . . . / It is rare that . . .
Es urgente que . . . / It is urgent that . . .

EXAMPLES:

Basta que sepan la verdad / It is sufficient that they know the truth.

Conviene que venga ahora mismo / It is proper that she come right now.

Es aconsejable que salga inmediatamente / It is advisable that she leave immediately.

Es probable que María regrese a las tres / It is probable that Mary will return at three o'clock.

Es necesario que Ud. escriba la composición / It is necessary that you write the composition *or* It is necessary for you to write the composition.

After verbs or expressions that indicate denial, doubt or lack of belief, and uncertainty

dudar que . . . / to doubt that . . .
negar que . . . / to deny that . . .
no creer que . . . / not to believe that . . .
Es dudoso que . . . / It is doubtful that . . .
Es incierto que . . / It is uncertain that . . .
Hay duda que . . . / There is doubt that . . .
No es cierto que . . . / It is not certain that . . .
No estar seguro que . . . / Not to be sure that . . .
No suponer que . . . / Not to suppose that . . .

EXAMPLES:

Dudo que mis amigos vengan a verme / I doubt that my friends are coming (will come) to see me.

No creo que sea urgente / I do not believe that it is urgent.

Es dudoso que Pablo lo haga / It is doubtful that Paul will do it.

After verbs or expressions that indicate an emotion of joy, gladness, happiness, sorrow, regret, fear, surprise

estar contento que . . . / to be happy that . . . , to be pleased that . . .
estar feliz que . . . / to be happy that . . .
estar triste que . . . / to be sad that . . .
alegrarse (de) que . . . / to be glad that . . .
sentir que . . . / to regret that . . . , to feel sorry that . . .
sorprenderse (de) que . . . / to be surprised that . . .
temer que . . . / to fear that . . .
tener miedo (de) que . . . / to be afraid that . . .

EXAMPLES:

Estoy muy contento que mis amigos vengan a verme / I am very pleased that my friends are coming (will come) to see me.

Me alegro de que ellos hayan venido / I am glad that they have come.

Siento mucho que su madre esté enferma / I am very sorry that your mother is ill.

After certain verbs that imply a wish or desire that something be done, including a command, order, preference, advice, permission, request, plea, insistence, suggestion

aconsejar / to advise
consentir / to consent
decir / to tell (someone to do something)
dejar / to allow, to let
desear / to want, to wish
esperar / to hope
exigir / to demand, to require
hacer / to make (someone do something or that something be done)
insistir (en) / to insist (on, upon)
mandar / to order, to command
pedir / to ask, to request
permitir / to allow, to permit
preferir / to prefer
prohibir / to forbid, to prohibit
querer / to want, to wish (someone to do something or that something be done)
recomendar / to recommend
rogar / to beg, to request
sugerir / to suggest
suplicar / to beg, to plead, to make a plea

EXAMPLES:

Les aconsejo a ellos que hagan el trabajo / I advise them to do the work.

Les digo a ellos que escriban los ejercicios / I am telling them to write the exercises.

Mi madre quiere que yo vaya a la escuela ahora / My mother wants me to go to school now.
BUT: **Yo quiero ir a la escuela ahora** / I want to go to school now.
NOTE: In this example, there is no change in subject; therefore, the infinitive **ir** is used. But in the previous example there is a new subject **(yo)** in the dependent clause and **ir** is in the subjunctive because the verb **querer** is used in the main clause.

El capitán me manda que yo entre / The captain orders me to come in.

OR: **El capitán me manda entrar** / The captain orders me to come in.
(NOTE that **mandar** can take a new clause in the subjunctive or it can take an infinitive.)

El coronel me permite que yo salga / The colonel permits me to leave.

OR: **El coronel me permite salir** / The colonel permits me to leave.
(NOTE that **permitir** can take a new clause in the subjunctive or it can take an infinitive. You can do the same with the verbs **dejar, hacer, mandar** and **prohibir.**)

Mi profesor exige que yo escriba los ejercicios / My professor demands that I write the exercises.

Espero que mi perrito vuelva pronto / I hope that my little dog returns soon.

Le ruego a usted que me devuelva mi libro / I beg you to return my book to me.

IN SUM, NOTE THAT:

(a) The subjunctive form of the verb in the dependent clause is used because what precedes is either a certain conjunction, a certain adverb, the expression **por + adj.** or **adv. + que,** a certain indefinite expression, an indefinite or negative antecedent, a superlative, an indirect wish or command or order introduced by **!Que . . . !** (which is short for "**Quiero que . . .** or "**Deje que . . .**"), **¡Ojalá que . . . !** or a certain impersonal expression, or a certain verb.

(b) When you are dealing with two different subjects, you need two clauses: the main clause (also known as independent clause) and the dependent clause which contains the new subject. When there is no change in subject, there is no need for a second clause.

(c) Generally speaking, only the verbs **dejar, hacer, mandar, permitir, prohibir** can be followed by just the infinitive or a new clause with its verb in the subjunctive.

(d) In English, it is possible not to use a second clause even when the subject changes and to use an infinitive, but this is not so in Spanish—except for what is noted. Example: I want you to leave / **Quiero que Ud. salga.**

EJERCICIOS

I. Escriba seis conjunciones en español que exigen el subjuntivo.

1. _____   4. _____

2. _____   5. _____

3. _____   6. _____

II. Cambie el verbo en infinitivo al presente de subjuntivo.

Modelo: Saldré a las tres y media a menos que (estar) lloviendo.

Escriba: Saldré a las tres y media a menos que esté lloviendo.

1. Se lo explico a ustedes a fin de que (poder) comprenderlo. _____

_____

2. Partiré a la una a menos que (estar) nevando. _____

_____

3. Le daré el dinero a Roberto cuando me lo (pedir). _____

4. Esperaré hasta que (llegar) el autobús. _____

_____

5. Trabajaré hasta que Ud. (venir). _____

_____

III. Escriba el verbo entre paréntesis en el presente de subjuntivo.

1. Tal vez ellos (haber) perdido. _____

2. Por más interesante que (ser), no quiero ver esa película. _____

3. No abriré la puerta, quienquiera que (ser). _____

4. Adondequiera que Ud. (ir), dígamelo. _____

5. Busco un libro que (ser) interesante. _____

6. No encuentro a nadie que (saber) la respuesta. _____

7. Quiero que Juan lo (hacer). _____

8. ¡Que lo (hacer) Jorge! _____

9. ¡Ojalá que ellos (venir)! _____

10. ¡Ojalá que Juan (llegar)! _____

OPTIONAL EXERCISE FOR ENRICHMENT

IV. Escriba seis expresiones impersonales en español que exigen el subjuntivo.

1. _____   4. _____

2. _____   5. _____

3. _____   6. _____

V. Complete las oraciones a continuación, usando en cada una el presente de subjuntivo de los verbos en la siguiente lista. Cada verbo debe usarse solamente una vez.

hacer	venir
ser	ir
estar	escribir

1. Dudo que mis amigos _____ a verme.

2. No creo que _____ urgente.

3. Es dudoso que Pablo lo _____

4. Siento mucho que su madre _____ enferma.

5. Les digo a ellos que _____ los ejercicios.

6. Mi madre quiere que yo _____ a la escuela ahora.

VI. Cambie el verbo entre paréntesis a la forma correcta. No es necesario escribir toda la oración.

Modelos: **Mi profesor exige que yo (escribir) los ejercicios.** _____ escriba _____

Yo quiero (ir) al cine ahora. _____ ir _____

Mi madre quiere que yo (ir) al cine ahora. _____ vaya _____

1. El capitán me manda que yo (entrar). _____

2. El profesor me permite que yo (salir). _____

3. Espero que mi perrito (volver) pronto. _____

4. Le ruego a usted que me (devolver) mis discos. _____

5. Quiero (salir) ahora. _____

6. Quiero que Ud. (salir) ahora. _____

Possessive pronouns

Definition: A possessive pronoun is a word that takes the place of a noun to show possession, as in English: *mine, yours,* etc., instead of saying *my mother, your car,* etc.

You form a possessive pronoun by using the appropriate definite article (**el, la, los, las**) + the long form of the possessive adjective. As you realize by now, a pronoun must agree in gender and number with the noun it takes the place of. Therefore, a possessive pronoun must agree in gender and number with the noun it replaces. It does not agree with the possessor.

The possessive pronouns are:

ENGLISH MEANING	SINGULAR FORM (agreement in gender and number with the noun it replaces)	PLURAL FORM (agreement in gender and number with the noun it replaces)
1. mine	**el mío, la mía**	**los míos, las mías**
2. yours *(fam. sing.)*	**el tuyo, la tuya**	**los tuyos, las tuyas**
3. yours, his, hers, its	**el suyo, la suya**	**los suyos, las suyas**
1. ours	**el nuestro, la nuestra**	**los nuestros, las nuestras**
2. yours *(fam. pl.)*	**el vuestro, la vuestra**	**los vuestros, las vuestras**
3. yours, theirs	**el suyo, la suya**	**los suyos, las suyas**

EXAMPLES:

Mi hermano es más alto que el suyo / My brother is taller than yours (his, hers, theirs).
Su hermana es más alta que la mía / Your sister is taller than mine.
Mi casa es más grande que la suya / My house is larger than yours (his, hers, theirs).

In order to clarify the meanings of **el suyo, la suya, los suyos, las suyas** (since they can mean *yours, his, hers, its, theirs*), do the following: drop the **suyo** form, keep the appropriate definite article (**el, la, los, las**), and add, appropriately, any of the following: **de Ud., de él, de ella, de Uds., de ellos, de ellas:**

mi libro y el de Ud., mi casa y la de él, mis amigos y los de ella, mis amigas y las de Uds., mis libros y los de ellos, mis cuadernos y los de ellas / my book and yours, my house and his, my friends and hers, my friends and yours, *etc.)*

¿De quién es . . . ? ¿De quiénes es . . . ? ¿De quién son . . . ? ¿De quiénes son . . . ?
Whose is . . . ? Whose are . . . ?

Whose, when asking a question (usually at the beginning of a sentence), is expressed by any of the above. If you believe that the possessor is singular, use **¿De quién es . . . ?** If you think that the possessor is plural, use **¿De quiénes es . . . ?** And if the noun you have in mind (**whose . . .**) is plural, use the third person plural form of **ser:**

¿De quién es esta casa? / Whose is this house? **Es de mi tío** / It is my uncle's.
¿De quiénes es esta casa? / Whose is this house? **Es de mis amigos** / It is my friends'.
¿De quién son estos guantes? / Whose are these gloves? **Son de Juan** / They are John's.
¿De quiénes son estos niños? / Whose are these children? **Son de los Señores Pardo** /
    They are Mr. and Mrs. Pardo's.

NOTE that the verb **ser** is used in these expressions showing possession.

ALSO NOTE that if a possessive pronoun is used with the verb **ser,** the definite article is dropped:

¿De quién es este lápiz? / Whose is this pencil? **Es mío** / It is mine.
¿De quién son estas camisas? / Whose are these shirts? **Son suyas** / They are theirs (yours,
    his, hers). OR, to clarify **suyas,** say: **Son de Ud., Son de él, Son de ella,** etc. / They are
    yours, They are his, They are hers, etc.

Relative pronouns

Definition: A pronoun is a word that takes the place of a noun. A relative pronoun is a pronoun that refers (relates) to an **antecedent.** An antecedent is something that comes before something; it can be a word, a phrase, a clause which is replaced by a pronoun or some other substitute. Example: *Is it Mary who did that?* In this sentence, *who* is the relative pronoun and *Mary* is the antecedent. Another example, a longer one: *It seems to me that you are right, which is what I had thought right along.* The relative pronoun in this example is *which* and the antecedent of it is the clause, *that you are right.*

In Spanish, a relative pronoun can refer to an antecedent which is a person or a thing, or an idea. A relative pronoun can be subject or object of a verb, or object of a preposition.

Common relative pronouns

que / who, that, whom, which. This is the most common relative pronoun.

As subject referring to a person: La muchacha **que** habla con Juan es mi hermana / The girl
    who is talking with John is my sister.

Here, the relative pronoun **que** is subject of the verb **habla** and it refers to **la muchacha,** which is the subject of the verb **es.**

As subject referring to a thing: El libro **que** está en la mesa es mío / The book **which (that)** is
    on the table is mine.

Here, the relative pronoun **que** is subject of the verb **está** and it refers to **el libro,** which is the subject of **es.**

As direct object of a verb referring to a person: El señor Molina es el profesor **que** admiro /
    Mr. Molina is the professor **whom** I admire.

Here, the relative pronoun **que** is object of the verb form **admiro.** It refers to **el profesor.**

As direct object of a verb referring to a thing: La composición **que** Ud. lee es mía / The
    composition **(that, which)** you are reading is mine.

Here, the relative pronoun **que** is object of the verb form **lee.** It refers to **la composición,** which is the subject of **es.** The subject of **lee** is **Ud.**

NOTE here, in the English translation of this example, that we do not always have to use a relative pronoun in English. In Spanish, it must be stated.

As object of a preposition referring only to a thing: La cama **en que** duermo es grande / The bed **in which** I sleep is large.

Here, the relative pronoun **que** is object of the preposition **en.** It refers to **la cama.** Other prepositions used commonly with **que** are **a, con, de.**

As object of a preposition, **que** refers to a thing only—not to a person. Use **quien** or **quienes** as object of a preposition referring to persons.

quien / who (after a preposition, whom)

As subject of a verb referring only to persons: Yo sé **quien** lo hizo / I know **who** did it.

Here, **quien** is the subject of **hizo.** It does not refer to a specific antecedent. Here, **quien** includes its antecedent.

When used as a subject, **quien** (or **quienes,** if plural) can also mean *he who, she who, the one who, the ones who, those who.* In place of **quien** or **quienes** in this sense, you can also use **el que, la que, los que, las que:**

Quien escucha oye / Who listens hears; He who listens hears; She who listens hears; The one who listens hears.

OR: **El que escucha** oye / He who listens hears; **La que escucha** oye / She who listens hears; The one who listens hears.

Quienes escuchan oyen / Who listen hear; Those who listen hear; The ones who listen hear.

OR: **Los que escuchan** oyen; **Las que escuchan** oyen / Those who listen hear; The ones who listen hear.

As subject of a verb, the relative pronoun **quien** may be used instead of **que** referring only to persons when it is the subject of a non-restrictive dependent clause set off by commas; La señora Gómez, **quien** (or **que**) es profesora, conoce a mi madre / Mrs. Gómez, who is a teacher, knows my mother.

As direct object of a verb referring only to persons, the relative pronoun **quien** or **quienes** may be used with the personal **a (a quien, a quienes)** instead of **que:** La muchacha **que** (*or* **a quien**) Ud. vio al baile es mi hermana / The girl **whom** you saw at the dance is my sister.

As object of a preposition referring only to persons: ¿Conoces a la chica **con quien** tomé el almuerzo? / Do you know the girl **with whom** I had lunch? ¿Conoces a los chicos **con quienes** María tomó el almuerzo? / Do you know the boys **with whom** Mary had lunch? ¿Conoce Ud. a los hombres **de quienes** hablo? / Do you know the men **of whom (about whom)** I am talking?

el cual, la cual, los cuales, las cuales / who, that, whom, which, the one which, the ones which, the one who, the ones who.

These relative pronouns may be used in place of **que.** This can be especially needed when it is desired to clarify the gender and number of **que:** La madre de José, **la cual** es muy inteligente, es dentista / Joseph's mother, **who** is very intelligent, is a dentist.

These substitute relative pronouns may also refer to things: El libro, **el cual** está sobre la mesa, es mío / The book, **which (the one which)** is on the table, is mine.

These relative pronouns may also be used as substitutes for **el que, la que, los que, las que** when used as the subject of a non-restrictive dependent clause set off by commas: La señora Gómez, **la cual** (or **la que,** or **quien,** or **que**) es profesora, conoce a mi madre / Mrs. Gómez, **who** is a teacher, knows my mother.

These relative pronouns, as well as **el que, la que, los que, las que,** are used as objects of prepositions except with **a, con, de, en**—in which case the relative pronoun **que** is preferred with things. These relative pronouns **(el cual, la cual, los cuales, las cuales** and **el que, la que, los que, las que)** are commonly used with the following prepositions: **para, por, sin,**

ya

Precio: 45 pesetas • LA EDITORIAL CATOLICA, S. A. • AÑO XLIX - N.º 14.378 - Depósito legal: M. 11-1958

Richard Burton muere en Suiza

El actor británico Richard Burton murió de una hemorragia cerebral en una clínica suiza, donde le ingresaron ya inconsciente. El famoso actor, nacido en Gales, tenía cincuenta y nueve años. Comenzó su carrera artística en el teatro, donde se especializó en las obras de Shakespeare. En su filmografía figuran títulos tan importantes como «La fierecilla domada», «Cleopatra», «El espía que vino del frío», «La túnica sagrada» y «¿Quién teme a Virginia Wool», que protagonizó con Elizabeth Taylor, con la que estuvo casado en varias ocasiones. (Página 26)

Primera medalla para España

Dos remeros españoles, Fernando Climent y Luis María Lasúrtegui, consiguieron ayer la medalla de plata en la prueba de dos sin timonel, la primera medalla española de estos Juegos Olímpicos y la primera medalla que consigue el remo español en unas Olimpiadas. La prueba fue ganada por la tripulación rumana.

También hubo españoles en la final de cuatro scull, pero en esta prueba hubo que conformarse con diploma olímpico, ya que nuestros representantes entraron en sexta posición. Empezaron bien, pero al final acabarían superados por el resto de los competidores.

(Página 17)

Cuadernillo especial sobre los Juegos Olímpicos, con coleccionable gráfico, en páginas centrales

Los jueces de Madrid piden «cerebros electrónicos»

Según el decano, «la capital de España es la población con mayor índice criminal del país»

Los datos de la última memoria judicial, a la que ha tenido acceso YA, revelan que se han incrementado los registros de domicilios y las intervenciones de teléfonos y correspondencia

(Página 4)

Muchas posibilidades para aprender idiomas en el extranjero

Precios y programas para casi todos los bolsillos

(Página 24)

Atentado contra el Palacio de Justicia de Amberes

La Policía belga sospecha de la organización terrorista ETA como posible autora de la colocación de una bomba en el Palacio de Justicia de Amberes, que causó importantes daños materiales, pero ninguna víctima. La bomba se encontraba en el despacho del presidente de la Cámara de Comercio, y destruyó los pisos segundo y tercero, los espesos muros del edificio e incluso parte del techo, como puede observarse en la fotografía de Efe/Ap, resultaron seriamente dañados. (Página 7)

Nieto, campeón del mundo 1984

Al entrar victorioso ayer en el, para otros temible, circuito inglés de Silverstone, a nuestro campeón le han sobrado carreras para ganar el Campeonato del Mundo 1984. Y van trece. Trece campeonatos mundiales, ochenta y nueve grandes premios, en todos los lugares del mundo han visto cómo el zamorano recorría en triunfo sus circuitos. La imagen de Nieto dejando atrás a sus rivales es ya a estas alturas algo cotidiano y no por ello menos meritorio. (Amplia información en página 21)

delante de, cerca de, and **sobre:** En este cuarto, hay una gran ventana **por la cual** se ve el sol por la mañana / In this room, there is a large window **through which** you (one, anyone) can see the sun in the morning.

These compound relative pronouns (**el cual, el que,** *etc.*) refer to persons as well as things and can be used as subject of a verb or direct object of a verb when used in a non-restrictive dependent clause separated from its antecedent and set off with commas.

lo cual / which; **lo que** / what, that which

These are neuter compound relative pronouns. They do not refer to an antecedent of any gender or number. That is why they are called *neuter.*

Lo cual or **lo que** are used to refer to a statement, a clause, an idea: Mi hijo Juan estudia sus lecciones todos los días, **lo cual** es bueno / My son John studies his lessons every day, **which** is good. Mi hija recibió buenas notas, **lo que** me gustó / My daughter received good marks, **which** pleased me.

Lo que is also used to express *what* in the sense of *that which:* Comprendo **lo que** Ud. dice / I understand **what (that which)** you say. **Lo que** Ud. dice es verdad / **What (That which)** you say is true.

cuanto = todo lo que / all that

As a relative pronoun, **cuanto** may be used in place of **todo lo que: Todo lo que** Ud. dice es verdad: OR: **Cuanto** Ud. dice es verdad / **All that (All that which)** you say is true.

cuyo, cuya, cuyos, cuyas / whose

This word (and its forms as given) refers to persons and things. Strictly speaking, **cuyo,** *etc.* is not regarded as a relative pronoun but rather as a relative possessive adjective. It agrees in gender and number with what is possessed (whose . . .), not with the possessor. Its position is directly in front of the noun it modifies. Examples:

El señor García, **cuyos hijos** son inteligentes, es profesor / Mr. García, **whose children** are intelligent, is a professor.

La muchacha, **cuyo padre** es profesor, es inteligente / The girl, **whose father** is a professor, is intelligent.

El muchacho, **cuya madre** es profesora, es inteligente / The boy, **whose mother** is a professor, is intelligent.

The forms of **cuyo** cannot be used as an interrogative when you ask: Whose is . . . ? You must use **de quién: ¿De quién es este libro?**

When referring to parts of the body, use **a quien** instead of **cuyo:** La niña, **a quien** la madre lavó las manos, es bonita / The child, **whose** hands the mother washed, is pretty.

EJERCICIOS

I. Escriba, en inglés, una definición de un pronombre posesivo. Dé ejemplos.

_____

_____

_____

_____

_____

_____

II. Llene los blancos con los pronombres posesivos, en español, naturalmente.

ENGLISH MEANING	SINGULAR FORM (agreement in gender and number with the noun it replaces)	PLURAL FORM (agreement in gender and number with the noun it replaces)
Singular		
1. mine	_____	_____
2. yours *(fam. sing.)*	_____	_____
3. yours, his, hers, its	_____	_____
Plural		
1. ours	_____	_____
2. yours *(fam. pl.)*	_____	_____
3. yours, theirs	_____	_____

III. Traduzca al español.

1. My brother is taller than yours. _____

2. Your sister is taller than mine. _____

3. My house is larger than theirs. _____

4. Whose is this house? It is my uncle's. _____

5. Whose is this car? It is my parents'. _____

6. Whose are these gloves? They are John's. _____

7. Whose are these children? They are Mr. and Mrs. Pardo's. _____

8. Whose is this pencil? It's mine. _____

9. Whose are these shirts? They're theirs. _____

10. Whose is this skirt? It's Jane's. _____

IV. Escriba, en inglés, una definición de un pronombre relativo. Dé ejemplos.

_____

_____

_____

_____

_____

_____

V. Llene los blancos con **quien** o **que.**

1. La muchacha _____ habla con Juan es mi hermana.

2. _____ escucha oye.

3. El libro _____ está en la mesa es mío.

4. El muchacho _____ Ud. vio al baile es mi hermano.

5. El señor Molina es el profesor _____ admiro.

VI. Llene los blancos con **el cual, la cual, los cuales,** o **las cuales.**

1. La madre de José, _____ es muy inteligente, es dentista.

2. El padre de Juana, _____ es médico, está enfermo hoy.

3. En este cuarto, hay dos ventanas por _____ se ve el sol por la mañana.

4. Aquellos hombres, cerca de _____ está mi padre, son mis tíos.

VII. Llene los blancos con **cuyo, cuya, cuyos,** o **cuyas.**

1. El señor García, _____ hijos son inteligentes, es profesor.

2. La muchacha, _____ padre es profesor, es inteligente.

3. El muchacho, _____ madre es profesora, es inteligente también.

4. El señor Villanueva, _____ hijas son bonitas, es muy rico.

VIII. En español hay muchas palabras que se escriben y se pronuncian idénticamente, pero un signo de acento es necesario para distinguir su significado.

Ejemplo:

mi *poss, adj., 1st pers., sing.* / my
mí *obj. of a prep.* / me

¡Es mi caramelo! ¡Es para mí! It's my caramel! It's for me!

---

este *dem. adj., masc., sing.* / this
éste *dem. pron., masc., sing.* / this one

Este té es para ti y éste es para él. This tea is for you and this one is for him.

Mnemonic tip	The accent mark on **éste** is a signal for *this one*.

---

estos *dem. adj., masc., pi.* / these
éstos *dem. pron., masc., pl.* / these (*not* these ones)

Estos caramelos son para mí y éstos son para ti. These caramels are for me and these are for you.

Mnemonic tip	The accent mark on **éstos** is a signal for *these*, a demonstrative pronoun.

IX. En español hay muchas palabras que se escriben y se pronuncian idénticamente, pero un signo de acento es necesario para distinguir su significado.

Ejemplo:

esta *dem. adj., fem., sing.* / this
ésta *dem. pron., fem., sing.* / this one

Esta bicicleta es para ti y ésta es para mí. This bicycle is for you and this one is for me.

> Mnemonic tip
>
> The accent mark on **ésta** is a signal for *this one.*

---

ese *dem. adj., masc., sing.* / that
ése *dem. pron., masc., sing.* / that one

Ese anzuelo es para él y ése es para ella. That fish hook is for him and that one is for her.

> Mnemonic tip
>
> The accent mark on **ése** is a signal for *that one.*

> Mnemonic tip
>
> The letter *t* on **este** (this) drops off and falls to the wayside on its way to **ese anzuelo** (that fish hook).

> Mnemonic tip
>
> *This* and *these* have the *t*'s and *that* and *those* don't:
>
> **este libro, estos libros** (this book, these books)
> **ese libro, esos libros** (that book, those books)
>
> **esta carta, estas cartas** (this letter, these letters)
> **esa carta, esas cartas** (that letter, those letters)

X. Complete este crucigrama.

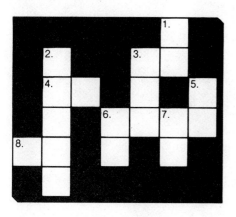

VERTICALES

1. Personal pron. as subject, 1st pers., sing.
2. Personal pron. as subject, 3rd pers., sing.
3. Indirect obj. pron., 3rd pers., pl.
5. Direct obj. pron., 3rd pers., sing., fem.
6. Personal pron., as object of a prep., 3rd pers., sing., masc.
7. Subject pron., 2nd pers., sing.

HORIZONTALES

3. Direct obj. pron., 3rd pers., sing., masc.
4. Reflexive pron., 3rd pers., sing. & pl.
6. Demonstrative pron., fem., sing.
8. Direct & indirect obj. pron., 1st pers., sing.

189

The Duchess of Alba *by Francisco José de GOYA y Lucientes (1746–1828)*
Courtesy of The Hispanic Society of America (Museum and Library), New York, N.Y.

Santuario de Loyola, Azpeitia (Guipúzcoa), España
Courtesy of Spanish National Tourist Office, New York, N.Y.

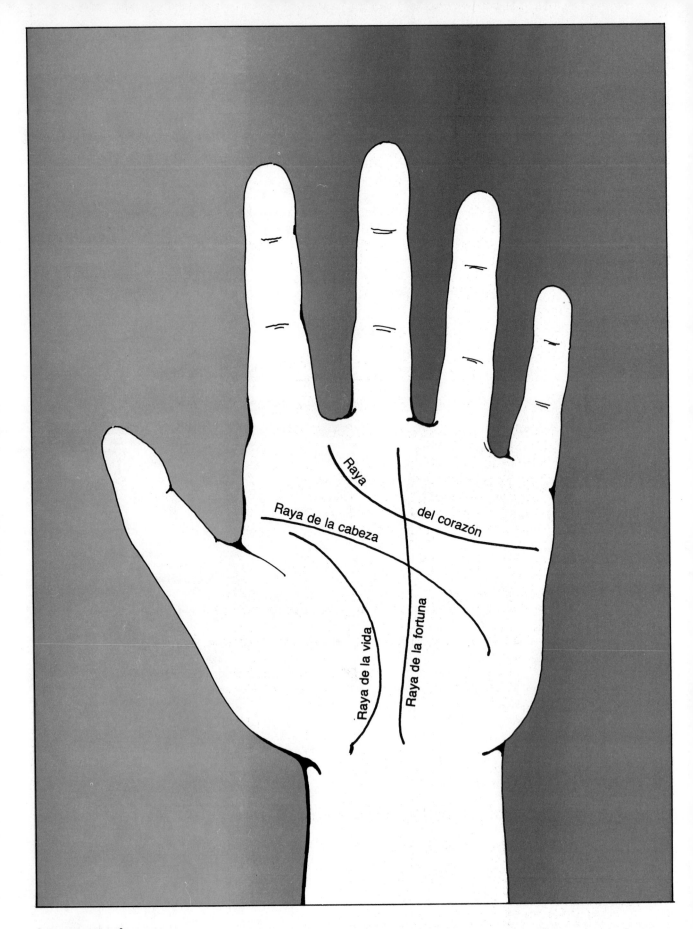

Los secretos de su mano

Some people like to have their palms read. It
can be fun—believe it or not.

Los secretos de su mano

Clara y Francisco Rodríguez fueron a la feria el sábado pasado. Allá, se divirtieron mucho. Vieron varias exposiciones, compraron muchas cosas, comieron mucho. También, entraron en la tienda de una quiromántica para que ella les leyera las rayas de las manos.

—¡Mira! ¡Francisco! ¡Una quiromántica!—exclamó Clara.

—¿Dónde?—le preguntó Francisco a Clara.   5

—Aquí, delante de nosotros. ¿No ves el anuncio?

> La señora Sabelotodo,
> quiromántica,
> revela los secretos de su mano.

—Francisco, yo quisiera entrar para saber el porvenir. ¿Quieres entrar conmigo?—preguntó su esposa.

—Sí, sí, estoy dispuesto. Pero, tú sabes bien que no creeré nada—dijo su esposo. Entraron en la tienda de la quiromántica.   10

—¿Podemos entrar, señora?—preguntó Clara.

—Sí, sí. ¡Entren! ¡Entren!—contestó la señora Sabelotodo.

—Me gustaría mucho que usted leyera las rayas de mi mano. Y las de mi marido también—dijo Clara.

—¡Bueno!—dijo la quiromántica—. Siéntese, señora, por favor. Y deme la mano,   15
señora.

La señora Sabelotodo mira fijamente la mano de Clara y comienza a leer las rayas.

—¡Ah! Veo en la raya de la fortuna que usted va a hacer un viaje a Australia con un hombre—, exclama la señora Sabelotodo.

—¡No me diga! ¡Es extraño! Mi marido y yo comenzamos a hacer preparaciones para un   20
viaje a Australia.

—Ahora—, dice la señora Sabelotodo, estoy mirando la raya del corazón. Veo que usted está enamorada de un hombre.

—¡No me diga! ¡Es extraño! Ud. tiene razón. ¡Estoy enamorada de mi marido!

—Ahora, señor, siéntese y deme la mano—, dice la señora Sabelotodo.   25
El señor Rodríguez se sienta y le da la mano a la quiromántica.

—¡Ah! Veo en la raya de la fortuna que usted va a hacer un viaje a Australia con una mujer—, exclama la señora Sabelotodo.

—¡No me diga! ¡Es extraño! Mi esposa y yo comenzamos a hacer preparaciones para un viaje a Australia.   30

—Ahora—, dice la señora Sabelotodo, estoy mirando la raya del corazón. Veo que usted está enamorado de una mujer.

—¡No me diga! ¡Es extraño! Ud. tiene razón. ¡Estoy enamorado de mi esposa! La mano revela todo, ¿no es verdad?

—Sí, señor, las rayas de la mano revelan los secretos de su vida. Cuesta cien pesetas   35
por las revelaciones.

Francisco da las cien pesetas a la señora Sabelotodo.

Afuera, Clara dice a Francisco:

—La señora Sabelotodo lo sabe todo, ¿no es verdad?

—Sí. La señora Sabelotodo lo sabe todo, pero yo no aprendí nada.   40

—Ni yo tampoco. Ya sabemos que vamos a hacer un viaje a Australia, y que estamos enamorados. ¿Verdad?

—¡Verdad! responde Francisco.

VOCABULARIO: Consult the vocabulary section in the back pages.

EJERCICIOS

I. Seleccione la respuesta correcta conforme al significado de la lectura en esta lección.

1. Clara y Francisco Rodríguez fueron a _____ el sábado pasado.
   (a) México (b) Australia (c) Inglaterra (d) la feria   _____

2. Delante de ellos, Clara y Francisco Rodríguez vieron
   (a) un anuncio (b) a una quiromántica (c) el porvenir (d) muchos secretos   _____

3. A Clara le gustaría mucho saber
   (a) si Francisco está dispuesto (b) el porvenir (c) cuando van a comer
   (d) cuando van a regresar a casa   _____

4. La quiromántica comienza a leer
   (a) el anuncio (b) un gran libro (c) las rayas de la mano (d) una carta   _____

5. La quiromántica ve en la raya de la fortuna de Clara que va a hacer un viaje
   (a) al Canadá (b) a Australia (c) a Puerto Rico (d) a los Estados Unidos   _____

6. Cuando la quiromántica examina la raya del corazón de la señora Rodríguez, ve que ésta
   (a) va a hacer un viaje (b) tiene dolor de cabeza (c) comienza a hacer preparaciones para un viaje (d) está enamorada de un hombre   _____

7. La señora Sabelotodo dice a Francisco que él está
   (a) enfermo (b) dispuesto (c) loco (d) enamorado   _____

8. Francisco está enamorado de
   (a) la quiromántica (b) Australia (c) su esposa (d) la señora Sabelotodo   _____

9. El señor Rodríguez paga _____ pesetas por las revelaciones.
   (a) diez (b) veinte (c) treinta (d) cien   _____

10. Cuando Clara y Francisco están afuera, dicen que
    (a) va a llover (b) van a regresar a casa (c) hace un tiempo magnífico (d) no
    aprendieron nada   _____

II. ¿Sí o No?

1. En la feria, Clara y Francisco se divirtieron mucho. _____

2. Clara y Francisco entraron en la tienda de la quiromántica para saber el porvenir. _____

3. Francisco no quiere entrar en la tienda de la quiromántica. _____

4. Francisco creerá todo lo que dirá la quiromántica. _____

5. Clara y Francisco están enamorados. _____

III. Sopa de letras (Alphabet soup). Busque las formas de los cuatro verbos expresados abajo en el imperfecto de subjuntivo, primera y tercera personas en el singular. Las cuatro formas pueden aparecer de derecha a izquierda, de izquierda a derecha, de abajo arriba y viceversa, y en diagonal.

dar   decir   leer   querer

D	I	E	R	A	L	A	E	I
I	A	E	A	R	E	J	I	D
D	J	I	E	R	Y	D	I	O
L	Y	E	R	A	E	N	A	M
P	R	E	T	Y	R	A	J	Y
D	I	J	E	P	A	L	C	O
Q	U	I	S	I	E	R	A	L

Estructuras de la lengua

Tense No. 7: Imperfecto de subjuntivo (Imperfect subjunctive)

This past tense is used for the same reasons as the **presente de subjuntivo**—that is, after certain verbs, conjunctions, impersonal expressions, etc., which were explained and illustrated in Work Unit 10. The main difference between these two tenses is the time of the action.

If the verb in the main clause is in the present indicative or future or present perfect indicative or imperative, the *present subjunctive* or the *present perfect subjunctive* is used in the dependent clause—provided, of course, that there is some element which requires the use of the subjunctive.

However, if the verb in the main clause is in the imperfect indicative, preterit, conditional, or pluperfect indicative, the *imperfect subjunctive* (this tense) or *pluperfect subjunctive* is ordinarily used in the dependent clause—provided, of course, that there is some element which requires the use of the subjunctive.

EXAMPLES:
1. *Insistí* en que María lo **hiciera** / I insisted that Mary *do* it.
2. Se lo *explicaba* a María **para que lo comprendiera** / I was explaining it to Mary *so that she might understand it*.

NOTE that the *imperfect subjunctive* is used after **como si** to express a condition contrary to fact.
EXAMPLE:
Me habla como si **fuera** un niño / He speaks to me as if *I were* a child.

NOTE: In this last example, the subjunctive is used in English also for the same reason.

Finally, note that **quisiera** (the imperfect subjunctive or **querer**) can be used to express in a very polite way, *I should like:* **Quisiera hablar ahora** / I should like to speak now.

The imperfect subjunctive is regularly formed as follows:
For all verbs, drop the **ron** ending of the 3rd pers. pl. of the preterit and add the following endings:

ra, ras, ra;   OR   **se, ses, se;**
ramos, rais, ran   **semos, seis, sen**

The only accent mark on the forms of the imperfect subjunctive is on the 1st pers. pl. form **(nosotros)** and it is placed on the vowel which is right in front of the ending **ramos** or **semos.**

EXAMPLES:

Preterit, 3rd pers. plural	Imperfect subjunctive
bebieron (beber)	bebiera, bebieras, bebiera; bebiéramos, bebierais, bebieran
	OR
	bebiese, bebieses, bebiese; bebiésemos, bebieseis, bebiesen
creyeron (creer)	creyera, creyeras, creyera; creyéramos, creyerais, creyeran
	OR
	creyese, creyeses, creyese; creyésemos, creyeseis, creyesen
dieron (dar)	diera, dieras, diera; diéramos, dierais, dieran
	OR
	diese, dieses, diese; diésemos, dieseis, diesen
dijeron (decir)	dijera, dijeras, dijera; dijéramos, dijerais, dijeran
	OR
	dijese, dijeses, dijese; dijésemos, dijeseis, dijesen
durmieron (dormir)	durmiera, durmieras, durmiera; durmiéramos, durmierais, durmieran
	OR
	durmiese, durmieses, durmiese; durmiésemos, durmieseis, durmiesen
hubieron (haber)	hubiera, hubieras, hubiera; hubiéramos, hubieras, hubieran
	OR
	hubiese, hubieses, hubiese; hubiésemos, hubieseis, hubiesen
hablaron (hablar)	hablara, hablaras, hablara; habláramos, hablarais, hablaran
	OR
	hablase, hablases, hablase; hablásemos, hablaseis, hablasen
hicieron (hacer)	hiciera, hicieras, hiciera; hiciéramos, hicierais, hicieran
	OR
	hiciese, hicieses, hiciese; hiciésemos, hicieseis, hiciesen

fueron (ir)	**fuera, fueras, fuera;** **fuéramos, fuerais, fueran**
	OR
	fuese, fueses, fuese; **fuésemos, fueseis, fuesen**
leyeron (leer)	**leyera, leyeras, leyera;** **leyéramos, leyerais, leyeran**
	OR
	leyese, leyeses, leyese; **leyésemos, leyeseis, leyesen**
recibieron (recibir)	**recibiera, recibieras, recibiera;** **recibiéramos, recibierais, recibieran**
	OR
	recibiese, recibieses, recibiese; **recibiésemos, recibieseis, recibiesen**
fueron (ser)	**fuera, fueras, fuera;** **fuéramos, fuerais, fueran**
	OR
	fuese, fueses, fuese; **fuésemos, fueseis, fuesen**
tuvieron (tener)	**tuviera, tuvieras, tuviera;** **tuviéramos, tuvierais, tuvieran**
	OR
	tuviese, tuvieses, tuviese; **tuviésemos, tuvieseis, tuviesen**

Using the first three examples given above **(beber, creer, dar),** the usual English equivalents are as follows:

(that I) might drink, (that you) might drink, (that he/she) might drink, *etc.*
(that I) might believe, (that you) might believe, (that he/she) might believe, *etc.*
(that I) might give, (that you) might give, (that he/she) might give, *etc.*

EJERCICIOS

I. Explique en inglés, en breve, cómo se forma regularmente el imperfecto de subjuntivo.

_____

_____

_____

II. Cambie el verbo en infinitivo al imperfecto de subjuntivo.

Modelo: **Clara entró en la tienda de la quiromántica para que ésta**
leer **las rayas de su mano.**

Escriba: **leyera**

1. Yo insistí en que María lo *hacer.*   _____

197

2. Se lo explicaba a María para que lo *comprender*. _____

3. Ud. me habla como si *ser* un niño. _____

4. La madre pidió a la niña que *beber* la leche. _____

5. El señor Rodríguez exigió que Pedro *estudiar* sus lecciones. _____

6. Dudé que José lo *aprender*. _____

7. Me alegraba de que *venir* Elena. _____

8. Temí que el alumno no *decir* la verdad. _____

9. La profesora no creía que Roberto *contestar* correctamente. _____

10. Cristóbal esperaba que Adela *telefonear*. _____

III. Acróstico. Complete enteramente en español los doce verbos expresados abajo en el imperfecto de subjuntivo, primera y tercera personas, en el singular.

1. querer	4. reír	7. aprender	10. invitar
2. usar	5. olvidar	8. nacer	11. caer
3. insistir	6. matar	9. tener	12. abrir

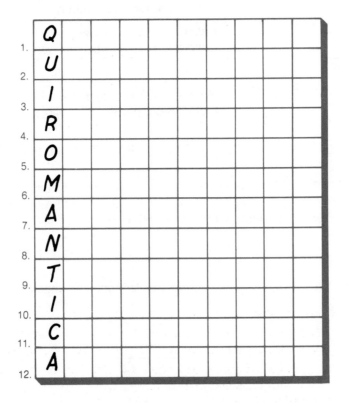

EXCLAMATORY ¡Qué . . . !

In English, when we exclaim *What a class! What a student!* we use the indefinite article *a* or *an*. In Spanish, however, we do not use the indefinite article:

¡Qué clase! ¡Qué alumno! ¡Qué alumna! ¡Qué idea!

If an adjective is used to describe the noun, we generally use **más** in front of the adjective, or **tan,** in order to intensify the exclamation:

¡Qué chica tan bonita! / What a pretty girl!
¡Qué libro más interesante! / What an interesting book!

When we use **¡Qué!** + an adjective, the meaning in English is *How . . . !*

¡Qué difícil es! / How difficult it is!

¿Para qué . . . ? and **¿Por qué . . . ?**
Both of these interrogatives mean *why* but they are not used interchangeably. If by *why* you mean *for what reason,* use **¿por qué . . . ?** If by *why* you mean *for what purpose (what for?)* use **¿para qué . . . ?**

Juanita, ¿Por qué lloras? / Jeanie, why [for what reason] are you crying?
Mamá, ¿para qué tenemos uñas? / Mom, why [what for, for what purpose] do we have fingernails?
¿Para qué sirven los anteojos? / What [why, what for, for what purpose] are eyeglasses used for?

EJERCICIOS

I. Escriba cuatro frases empleando **¡Qué . . . !**

1. ¡Qué _____!   3. ¡Qué _____!

2. ¡Qué _____!   4. ¡Qué _____!

II. Escriba dos oraciones empleando **¿Por qué . . .** y dos oraciones empleando **¿Para qué . . .**

1. ¿Por qué _____?   3. ¿Para qué _____?

2. ¿Por qué _____?   4. ¿Para qué _____?

III. Conteste las siguientes preguntas con oraciones completas.

1. ¿Por qué lloras? _____

2. ¿Para qué sirven los anteojos? _____

_____

3. ¿Por qué llora el niño? _____

GUSTAR

(a) Essentially, the verb **gustar** means *to be pleasing to . . .*

(b) In English, we say, for example, *I like ice cream.* In Spanish, we say **Me gusta el helado;** that is to say, "Ice cream is pleasing to me" [To me ice cream is pleasing].

(c) In English, the thing that you like is the direct object. In Spanish, the thing that you like is the subject. Also, in Spanish, the person who likes the thing is the indirect object: to me, to you, *etc.:* **A Roberto le gusta el helado** / Robert likes ice cream; in other words, "To Robert, ice cream is pleasing to him."

(d) In Spanish, therefore, the verb **gustar** is used in the third person, either in the singular or plural, when you talk about something that you like—something that is pleasing to you. Therefore, the verb form must agree with the subject; if the thing liked is singular, the verb is third person singular; if the thing liked is plural, the verb **gustar** is third person plural: **Me gusta el café** / I like coffee; **Me gustan el café y la leche** / I like coffee and milk ["Coffee and milk are pleasing to me."]

(e) When you mention the person or the persons who like something, you must use the preposition **a** in front of the person; you must also use the indirect object pronoun of the noun which is the person:

A los muchachos y a las muchachas les gusta jugar / Boys and girls like to play; that is to say, "To play is pleasing to them, to boys and girls."

(f) Review the indirect object pronouns. They are: **me, te, le; nos, os, les.**

(g) Other examples:

Me gusta leer / I like to read.
Te gusta leer / You *(familiar)* like to read.
A Felipe le gusta el helado / Philip likes ice cream.
Al chico le gusta la leche / The boy likes milk.
A Carlota le gusta bailar / Charlotte likes to dance.
A las chicas les gustó el libro / The girls liked the book.
Nos gustó el cuento / We liked the story.
¿Le gusta a Ud. el español? / Do you like Spanish?
A Pedro y a Ana les gustó la película / Peter and Anna liked the film.
A mi amigo le gustaron los chocolates / My friend liked the chocolates; that is to say, the chocolates were pleasing [pleased] to him (to my friend).

EJERCICIOS

I. Traduzca las siguientes oraciones.

1. Me gusta el helado. _____

2. A Roberto le gusta el chocolate. _____

3. A Miguel le gusta la cereza. _____

4. Me gustan el café y la leche. _____

5. A los muchachos y a las muchachas les gusta jugar. _____

6. ¿Le gusta a usted leer? _____

7. Sí, me gusta leer. _____

8. ¿Te gusta comer? _____

9. ¿Le gusta a Ud. el español? _____

10. A Pedro y a Ana les gustó la película. _____

II. Conteste las siguientes preguntas afirmativamente con oraciones completas. En la oración (a) use la palabra **Sí.** En la oración (b) use la palabra **también,** según los modelos.

Modelos: a. **¿Le gusta a Ud. el helado?**   Escriba: a. **Sí. Me gusta el helado.**
        b. **¿Y a los chicos?**   b. **Sí. A los chicos, también, les gusta el helado.**

1. a. ¿Le gusta a Ud. el español? _____

   b. ¿Y a los otros alumnos? _____

2. a. ¿Te gusta leer? _____

   b. ¿Y a tu hermano? _____

     _____

3. a. ¿A Carlota le gustan los pasteles y el helado? _____

     _____

   b. ¿Y a usted? _____

     _____

III. Varias palabras en una sola. Utilizando las letras en **PUERTO RICO,** ¿cuántas palabras puede usted escribir? Escriba cinco palabras, por lo menos.

PUERTO RICO

1. _____   2. _____   3. _____

    4. _____   5. _____

IV. Algunos alumnos confunden las palabras jueves y huevos.

jueves *n.m.* Thursday
huevos *n.m., pl.* eggs

Me gusta comer huevos los jueves. I like to eat eggs on Thursdays.

Mnemonic tip

Jueves is the day before **viernes;**
j precedes **v** in the alphabet;
jueves and **viernes** both end in **es.**
Huevos, therefore, is the word that
means eggs. Pronounce the j in **jueves**
as the English *h* in *hello* but do not
pronounce the *h* in **huevo** or **huevos.**

¿Qué palabras españolas confunde usted? ¿Puede Ud. dar un "mnemonic tip"?

V. En español hay muchas palabras que se escriben y se pronuncian idénticamente, pero un signo de acento es necesario para distinguir su significado.

Ejemplo:

te *reflexive pronoun, 2nd person, singular* / yourself
 also direct & indirect object pronoun, 2nd person, singular / you, to you

té *n.m.* tea

 ¿Te gusta el té? / Do you like tea?

 ¿Cuántas palabras españolas puede Ud. decir y escribir?

VI. Practique el uso del verbo gustar en el condicional, por ejemplo: Me gustaría una taza de café / I would like a cup of coffee.

Ejemplo:

Me gustaría tener (I would like to have)	**mantequilla** / butter **pan** / bread **pimienta** / pepper **chile con carne** / chili with meat **sal** / salt **una servilleta** / a napkin **una rosa** / a rose **una casita** / a little house **una muñeca** / a doll **un tenedor** / a fork

¿Cuántos nombres puede Ud. añadir?

Mnemonic tip	**Una moneda** is a coin. **El dinero** is money. You need **dinero** to buy yourself a dinner.

VII. HUMOR. La adivinanza para hoy.

Vuelo como un pájaro. ¿Qué soy?

Respuesta: _____

Sequence of tenses when the subjunctive is required: a summary

When the verb in the main clause is in the:	The verb in the following clause (the dependent clause) most likely will be in the:
1. Present Indicative or Future or Present Perfect Indicative or Imperative (Command)	1. Present Subjunctive or Present Perfect Subjunctive
2. Conditional or a past tense (Imperfect Indicative or Preterit or Pluperfect Indicative)	2. Imperfect Subjunctive or Pluperfect Subjunctive

EXAMPLES:

Deseo que Ana cante / I want Anna to sing.

Le diré a Ana que baile / I will tell Anna to dance.

Le he dicho a Ana que cante y baile / I have said to Anna to sing and dance.

Dígale a Ana que cante y baile / Tell Anna to sing and dance.

Dudo que mi madre tome el tren / I doubt that my mother is taking (or will take) the train.

Dudo que mi madre haya tomado el tren / I doubt that my mother has taken the train.

Le gustaría al profesor que los alumnos hicieran los ejercicios / The professor would like the pupils to do the exercises.

Sentía que su madre estuviera enferma / I felt sorry that your mother was ill.

Dudé que mi madre hubiera tomado el tren / I doubted that my mother had taken the train.

Si clause: a summary of contrary-to-fact conditions

When the verb in the **Si** clause is:	The verb in the main or result clause is:
1. Present Indicative	1. Future

EXAMPLE:

Si tengo bastante tiempo, vendré a verle / If I have enough time, I will come to see you.

Note that the present subjunctive form of a verb is never used in a clause beginning with the conjunction *si*.

2. Imperfect Subjunctive (**-se** form or **-ra** form)	2. Conditional or Imperfect Subjunctive (**-ra** form)

EXAMPLE:

Si yo tuviese (or **tuviera**) **bastante tiempo, vendría a verle** / If I had enough time, I would come to see you.

OR: **Si yo tuviese** (or **tuviera**) **bastante tiempo, viniera a verle** / If I had enough time I would come to see you.

3. Pluperfect Subjunctive (**-se** form or **-ra** form)	3. Conditional Perfect or Pluperfect Subjunctive (**-ra** form)

EXAMPLE:

Si yo hubiese tenido (or **hubiera tenido**) **bastante tiempo, habría venido a verle** / If I had had enough time, I would have come to see you.

OR: **Si yo hubiese tenido** (or **hubiera tenido**) **bastante tiempo, hubiera venido a verle** / If I had had enough time, I would have come to see you.

Catedral de JAEN (Andalucía) España
Courtesy of Spanish National Tourist Office, New York, N. Y.

¡Adiós, señor! ¡Hasta mañana, señor!

*Have you ever received a note from a boy
or girl in a class at school? In this scene,
Pedro is reading a note that Lolita just
passed to him.*

Lolita

Pedro está en clase de matemáticas. Está leyendo una nota escondida en las páginas de su libro. He aquí la nota:

Pedro, querido mío;
   Detesto esta asignatura y detesto al profesor. Es un mal profesor de matemáticas. Es un hombre monstruoso.   5
   Te quiero, te amo, te adoro.

                                                                              Lolita

El maestro de matemáticas dice a Pedro:
   —Tú no has hecho la lección, tú no has escuchado nada esta mañana en la clase, tú no has aprendido nada hoy, tú no has escrito nada. No tienes nada   10
en la cabeza. ¿Qué tienes escondido en las páginas de tu libro?

   —Nada, señor, nada.

   —Sí, sí, tienes algo que estás leyendo. Es una nota, un billete como ayer y como anteayer. ¡Dámela!

Pedro se pone rojo. Mira hacia Lolita, su novia bonita, y ella le pide   15
cariñosamente con sus ojos azules, que Pedro no revele el amor secreto entre los dos, y que no entregue la nota al profesor.

En este momento, toca el timbre. La lección de matemáticas ha terminado. Todos los alumnos salen de la sala de clase inmediatamente y Pedro, también, con la nota escondida en las páginas de su libro.   20

Cuando Pedro está cerca de la puerta para salir, exclama:

   —¡Adiós, señor! ¡Hasta mañana, señor! ¡A buen fin no hay mal principio!

En el pasillo, Lolita dice a Pedro:

   —Querido mío, ¡eres magnífico!

   —Lolita, te amo. ¿Qué haces esta noche? ¿Vamos al cine?   25

VOCABULARIO: Consult the vocabulary section in the back pages.

EJERCICIOS

I. Seleccione la respuesta correcta conforme al significado de la lectura en esta lección.

1. Pedro y Lolita están (a) en casa (b) en la biblioteca (c) en la hierba
   (d) en la escuela   _____

2. Pedro está (a) estudiando su libro de matemáticas (b) escribiendo la lección
   (c) escuchando (d) enamorado de Lolita   _____   **207**

3. Lolita está (a) enferma (b) estudiando (c) escribiendo (d) enamorada de Pedro _____

4. Lolita ha escrito (a) la lección de matemáticas (b) en la pizarra (c) una nota (d) una carta al maestro de matemáticas _____

5. En la nota Lolita dice que (a) a ella le gusta mucho la asignatura (b) el maestro de matemáticas es simpático (c) el maestro de matemáticas es un hombre monstruoso (d) quiere al profesor

II. ¿Sí o No?

1. Lolita piensa que Pedro es magnífico. _____

2. Pedro quiere a Lolita. _____

3. Lolita quiere a Pedro. _____

4. El maestro de matemáticas es muy amable. _____

5. El maestro de esta asignatura es un hombre monstruoso. _____

III. **Sopa de letras** (Alphabet soup). **La palabra misteriosa** (the mystery word). En esta sopa de letras, busque las palabras expresadas abajo. Las palabras pueden aparecer de derecha a izquierda, de izquierda a derecha, de abajo arriba y viceversa, y en diagonal. La palabra que queda es la palabra misteriosa y contiene cuatro letras.

A	D	O	R	A	R	B
M	A	F	H	L	L	U
A	Z	I	A	G	E	E
R	U	N	Y	O	S	N
E	L	L	A	S	O	Y
P	O	R	A	M	O	R
A	Y	E	R	M	A	L

adorar   fin
algo   hay
amar   soy
ayer   mal
azul   buen
por   les
ella

Estructuras de la lengua

Tense No. 8: Perfecto de indicativo (Present perfect indicative)

This is the first of the seven compound tenses. This tense expresses an action that took place at no definite time in the past. It is also called Past Indefinite. It is a compound tense because it is formed with the present indicative of **haber** (the auxiliary or helping verb) plus the past participle of the verb you have in mind. Note the translation into English in the examples that follow.

1. (Yo) **he hablado** / I have spoken.
2. (Tú) no **has venido** a verme / You have not come to see me.
3. Elena **ha ganado** el premio / Helen has won the prize.

Es preciso saber las seis formas del verbo **haber** en el presente de indicativo para formar el perfecto de indicativo.

Singular	Plural
1. **he**	1. **hemos**
2. **has**	2. **habéis**
3. **ha**	3. **han**

Past participle: A past participle is a verb form which, in English, usually ends in -ed: for example, *worked, talked, arrived,* as in *I have worked, I have talked, I have arrived.* There are many irregular past participles in English; for example: *gone, sung,* as in *She has gone, We have sung.* In Spanish, a past participle is regularly formed as follows:

drop the **ar** of an **-ar** ending verb, like **trabajar,** and add **-ado: trabajado** / worked
drop the **er** of an **-er** ending verb, like **comer,** and add **-ido: comido** / eaten
drop the **ir** of an **-ir** ending verb, like **recibir,** and add **-ido: recibido** / received

Common irregular past participles are as follows.

Infinitive	Past Participle
abrir / to open	**abierto** / opened
caer / to fall	**caído** / fallen
creer / to believe	**creído** / believed
cubrir / to cover	**cubierto** / covered
decir / to say, to tell	**dicho** / said, told
descubrir / to discover	**descubierto** / discovered
deshacer / to undo	**deshecho** / undone
devolver / to return (something)	**devuelto** / returned (something)
escribir / to write	**escrito** / written
hacer / to do, to make	**hecho** / done, made
imponer / to impose	**impuesto** / imposed
imprimir / to print	**impreso** / printed
ir / to go	**ido** / gone
leer / to read	**leído** / read
morir / to die	**muerto** / died
oír / to hear	**oído** / heard
poner / to put	**puesto** / put
rehacer / to redo, to remake	**rehecho** / redone, remade
reír / to laugh	**reído** / laughed
resolver / to resolve, to solve	**resuelto** / resolved, solved
romper / to break	**roto** / broken
traer / to bring	**traído** / brought
ver / to see	**visto** / seen
volver / to return	**vuelto** / returned

Uses of the past participle

To form the compound tenses:

As in English, the past participle is needed to form the compound tenses in Spanish, of which there are seven.

The Compound Tenses / Los Tiempos compuestos

Name of tense in Spanish / English	Example (1st pers., sing.)
Perfecto de Indicativo / Present Perfect Indicative	**he hablado**
Pluscuamperfecto de Indicativo / Pluperfect Indicative	**había hablado**
Pretérito Anterior / Preterit Perfect	**hube hablado**
Futuro Perfecto / Future Perfect	**habré hablado**
Potencial Compuesto / Conditional Perfect	**habría hablado**
Perfecto de Subjuntivo / Present Perfect Subjunctive	**haya hablado**
Pluscuamperfecto de Subjuntivo / Pluperfect Subjunctive	**hubiera hablado** *or* **hubiese hablado**

To form the Perfect Infinitive: **haber hablado** / to have spoken

To form the Perfect Participle: **habiendo hablado** / having spoken

To serve as an adjective, which must agree in gender and number with the noun it modifies: **El señor Molina es muy respetado de todos los alumnos** / Mr. Molina is very respected by all the students; **La señora González es muy conocida** / Mrs. González is very well known.

To express the result of an action with **estar** and sometimes with **quedar** or **quedarse: La puerta está abierta** / The door is open; **Las cartas están escritas** / The letters are written; **Los niños se quedaron asustados** / The children remained frightened.

To express the passive voice with **ser: La ventana fue abierta por el ladrón** / The window was opened by the robber.

EJERCICIOS

I. Escriba el participio pasado (past participle) de los siguientes verbos.

1. trabajar _____
2. hablar _____
3. comer _____
4. aprender _____
5. recibir _____
6. vivir _____
7. abrir _____
8. caer _____
9. creer _____
10. cubrir _____

11. decir _____
12. escribir _____
13. hacer _____
14. ir _____
15. leer _____
16. morir _____
17. oír _____
18. poner _____
19. reír _____
20. resolver _____

II. Escriba el gerundio (present participle) y el participio pasado (past participle) de los siguientes verbos, según el modelo.

Modelo: descubrir ⟶ ___descubriendo, descubierto___

	gerundio	participio pasado
1. hacer	_____	_____
2. escribir	_____	_____
3. volver	_____	_____
4. devolver	_____	_____
5. poner	_____	_____
6. traer	_____	_____

7. abrir   _____   _____

8. ir   _____   _____

9. romper   _____   _____

10. traer   _____   _____

11. ver   _____   _____

12. decir   _____   _____

13. hablar   _____   _____

14. aprender   _____   _____

15. vivir   _____   _____

III. Escriba el infinitivo compuesto (perfect infinitive) de los siguientes infinitivos simples, según el modelo.

Modelo: hablar   **Escriba: haber hablado**

1. trabajar _____   4. comer _____

2. recibir _____   5. hacer _____

3. decir _____   6. escribir _____

IV. Escriba el gerundio compuesto (perfect participle) de los siguientes infinitivos simples, según el modelo.

Modelo: hablar   **Escriba: habiendo hablado**

1. amar _____   6. ir _____

2. escribir _____   7. decir _____

3. tener _____   8. romper _____

4. estudiar _____   9. ver _____

5. recibir _____   10. poner _____

V. Escriba las seis formas del verbo **haber** en el presente de indicativo. Es preciso saber estas formas para formar el perfecto de indicativo.

VI. Traduzca al español.

1. I have spoken. _____

2. You **(tú)** have learned. _____

3. You **(Ud.)** have eaten. _____

4. He has come. _____

5. She has received. _____

6. Helen has left. _____

7. We have believed. _____

8. You **(vosotros)** have heard. _____

9. You **(Uds.)** have laughed. _____

10. They **(ellos)** have seen. _____

VII. Conteste las siguientes preguntas afirmativamente con oraciones completas. En la oración (a) use la palabra **Sí.** En la oración (b) use la palabra **también**, según los modelos.

> **Modelos: a. ¿Ha escrito Ud. la carta?**   **Escriba: a. Sí, yo he escrito la carta.**
> **b. ¿Y Pablo?**   **b. Sí, Pablo ha escrito,**
> **   también, la carta.**

1. a. ¿Han comido los chicos? _____

   b. ¿Y María? _____

2. a. ¿Ha abierto la profesora la ventana? _____

   b. ¿Y usted? _____

3. a. ¿Han leído los alumnos la lección? _____

   b. ¿Y Juana? _____

4. a. ¿Ha puesto María el vaso en la mesa? _____

   _____

   b. ¿Y nosotros? _____

   _____

5. a. ¿Ha devuelto Ud. el libro a la biblioteca? _____

   _____

   b. ¿Y su hermano? _____

   _____

6. a. ¿Han estudiado Uds. los problemas de matemáticas? _____

   _____

   b. ¿Y Carlos? _____

_____

7. a. ¿Ha muerto el pobre viejo? _____

_____

b. ¿Y su esposa? _____

_____

8. a. ¿Han bebido los niños la leche? _____

_____

b. ¿Y tú? _____

_____

9. a. ¿Ha hablado el hombre monstruoso? _____

_____

b. ¿Y Pedro y Lolita? _____

_____

10. a. ¿Ha escrito Lolita una nota? _____

_____

b. ¿Y las otras alumnas? _____

_____

VIII. Acróstico. Complete cada palabra en español, escribiendo el participio (past participle) de los siguientes infinitivos simples.

1. escribir
2. nacer
3. abrir
4. morir
5. oír
6. reír
7. aprender
8. decir
9. obtener

1. E
2. N
3. A
4. M
5. O
6. R
7. A
8. D
9. O

IX. En español hay muchas palabras que se escriben y se pronuncian idénticamente, pero tienen distinto significado.

EJEMPLO:

pescado *past participle of* **pescar** / to fish
pescado *n.m.* fish (caught for eating)
**¡Mire este pescado! He pescado toda
la mañana.**
Look at this fish! I have fished all morning.

pescar / to fish
perfecto de indicativo

yo	he pescado	nosotros hemos pescado
tú	has pescado	vosotros habéis pescado
Ud. ⎫		Uds. ⎫
él ⎬	ha pescado	ellos ⎬ han pescado
ella ⎭		ellas ⎭

Mnemonic tip	**El pez (los peces)** is the word for fish in the water; **el pescado** is the word for fish caught, taken out of the water intended for eating.

Una adivinanza / a riddle	Tengo ojos pero no tengo párpados. Vivo en el agua. ¿Quién soy?

X. En español hay muchas palabras que se escriben y se pronuncian idénticamente, pero tienen distinto significado.

EJEMPLO:

cuidado *n.m.* care, concern
cuidado *past part. of* **cuidar** / to care for, take care of, look after
He cuidado la ropa con gran cuidado. I have taken care of the clothes with great care.

perfecto de indicativo
cuidar

yo	he cuidado	nosotros	hemos cuidado
tú	has cuidado	vosotros	habéis cuidado
Ud. ⎫		Uds. ⎫	
él ⎬	ha cuidado	ellos ⎬	han cuidado
ella ⎭		ellas ⎭	

¿Tiene Ud. otros ejemplos?

HABER, HABER DE + INF., AND TENER

The verb **haber** (to have) is used as an auxiliary verb (or helping verb) in order to form the seven compound tenses, which are as follows:

Compound Tenses	Example (in the 1st person sing.)
Present Perfect (or Perfect) Indicative	**he hablado** (I have spoken)
Pluperfect (or Past Perfect) Indicative	**había hablado** (I had spoken)
Preterit Perfect (or Past Anterior)	**hube hablado** (I had spoken)
Future Perfect (or Future Anterior)	**habré hablado** (I will have spoken)
Conditional Perfect	**habría hablado** (I would have spoken)
Present Perfect (or Past) Subjunctive	**haya hablado** (I may have spoken)
Pluperfect (or Past Perfect) Subjunctive	**hubiera hablado** *or* **hubiese hablado** (I might have spoken)

The verb **haber** is also used to form the Perfect (or Past) Infinitive: **haber hablado** (to have spoken). As you can see, this is formed by using the infinitive form of haber + the past participle of the main verb.

The verb **haber** is also used to form the Perfect Participle: **habiendo hablado** (having spoken). As you can see, this is formed by using the present participle of **haber** + the past participle of the main verb.

The verb **haber + de + inf.** is equivalent to the English use of "to be supposed to . . ." or "to be to . . ." EXAMPLES:

María ha de traer un pastel, yo he de traer el helado, y mis amigos han de traer sus discos / Mary is supposed to bring a pie, I am supposed to bring the ice cream, and my friends are to bring their records.

The verb **tener** is used to mean *to have* in the sense of *to possess* or *to hold:* **Tengo un perro y un gato** / I have a dog and a cat; **Tengo un lápiz en la mano** / I have (am holding) a pencil in my hand.

In the preterit tense, **tener** can mean *received:* **Ayer mi padre tuvo un cheque** / Yesterday my father received a check.

HAY AND HAY QUE + INF.

The word **hay** is not a verb. You might regard it as an impersonal irregular form of **haber.** Actually, the word is composed of **ha** + the archaic **y,** meaning *there.* It is generally regarded as an adverbial expression because it points out that something or someone "is there". Its English equivalent is *There is . . .* or *There are . . . ,* for example:

Hay muchos libros en la mesa / There are many books on the table; **Hay una mosca en la sopa** / There is a fly in the soup; **Hay veinte alumnos en esta clase** / There are twenty students in this class.

Hay que + inf. is an impersonal expression that denotes an obligation and it is commonly translated into English as: *One must . . .* or *It is necessary to . . .* EXAMPLES:

Hay que estudiar para aprender / It is necessary to study in order to learn; **Hay que comer para vivir** / One must eat in order to live.

EJERCICIOS

I. Componga dos oraciones empleando **haber + de + inf.**

1. _____

2. _____

II. Componga dos oraciones empleando **hay.**

1. _____

2. _____

III. Componga dos oraciones empleando **hay que + inf.**

1. _____

2. _____

IV. Componga dos oraciones empleando **tener** en el presente de indicativo y en el pretérito.

1. _____

2. _____

V. Traduzca al inglés los siguientes verbos que están en el perfecto de indicativo.

Modelo: María ha trabajado.   Escriba: Mary has worked.

1. Yo he hablado. _____ 7. Nosotros hemos viajado. _____

2. Tú has aprendido. _____ 8. Vosotros habéis hecho. _____

3. Ud. ha escrito. _____ 9. Uds. han visto. _____

4. Él ha recibido. _____ 10. Ellos han ido. _____

5. Ella ha puesto. _____ 11. Ellas han cubierto. _____

6. Juan ha dicho. _____ 12. Juan y Juana han vuelto. _____

VI. Dictado. Escriba las oraciones que su profesor de español va a leer.

1. _____

2. _____

3. _____

VII. ¿Qué estás haciendo? ¿Dónde estás?

Respuesta: _____

Saint Martin and the Beggar *by EL GRECO (1541–1614)*
Courtesy of The National Gallery of Art, Washington, D.C.

Cuando el gato va a sus devociones, bailan los ratones.

El apetito se abre al comer.

Veinte Proverbios (Refranes)

Here are a few common proverbs in Spanish that you ought to be familiar with in case you come across them in the reading selections on the next standardized test that you take in Spanish. They also contain some essential Spanish words which you ought to look up in the back pages of this book.

A Dios rogando y con el mazo dando / Put your faith in God and keep your powder dry. OR: Praise the Lord and pass the ammunition.

El apetito se abre al comer / The more you have, the more you want; *ie.,* Appetite comes while eating.

Cuando el gato va a sus devociones, bailan los ratones / When the cat is away, the mice will play.

Dicho y hecho / No sooner said than done.

Dime con quien andas y te diré quien eres / Tell me who your friends are and I will tell you who you are.

La práctica hace maestro al novicio / Practice makes perfect.

El que mucho abarca poco aprieta / Do not bite off more than you can chew.

El que no se aventura no cruza la mar / Nothing ventured, nothing gained.

El tiempo da buen consejo / Time will tell.

Más vale pájaro en mano que ciento volando / A bird in the hand is worth two in the bush.

Más vale tarde que nunca / Better late than never.

Mientras hay vida hay esperanza / Where there is life there is hope.

Mucho ruido y pocas nueces / Much ado about nothing.

Perro que ladra no muerde / A barking dog does not bite.

Piedra movediza, el moho no la cobija / A rolling stone gathers no moss.

Quien canta su mal espanta / When you sing you drive away your grief.

Quien siembra vientos recoge tempestades / If you sow the wind, you will reap the whirlwind.

Si a Roma fueres, haz como vieres / When in Rome do as the Romans do. [Note that it is not uncommon to use the future subjunctive in proverbs, as in *fueres* (*ir* or *ser*) and *vieres* (*ver*).]

Tal madre, tal hija / Like mother, like daughter.

Tal padre, tal hijo / Like father, like son.

VOCABULARIO: Consult the vocabulary section in the back pages.

EJERCICIOS

I. Escriba en español los siguientes refranes.

1. When the cat is away, the mice will play. _____

---

2. Tell me who your friends are and I will tell you who you are. _____

_____

3. Practice makes perfect. _____

_____

4. Time will tell. _____

5. A bird in the hand is worth two in the bush. _____

_____

6. Better late than never. _____

7. A barking dog does not bite. _____

8. Much ado about nothing. _____

9. When in Rome do as the Romans do. _____

10. Like father, like son. _____

II. Llene los blancos con la palabra correcta según los refranes de esta lección.

1. A Dios _____ y con el mazo dando.

2. Cuando el _____ va a sus devociones, _____ los ratones.

3. El tiempo da _____ consejo.

4. Perro _____ ladra no _____.

5. Si a Roma _____, haz como _____.

6. Más vale _____ que _____.

7. Quien _____ su mal _____.

8. La práctica hace maestro _____ novicio.

9. Dicho y _____.

10. Tal padre, tal _____.

III. Una los refranes en inglés con los equivalentes en español.

1. Better late than never.   _____ Mucho ruido y pocas nueces.

2. Time will tell.   _____ Perro que ladra no muerde.

3. No sooner said than done.   _____ Más vale tarde que nunca.

4. Much ado about nothing.   _____ El tiempo da buen consejo.

5. A barking dog does not bite. _____ Dicho y hecho.

6. The more you have, the more you want. _____ El apetito se abre al comer.

Estructuras de la lengua

Tense No. 9: Pluscuamperfecto de indicativo (Pluperfect or Past perfect indicative)

This is the second of the compound tenses. In Spanish and English, this past tense is used to express an action which happened in the past *before* another past action. Since it is used in relation to another past action, the other past action is ordinarily expressed in the preterit. However, it is not always necessary to have the other past action expressed, as in example no. 2 below.

In English, this tense is formed with the past tense of *to have* (had) plus the past participle of the verb you have in mind. In Spanish, this tense is formed with the imperfect indicative of **haber** plus the past participle of the verb you have in mind. Note the translation into English in the examples that follow.

1. Cuando **llegué** a casa, mi hermano **había salido** / When I *arrived* home, my brother *had gone out.*

NOTE: *First,* my brother went out; *then,* I arrived home. Both actions happened in the past. The action that occurred in the past *before* the other past action is in the pluperfect, and in this example it is *my brother had gone out* **(mi hermano había salido).**

NOTE ALSO that **llegué** *(I arrived)* is in the preterit because it is an action that happened in the past and it was completed.

2. Juan lo **había perdido** en la calle / John *had lost* it in the street.

NOTE: In this example, the pluperfect indicative is used even though no other past action is expressed. It is assumed that John *had lost* something **before** some other past action.

Es preciso saber las seis formas del verbo **haber** en el imperfecto de indicativo para formar el pluscuamperfecto de indicativo.

Singular	Plural
1. **había**	1. **habíamos**
2. **habías**	2. **habíais**
3. **había**	3. **habían**

INFINITIVES

Definition: In English, an infinitive is identified as a verb with the preposition *to* in front of it: *to talk, to eat, to live.* In Spanish, an infinitive is identified by its ending: those that end in **-ar, -er, -ir,** for example, **hablar** (to talk, to speak), **comer** (to eat), **vivir** (to live).

Negation: To make an infinitive negative, place **no** in front of it: **No entrar** / Do not enter; **No fumar** / Do not smoke or No smoking; **No estacionar** / Do not park or No Parking.

As a verbal noun: In Spanish, an infinitive may be used as a noun. This means that an infinitive may be used as a subject, a direct object, a predicate noun, or object of a preposition. A verbal noun is a verb used as a noun.

EXAMPLES:

● **As a subject: Ser o no ser es la cuestión** / To be or not to be is the question. In this sentence, the subject is **ser** and **no ser.**

● **El estudiar es bueno** or **Estudiar es bueno** / Studying (to study) is good. Here, when the infinitive is a subject and it begins the sentence, you may use the definite article **el** in front of the inf. or you may omit it.

But if the sentence does not begin with the infinitive, do not (as a general rule) use the def. art. **el** in front of it: **Es bueno estudiar** / It is good to study.

● **As a direct object: No deseo comer** / I do not want to eat. Here, the inf. **comer** is used as a noun and it functions as the direct object of the verb **deseo.**

● **As a predicate noun: Ver es creer** / Seeing is believing (To see is to believe). Here, the inf. **ver** is used as a noun and it functions as the subject. The inf. **creer** is used as a noun and it functions as the predicate noun because the verb is a form of **ser,** which takes a predicate noun or predicate adjective.

Do you know what these grammatical terms mean? A predicate noun is a noun which has the same referent as the subject; in other words, the predicate noun and the subject are pretty much the same thing; for example, in English: He is a father. A predicate adjective is an adjective which is attributive to the subject; in other words, the predicate adjective describes the subject in some way; for example, in English: She is pretty; She is tall. A predicate adjective is also known as an attribute complement because, as an adjective, it is attributive to the subject and it complements (describes) it in some way.

One last comment: In English, we can use an infinitive as a verbal noun, as in the above examples. In English, we can also use a gerund as a noun. A gerund in English looks like a present participle (ends in *-ing,* like *seeing, believing*) and it is used as a noun. But in Spanish, we do not use gerunds as nouns; we use only infinitives as nouns, as in the above examples. The Spanish word **gerundio** is normally translated into English as *gerund.* In a word, when we use a gerund as a noun in English its equivalent use is the infinitive in Spanish: Seeing is believing / **Ver es creer.**

As object of a preposition: después de llegar / after arriving. Here, the infinitive (verbal noun) **llegar** is object of the prep. **de.** In English, the word *arriving* in this example is a present participle, not a gerund. In English, present participles and gerunds both end in *-ing* but there is a distinct difference in their use. The point here is that in Spanish, only an infinitive can be used as a verbal noun, not a present participle and not a gerund in the English sense of these two terms.

In Spanish, an infinitive is ordinarily used after such verbs as, **dejar, hacer, mandar,** and **permitir** with no preposition needed: **Luis dejó caer sus libros** / Louis dropped his books; **Mi madre me hizo leerlo** / My mother made me read it; **Mi padre me mandó comerlo** / My father ordered me to eat it; **Mi profesor me permitió hacerlo** / My teacher permitted me to do it. Note that when **dejar** is followed by the prep. **de** it means *to stop* or *to cease:* **Luis dejó de trabajar** / Louis stopped working.

The verb **pensar** is directly followed by an infinitive with no preposition required in front of the infinitive when its meaning is *to intend:* **Pienso ir a Chile** / I intend to go to Chile.

Ordinarily, the infinitive form of a verb is used right after a preposition: **Antes de estudiar, Rita telefoneó a su amiga Beatriz** / Before studying, Rita telephoned her friend Beatrice; **El alumno salió de la sala de clase sin decir nada** / The pupil left the classroom without saying anything. Here, note **de estudiar** and **sin decir.**

The infinitive form of a verb is ordinarily used after certain verbs of perception, such as **ver** and **oír: Las vi salir** / I saw them go out; **Las oí cantar** / I heard them singing.

After **al,** a verb is used in the infinitive form: **Al entrar en la escuela, Dorotea fue a su clase de español** / Upon entering the school, Dorothy went to her Spanish class.

The Perfect Infinitive (also known as the Past Infinitive) is formed by using **haber** in its inf. form + the past participle of the main verb: **haber hablado** (to have spoken), **haber comido** (to have eaten), **haber escrito** (to have written).

Paseo a orillas del mar (Stroll along the seashore) *by Joaquín SOROLLA y Bastida (1863–1923)*
Reprinted with permission of Oficina Nacional Española de Turismo, Paris.

EJERCICIOS

I. Escriba las seis formas de **haber** en el imperfecto de indicativo. Es preciso saber estas formas para formar el pluscuamperfecto de indicativo.

Singular   Plural

1. _____   1. _____

2. _____   2. _____

3. _____   3. _____

II. Cambie los siguientes verbos al pluscuamperfecto de indicativo.

Modelo: Los chicos han comido.   Escriba: Los chicos habían comido.

1. El alumno ha leído la página. _____

2. Los alumnos han escrito en la pizarra. _____

   _____

3. La profesora abrió la ventana. _____

4. María puso el vaso en la mesa. _____

5. Ud. devolvió el libro a la biblioteca. _____

   _____

6. Uds. estudiaron la lección. _____

7. El pobre viejo murió. _____

8. Juana dice siempre la verdad. _____

9. Lolita escribió una nota. _____

10. Clara y Francisco hacen un viaje a Australia. _____

    _____

III. Conteste las siguientes preguntas en el afirmativo con oraciones completas. En la oración (a) use la palabra **Sí.** En la oración (b) use la palabra **también,** según los modelos.

Modelos: a. ¿Había recibido Ud. una carta?   Escriba: a. Sí. Yo había recibido
**   b. ¿Y el señor Vargas?   una carta.**
**   b. El señor Vargas**
**   había recibido una**
**   carta también.**

1. a. ¿Habían pedido los alumnos el libro a la profesora? _____

   _____

b. ¿Y Ud.? _____

2. a. ¿Habíamos visto esa película? _____

_____

b. ¿Y ellos? _____

3. a. ¿Había hecho Ud. un viaje a Inglaterra? _____

_____

b. ¿Y Uds.? _____

4. a. ¿Habían escrito los estudiantes las lecciones? _____

_____

b. ¿Y vosotros? _____

5. a. ¿Había abierto el profesor la puerta? _____

b. ¿Y nosotros? _____

IV. Ordene las palabras para hallar una oración significativa.

Modelo:

visto	habíamos	la película	nosotros

Escriba: Nosotros habíamos visto la película.

1.

recibido	había	una carta	Ud.

_____

2.

puesto	habían	de flores	el vaso	la mesa	en

_____

3.

padre	mi	vuelto	había	a medianoche

_____

4.

yo llegué	cuando	a casa	hermano	mi	salido	había

_____

V. Traduzca.

1. When I arrived home, my brother had gone out. _____

_____ **225**

2. John had lost it in the street. _____

3. To be or not to be is the question. _____

4. Studying (to study) is good. _____

5. It is good to study. _____

6. I do not want to eat. _____

7. Seeing is believing. _____

8. Tell me who your friends are and I will tell you who you are. _____

_____

9. The more you have, the more you want (*i.e.,* Appetite comes while eating.) _____

_____

10. After arriving home, Mr. Rodríguez went to the bathroom and washed himself. _____

_____

VI. Traduzca al inglés.

1. Luis dejó caer sus libros. _____

2. Mi padre me mandó comerlo. _____

3. Mi profesor me permitió hacerlo. _____

4. Luis dejó de trabajar. _____

5. Pienso ir a Inglaterra. _____

6. Antes de estudiar, Rita telefoneó a su amiga Beatriz. _____

_____

7. El alumno salió de la sala de clase sin decir nada. _____

_____

8. Las vi salir. _____

9. Las oí cantar. _____

10. Al entrar en la escuela, Dorotea fue a su clase de español. _____

_____

VII. Traduzca al inglés los siguientes verbos que están en el pluscuamperfecto de indicativo.

Modelo: María había hablado.   Escriba: Mary had spoken.

1. Yo había trabajado doce horas. _____

2. Tú habías cerrado la puerta. _____

3. Vd. había terminado la lección. _____

4. El había aprendido el poema. _____

5. Ella había vivido ochenta años. _____

6. José había escrito una carta a sus amigos. _____

_____

7. Nosotros habíamos hecho el trabajo. _____

8. Vosotros habíais puesto los libros en la mesa. _____

9. Uds. habían dicho la verdad. _____

10. Ellos habían muerto. _____

11. Ellas habían abierto las ventanas. _____

12. María y José habían leído cartas de sus amigos en España. _____

_____

VIII. Discriminación de los sonidos. Su profesor de español va a pronunciar una sola palabra, sea la letra A, sea la letra B. Escoja la palabra que su profesor pronuncia escribiendo la letra en la línea.

Modelo: **A. lama**
        B. llama   <u> B </u>

He escrito la letra B en la línea porque mi profesor de español ha pronunciado la palabra de la letra B.

1. A. bosque
   B. busque _____

2. A. hambre
   B. hombre _____

3. A. cuando
   B. ¿cuando? _____

4. A. hacía
   B. hacia _____

5. A. como
   B. coma _____

6. A. ya
   B. yo _____

IX. Varias palabras en una sola. Utilizando las letras en la palabra **MEXICO** ¿cuántas palabras puede usted escribir? Escriba tres palabras, por lo menos.

MEXICO

1. _____ 2. _____ 3. _____

X. ¿Cuántos infinitivos y palabras puede Ud. añadir a **al?**

EJEMPLOS:

Al entrar en la escuela, . . .   Al llegar al cine, . . .

Al salir de la biblioteca, . . .   Al partir de Nueva York, . . .

227

Escriba diez, por lo menos.

1. _____   6. _____

2. _____   7. _____

3. _____   8. _____

4. _____   9. _____

5. _____   10. _____

| Mnemonic tip | If you confuse the English meaning of **verano** and **invierno**, remember this: |

```
    ┌─────┐
  I N│ V I│E R N O
  W  │ I N│T E R
    └─────┘
```

CAMPO, PAÍS, PATRIA, NACIÓN

The first three nouns (**el campo, el país, la patria**) all mean *country*. However, note the following:

(a) **campo** means *country* in the sense of countryside, where you find farmlands, as opposite to life in a city: **en el campo** / in the country; **Vamos a pasar el fin de semana en el campo** / We are going to spend the weekend in the country; **Voy al campo este verano** / I am going to the country this summer.

(b) **país** means *country* in the meaning of a *nation*: **¿En qué país nació Ud.?** / In what country were you born?

(c) **patria** means *country* in the sense of *native land*: **El soldado defendió a su patria** / The soldier defended his country.

(d) **nación** means *country* in the sense of *nation*: **Las Naciones Unidas** / the United Nations; **La Sociedad de las Naciones** / The League of Nations.

CONOCER AND SABER

These two verbs mean *to know* but they are used in a distinct sense:

(a) Generally speaking, **conocer** means to know in the sense of *being acquainted* with a person, a place, or a thing: **¿Conoce Ud. a María?** / Do you know Mary? **¿Conoce Ud. bien los Estados Unidos?** / Do you know the United States well? **¿Conoce Ud. este libro?** / Do you know (Are you acquainted with) this book?

In the preterit tense, **conocer** means *met* in the sense of *first met, first became acquainted with someone:* **¿Conoce Ud. a Elena?** / Do you know Helen? / **Sí, (yo) la conocí anoche en casa de un amigo mío** / Yes, I met her [for the first time] last night at the home of one of my friends.

(b) Generally speaking, **saber** means to know a fact, to know something thoroughly: **¿Sabe Ud. qué hora es?** / Do you know what time it is? **¿Sabe Ud. la lección?** / Do you know the lesson?

When you use **saber + inf.**, it means *to know how:* **¿Sabe Ud. nadar?** / Do you know how to swim? **Sí, (yo) sé nadar** / Yes, I know how to swim.

In the preterit tense, **saber** means *found out;* **¿Lo sabe Ud.?** / Do you know it? **Sí, lo supe ayer** / Yes, I found it out yesterday.

| Mnemonic tip | If you're not sure about the difference in use between **conocer** and **saber**, remember that **conocer** means to know in the sense of to be acquainted with. Associate the letter c in **conocer** and **acquainted**. |

If you have to, memorize this:

—¿Conoces a Carlos?
—Sí, lo conozco.
—¿Sabes qué es un sabichoso? (a know-it-all)
—Sí lo sé.

DEBER, DEBER DE AND TENER QUE

Generally speaking, use **deber** when you want to express a moral obligation, something you ought to do but you may or may not do it: **Debo estudiar esta noche pero estoy cansado y no me siento bien** / I ought to study tonight but I am tired and I do not feel well.

Generally speaking, **deber de + inf.** is used to express a supposition, something that is probable: **La señora Gómez debe de estar enferma porque sale de casa raramente** / Mrs. Gomez must be sick (is probably sick) because she goes out of the house rarely.

Generally speaking, use **tener que** when you want to say that you *have to* do something: **No puedo salir esta noche porque tengo que estudiar** / I cannot go out tonight because I have to study.

EJERCICIOS

I. Componga oraciones usando las siguientes palabras.

1. campo: _____

2. país: _____

3. patria: _____

4. nación: _____

II. Traduzca al español.

1. Do you know Mary? _____

2. I know Michael very well. _____

3. Do you know the United States well? _____

_____

4. Do you know this book? _____

5. I know this book. It's a very good book. _____

_____

6. Do you know Christopher? Yes, I met him last night at the home of one of my friends. _____

_____

7. Do you know what time it is? _____

_____

8. Do you know the lesson for today? _____

_____

9. Do you know how to swim? _____

10. Yes, I know how to swim. _____

11. Do you know it? Yes, I found it out yesterday. _____

_____

12. I ought to study tonight but I am tired and I do not feel well. _____

_____

13. Mrs. Gómez must be sick because she goes out of the house rarely. ____

_____

14. I cannot go out tonight because I have to study. _____

_____

III. Componga oraciones empleando las siguientes palabras en español.

1. deber: _____

_____

2. deber de + inf.: _____

_____

3. tener que: _____

_____

4. conocer: _____

_____

5. saber: _____

IV. **Varias palabras en una sola.** Utilizando las letras en la palabra **AGRADABLE**, ¿cuántas palabras puede usted escribir? Escriba diez palabras, por lo menos.

AGRADABLE

1. _____   3. _____   5. _____   7. _____   9. _____

2. _____   4. _____   6. _____   8. _____   10. _____

V. **LETRA RELOJ.** Cuatro palabras se esconden en este reloj: una palabra de las doce a las tres, una palabra de las tres a las seis, una palabra de las seis a las nueve y, por fin, una palabra de las nueve a las doce.

La misma letra es común a la palabra que sigue.

Este reloj no tiene agujas. ¡Es un reloj de palabras!

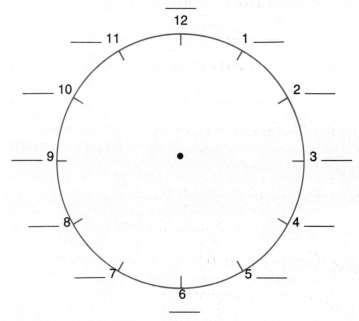

De las doce a las tres es el número entre diez y doce.

De las tres a las seis es la forma masculina, singular, de **esta.**

De las seis a las nueve es el pronombre demostrativo, neutro.

De las nueve a las doce es la forma masculina, singular, de **otra.**

VI. Dictado. Escriba las oraciones que su profesor de español va a leer.

1. _____

2. _____

3. _____

VII. ¿Qué está haciendo Ud.? ¿Dónde está Ud.? ¿En un parque?

Respuesta: _____

_____

VIII. En este diálogo, Juanita y usted hablan de los exámenes de junio y de las vacaciones de verano.

Complete el diálogo.

Juanita: ¿Estás bien preparado para tus exámenes?

Usted: _____

Juanita: Mañana tengo un examen más y luego empiezan las vacaciones.

Usted: _____

Juanita: En julio hacemos un viaje a Puerto Rico.

Usted: _____

Juanita: El verano pasado lo pasamos en las montañas.

Usted: _____

Juanita: Voy a mandarte una tarjeta postal desde San Juan si me das tu
dirección.

Usted: _____

IX. Escoja la palabra apropiada para completar los siguientes proverbios (refranes).

1. Mucho ruido y pocas _____.
   A. casas
   B. peras
   C. calles
   D. nueces

2. El tiempo da buen _____.
   A. tiempo
   B. hora
   C. consejo
   D. conejo

3. Si a Roma fueres, _____ como vieres.
   A. hace
   B. haga
   C. haces
   D. haz

4. Más vale pájaro en mano que _____ volando.
   A. cien
   B. ciento
   C. cientos
   D. un cien

5. Dime con quien andas y te diré quien _____.
   A. es
   B. esta
   C. eres
   D. fueres

X. ¿Qué palabras españolas tienen las siguientes letras?

EJEMPLO: **CHE** noche, coche, chiste

1. MJR _____   4. AGA _____

2. CSA _____   5. TPO _____

3. PTL _____   6. AHR _____

| Mnemonic tip | If you confuse the meaning of **vieja** (old, *fem., sing.*) and **viaje** (trip), remember this statement: **Esta mujer vieja hace un viaje por autobús** / This old woman is taking a trip by bus. |

Madrid. Interior del Museo del Prado.
Courtesy of Oficina Nacional Española de Turismo, Paris.

Museo del Prado, Madrid (Fachada principal)
Courtesy of Spanish National Tourist Office, New York, N.Y.

A Pedro le gustan los deportes. Su deporte favorito es el fútbol.

Are you as eager as Pedro to play in a soccer game?

¡Sorpresa! ¡Sorpresa!

A Pedro le gustan los deportes. Su deporte favorito es el fútbol. Siempre quiere que su cuerpo esté en buena forma porque as guardameta del equipo de fútbol de su escuela. Quiere estar siempre dispuesto para jugar bien. Siempre cuida su salud; por ejemplo, Pedro come solamente alimentos que son buenos para la salud. Cuando juega al fútbol, evita el helado, las patatas fritas y los pasteles. Es un buen muchacho y buen futbolista.   5

Pedro se acuesta temprano todas las noches, se despierta temprano, se levanta con el sol, se lava cuidadosamente, se viste pronto y toma un buen desayuno todas las mañanas.

Pedro anuncia a sus padres:

—Hoy es el gran partido de fútbol. Tendrá lugar después de clase.

Pedro dice a Juana: 10

—Juanita, tú vas a jugar en el equipo con los muchachos y las muchachas también, ¿no es verdad?

—Sí—, contesta Juana—. A las muchachas nos gustan los deportes también. Estaré en el estadio esta tarde para jugar con los muchachos y mis amigas.

Pedro se apresuró para llegar temprano al gran campo de la escuela. Corrió un kilómetro en la 15 pista antes de entrar en la escuela.

Para Pedro, el fútbol es todo. Se acuerda de los buenos consejos de su entrenador de fútbol:

—¡Guárdate de la red! ¡Guárdate de la red! ¡El gol! ¡El gol!

Pedro juega extremadamente bien. Es un muchacho admirable. Nos gusta más. Es todo un 20 hombre. Es un buen estudiante, buen jugador, futbolista excelente. Los compañeros de Pedro lo quieren.

Después de la última clase, Pedro fue al gimnasio. Se preparó para el gran partido de fútbol. Se puso su traje de gimnasio, hizo ejercicios para estar en buena forma antes de comenzar el partido.   25

Padro hizo ejercicios por tres horas. ¡Ahora está listo para el gran partido!

Pedro corre a toda velocidad al estadio. Cuando llega al estadio, ve que todo el mundo parte.

—¡Pedro! ¿Por qué llegas tarde?—pregunta el entrenador.

Pedro no contesta. Está estupefacto.

—¿Por qué llegas tarde?—repite el entrenador.   30

—¿Tarde? ¿Tarde?—pregunta Pedro con sorpresa.

—El partido ha terminado—, dice el entrenador.

—¡El partido ha terminado!—exclama Pedro.

—Sí, sí. ¡Terminado! ¡Se acabó! ¡Hemos ganado! ¡Sorpresa! ¡Sorpresa!

VOCABULARIO: Consult the vocabulary section in the back pages.

EJERCICIOS

I. Conteste las siguientes preguntas conforme a la lectura de esta lección.

1. ¿Cuál es el deporte favorito de Pedro? _____

_____

2. ¿Por qué quiere Pedro estar siempre en buena forma? _____

_____

3. ¿Qué alimentos come Pedro? _____

_____

4. ¿Qué alimentos evita él? _____

_____

5. ¿Se levanta Pedro temprano o tarde? _____

_____

6. ¿Va a jugar Juanita en el equipo? _____

_____

·7. ¿Cómo se lava Pedro? _____

_____

8. ¿Cuándo tendrá lugar el gran partido de fútbol? _____

_____

9. ¿Por qué llegó tarde Pedro al gran partido de fútbol? _____

_____

10. Cuando Pedro llegó tarde al estadio, ¿quién le dice a él que el partido ha terminado? _____

_____

II. Conteste las siguientes preguntas. Son preguntas personales.

1. ¿Le gustan a usted los deportes? _____

_____

2. ¿Cuál es su deporte favorito? _____

_____

3. ¿Se acuesta usted temprano o tarde? _____

_____

4. Por lo general, ¿a qué hora se levanta usted todas las mañanas? _____

_____

5. Y, por lo general, ¿a qué hora se acuesta usted todas las noches? _____

_____

6. Por lo general, ¿se apresura Ud. por la mañana? _____

_____

7. ¿Se lava Ud. todas las mañanas con cuidado o sin cuidado? _____

_____

8. Por lo general, ¿qué toma Ud. en el desayuno todas las mañanas? _____

_____

9. ¿Se viste Ud. pronto o lentamente? _____

_____

10. ¿Prefiere Ud. helado o pastel? _____

_____

III. ¿Sí o No?

1. El deporte predilecto de Pedro es el tenis. _____

2. Pedro es guardameta de su equipo de fútbol. _____

3. A Juanita le gustan los deportes también. _____

4. Pedro se despierta tarde. _____

5. Pedro se viste pronto. _____

6. Pedro se lava con cuidado. _____

7. Pedro desea estar en buena forma. _____

8. El gran partido de fútbol tendrá lugar por la mañana antes de las clases. _____

9. Pedro es todo un hombre. _____

10. Pedro está listo para el gran partido despúes de hacer ejercicios por tres horas. _____

IV. Acróstico. Traduzca al español horizontalmente las palabras inglesas expresadas abajo.

1. slowly
2. to offer
3. health
4. sports
5. team
6. track (race)
7. to occupy
8. to repeat
9. suit
10. to avoid
11. surprise

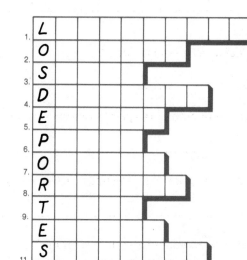

LOS ANGELES-84

Un gran espectáculo alrededor del deporte

En Los Angeles todo el mundo vive pendiente de la Olimpiada, pero al margen de la competición, los miles de turistas llegados de todas partes dan el toque de color al gran acontecimiento. El vaivén de la gente, los souvenirs, las anécdotas de todo tipo unido a la presencia casi constante de los famosos de Hollywood entre el público son ya casi tan importantes como los propios récords y medallas.

LOS ANGELES. Diana Domken

TODAS las previsiones catastrofistas que anunciaban unos Juegos Olímpicos cargados de problemas, ahogados por la polución, congestionados por el tráfico de las autopistas, atemorizados por la masiva seguridad y el acecho del terrorismo, han caído por su propio peso. Ni siquiera el boicot soviético y de los países del este se está notando en algo más que no sean las frías cifras de los récords y mejores tiempos. Las calles y autopistas de Los Angeles, están más vacías que nunca. Ni los más viejos del lugar recuerdan la facilidad con que se circula. El terrorismo no ha hecho su aparición, y la polución, la temible nube amarilla que se concentra en los días más calurosos del verano, se mantiene bajo control.

Al contrario, las competiciones están llenas de bote en bote. A pesar de las distancias y los extravagantes horarios impuestos por la cadena de televisión que transmite los Juegos (incluso a las ocho de la mañana, en deportes como el Hockey sobre Hierba o el Balonmano, que en Estados Unidos son totalmente desconocidos),la demanda de entradas es extraordinaria.

Claro que, entre el público, están, muy a menudo, las grandes atracciones. El día de la espectacular ceremonia de inauguración en el viejo Coliseo de Los Angeles, que ya había sido la sede de los Juegos de 1932, justo en el punto opuesto del lugar donde se hallaban las autoridades, se encontraban sentadas Brooke Shields, Linda Evans y John Forsythe.

Estructuras de la lengua

Tense No. 10: Pretérito anterior (Past anterior *or* Preterit perfect)

This is the third of the compound tenses. This past tense is compound because it is formed with the preterit of **haber** plus the past participle of the verb you are using. It is translated into English like the pluperfect indicative explained above. This tense is not used much in spoken Spanish. Ordinarily, the pluperfect indicative is used in spoken Spanish (and sometimes even the simple preterit) in place of the past anterior.

This tense is ordinarily used in formal writing, such as history and literature. It is normally used after certain conjunctions of time, *e.g.,* **después que, cuando, apenas, luego que, en cuanto.**

You must become familiar with this tense because you will have to recognize its meaning in reading comprehension selections. Remember that it is translated into English the same as the pluperfect indicative. It is used in literature and formal writings, rarely in informal conversation.

EXAMPLE:

Después que **hubo hablado,** salió / After *he had spoken,* he left.

Es preciso saber las seis formas del verbo **haber** en el pretérito para formar el pretérito perfecto (pretérito anterior).

	Singular		Plural
1.	**hube**	1.	**hubimos**
2.	**hubiste**	2.	**hubisteis**
3.	**hubo**	3.	**hubieron**

PASSIVE VOICE **AND USES OF SE**

Passive voice means that the action of the verb falls on the subject; in other words, the subject receives the action: **La ventana fue abierta por el ladrón** / The window was opened by the robber. NOTE that **abierta** (really a form of the past part. **abrir / abierto**) is used as an adjective and it must agree in gender and number with the subject that it describes.

Active voice means that the subject performs the action and the subject is always stated: **El ladrón abrió la ventana** / The robber opened the window.

To form the true passive, use **ser** + the past participle of the verb you have in mind; the past part. then serves as an adjective and it must agree in gender and number with the subject that it describes. In the true passive, the agent (the doer) is always expressed with the prep. **por** in front of it. The formula for the true passive construction is: subject + tense of **ser** + past participle + **por** + the agent (the doer): **Estas composiciones fueron escritas por Juan** / These compositions were written by John.

The reflexive pronoun **se** may be used to substitute for the true passive voice construction. When you use the **se** construction, the subject is a thing (not a person) and the doer (agent) is not stated: **Aquí se habla español** / Spanish is spoken here; **Aquí se hablan español e inglés** / Spanish and English are spoken here; **Se venden libros en esta tienda** / Books are sold in this store.

There are a few standard idiomatic expressions that are commonly used with the pronoun **se.** These expressions are not truly passive, the pronoun **se** is not truly a reflexive pronoun, and the verb form is in the 3rd pers. sing. only. In this construction, there is no subject expressed; the subject is contained in the use of **se** + the 3rd pers. sing. of the verb at all times and the common translations into English are: it is . . . , people . . . , they . . . , one . . . :

Se cree que . . . / It is believed that . . . , people believe that . . . , they believe that . . . , one believes that . . .

Se cree que este criminal es culpable / It is believed that this criminal is guilty.

Se dice que . . . / It is said that . . . , people say that . . . , they say that . . . , one says that . . .

Se dice que va a nevar esta noche / They say that it's going to snow tonight; **¿Cómo se dice en español** *ice cream*? / How do you say *ice cream* in Spanish?

Se sabe que . . . / It is known that . . . , people know that . . . , they know that . . .

Se sabe que María va a casarse con Juan / People know that Mary is going to marry John.

The **se** reflexive pronoun construction is avoided if the subject is a person because there can be ambiguity in meaning. For example, how would you translate into English the following: **Se da un regalo.** Which of the following two meanings is intended? She (he) is being given a present, *or* She (he) is giving a present to himself (to herself). In correct Spanish you would have to say: **Le da (a María, a Juan,** *etc.***) un regalo** / He (she) is giving a present to Mary (to John, *etc.*) Avoid using the **se** construction in the passive when the subject is a person; change your sentence around and state it in the active voice to make the meaning clear. Otherwise, the pronoun **se** seems to go with the verb, as if the verb itself is reflexive, which gives an entirely different meaning. Another example: **Se miró** would mean *He (she) looked at himself (herself),* not *He (she) was looked at!* If you mean to say *He (she) looked at him (at her),* say: **La miró** or, if in the plural, say: **La miraron** / They looked at her.

Mnemonic tip

Se venden libros en una librería / Books are sold in a bookstore. Associate **libros** with **librería**. The ending **ría** is used to denote the store where something is sold; e.g., **una panadería** (where **pan** is sold), **una lechería** (where **leche** is sold), **una librería** (where books are sold).

Una biblioteca is a library.

EJERCICIOS

I. Escriba las seis formas de **haber** en el pretérito. Es preciso saber estas formas para formar el pretérito perfecto (pretérito anterior).

Singular	Plural
1. _____	1. _____
2. _____	2. _____
3. _____	3. _____

II. Cambie los siguientes verbos que están en el pluscuamperfecto de indicativo al pretérito perfecto (pretérito anterior), y traduzca este cambio al inglés.

Modelo: María había hablado.   **Escriba:** (a) **María hubo hablado.**
(b) Mary had spoken.

1. Yo había trabajado toda la noche. (a) _____

   (b) _____

2. Tú habías hablado incesantemente. (a) _____

   (b) _____

3. Ud. había abierto todas las ventanas. (a) _____

(b) _____

4. Él había caído en la calle. (a) _____

   (b) _____

5. Ella había creído la verdad. (a) _____

   (b) _____

6. Roberto había cubierto su bicicleta. (a) _____

   (b) _____

7. Nosotros habíamos dicho la verdad. (a) _____

   (b) _____

8. Vosotros habíais descubierto la mentira. (a) _____

   (b) _____

9. Uds. habían escrito las lecciones. (a) _____

   (b) _____

10. Ellos habían roto la silla. (a) _____

   (b) _____

III. Explique en breve, en inglés, cómo se forma el pretérito perfecto (pretérito anterior).

_____

_____

_____

_____

IV. Traduzca al español.

1. The window was opened by the robber. _____

_____

2. The robber opened the window. _____

_____

3. These compositions were written by John. _____

_____

4. John wrote these compositions. _____

_____

5. Spanish is spoken here. _____

_____

6. Spanish and English are spoken here. _____

_____

7. Books are sold in this store. _____

_____

8. It is believed that this criminal is guilty. _____

_____

9. They say that it's going to snow tonight. _____

_____

10. How do you say *ice cream* in Spanish? _____

_____

V. Traduzca al inglés.

1. Se venden zapatos en una zapatería. _____

_____

2. Se venden pasteles en una pastelería. _____

_____

3. Se venden libros en una librería. _____

_____

4. Se vende pan en una panadería. _____

_____

5. Se venden medicamentos en una farmacia. _____

_____

VI. Conteste las siguientes preguntas en español con oraciones completas.

Modelo: ¿Dónde se venden zapatos?   Escriba: Se venden zapatos en una zapatería.

1. ¿Dónde se venden pasteles? _____

_____

2. ¿Cómo se dice *ice cream* en español? _____

_____

3. ¿Dónde se vende pan? _____

_____

Carl Lewis ya tiene su primera medalla de oro

Printed with permission of YA (periódico), Madrid.

4. ¿Dónde se venden libros? _____

_____

5. ¿Quién escribió estas composiciones? _____

_____

DEJAR, SALIR, AND SALIR DE

These verbs mean *to leave,* but notice the difference in use:

Use **dejar** when you leave someone or when you leave something behind you: **El alumno dejó sus libros en la sala de clase** / The pupil left his books in the classroom.

Dejar also means *to let* or *to allow* or *to let go:* **¡Déjelo!** / Let it! (Leave it!)

Use **salir de** when you mean *to leave* in the sense of *to go out of* (a place): **El alumno salió de la sala de clase** / The pupil left the classroom; **¿Dónde está su madre? Mi madre salió** / Where is your mother? My mother went out.

DEJAR DE + INF. AND DEJAR CAER

Use **dejar de + inf.** when you mean *to stop* or *to fail to:* **Los alumnos dejaron de hablar cuando la profesora entró en la sala de clase** / The students stopped talking when the teacher came into the classroom.

¡No deje Ud. de llamarme! / Don't fail to call me!
Dejar caer means *to drop:* **Luis dejó caer sus libros** / Louis dropped his books.

IR, IRSE

Use **ir** when you simply mean *to go:* **Voy al cine** / I am going to the movies.

Use **irse** when you mean *to leave* in the sense of *to go away:* **Mis padres se fueron al campo para visitar a mis abuelos** / My parents left for (went away to) the country to visit my grandparents.

EJERCICIOS

I. Conteste las siguientes preguntas con oraciones completas.

Modelo: **¿Quién dejó estos libros en la mesa?**
Escriba: **Pedro dejó estos libros en la mesa.**

1. ¿Quién dejó sus libros en la sala de clase? _____

_____

2. ¿Quién salió del cuarto? _____

_____

3. ¿Dónde está su madre? ¿Salió? _____

_____

4. ¿Quién dejó de hablar cuando la profesora entró en la sala de clase? _____

_____

5. ¿Quién dejó caer sus libros? _____

_____

6. ¿Adónde va Ud. esta tarde? _____

_____

7. ¿Adónde se fueron sus padres? _____

_____

8. ¿Por qué se fueron sus padres al campo? _____

_____

9. ¿Quién abrió la ventana? _____

_____

10. ¿Quién rompió esta silla? _____

_____

II. **Sopa de letras** (Alphabet soup). En esta sopa de letras, busque los verbos **ver, abrir, escribir** en el pretérito perfecto. Las formas de estos verbos pueden aparecer de derecha a izquierda, de izquierda a derecha, de abajo arriba y viceversa, y en diagonal.

B	U	H	O	H	B	U	T	O
H	B	U	A	G	I	R	O	T
H	U	B	E	V	I	S	T	O
R	I	O	E	S	C	I	R	T
H	U	E	B	I	M	O	E	S
O	R	S	E	I	B	U	I	H
E	S	C	R	I	O	T	B	U
V	I	R	T	O	A	B	A	E
H	A	I	B	A	B	I	E	R
I	S	T	O	V	H	U	B	E
R	O	O	T	R	O	T	U	I
R	C	S	E	E	B	U	H	O

III. Discriminación de los sonidos. Su profesor de español va a pronunciar una sola palabra, sea la letra A, sea la letra B. Escoja la palabra que su profesor pronuncia y escriba la letra en la línea.

Modelo: **A. lama**
B. llama _A_

He escrito la letra A en la línea porque mi profesor de español ha pronunciado la palabra de la letra A.

1. A. fuego
   B. luego _____

2. A. llana
   B. lana _____

3. A. amó
   B. amo _____

4. A. digo
   B. dijo _____

5. A. aun
   B. aún _____

6. A. cesta
   B. sexta _____

IV. Uno por tres. Ponga en las casillas una palabra que, con la palabra ya inscrita, permitirá formar otra palabra. La tercera palabra será el resultado de la palabra ya inscrita y de la palabra que usted va a escribir.

Modelo: | P | A | S | A | + | | | | | | = _____

Solución: | P | A | S | A | + | T | I | E | M | P | O | = PASATIEMPO

1. | | | + | C | A | R | E | C | E | R | = _____

2. | | | | + | S | O | L | = _____

3. | | | | + | T | A | L | = _____

V. Varias palabras en una sola. Utilizando las letras en la palabra **CHILE,** ¿cuántas palabras puede usted escribir? Escriba dos palabras, por lo menos.

CHILE

1. _____ 2. _____

VI. Las palabras escondidas. En la rejilla, busque las palabras en español por las palabras en inglés. Cuando las haya encontrado, ráyelas. Las palabras, pueden estar inscritas en todas las direcciones: de abajo arriba, de arriba abajo, de derecha a izquierda, de izquierda a derecha, al derecho y al revés, y en diagonal.

246   La misma letra puede ser común a varias palabras.

M	A	D	O	M	A	D	R	E	I
H	E	R	A	H	E	R	D	A	P
B	U	E	H	I	J	O	T	Í	O
H	I	J	E	J	A	E	O	I	U
P	A	D	R	A	B	U	E	L	A
H	E	R	M	A	N	A	T	Í	A
P	A	D	A	E	R	B	U	E	L
E	H	M	N	O	L	E	U	B	A
T	O	I	O	I	T	A	O	T	O

mother	grandmother	son	uncle	brother
father	grandfather	daughter	aunt	sister

VII. Dictado. Escriba las oraciones que su profesor de español va a leer.

1. _____

2. _____

3. _____

VIII. ¿Qué tiempo hace?

Respuesta: _____

IX. ¿Qué están haciendo Uds.?

Respuesta: _____

X. ¿Qué está haciendo usted ?

Respuesta: _____

XI. Seleccione la respuesta correcta para completar cada oración.

1. Ayer no nos visitó   (1) alguien   (2) nadie   (3) algunos   (4) ningunos   _____

2. El Año Nuevo empieza el . . . de enero.   (1) un   (2) uno   (3) primero
   (4) primer   _____

3. Antes de . . . las noticias, el joven estaba bastante nervioso. (1) oyera (2) oír
(3) oiga (4) oyendo   _____

4. María es . . . guapa como las otras chicas. (1) tan (2) tanto (3) más
(4) menos   _____

5. Me pidió que lo . . . a clase. (1) traer (2) traeré (3) traje (4) trajera   _____

XII. En este diálogo, usted trabaja en una librería. Usted es librero. Un señor entra en la librería
para comprarle un libro a su primo. Usted le recomienda varios libros. El señor escoge un libro
de historia.

Complete el diálogo.

Usted: Buenos días, señor. ¿Qué clase de libro busca?

El cliente: _____

Usted: Muchos clientes prefieren libros de arte.

El cliente: _____

Usted: Tenemos un magnífico libro sobre los toros.

El cliente: _____

Usted: ¿A su primo le gusta la música?

El cliente: _____

Usted: Aquí tiene usted un nuevo libro sobre nuestra Guerra Civil.

El cliente: _____

XIII. Lea el siguiente párrafo dos veces, por lo menos. Entonces, escoja la palabra más apropiada
para completar la frase.

A Pedro le gustan los deportes. Su deporte favorito es el fútbol. Siempre quiere que su
_____ esté en buena forma porque es

1. A. cuerda
   B. cuerpo
   C. cuenta
   D. cuesta

guardameta del _____ de fútbol de su escuela. Quiere _____

2. A. equipaje   3. A. estar
   B. equipo   B. ser
   C. tema   C. tener
   D. tempestad   D. haber

siempre dispuesto para jugar bien. Siempre cuida su salud; por ejemplo, Pedro
_____ solamente alimentos que son buenos para la salud. Cuando _____

4. A. come   5. A. jugo
   B. bebe   B. juega
   C. compra   C. juego
   D. vende   D. jugar

al fútbol, evita el helado, las patatas fritas y los pasteles.

HOGAREÑA EN VACACIONES

Tras un año de duro y diario esfuerzo en el Trabajo el Hogar y el Colégio, han llegado por fin y para todos, esas bien ganadas vacaciones.

Hogareña, la nueva galleta de Cuétara, quiere estar con todos y en todos los momentos más felices de este verano.

Hogareña es siempre ideal para el desayuno y la merienda en cualquier época, porque está elaborada con harina, leche, huevos, mantequilla y azúcar, ingredientes todos ellos con un alto valor nutritivo y energético. Hogareña es además cremosa, crujiente, riquísima y no hay quien se resista.

Y ahora, el paquete de aluminio de 200 grs., que cabe en cualquier sitio, no puede faltar entre lo más imprescindible para ir a la Playa, la Sierra o la Excursión.

Los momentos más felices de sus vacaciones saben mejor con Hogareña.

Hogareña la podrá encontrar en su proveedor habitual con las siguientes presentaciones:
ESTUCHE FAMILIAR de 600 grs.
PAQUETE DE ALUMINIO de 200 grs.

Cuétara
Todo en galletas

APPENDIX

A GUIDE TO PRONOUNCING SPANISH SOUNDS

PURE VOWEL SOUNDS

Phonetic Symbol	Pronounced as in the Spanish word	English word
a	*la*	father
e	*le*	ate
i	*ti*	see
o	*yo*	order
u	*tu*	too

OTHER SOUNDS

h	*justo* *general* *gigante*	help

The letter *h* in a Spanish word is not pronounced.

y	*yo* *llave*	yes

DIPHTHONGS (2 vowels together)

ai	*baile* *hay*	eye
au	*aula*	cow
ei	*reino* *ley*	they
eu	*Europa*	wayward
ya	*enviar* *ya*	yard
ye	*tiene* *yendo*	yes
yo	*iodo* *yodo*	yore
yu	*viuda* *yugo*	you
oy	*oigo* *estoy*	toy
wa	*cuando*	want
we	*bueno*	way
wi	*suizo*	week
wo	*cuota*	woke

The pronunciation given in phonetic symbols is that of most Latin American countries and of certain regions in Spain.

CONSONANT SOUNDS

Phonetic Symbol	Pronounced as in the Spanish word	English word
b	*bien* *va*	boy
d	*dar*	this
f	*falda*	fan
g	*gato* *goma* *gusto*	gap
k	*casa* *culpa* *que* *quito*	cap
l	*la*	lard
m	*me*	may
n	*no*	no
ɲ	*niño*	canyon
p	*papá*	papa
R	*pero*	April
RR	*perro*	burr, gr-r-r
s	*sopa* *cero* *cita* *zumo*	soft
t	*tu*	sit
tʃ	*mucho*	church

TRIPHTHONGS (3 vowels together)

yai	*enviáis*	yipe
yau	*miau*	meow
yei	*enviéis*	yea
wai	*guaina* *Uruguay*	wise
wau	*guau*	wow
wei	*continuéis* *buey*	wait

The accent mark (´) over a vowel sound indicates that you must raise your voice on that vowel sound.

English words given here contain sounds that only approximate Spanish sounds.

FIVE COMMONLY USED SPANISH VERBS CONJUGATED IN ALL 14 TENSES

Here are some commonly used irregular verbs conjugated fully in all the tenses and moods. If any verbs *not* given here are of interest to you, consult my book *501 Spanish verbs fully conjugated in all the tenses in a new easy to learn format*, Second Edition, which contains them all, also published by Barron's.

In the format of the verbs that follow, the subject pronouns have been omitted in order to emphasize the verb forms. The subject pronouns are, as you know:

Subject Pronouns

singular	*plural*
yo	nosotros (nosotras)
tú	vosotros (vosotras)
Ud. (él, ella)	Uds. (ellos, ellas)

estar to be

Gerundio **estando**   Part. pas. **estado**

The Seven Simple Tenses		The Seven Compound Tenses	
Singular	Plural	Singular	Plural

1 presente de indicativo		8 perfecto de indicativo	
estoy	estamos	he estado	hemos estado
estás	estáis	has estado	habéis estado
está	están	ha estado	han estado

2 imperfecto de indicativo		9 pluscuamperfecto de indicativo	
estaba	estábamos	había estado	habíamos estado
estabas	estabais	habías estado	habíais estado
estaba	estaban	había estado	habían estado

3 pretérito		10 pretérito anterior	
estuve	estuvimos	hube estado	hubimos estado
estuviste	estuvisteis	hubiste estado	hubisteis estado
estuvo	estuvieron	hubo estado	hubieron estado

4 futuro		11 futuro perfecto	
estaré	estaremos	habré estado	habremos estado
estarás	estaréis	habrás estado	habréis estado
estará	estarán	habrá estado	habrán estado

5 potencial simple		12 potencial compuesto	
estaría	estaríamos	habría estado	habríamos estado
estarías	estaríais	habrías estado	habríais estado
estaría	estarían	habría estado	habrían estado

6 presente de subjuntivo		13 perfecto de subjuntivo	
esté	estemos	haya estado	hayamos estado
estés	estéis	hayas estado	hayáis estado
esté	estén	haya estado	hayan estado

7 imperfecto de subjuntivo		14 pluscuamperfecto de subjuntivo	
estuviera	estuviéramos	hubiera estado	hubiéramos estado
estuvieras	estuvierais	hubieras estado	hubierais estado
estuviera	estuvieran	hubiera estado	hubieran estado
OR		OR	
estuviese	estuviésemos	hubiese estado	hubiésemos estado
estuvieses	estuvieseis	hubieses estado	hubieseis estado
estuviese	estuviesen	hubiese estado	hubiesen estado

imperativo

—	estemos
está; no estés	estad; no estéis
esté	estén

Common idiomatic expressions using this verb

— ¿Cómo está Ud.?
— Estoy muy bien, gracias. ¿Y usted?
— Estoy enfermo hoy.

estar para + inf.   to be about + inf.
   Estoy para salir.   I am about to go out.
estar por   to be in favor of

haber to have (as an auxiliary verb to form compound tenses)
Gerundio **habiendo**   Part. pas. **habido**

The Seven Simple Tenses		The Seven Compound Tenses	
Singular	Plural	Singular	Plural
1 presente de indicativo		**8 perfecto de indicativo**	
he	hemos	he habido	hemos habido
has	habéis	has habido	habéis habido
ha	han	ha habido	han habido
2 imperfecto de indicativo		**9 pluscuamperfecto de indicativo**	
había	habíamos	había habido	habíamos habido
habías	habíais	habías habido	habíais habido
había	habían	había habido	habían habido
3 pretérito		**10 pretérito anterior**	
hube	hubimos	hube habido	hubimos habido
hubiste	hubisteis	hubiste habido	hubisteis habido
hubo	hubieron	hubo habido	hubieron habido
4 futuro		**11 futuro perfecto**	
habré	habremos	habré habido	habremos habido
habrás	habréis	habrás habido	habréis habido
habrá	habrán	habrá habido	habrán habido
5 potencial simple		**12 potencial compuesto**	
habría	habríamos	habría habido	habríamos habido
habrías	habríais	habrías habido	habríais habido
habría	habrían	habría habido	habrían habido
6 presente de subjuntivo		**13 perfecto de subjuntivo**	
haya	hayamos	haya habido	hayamos habido
hayas	hayáis	hayas habido	hayáis habido
haya	hayan	haya habido	hayan habido
7 imperfecto de subjuntivo		**14 pluscuamperfecto de subjuntivo**	
hubiera	hubiéramos	hubiera habido	hubiéramos habido
hubieras	hubierais	hubieras habido	hubierais habido
hubiera	hubieran	hubiera habido	hubieran habido
OR		OR	
hubiese	hubiésemos	hubiese habido	hubiésemos habido
hubieses	hubieseis	hubieses habido	hubieseis habido
hubiese	hubiesen	hubiese habido	hubiesen habido

imperativo

—	hayamos
he; no hayas	habed; no hayáis
haya	hayan

Words and expressions related to this verb

el haber   credit (in bookkeeping)
los haberes   assets, possessions, property
habérselas con alguien   to have a showdown with someone

hacer to do, to make
Gerundio **haciendo**   Part. pas. **hecho**

The Seven Simple Tenses		The Seven Compound Tenses	
Singular	Plural	Singular	Plural
1 presente de indicativo		**8 perfecto de indicativo**	
hago	hacemos	he hecho	hemos hecho
haces	hacéis	has hecho	habéis hecho
hace	hacen	ha hecho	han hecho
2 imperfecto de indicativo		**9 pluscuamperfecto de indicativo**	
hacía	hacíamos	había hecho	habíamos hecho
hacías	hacíais	habías hecho	habíais hecho
hacía	hacían	había hecho	habían hecho
3 pretérito		**10 pretérito anterior**	
hice	hicimos	hube hecho	hubimos hecho
hiciste	hicisteis	hubiste hecho	hubisteis hecho
hizo	hicieron	hubo hecho	hubieron hecho
4 futuro		**11 futuro perfecto**	
haré	haremos	habré hecho	habremos hecho
harás	haréis	habrás hecho	habréis hecho
hará	harán	habrá hecho	habrán hecho
5 potencial simple		**12 potencial compuesto**	
haría	haríamos	habría hecho	habríamos hecho
harías	haríais	habrías hecho	habríais hecho
haría	harían	habría hecho	habrían hecho
6 presente de subjuntivo		**13 perfecto de subjuntivo**	
haga	hagamos	haya hecho	hayamos hecho
hagas	hagáis	hayas hecho	hayáis hecho
haga	hagan	haya hecho	hayan hecho
7 imperfecto de subjuntivo		**14 pluscuamperfecto de subjuntivo**	
hiciera	hiciéramos	hubiera hecho	hubiéramos hecho
hicieras	hicierais	hubieras hecho	hubierais hecho
hiciera	hicieran	hubiera hecho	hubieran hecho
hiciese	hiciésemos	hubiese hecho	hubiésemos hecho
hicieses	hicieseis	hubieses hecho	hubieseis hecho
hiciese	hiciesen	hubiese hecho	hubiesen hecho

	imperativo	
—	hagamos	
haz; no hagas	haced; no hagáis	
haga	hagan	

Common idiomatic expressions using this verb

Dicho y hecho.   No sooner said than done.
La práctica hace maestro al novicio.   Practice makes perfect.
Si a Roma fueres, haz como vieres.   When in Rome do as the Romans do. Note that it is
  not uncommon to use the future subjunctive in proverbs, as in *fueres* (**ir** or **ser**) and
  vieres (**ver**).

ir to go
Gerundio **yendo**   Part. pas. **ido**

The Seven Simple Tenses		The Seven Compound Tenses	
Singular	Plural	Singular	Plural
1 presente de indicativo		**8 perfecto de indicativo**	
voy	vamos	he ido	hemos ido
vas	vais	has ido	habéis ido
va	van	ha ido	han ido
2 imperfecto de indicativo		**9 pluscuamperfecto de indicativo**	
iba	íbamos	había ido	habíamos ido
ibas	ibais	habías ido	habíais ido
iba	iban	había ido	habían ido
3 pretérito		**10 pretérito anterior**	
fui	fuimos	hube ido	hubimos ido
fuiste	fuisteis	hubiste ido	hubisteis ido
fue	fueron	hubo ido	hubieron ido
4 futuro		**11 futuro perfecto**	
iré	iremos	habré ido	habremos ido
irás	iréis	habrás ido	habréis ido
irá	irán	habrá ido	habrán ido
5 potencial simple		**12 potencial compuesto**	
iría	iríamos	habría ido	habríamos ido
irías	iríais	habrías ido	habríais ido
iría	irían	habría ido	habrían ido
6 presente de subjuntivo		**13 perfecto de subjuntivo**	
vaya	vayamos	haya ido	hayamos ido
vayas	vayáis	hayas ido	hayáis ido
vaya	vayan	haya ido	hayan ido
7 imperfecto de subjuntivo		**14 pluscuamperfecto de subjuntivo**	
fuera	fuéramos	hubiera ido	hubiéramos ido
fueras	fuerais	hubieras ido	hubierais ido
fuera	fueran	hubiera ido	hubieran ido
OR		OR	
fuese	fuésemos	hubiese ido	hubiésemos ido
fueses	fueseis	hubieses ido	hubieseis ido
fuese	fuesen	hubiese ido	hubiesen ido

imperativo

—	vamos (no vayamos)
ve; no vayas	id; no vayáis
vaya	vayan

Common idiomatic expressions using this verb

ir de compras   to go shopping
ir de brazo   to walk arm in arm
¿Cómo le va?   How goes it? How are you?
Cuando el gato va a sus devociones, bailan los ratones.   When the cat is away, the mice will play.

ir a caballo   to ride horseback
un billete de ida y vuelta   return ticket
¡Qué va!   Nonsense!

ser to be
Gerundio **siendo**   Part. pas. **sido**

The Seven Simple Tenses		The Seven Compound Tenses	
Singular	Plural	Singular	Plural

1 presente de indicativo

soy	somos		
eres	sois		
es	son		

8 perfecto de indicativo

he sido	hemos sido
has sido	habéis sido
ha sido	han sido

2 imperfecto de indicativo

era	éramos
eras	erais
era	eran

9 pluscuamperfecto de indicativo

había sido	habíamos sido
habías sido	habíais sido
había sido	habían sido

3 pretérito

fui	fuimos
fuiste	fuisteis
fue	fueron

10 pretérito anterior

hube sido	hubimos sido
hubiste sido	hubisteis sido
hubo sido	hubieron sido

4 futuro

seré	seremos
serás	seréis
será	serán

11 futuro perfecto

habré sido	habremos sido
habrás sido	habréis sido
habrá sido	habrán sido

5 potencial simple

sería	seríamos
serías	seríais
sería	serían

12 potencial compuesto

habría sido	habríamos sido
habrías sido	habríais sido
habría sido	habrían sido

6 presente de subjuntivo

sea	seamos
seas	seáis
sea	sean

13 perfecto de subjuntivo

haya sido	hayamos sido
hayas sido	hayáis sido
haya sido	hayan sido

7 imperfecto de subjuntivo

fuera	fuéramos
fueras	fuerais
fuera	fueran
OR	
fuese	fuésemos
fueses	fueseis
fuese	fuesen

14 pluscuamperfecto de subjuntivo

hubiera sido	hubiéramos sido
hubieras sido	hubierais sido
hubiera sido	hubieran sido
OR	
hubiese sido	hubiésemos sido
hubieses sido	hubieseis sido
hubiese sido	hubiesen sido

imperativo

—	seamos
sé; no seas	sed; no seáis
sea	sean

Common idiomatic expressions using this verb

Dime con quien andas y te diré quien eres. Tell me who your friends are and I will tell you who you are.
es decir that is, that is to say; **Si yo fuera usted. . .** If I were you. . .
¿Qué hora es? What time is it?   **Es la una.** It is one o'clock.   **Son las dos.** It is two o'clock.

VOCABULARY SPANISH AND ENGLISH WORDS IN ONE ALPHABETICAL LISTING

This list of vocabulary contains words and expressions in Spanish and English in one alphabetical order because I think it is convenient if you look in one place instead of two for an entry. One listing prevents you from looking inadvertently in a Spanish listing for an English word or in an English listing for a Spanish word. Also, cognates and near-cognates in both languages are reduced to a single entry. All Spanish words are printed in bold face.

The preposition *to* in an English infinitive is omitted, e.g., *to eat* is listed under *eat*.

Note that the Spanish alphabet contains the letters, **ch, ll, ñ,** and **rr** which are considered separately. A Spanish word, therefore, that contains or begins with **ch** is alphabetized *after* the letter **c; ll** is alphabetized *after* the letter **l**; and **ñ** is alphabetized *after* the letter **n.** Therefore, in the alphabetical listing of words given below, you will find **mañana** after **manzana, ochenta** after **ocupar.** This rule does not apply to the double consonant **rr.** English words are alphabetized in this vocabulary list according to these rules, *e.g., Christmas* is listed under the separate letter **CH,** which comes after **C.** This is done for the sake of consistency.

Vowels placed in parentheses after an infinitive in the following list, *e.g.,* **(ue), (ie, i)** mean that the vowel in the stem of the verb form changes when stressed. These are called stem-changing verbs. For example, the entry **pensar (ie)** means that the vowel **e** in the stem changes to **ie** when stressed, as in **pienso.** See the entry *stem-changing verbs* in the index. Also, consult the table of contents for work units where stem-changing verbs and verbs that change in spelling (orthographical-changing verbs) are presented. Consonants placed in parentheses after an infinitive, *e.g.,* **(c), (j)** mean that the verb form changes in spelling.

For a list of names of boys and girls in Spanish, see Work Unit 8.

If you do not understand the meaning of an abbreviation, look it up in the list of abbreviations in the beginning pages of this book. Entries in this vocabulary pertain to words used in this book. For any not listed here, consult a standard Spanish-English/English-Spanish dictionary.

A

a *prep.* at, to, in; **a cargo de** in care of; **¡A ver!** let's see! also used as personal **a** in front of a dir. obj. n. referring to a person, *e.g.,* **Conozco a María.** I know Mary; **A buen fin no hay mal principio.** All's well that ends well.

abajo *adv.* down, downstairs, below; **de abajo arriba** from bottom to top

abarca *pres. indic. of* **abarcar (qu)** *v.* to embrace, clasp, grasp

abierto *past part.* (*participio*) *of* **abrir** *v.* to open; *also adj.,* **abierto, -a, -os, -as** open, opened

able, to be *v.* **poder (ue)**

abrazar (c) *v.* to embrace; **el abrazo** hug, embrace; **abrazarse a** to embrace; **dar un abrazo a** to embrace; **darse un abrazo** to embrace (hug) each other

abre *pres. indic. of* **abrir;** **abrirse** *refl. v.* to open up

abrelatas *n.m., s. pl.* can opener

abrigo *n.m.* coat, overcoat; shelter

abril *n.m.* April

abrir *v.* to open

absence **la ausencia**

absent *adj.* **ausente**

absolutamente *adv.* absolutely

absoluto, -a, -os, -as, *adj.* absolute; **en absoluto** absolutely

absurdo, -a, -os, -as *adj.* absurd

abuela *n.f.* grandmother; **abuelo** *n.m.* grandfather; **los abuelos** grandparents

abundancia *n.f.* abundance; **abundante** *adj.* abundant, plentiful

acabar *v.* to finish, end, complete; **acabó** *pret.;* **Se acabó.** It has ended; It has finished; It's finished; It's over; **acabar de +**

inf. to have just + past part.; **Acabo de comer.** I have just eaten. I just ate; **Acababa de comer cuando el teléfono sonó.** I had just eaten when the telephone rang.

acaso *adv.* perhaps

accept *v.* **aceptar; aceptara** *imperf. sub.*

accompany *v.* **acompañar**

according to **según**

accuse *v.* **acusar; Acuso recibo . . .** I acknowledge receipt . . .

acento *n.m.* accent

aceptara *imperf. sub. of* **aceptar** *v.* to accept; **acepto** *pres. indic.*

acerca de *prep.* about, concerning; **acercarse (qu) (a + obj.)** *refl. v.* to approach, get near (close)

acknowledge receipt of *v.* **acusar recibo de**

acknowledgment **el agradecimiento**

aconsejar *v.* to advise

acordarse (ue) (de + obj.) *refl. v.* to remember

acostado, -a, -os, -as *adj.* lying down

acostarás *fut. of* **acostar (ue)** *v.* to put to bed; **acostarse (ue)** to go to bed (to put oneself to bed), to lie down

acróstico *n.m.* acrostic (word game)

actividad *n.f.* activity

actual *adj.* present (now), present-day; **el español actual** *Spanish Now*

acuerda, acuerdo *pres. indic. of* **acordar (ue)** *v.* to agree, agree upon, grant; **el acuerdo** agreement; **de acuerdo** okay, agreed; **estar de acuerdo** to agree, be in agreement; **acuérdese** *imper. of* **acordarse (ue)** remember

acuesta, acuesto, *pres. indic. of* **acostar (ue)**

acusar *v.* to accuse; **acuso** *pres. indic.;* **Acuso recibo . . .** I acknowledge receipt. . .

add *v.* **añadir**

address **la dirección**

adelantar *v.* to go forward, advance; **adelante** *adv.* forward, onward; **¡Adelante con . . . !** On with . . . ! **adelantarse a** to go ahead of

además *adv.* besides, furthermore; **además de** *prep.* in addition to, besides

adiós *interj.* good-bye; **Dios** God

adivinanza *n.f.* riddle

adivinar *v.* to guess, solve (a riddle), foretell the future

adjetivo *n.m.* adjective

admiración *n.f.* admiration; **signo de admiración** exclamation mark

admirar *v.* to admire

admitir *v.* to admit

adonde *adv.* (to) where; **¿adónde?** where? where (to)? to where?

adondequiera see this word in the index.

adoptar *v.* to adopt

adorar *v.* to adore, worship; **Te adoro, Juan.** I adore you, John; **la adoración** adoration

adornar de *v.* to adorn with, decorate with

advenir *v.* to happen (come, arrive)

adverbio *n.m.* adverb; see *adverbs* in the index.

advertir (ie, i) *v.* to warn, advise

aeroplano *n.m.* airplane; **el aeropuerto** airport

afectar *v.* to affect; **el afecto** affection, fondness

aficionado *n.m.* fan (of sports, *etc.*); **ser aficionado (aficionada) a** to be a fan of, to be fond of

afirmativo *n.m.* affirmative

aflicción *n.f.* affliction, sorrow

afortunadamente *adv.* fortunately; see *adverbs* in the index.

after *adv., prep.* **después (de); tras**

afternoon **la tarde**

afuera *adv.* outside

age **la edad**

agitar *v.* to agitate, move, stir

agosto *n.m.* August

agradable *adj.* pleasant, enjoyable, agreeable

agradecer (zc) *v.* to be grateful, thankful; **agradecido, -a, -os, -as** *adj.* grateful

agreeable *adj.* **grato, -a, -os, -as agradable**

agreed (okay) **de acuerdo**

agua *n.f.* **el agua; agua mineral** mineral water; **agua fresca** fresh water

aguardar *v.* to wait (for), await

aguja *n.f.* needle

ahora *adv.* now; **ahora mismo** right away, right now

ahorrar *v.* to economize, save (money)

aid *v.* **ayudar**

air **el aire; al aire libre** outdoors, in the open air

airplane **el avión, el aeroplano**

al (a + el, *def.art.)* at the, to the; **al teatro** to the theater; **al cine** to the movies; **al muchacho** to the boy; **al amanecer** at dawn; **al mismo tiempo** at the same time; **al siguiente día** on the following day; **al + inf.** on (upon) + pres. part., **al ver** on (upon) seeing, **al comer** on (upon) eating; *see* **al** in the index.

alcanzar (c) *v.* to attain, reach

alcoba *n.f.* bedroom

alegraría *potencial of* **alegrar; alegrarse de + inf.** *refl.v.* to rejoice, to be glad; **Me alegraría . . .** I would be glad . . . ; **alegrarse de que + sub.** to be glad that . . .

alegre *adj.* happy, gay, joyful; **alegremente** *adj.* happily, joyfully

alegría *n.f.* joy, happiness

Alejandro Alexander

alfabeto *n.m.* alphabet; alphabet soup **la sopa de letras**

alfombra *n.f.* carpet

algo *indef. pron.* something, anything; *see* **algo** in the index.

alguien *indef. pron.* someone, somebody, anybody, anyone; *see* **alguien** in the index.

algún *adj., shortened form of* **alguno,** *used in front of a m. sing. n.,* **algún día** some day; **alguno, -a, -os, -as** *adj., pron.* some, a few; **algunas veces** sometimes; *see* **algún** in the index.

alhaja *n.f.* jewel

alimentarse *refl.v.* to nourish (feed) oneself

alimento *n.m.* food

alma *n.f.* **(el alma)** soul; **un alma bondadosa** a kind, helpful soul

almacén *n.m.,* **los almacenes** store, department store

almorzar (ue, c) *v.* to lunch, have (eat) lunch; **ir a almorzar** to go to lunch

almuerzo *n.m.* lunch; **tomar el almuerzo** to have (eat) lunch; **para el almuerzo** for lunch; **tomar el almuerzo** to have lunch; **almuerzo** *is also pres. indic. of* **almorzar (ue, c); ¡Qué almuerzo!** What a lunch!

alone *adj.* **solo, -a, -os, -as**

alphabet **el alfabeto;** alphabet soup **la sopa de letras**

alrededor *adv.* around

also *adv.* **también;** also (as well) **igualmente**

alternativa *n.f.* alternative; **alternativamente** *adv.* alternately

alto, -a, -os, -as *adj.* high, tall; **en voz alta** loudly, in a loud voice

alumbrar *v.* to illuminate, light, enlighten

alumna *n.f.* **alumno** *n.m.* pupil, student

always *adv.* **siempre**

allá *adv.* there; **allí** *adv.* there

allow *v.* **dejar, permitir**

amable *adj.* friendly, kind, likable

amar *v.* to love; **Te amo, Juana.** I love you, Jean.

amarillo, -a, -os, -as *adj.* yellow

ambulancia *n.f.* ambulance

amiga *n.f.* (girl) friend; **amigo** *n.m.* (boy) friend; **amigo mío, amiga mía** my friend: **amigos míos, amigas mías** my friends (used in direct address), e.g., **Amigo mío, ¿qué tal?** My friend, how are things? See **amigo mío** in the index.

amo *pres. indic. of* **amar; amó** *pret.*

amor *n.m.* love

amuse oneself *refl.v.* **divertirse (ie, i)**

amusing *adj.* **divertido, -a, -os, -as**

anciano, -a, -os, -as *adj.* elderly, old

ancho, -a, -os, -as *adj.* wide, broad

and *conj.* **y** *or* **e** (**e** is used instead of **y** to mean *and* when in front of a word beginning with **i-** or **hi-,** *e.g.,* **hermosa e inteligente** beautiful and intelligent; **madres e hijas** mothers and daughters

andar *v.* to walk, run (machine); **andar a pie** to walk; (sinónimo de **andar: marchar**)

Andrés Andrew

anger *v.* **enojar**

animal *n.m.* animal; **animalito** small animal; see *diminutive endings* -ito & -illo in the index.

aniversario *n.m.* anniversary

announce *v.* **anunciar**

annoy *v.* **enojar**

anoche *adv.* last night, yesterday evening

answer *v.* **contestar, responder;** *as a n.,* **la con-**

testación, la respuesta

anteayer *adv.* day before yesterday

anteojos *n.m., pl.* eye glasses

antes *adv.* before; **antes de** before; **antes de + inf.** **antes de cerrar** before closing, **antes de comenzar** before beginning; see **antes de** in the index.

anticonstitucionalmente *adv.* anticonstitutionally

antónimo *n.m.* antonym, opposite (in meaning)

anunciar *v.* to announce; **anunció** *pret.;* **el anuncio** advertisement, sign

añadir *v.* to add

año *n.m.* year; **el año pasado** last year; **el año nuevo** New Year; **años** years; sinónimo de **años: la edad** age

aparecer (zc) *v.* to appear

apariencia *n.f.* appearance

apartamento *n.m.* apartment

apetito *n.m.* appetite

aplastar *v.* to crush, smash; **aplastado, -a, -os, -as** *adj.* crushed

apoyar *v.* to support, favor, advocate

appear *v.* **aparecer (zc)**

appearance **la apariencia**

apple **la manzana**

appreciate *v.* **apreciar**

apprentice **el novicio**

approach *v.* **acercarse (qu) (a + obj.)** *refl.v.*

aprender *v.* to learn; **aprender a + inf.** to learn (to); **Aprendo a leer.** I am learning to read; **aprendí** *pret.;* **aprendido** *past part.* **(participio); Tú no has aprendido nada.** You have not learned anything.

apresurarse *refl. v.* to hurry, rush; **se apresuró** *pret.*

apretar (ie) *v.* to squeeze, compress, tighten, press

aprieta *pres. indic. of* **apretar (ie)**

aquel, aquella, aquellos, aquellas *dem. adj.* that, those (farther away)

aquel hombre that man (over there), **aquella mujer** that woman (over there), **aquellos libros** those books, **aquellas casas** those houses; see **aquel** in the index.

aquí *adv.* here; **He aquí . . .** Here is . . . ; **Aquí tiene Ud. . . .** Here is . . . , Here are . . . ; **por aquí** this way, around here

árbol *n.m.* tree

arena *n.f.* sand

arm **el brazo;** armchair **el sillón,** la butaca

arrancar (qu) *v.* to pull away, snatch, tear out

arrange *v.* **arreglar;** *can also mean* to fix, regulate, adjust

arriba *adv.* top, up, above; **de arriba abajo** from top to bottom; **desde arriba** from above

arroz *n.m.* rice; **arroz con pollo** rice with chicken

arte *n.m.f.* art

articular *v.* to articulate, pronounce distinctly

artículo *n.m.* article; **artículo determinado** definite article; **artículo indeterminado** indefinite article; see the entry *articles* in the index.

artista *n.m., n.f.* artist

as *conj.* **como;** *as well (also)* **igualmente**

así *adv.* so, thus, like this, in this manner; **así, así** so so; **así como** as well as

asiento *n.m.* seat; **tomar asiento** to take a seat

asignatura *n.f.* course (subject studied)

asistir a *v.* to attend, be present at

ask *v.* **preguntar;** ask for **pedir (i)**

aspecto *n.m.* aspect

assist *v.* **ayudar;** assistance **la ayuda;** assistant **el (la) ayudante**

at *prep.* **a;** at the **al, a los, a las;** see **a** in the index.

atacar (qu) *v.* to attack

atención *n.f.* attention; **prestar atención a** to pay attention to

atentamente *adv.* attentively, very truly yours (used in signing letters as a complimentary closing); see the entry *letter writing* in the index.

atrás *adv.* behind, towards the back, backward; **hacia atrás** backwards

attack *v.* **atacar (qu)**

attend *v.* **asistir a**

attention **la atención;** to pay attention to **prestar atención a, hacer caso**

auction sale **una venta pública; A la señora Rodríguez le gustan las ventas públicas.** Mrs. Rodríguez likes auction sales (To Mrs. Rodríguez auction sales are pleasing.)

auctioneer **el subastador**

auditorio *n.m.* auditorium

aula *n.f.* **(el aula)** classroom, lecture hall

aun, aún *adv.* as yet, still, yet, even

aunque *conj.* although, even though

aunt **la tía**

ausencia *n.f.* absence

ausente *adj.* absent

author **el autor, la autora**

auto *n.m.* auto, car

autobús *n.m.* bus; **los autobuses; en autobús** by bus

autógrafo *n.m.* autograph

automobile **el automóvil, el auto, el coche**

autor *n.m.,* **autora** *n.f.* author

avanzar (c) *v.* to advance, go forward

avenida *n.f.* avenue

aventura *n.f.* adventure

aventurarse *refl.v.* to risk, venture

averiguar (gü) *v.* to find out, inquire

avión *n.m.* airplane, plane; **los aviones**

avoid *v.* **evitar**

¡Ay! *excl.* My! Oh! Wow!

ayer *adv.* yesterday; **ayer**

por la tarde yesterday afternoon; **anteayer** day before yesterday; **ayer por la noche** yesterday evening

ayuda *n.f.* help, aid, assistance

ayudante *n.m., f.* assistant; **ayudar a + inf.** *v.* to help (to), aid (to)

azúcar *n.m.* sugar

azul, azules *adj.* blue

B

babysitter **la niñera, el niñero**

back (of an animal) **el lomo**

bailar *v.* to dance; **bailaremos** *fut.*

baile *n.m.* dance, dancing

¡Bailen! Dance! *imper. of* **bailar**

bajar *v.* to come (go) down, descend

bajo *adv.* beneath, below, under

bajo, -a, -os, -as *adj.* low, short; **en voz baja** in a low voice; **hablar bajo** to speak softly, in a low voice

bakery **la panadería**

balcón *n.m.* balcony; **los balcones**

banco *n.m.* bench; bank

bañarse *refl.v.* to bathe oneself, take a bath

baño *n.m.* bath; **el cuarto de baño** bathroom

barato, -a, -os, -as *adj.* cheap, inexpensive

barco *n.m.* boat

bark *v.* **ladrar** (said of a dog)

baseball **el béisbol**

básico, -a, -os, -as *adj.* basic

basket **la cesta**

básquetbol *n.m.* basketball

¡Basta! Enough!

bastante *adj.* enough, sufficient; *adv.*, sufficiently

bastar *v.* to be enough, be sufficient

bastón (de mando) *n.m.* baton stick (used to give an order, a command)

basura *n.f.* garbage, rubbish

bathe oneself *refl.v.* **bañarse**

bathroom **el cuarto de baño**

be *v.* **ser, estar;** see these two words in the index; be called, call oneself *refl.v.* **llamarse;** be glad *refl.v.* **alegrarse;** be in love with *v.* **estar enamorado, -a de;** be lacking *v.* **faltar;** be named *refl.v.* **llamarse;** be present at *v.* **asistir a;** be wanting *v.* **faltar;** be worth *v.* **valer;** see the entry *be* in the index.

beach **la playa**

bear up (endure) *v.* **sufrir**

beautiful *adj.* **hermoso, -a, -os, -as**

beber *v.* to drink; **bebió** *pret.;* **bebiendo** *gerundio of* **beber; una bebida** a drink, beverage

because *conj.* **porque**

bed **la cama**

beef steak **el bistec**

before *adv.* **antes (de);** before + *pres. part.* **antes de + inf.;** before closing **antes de cerrar;** before beginning **antes de comenzar**

begin *v.* **comenzar (ie; c), empezar (ie; c), principiar a + inf.** begin + inf.; **ponerse a + inf.;** beginner *n.m.* **novicio**

behave oneself *refl.v.* **comportarse**

behind *adv.* **tras, atrás**

béisbol *n.m.* baseball

belief **la creencia**

believe *v.* **creer (y)**

belong to *v.* **pertenecer (zc) a**

below adv. **abajo, debajo (de)**

bello, -a, -os, -as *adj.* beautiful

besar *v.* to kiss

beso *n.m.* kiss; **dar un beso a** give a kiss to, to kiss; **a besos** with kisses

best *adj.* **el (la) mejor, los (las) mejores**

better *adj.* **mejor, mejores**

between *prep.* **entre**

beverage **la bebida**

biblioteca *n.f.* library

bicicleta *n.f.* bicycle; **en bicicleta** by bicycle

bid **la oferta;** the last bid **la última oferta**

bien *adv.* well, all right; **Está bien.** Okay. See **bien** in the index.

big *adj.* **gran, grande;** see these two Spanish words in the index.

bill (that you pay, *e.g.,* in a restaurant) **la cuenta**

billete *n.m.* note (short letter); bill (currency, paper money); ticket

bird **el pájaro**

birthday **el aniversario (de cumpleaños), el cumpleaños, la fecha de nacimiento**

biscuit **el bizcocho**

bistec *n.m.* steak, beef steak

bite *v.* **morder (ue)**

bizcocho *n.m.* cookie, cake, sponge cake, biscuit, sponge biscuit

black *adj.* **negro, -a, -os, -as**

blanco, -a, -os, -as *adj.* white; **los blancos** blank spaces, blank lines

block **el bloque**

blue *adj.* **azul, azules**

blush *refl.v.* **ponerse rojo**

boat **el barco, el buque**

boca *n.f.* mouth

bocadillo *n.m.* sandwich, snack, a bite to eat; *cf.* **la boca** mouth; **¿Qué bocadillos?** What sandwiches?

body (human) **el cuerpo**

bolsa *n.f.* pouch, purse, pocketbook

bolsillo *n.m.* pocket

bondadoso, -a, -os, -as *adj.* kind, helpful

bonito, -a, -os, -as *adj.* pretty

book **el libro;** bookstore **la librería;** bookseller **el librero, la librera**

born, to be *v.* **nacer (zc)**

borrar *v.* to erase

bosque *n.m.* forest

bota *n.f.* boot, shoe

botar *v.* to fling, cast (away), throw (away), launch

263

botella *n.f.* bottle; **una bote-lla de agua mineral** a bottle of mineral water

box **la caja**

boy **el chico, el muchacho**

branch (of a tree) **la rama**

Brasil (el Brasil) Brazil

brazo *n.m.* arm

bread **el pan**

break *v.* **romper;** *past part.* is **roto;** see the entry *participles* in the index.

breakfast **el desayuno;** to have breakfast **tomar el desayuno, desayunar**

breve *adj.* brief; **en breve** briefly; **breve-mente** briefly

bring *v.* **traer**

broom **la escoba**

brother **el hermano;** little brother **el hermanito**

brush *v.* **cepillar; un cepi-llo** a brush

bucket **el cubo**

buddy **el compañero**

buen, bueno, -a, -os, -as *adj.* good; **A buen fin no hay mal principio.** All's well that ends well; **bue-nas noches** good evening, good night; **bue-nos días** good morning, good day; **buenas tardes** good afternoon; see **buen** in the index.

¡Bueno! *excl.* Good!

bull **el toro**

burlador *n.m.* jester

burn *v.* **quemar;** burned **quemado**

bus **el autobús; los auto-buses**

buscando *gerundio* of **bus-car (qu)** *v.* to look for, to search for, seek; **Estoy buscando . . .** I am look-ing for . . .; see **buscar** in the index.

but *conj.* **pero**

butaca *n.f.* armchair

butter **la mantequilla**

buy *v.* **comprar**

by *prep.* **por**

C

cabello *n.m.* hair

cabeza *n.f.* head; **tener do-**

lor de cabeza to have a headache; see the entry **tener** in the index.

cacerola *n.f.* pot, casserole

cada *adj.* each

caer(se) *v.* to fall (down); **dejar caer** to drop (let fall); see **dejar** in the in-dex.

café *n.m.* coffee, café; cafe-teria **la cafetería**

caído *past part.* **(participio)** of **caer**

caja *n.f.* box

cajero *n.m.,* **cajera** *n.f.* cashier; bank teller

cake **el pastel, el bizco-cho**

caliente *adj.* warm, hot

calm *adj.* **tranquilo, quito**

calor *n.m.* heat, warmth; **hacer calor** to be warm (weather)

call *v.* **llamar;** call my-self *refl.v.* **llamarme;** to call oneself *refl.v.* **lla-marse**

callarse *refl.v.* to be (keep) quiet, silent; **¡Cállese! ¡Cállate!** Be quiet!

calle *n.f.* street

called, to be *refl.v.* **llamarse**

cama *n.f.* bed

camarero *n.m.* waiter

cambiar *v.* to change; **cam-bie** *imper.;* **el cam-bio** change

caminar *v.* to walk, move along; **el camino** road, route

camión *n.m.* truck

camisa *n.f.* shirt

campo *n.m.* field, country (as opposed to city); see **campo** in the index.

can opener **el (los) abrela-tas**

canción *n.f.* song

candy **los dulces**

canguro *n.m.* kangaroo

cansado, -a, -os, -as *adj.* tired; **cansar** *v.* to tire; **es-tar cansado** to be tired; see **estar** in the index.

cantante *n.m.f.* singer

cantar *v.* to sing; **cantare-mos** *fut.;* **¡Canten!** Sing!

capa *n.f.* cape

capitán *n.m.* captain

caprichoso, -a, -os, -as *adj.* capricious

car **el coche**

cara *n.f.* face

¡Caramba! *excl.* Gosh darn it! Good heavens!

carcajada *n.f.* burst of laugh-ter; **reír a carcajadas** to burst out laughing

card **la tarjeta**

care of **a cargo de**

carecer (zc) *v.* to lack, to be wanting, to be in need

carefully **cuidadosamente, con cuidado**

cargo *n.m.* charge, burden; **a cargo de** care of

cariñosamente *adv.* tenderly

Carlos Charles

carne *n.f.* meat; **carne de cerdo** pork

carpet **la alfombra**

carta *n.f.* letter (that you write); see the entry *letter writing* in the index.

casa *n.f.* house; **a casa** home; **en casa** at home

casarse *refl.v.* to marry; **ca-sarse con alguien** to marry someone

cashier **el cajero, la cajera**

casilla *n.f.* box, square

caso *n.m.* case; **hacer caso (de)** to pay attention (to); **¡Hazme caso!** Pay atten-tion to me!

cast *v.* **echar;** to cast (away) *v.* **botar**

casualidad *n.f.* chance, ca-sualty; **por casuali-dad** by chance

cat **el gato;** little cat **el gatito**

catedral *n.f.* cathedral

celebrar *v.* to celebrate

cellar **el sótano**

cena *n.f.* dinner, supper

cenar *v.* to sup, have dinner, dine, eat supper

center (middle) **el medio**

centro *n.m.* center, down-town; **al centro** down-town; **Voy al centro.** I'm going downtown.

cepillar *v.* to brush; **un ce-pillo** a brush; **con los**

cabellos al cepillo brush haircut

cerca *adv.* near, close by; **cerca de** + *n., pron.* near, close to + *n., pron.;* **cerca de la escuela** near (the) school

cerdo *n.m.* hog, pig; **la carne de cerdo** pork

cereza *n.f.* cherry

cerrar (ie) *v.* to close; *past part.* **(participio)** & *adj.,* **cerrado, -a, -os, -as**

certain *adj.* **cierto, -a, -os, -as;** certainly *adv.* **ciertamente**

cesta *n.f.* basket

cielo *n.m.* sky

cien(to) *num.* a (one) hundred; **cien, ciento, cientos, cientas;** see **cien, ciento** and the word *numbers* in the index.

cierro *pres. indic.* of **cerrar (ie)**

cierto, -a, -os, -as *adj.* certain, true; **ciertamente** *adv.* certainly; see **cierto, cierta** in the index.

cinco *num.* five; **cincuenta** fifty; see the entry *numbers* in the index.

cine *n.m.* movies (theater); **Voy al cine.** I'm going to the movies.

circulación *n.f.* traffic (vehicles)

cita *n.f.* appointment, date; **tener cita** to have a date, an appointment; see **tener** in the index.

city **la ciudad**

¡Claro! *excl.* Of course! Sure! **¡Claro que sí!** Yes, of course!

clase *n.f.* class; type, kind; **la sala de clase** classroom; **la clase de español** Spanish class; **el aula** *n.f.* classroom, lecture hall

clásico, -a, -os, -as *adj.* classical

cliente *n.m.f.* client, customer

clock (watch) **el reloj**

close *v.* **cerrar (ie)**; closed *past part.* & *adj.* **cerrado, -a, -os, -as**

close to **cerca de**

closet (clothing) **el guardarropa**

clothes (clothing) **los vestidos**

coat, overcoat **el abrigo**

cobija *pres. indic.* of **cobijar** *v.* to cover, shelter, protect

cocer (ue) *v.* to cook; **cocido** *past part.* **(participio)** & *adj.;* **bien cocido** well cooked

cocina *n.f.* kitchen

cocinar *v.* to cook

cock, rooster **el gallo;** hen **la gallina**

coche *n.m.* car, automobile

coffee **el café**

coger (j) *v.* to grab, take, pick up

coin **una moneda, una pieza**

coja *imper.* & *pres. sub.* of **coger (j)**

colegio *n.m.* college; school

colocar (qu) *v.* to put, place

colonel **el coronel**

coma *imper.* & *pres. sub.* of **comer;** *also n.f.* comma

come *v.* **venir;** come across (find) *v.* **hallar;** come in *v.* **entrar (en); come** is *imper.* & *pres. indic.* of **comer** *v.* to eat

comedia *n.f.* play (theater), comedy

comedor *n.m.* dining room

comenzar (ie, c) (a + inf.) to begin, commence, start; **comenzó** *pret.*

comer *v.* to eat; **al comer** on (upon) eating; **comerse** *refl. v.* to eat up; **¡Cómete . . . !** Eat up . . . !

comestibles *n.m.pl.* foods, groceries

comida *n.f.* meal, food, dinner

comiendo *pres. part.* **(gerundio)** *of* comer; **Coco se está comiendo . . .** Coco is eating up . . .

comienza *pres. indic.* of **comenzar (ie, c)**

comió *pret.* of **comer**

comma **la coma**

commence *v.* **comenzar (ie, c)** (a + inf.)

common *adj.* **común; en común** in common

como *adv., conj.* as, like; **¿Cómo . . . ?** How . . .? **¿Cómo se llama Ud.?** What's your name? **como** is also pres. indic. of **comer;** see **¿cómo . . . ?** in the index.

compañero *n.m.* friend, buddy, pal

comparar *v.* to compare

comparativo *adj.* comparative; see *comparatives & superlatives* in the index.

competencia *n.f.* contest, competition

complemento *n.m.* complement; **complemento directo** direct object; **complemento indirecto** indirect object; see the entry *attribute complement* in the index.

completar *v.* to complete

complete *imper.* of **completar**

complete *v.* **completar, acabar;** complete, *as adj.* **completo, -a, -os, -as**

componga *imper.* & *pres. sub.* of **componer** *v.* to compose

comportarse *refl.v.* to behave oneself

composición *n.f.* composition

compota *n.f.* jam, preserves

compra *n.f.* purchase; **ir de compras, hacer compras** to do (go) shopping

comprar *v.* to buy, purchase

comprender *v.* to understand

común *adj.* common, ordinary; **en común** in common

con *prep.* with; **con frecuencia** frequently; **conmigo** with me; **contigo** with you *(fam.);* **con Juan** with John; **con él** with him; **con María** with Mary; **con ella** with her; see **con** in the index.

conditional *(verb form)* **el potencial;** see the entry *conditional* in the index.

condolencia *n.f.* condolence, sympathy; **una carta de condolencia** a letter of sympathy

conducir (zc, j) *v.* to drive (a car), conduct, lead

conejo *n.m.* rabbit

conforme a conforming to, in accordance with

conjunción *n.f.* conjunction; see the entry *conjunctions, conjunctive locutions* in the index.

conmigo with me; see **conmigo, contigo, consigo** in the index.

connect *v.* **unir**

conocer (zc) *v.* to know (be acquainted with); see **conocer & saber** in the index.

conozco *pres. indic. of* **conocer; Yo conozco muy bien a Juan.** I know John very well.

consejo *n.m.* advice, counsel; **aconsejar** *v.* to advise, to counsel

consent *v.* **consentir (ie, i); consintiera** *imperf. sub.*

construya *imper. of* **construir (y)** *v.* to build, construct

consultar *v.* to consult; **consulte** *imper. & pres. sub. of* **consultar**

contar (ue) *v.* to count, relate, tell about

contener *v.* to contain, hold

contentamiento *n.m.* contentment

contentísimo, -a, -os, -as *adj.,* absolute superlative very (extremely) content, happy, pleased; see *absolute superlative* and *comparatives & superlatives* in the index.

contento, -a, -os, -as *adj.* content, happy, pleased; (synonyms: **satisfecho, feliz, plácido, encantado**)

contest **la competencia, la competición;** also **concurso**

contestación *n.f.* reply, answer

contestar *v.* to answer, reply

conteste *imper. of* **contestar; contestó** *pret.*

contiene *pres. indic. of* **contener**

contigo with you *(fam.);* see **conmigo, contigo, consigo** in the index.

continúa *pres. indic. of* **continuar (ú);** see **continuar** in the index.

continuación *n.f.* continuation; **a continuación** listed, one after the other (in a list)

continuar (ú) *v.* to continue; see **continuar** in the index.

contrario, -a, -os, -as *adj.* contrary, opposite; **lo contrario** the opposite

convenga *pres. sub. & imper. of* **convenir** *v.* to agree, be appropriate, be convenient; **según convenga** according to what is appropriate

conversación *n.f.* conversation

conviene *pres. indic. of* **convenir**

cook *v.* **cocinar, cocer (ue);** cooked **cocido** *past part. (participio) & adj.*

cookie **el bizcocho; una galleta, una galletita**

cool *adj.* **fresco, -a, -os, -as**

corazón *n.m.* heart

corbata *n.f.* necktie

cordialmente *adv.* cordially

coronel *n.m.* colonel

correct *v.* **corregir (i, j)**

correctamente *adv.* correctly

correcto, -a, -os, -as *adj.* correct

corregir (i, j) *v.* to correct

correr *v.* to run, race, flow

corresponder *v.* to correspond

corridor **el pasillo**

corriendo *pres. part. (gerundio) of* **correr**

corriente *adj.* ordinary, common

corrigieron *pret. of* **corregir (i, j)**

corrió *pret. of* **correr**

cortar *v.* to cut, cut off, cut out

corte *n.m.* cut; **un corte de pelo** haircut

corto, -a, -os, -as *adj.* short

cosa *n.f.* thing

cost *v.* **costar (ue)**

count *v.* **contar (ue)**

country (as opposed to city) **el campo;** nation **el país;** see the entry *country* in the index.

course (study of a subject matter) **la asignatura**

cousin **el primo, la prima**

cover *v.* **cubrir;** *past part.* **cubierto**

cow **la vaca**

crazy *adj.* **loco, -a, -os, -as;** to be crazy **estar loco (loca);** to go crazy **volverse (ue) loco (loca)**

creak *v.* **gruñir**

creencia *n.f.* belief, credence

creer (y) *v.* to believe; **creeré** *fut.;* **creía** *imperf. indic.;* **creído** *past part. (participio)*

cría *n.f.* suckling, baby animal

cristal *n.m.* window pane

Cristóbal Christopher, Chris

cross *v.* **cruzar (c), atravesar**

crush *v.* **aplastar**

cry (weep) *v.* **llorar**

cry out *v.* **gritar**

cuaderno *n.m.* notebook

cuadro *n.m.* picture

cual, ¿cuál? *pron.* which, what **¿Cuál es su deporte favorito?** What (which, which one of all sports) is your favorite sport?

cuando *adv.* when; **de vez en cuando** from time to time; see **cuando** in the index.

cuánto, -a, -os, -as *adj. & adv.* how much . . . ? how many . . . ? See the word **cuanto** in the index.

cuarto *n.m.* room, (living) quarters; **el cuarto de baño** bathroom

cubo *n.m.* bucket, pail, basket, barrel, drum; **el cubo de basura** the garbage can

cubrir *v.* to cover; **cubierto** *past part.*

cucharada *n.f.* spoonful

cuello *n.m.* neck

cuenta *n.f.* bill, check (which you pay, *e.g.,* in a restaurant)

cuento *n.m.* story (literature); also *pres. indic. of* **contar (ue)**

cuerpo *pres. indic. of* **costar (ue)**

cuesta *pres. indic. of* **costar (ue)**

cuidado *n.m.* care; **con cuidado** carefully, with care; **sin cuidado** carelessly, without care; **cuidadosamente** *adv.* carefully; **cuidar** *v.* to take care of

cumpleaños *n.m.* birthday

cumplir *v.* to fulfill, to keep (a promise, one's word); to reach one's birthday (use with **años**); ¡**Ah! Hoy es tu cumpleaños. ¿Cuántos años cumples (tú)?** Ah! Today is your birthday. How old are you? ¿**Cuántos años tiene Ud.?** How old are you?

cup **la taza;** a cup of tea **una taza de té;** a cup of coffee **una taza de café**

cura *n.m.* priest

curiosidad *n.f.* curiosity

curious *adj.* **curioso, -a, -os, -as; extraño, -a, -os, -as**

cursivo, -a, -os, -as *adj.* cursive; **en letras cursivas** in italics

customer **el, la cliente**

cut, cut off, cut out *v.* **cortar**

cuyo, -a, -os, -as *rel. pron. indicating possession* whose; see the word **cuyo** in the index.

CH

chair **la silla**

chalk **la tiza;** chalkboard **la pizarra**

champú *n.m.* shampoo

change *v.* **cambiar;** change *n.* **el cambio**

charlar *v.* to chat, prattle

Charles **Carlos**

---

charming *adj.* **gracioso, -a, -os, -as**

chat *v.* **charlar**

check (that you pay, *e.g.,* in a restaurant) **la cuenta**

chemistry **la química**

cherry **la cereza**

chica *n.f.* girl

chicken **el pollo**

chico *n.m.* boy

child **el niño, la niña;** children **los niños**

chimenea *n.f.* chimney

chistar *v.* to mumble, mutter

chocolate **el chocolate**

choose *v.* **escoger (j)**

Christmas **la Navidad**

Christopher **Cristóbal**

chuleta *n.m.* chop; **las chuletas de ternera** veal chops

church **la iglesia**

D

da *pres. indic. & imper. of* **dar; El alumno da el libro a la maestra.** The pupil gives the book to the teacher; **El padre dice a su hijo:—¡Dámelo!** Give it to me!

daba *imperf. indic. of* **dar**

dad **el papá**

dama *n.f.* lady

dame give me; ¡**Dámela!** Give it to me!

dance *v.* **bailar;** dance *n.* **el baile**

dando *pres. part.* (*gerundio*) *of* **dar**

danger **el peligro;** dangerous *adj.* **peligroso, -a, -os, -as**

dar *v.* to give

dará *fut. of* **dar**

dare *v.* **osar**

darkness **la oscuridad**

darling **querido mío, querida mía**

das *pres. indic. of* **dar**

date (appointment) **la cita; tener cita** to have a date, an appointment; date (on the calendar) **la fecha**

daughter **la hija**

dawn **la madrugada**

day **el día; todo el día** all

---

day long; **todos los días** every day

day before yesterday *adv.* **anteayer**

daybreak **la madrugada**

daylight **la luz; las luces,** *pl.*

de *prep.* of, from; **de acuerdo** okay, agreed; **de repente** suddenly; **de seguro** surely; **de veras** really; **de todos modos** at any rate, anyhow; see the entry **de** in the index.

dé *imper. of* **dar; Deme la mano.** Give me your hand.

dead *adj.* **muerto, -a, -os, -as;** This dog is dead. **Este perro está muerto;** see **estar** in the index.

dear **querido, querida;** my dear **querido mío, querida mía**

death **la muerte**

debajo de *adv., prep.* underneath, below

deber *v.* to owe, ought to, should, must; *as a n.,* duty; **los deberes** duties, homework, obligations; see **deber** in the index.

December **diciembre**

decidir *v.* to decide

decir *v.* to say, tell; **decirse** *refl.v.* to say to oneself

declarar *v.* to declare

dedo *n.m.* finger; **el dedo del pie** toe

definición *n.f.* definition

deja *imper. & pres. indic. of* **dejar; ¡Déjame!** Let me!

dejar *v.* to leave, let, let go, permit, allow, leave (something behind you; takes a dir. obj. n. or pron.); **dejar caer** *v.* to drop; **dejar de + inf.** to stop + pres. part.; **Pablo dejó de hablar.** Paul stopped talking. See **dejar** in the index.

dejaron *pret. of* **dejar**

del of the, from the (combination of **de + el,** def.art.); **del teatro** from the theater; **del autor** of the author. See the entry **de** in the index.

delante *adv.* forward, in front; **delante de** in front of

delicado, -a, -os, -as *adj.* delicate, weak, sickly (synonyms: **débil, tierno, frágil, enfermizo**)

delicioso, -a, -os, -as *adj.* delicious

delineate *v.* **describir**

demand *v.* **exigir**

demasiado *adv.* too, too much; **demasiado cocido** too (over)cooked

Deme la mano. Give me your hand.

demostrativo *adj.* demonstrative; see the entry *demonstrative* in the index.

denounce *v.* **denunciar**

dentista *n.m.f.* dentist; **Este señor es dentista; Esta señora es dentista.**

dentro *adv.* inside, within; **dentro de unos días** within a few days

depart *v.* **partir**

depend *v.* **depender**

deporte *n.m.* sport

depravado, -a, -os, -as *adj.* depraved

derecha *n.f.* right (as opposed to *left*)

derecho *n.m.* right (privilege)

desayuno *n.m.* breakfast; **tomar el desayuno** to have breakfast

descansar *v.* to rest; see **cansado** in this vocabulary list.

descend *v.* **bajar**

describir *v.* to describe, sketch, delineate; **descrito** *past part.* **(participio)**

descubrir *v.* to discover; **descubierto** *past part.* **(participio)**

desde *prep.* from, after, since; **desde Puerto Rico** from Puerto Rico; **desde arriba** from above; see **desde** in the index.

desear *v.* to desire, want

desembrollar *v.* to unscramble, unravel

deserve *v.* **merecer (zc)**

desfile *n.m.* parade

desgraciada *adj.* unfortunate

desierto *adj.* empty, deserted

design *v.* **dibujar**

desire *v.* **desear**

deslumbrante *adj.* dazzling

desorden *n.m.* disorder

desordenado *participio* of **desordenar** wild, unruly, disordered

despacio *adv.* slowly

despedirse (i) de *refl.v.* to take leave of, say goodbye to

despertarse (ie) *refl.v.* to wake (oneself) up

despido *pres. indic.* of **despedir (i)** *v.* to dismiss

despierta *pres. indic.* of **despertar (ie)** *v.* to awaken, to wake up (someone); **despertarse (ie)** *refl.v.* to wake (oneself) up

despite **a pesar de**

después *adv.* after; **después de + inf.** after + pres. part.; **después de cenar** after having dinner; **después de llegar** after arriving; **después de perder** after wasting (losing); **después de trabajar** after working; **después de + haber + past part. (participio)** after having worked; **después de haber comido** after having eaten; **después (de) que** *conj.* after + new clause; see the entry *participles* in the index.

dessert **el postre**

detach *v.* **separar**

determinado, -a, -os, -as *adj.* determined, definite; **el artículo determinado** definite article **(el, la, los, las)**; see *articles* in the index.

detest *v.* **detestar; Te detesto, Miguel;** I hate you, Michael.

devoción *n.f.* devotion; **las devociones,** *pl.*

devolver (ue) *v.* to return, give back (something to someone or to some place)

devuelve *imper.* of **devolver (ue); ¡Devuélvemelos!** Return them to me!

di *pret.* of **dar; Se los di a Ana.** I gave them to Anna; **di** *is also imper.* of **decir; Dime.** Tell me; **Dímelo.** Tell it to me. **Dime lo que (tú) comes y te diré lo que (tú) eres.** Tell me what you eat and I'll tell you what you are.

día *n.m.* day; **todo el día** all day long; **todos los días** every day; **en pocos días** in a few days; **buenos días** good day, good morning; **de hoy en ocho días** a week from today; **hoy día** nowadays; **al día siguiente** on the following day

diálogo *n.m.* dialogue

dibujar *v.* to design, draw, sketch; **un dibujo** a drawing, sketch

dice *pres. indic.* of **decir**

diciembre *n.m.* December

diciendo *pres. part.* **(gerundio)** *of* **decir; dicho** *past part.* **(participio)**

dictado *n.m.* dictation

dicho *n.m.* proverb, saying; **dicho** *is also past part.* **(participio)** *of* **decir**

die *v.* **morir**

dieciocho *num.* eighteen; see *numbers* in the index.

diente *n.m.* tooth

dieron *pret.* of **dar; diera, diese** *imperf. sub.* of **dar**

diferencia *n.f.* difference; **diferente** *adj.* different

difícil, difíciles *adj.* difficult

dificultad *n.f.* difficulty

diga *pres. sub. & imper.* of **decir; ¡No me diga!** You don't say! Don't tell me! **¡Diga!** *excl.,* meaning *Hello!* when answering the telephone; **¡Dígame!** Tell me! **¡Dígamelo!** Tell it to me!

digo *pres. indic.* of **decir**

dijo *pret.* of **decir**

Dime lo que (tú) comes y te diré lo que (tú) eres. Tell me what you eat and I'll tell you what you are.

dine (to have dinner) *v.* **cenar**

dinero *n.m.* money

dining room **el comedor**

dinner **la comida, la cena;** to have dinner, to dine **cenar, tomar la comida**

dio *pret. of* **dar; Susana los dio a Ana.** Suzanne gave them to Anna.

Dios *n.m.* God; **¡Dios mío!** *excl.* My God! **¡Adiós!** Good-bye! (See **Dios mío** in the index.)

diré *fut. of* **decir**

dirección *n.f.* address; **direcciones** directions, addresses

direct object **el complemento directo;** indirect object **el complemento indirecto;** see the entry *attribute complement* in the index.

director, directora *n.m.f.* principal, director

dirige *pres. indic. of* **dirigir (j)** *v.* to direct, to conduct, to address; **dirigir la palabra a** to talk to (to address); **dirigirse (j) a** *refl.v.* to go to, to direct oneself to (a place); **El maestro se dirigió a la puerta para abrirla.** The teacher went to open the door (went to the door to open it).

dirty *adj.* **sucio, -a, -os, -as**

disco *n.m.* disc, record (that you play on a record player)

discover *v.* **descubrir**

discuss *v.* **discutir**

dish **el plato**

disorder **el desorden**

dispénseme *imper. of* **dispensar** + **me** *v.* to excuse; Excuse me.

display *v.* **presentar**

dispuesto, -a, -os, -as *adj.* prepared, ready, willing

diste *pret. of* **dar**

divertido, -a, -os, -as *adj.* amusing

divertirse (ie, i) *refl.v.* to have a good time; have a lot of fun, amuse oneself; **Nos divertiremos.** We will have a good time.

divide *v.* **partir, dividir**

do *v.* **hacer;** see **hacer** in the index.

doctor **el médico, el doctor**

dog **el perro;** doggie, little dog **el perrito;** see the entry *diminutive endings -ito & -illo* in the index.

dólar *n.m.* dollar

dolor *n.m.* pain, grief, sorrow; **dolor de estómago** stomach ache; see **tener** in the index.

donde; ¿dónde . . . ? *adv.* where; where? See **¿dónde . . . ?** in the index.

Don't tell me! **¡No me diga!**

door **la puerta**

dormía *imperf. indic. of* **dormir (ue, u);** read the introduction to this vocabulary list.

dormir (ue, u) *v.* to sleep

dormitorio *n.m.* bedroom

dos *num.* two; **dos por dos** two by two; see the entry *numbers* in the index.

doubt **la duda;** *v.* **dudar**

downtown **al centro; Voy al centro.** I'm going downtown.

drama *n.m.* drama, play (theater)

draw (sketch) *v.* **dibujar;** a drawing, sketch **un dibujo**

dread *v.* **temer**

dresser (chest of drawers) **el tocador**

drink *v.* **beber;** drinking glass **el vaso;** *as a n.,* beverage **la bebida**

drive away (scare away) *v.* **espantar**

drop *v.* **dejar caer**

drug store **la farmacia**

dry *v.* **secar (qu);** *adj.* **seco, -a, -os, -as**

duda *n.f.* doubt; **dudar** *v.* to doubt

dueña *n.f.* duenna; governess, an older woman who serves as chaperon of a young lady

duermo *pres. indic. of* **dormir (ue, u)**

dulces *n.m.* candy, candies, sweets

dumb thing **una tontería**

durante *prep.* during

duró *pret. of* **durar** *v.* to last

dwell (reside) *v.* **habitar**

E

e *conj.* and; **e** instead of **y** is used in front of a word that begins with **i** or **hi,** as in **español e inglés, madres e hijas, padres e hijos;** see the entry **e** and **y** in the index.

each **cada**

earn *v.* **ganar;** earn one's living **ganarse la vida**

easy **fácil, fáciles**

eat *v.* **comer;** eat supper *v.* **cenar**

echar *v.* to cast, fling, hurl, pitch, throw; **eché** *pret.;* **echar una carta al correo** to mail (post) a letter

edad *n.f.* age; (**años** years)

egg **el huevo;** soft boiled egg **un huevo pasado por agua**

eight *num.* **ocho; a las ocho** at 8 o'clock; **a las ocho y cuarto** at 8:15; **a las ocho y media** at 8:30

eighteen *num.* **dieciocho;** see the entry *numbers* in the index.

eighty *num.* **ochenta;** see the entry *numbers* in the index.

ejemplo *n.m.* example; **por ejemplo** for example

ejercicio *n.m.* exercise, practice

él *pron.* he (as subject); him, it *m.* (as obj. of a prep.); see *pronouns* in the index.

el *def.art.m.s.* the (*pl.,* **los**); **el que . . .** he who . . . ,

269

the one who . . . ; see the entries *articles* and **el cual, el de, el que** in the index.

elect *v.* **elegir**

elegante *adj.* elegant

elegido *participio* of **elegir** *v.* to elect, select, choose

ella *pron.* she (as subject); her, it *f.* (as obj. of a prep.); see *pronouns* in the index.

embajada *n.f.* embassy

embargo *n.m.* **sin embargo** nevertheless, all the same; however

embrace **el abrazo;** *v.* **abrazar (c)**

emoción *n.f.* emotion

empezar (ie, c) a + inf. *v.* to begin, start + inf.; **empiece** *imper.*

empleando *pres. part.* (gerundio) of **emplear** *v.* to use, employ; **emplee** *imper.*

empty *adj.* **vacío, -a, -os, -as**

en *prep.* in, at, on; **en casa** at home; **en seguida** immediately, at once; see the entry **en** in the index.

enamorado, -a, -os, -as *adj.* in love; **estar enamorado (de)** to be in love (with); see **estar** in the index.

encantado, -a, -os, -as *adj.* content, happy, pleased

encargarse *refl.v.* to take charge of, take care of

encima *adv.* above; **por encima** at the top

encontrado *past part.* (participio) of **encontrar (ue)** *v.* to encounter, meet, find; **encontrará** *fut.* of **encontrar; encontrarse** *refl.v.* to find oneself; **encuentro** *n.m.* encounter, meeting

end *v.* **acabar, terminar;** see **acabar** in the index.

endure *v.* **sufrir**

enero *n.m.* January

enfermarse *refl.v.* to become (get) sick. **Voy a enfermarme.** I'm going to get sick.

enfermo, -a, -os, -as *adj.* sick, ill

England **Inglaterra**

English **el inglés** (language); *as adj.,* **inglés, inglesa, ingleses, inglesas;** see the entries *name of language* and *nationality* in the index.

enjoy *v.* **gozar (c) de** + dir. obj.

enjoyable *adj.* **agradable**

enlighten *v.* **alumbrar**

enojar *v.* to anger, annoy, vex; **enojarse** *refl.v.* to get annoyed; **el enojo** anger

enough **bastante;** Enough! **¡Basta!**

ensalada *n.f.* salad

enseñar a + inf. *v.* to point out, teach, show how + inf.; **enséñeme** *imper.* show me

enter *v.* **entrar (en** + **obj.)** to enter (in, into), go (come) in

enteramente *adv.* entirely

entiendes *pres. indic.* of **entender (ie)** *v.* to understand, hear

entonces *adv.* then

entrar (en + **obj.)** *v.* to enter (in, into), go (come) in; **entraron** *pret.*

entre *prep.* between; *also, imper.* of **entrar;** see **entre** in the index.

entreacto *n.m.* intermission

entregue *pres. sub.* of **entregar (gu)** *v.* to hand over, give, deliver

¡Entren! *imper.* of **entrar;** Come in!

entrenador *n.m.* trainer, coach

entretanto *adv.* meanwhile

enviar (í) *v.* to send; **enviar por** to send for

equipo *n.m.* team

era *imperf. indic.* of **ser;** see **ser** in the index.

erase *v.* **borrar**

eres *pres. indic.* of **ser**

es *pres. indic.* of **ser**

esbelto, -a, -os, -as *adj.* slim, slender

escalera *n.f.* stairs, stairway

escena *n.f.* scene

escoba *n.f.* broom

escoger (j) *v.* to choose, select

escojas *imper.* of **escoger (j)**

escondido, -a, -os, -as *adj.* hidden; **esconder** *v.* to hide, conceal; **esconderse** *refl.v.* to hide oneself

escriba *imper. & pres. sub.* of **escribir** *v.* to write; **escribiste** *pret;* **escribiendo** *gerundio* writing

escrito *past part.* (participio) of **escribir; Tú no has escrito nada.** You have written nothing; You have not written anything; *as adj.,* **escrito, -a, -os, -as** written; **escritor, escritora** *n.m.f.* writer; see **escrito** in the index.

escuchar *v.* to listen (to); **Escucho la música.** I'm listening to the music; **Tú no has escuchado.** You have not listened.

escuela *n.f.* school; **a la escuela** to school; **en la escuela** in (at) school

eso *neuter dem. adj.* that **¡Eso es!** That's right! See **eso** in the index.

espantar *v.* to drive away, scare away

España *n.f.* Spain

español *n.m.* Spanish (language); *as adj.,* **español, española, españoles, españolas;** see the entries *name of language* and *nationality* in the index.

especial *adj.* special

especie *n.f.* species, kind, type

espectáculo *n.m.* show (theatrical)

espectador, espectadora *n.m.f.* spectator

esperanza *n.f.* hope

esperar *v.* to wait (for), expect, hope; **¡Espera!** Wait!

esposa *n.f.* wife, spouse; (sinónimo: **la mujer**)

esposo *n.m.* husband, spouse; (sinónimo: **el marido**)

esquina *n.f.* corner

esta *dem.adj.f.s.* this; **esta casa** this house; **ésta** *dem.pron.f.s.* the latter (this one); see **esta, ésta** in the index.

está *pres. indic. of* **estar** *v.* to be; **está buscando** *pres. prog. of* **buscar;** **El señor Rodríguez está buscando su sombrero.** Mr. Rodríguez is looking for his hat; **Juan está hablándome.** John is talking to me. See **estar** in the index.

estaba *imperf. indic. of* **estar**

estadio *n.m.* stadium

estado *n.m.* state; **los Estados Unidos (de Norteamérica)** the United States of America

estanque *n.m.* pond, pool, basin

estar *v.* to be; **estar enamorado, -a (de)** to be in love (with); See **estar** in the index and the appendix.

este *dem. adj., m.s.* this; **este libro** this book; **éste** *dem.pron.* this one; see the following words in the index: **estas, éstas, este, éste, esto, estos, éstos.**

esteem *v.* **estimar**

estén *pres. sub. of* **estar**

estimado, -a, -os, -as *adj.* esteemed, dear (as a salutation in writing a letter)

estimar *v.* to estimate, esteem, respect, value

esto *pron. dem. neut.* this; **¿Qué es esto?** What is this?

estómago *n.m.* stomach; **dolor de estómago** stomach ache

estoy *pres. indic. of* **estar;** see **estar** in the index.

estropear *v.* to spoil

estructura *n.f.* structure

estudiante *n.f.m.* student

estudiar *v.* to study

estupefacto, -a, -os, -as *adj.* stupefied

evening **la noche;** in the evening **por la noche;** **ayer por la noche** yes-terday evening; see **por** in the index.

every day **todos los días;** every morning **todas las mañanas;** every night **todas las noches;** everybody **todo el mundo;** everywhere **por todas partes**

evil **el mal**

evitar *v.* to avoid

exactamente *adv.* exactly

examen *n.m.* examination; *pl.,* **exámenes**

examinar *v.* to examine; **examinándola** examining her; **examinando** *pres. part. (gerundio)*

example **el ejemplo;** for example **por ejemplo**

excelente *adj.* excellent

exclaim *v.* **exclamar(se)**

excuse *v.* **perdonar, dispensar; Dispénseme.** Excuse me.

exercise *n.m.* **ejercicio**

exhibir *v.* to exhibit

exigió *pret. of* **exigir (j)** *v.* to require, demand

existir *v.* to exist

expect *v.* **esperar;** expectancy, expectation **la espera; en espera de** hoping for, waiting for

explain *v.* **explicar (qu)**

exposición *n.f.* exposition, exhibit

expresado, -a, -os, -as *adj.* expressed

expresar *v.* to express

extranjero, -a, -os, -as *adj.* foreign; *as n.,* foreigner

extraño *adj.* strange, odd, curious

extraordinario *adj.* extraordinary

extremadamente *adv.* extremely

eye **el ojo;** eyelid **el párpado;** eye glasses **los anteojos**

F

face **la cara**

fácil, fáciles *adj.* easy; **fácilmente** easily

fachada *n.f.* façade, face of a building

fair (bazaar) **la feria**

falda *n.f.* skirt

falso, -a, -os, -as *adj.* false

falta *n.f.* lack, need, fault, deficiency

faltar *v.* to be lacking, wanting; to lack, miss, need; see **faltar** in the index.

familia *n.f.* family

fantástico, -a, -os, -as *adj.* fantastic

far *adv.* **lejos**

farmacia *n.f.* pharmacy, drug store

fast *adv.* **pronto;** *as adj.,* **pronto, -a, -os, -as**

fat *adj.* **gordo, gorda**

father **el padre; los padres** parents

fatiga *n.f.* fatigue

fault **la falta;** see **faltar** in the index.

favor *n.m.* **favor; por favor** please; see **por** in the index.

favorite *adj.* **favorito, -a, -os, -as; predilecto, -a, -os, -as**

fear *v.* **temer;** *as a n.,* **el temor;** to be afraid **tener miedo**

fecha *n.f.* date (on a calendar)

feel *v.* **tocar (qu), sentir (ie, i);** to feel nausea *v.* **sentir náuseas;** see **tocar** in the index.

felicidad *n.f.* happiness, felicity

feliz *(pl.,* **felices)** *adj.* happy, content; **Feliz Navidad (Felices Navidades)** (Merry Christmas); **felizmente** *adv.* happily **(con felicidad)**

femenino *n.m.* feminine; *as an adj.,* **femenino, -a, -os, -as;** see the entry *gender* in the index.

feo, -a, -os, -as *adj.* ugly

feria *n.f.* fair (bazaar)

festividad *n.f.* festivity

field **el campo;** see **campo** in the index.

fiesta *n.f.* holiday, celebration, party

fifth *num.* **quinto, -a;** see *numbers* in the index.

fifty *num.* **cincuenta;** see *numbers* in the index.

figuran a continuación contained in the list; **figurar** *v.* to be contained, to figure (in)

fijamente *adv.* fixedly, staringly; **mirar fijamente** to stare (at)

fila *n.f.* row (of seats)

fill *v.* **llenar, rellenar;** filled, full *adj.* **lleno, -a, -os, -as**

film (movie) **la película;** movies **el cine** (theater); **Me gusta ir al cine.** I like going (to go) to the movies.

fin *n.m.* end; **A buen fin no hay mal principio.** All's well that ends well; **el fin de semana** weekend; **por fin** at last, finally

finalmente *adv.* finally

find *v.* **hallar;** to be found **hallarse;** to find oneself **encontrarse (ue)**

finger **el dedo**

finish *v.* **terminar, acabar; Se acabó.** It's finished. It's all over.

fire (burn) *v.* **quemar;** *as a n.,* **el fuego**

first *adj.* **primer, primero, -a, -os, -as; el primer libro** the first book; **la primera casa** the first house; **Hoy es el primero de enero.** Today is January first. See the entry *numbers* in the index.

fish **el pescado;** *v.* **pescar (qu);** *as a n.,* **el pescado** (which is caught from the waters, cooked, and eaten); **el pez** (fish swimming in water; *pl.,* **peces**)

five *num.* **cinco;** See the entry *numbers* in the index.

fling *v.* **botar, echar**

float *v.* **flotar**

flor, flores *n.f.* flower, flowers

flow *v.* **correr**

fly *v.* **volar (ue);** to fly away **volarse**

fly (insect) **la mosca**

follow *v.* **seguir (i);** following **siguiente**

food **el alimento**

foolish *adj.* **tonto, -a, -os, -as;** foolish thing **una tontería**

foot **el pie;** football player *n.m.f.* **futbolista**

for *prep.* **para, por;** see **para** and **por** in the index.

forbid *v.* **prohibir**

forehead **la frente**

foreign *adj.* **extranjero, -a, -os, -as**

forest **el bosque**

forget *v.* **olvidar**

forgive *v.* **perdonar**

form *v.* **formar;** *as a n.,* **la forma;** in good form, in good shape **en buena forma**

fortuna *n.f.* luck, chance, fortune; **¡Qué fortuna!** What luck! fortunately **afortunadamente**

forward *adv.* **adelante**

foto *n.f.* photo

fountain **la fuente**

francés *n.m.* French (language); *as adj.,* **francés, francesa, franceses, francesas;** see *name of language* and *nationality* in the index.

Francia *n.f.* France

frase *n.f.* sentence, phrase

frecuencia *n.f.* frequency; **con frecuencia** frequently

freeze *v.* **helar (ie)**

freír (i) *v.* to fry

frente *n.f.* forehead; **en frente** opposite, facing; **en la página en frente** on the facing (opposite) page

fresco, -a, -os, -as *adj.* cool, fresh

fresh (cool) water **el agua fresca**

friend (close) **el compañero, la compañera; el amigo, la amiga**

frío *n.m.* cold; **Hace mucho frío.** It's very cold (weather); *as adj.,* **frío, -a, -os, -as**

frito, -a, -os, -as *adj.* fried; **patatas fritas** fried potatoes; **freír (i)** *v.* to fry

from *prep.* **de, desde;** from

the **del, de la, de los, de las;** from time to time **de vez en cuando; desde Puerto Rico** from Puerto Rico; **desde arriba** from above; see **de** and **desde** in the index.

front of **delante de**

fruta *n.f.* fruit

fue *pret.* of **ir** and of **ser**

fuego *n.m.* fire

fuente *n.f.* fountain

fueres *fut. sub.* of **ir** and of **ser; fueron** *pret.* of **ir** and of **ser**

fulfill *v.* **cumplir;** full, filled *adj.* **lleno, -a, -os, -as**

fumar *v.* to smoke

function (machine) *v.* **marchar**

fútbol *n.m.* soccer

futbolista *n.m.f.* football (soccer) player

future *n.m.* **el futuro, el porvenir**

G

gafas *n.f.pl.* sunglasses

gain *v.* **ganar**

gallo *n.m.* cock, rooster; **El gallo de oro** The Golden Cock (name of a restaurant)

game **el juego;** (sports) **el partido**

ganado *past part.* (participio) of **ganar** *v.* to win, gain, earn; **¡Hemos ganado!** We have won! **ganarse la vida** to earn one's living

garaje *n.m.* garage

garbage **la basura**

garden **el jardín;** gardener **el jardinero**

gastado *past part.* (participio) of **gastar** *v.* to spend (money), wear out, waste; **gastando** *pres. part.* (gerundio) of **gastar** spending; **gasté** *pret.*

gather *v.* **recoger (j)**

gato *n.m.* cat; **el gatito** kitten; see the entry *diminutive endings -ito & -illo* in the index.

gem **la joya**

general *n., adj.* **general; por**

lo general in general, generally; **generalmente** generally

generoso, -a, -os, -as *adj.* generous

genio *n.m.* genius

gente *n.f.* people; **mucha gente** many people

geografía *n.f.* geography

George **Jorge**

gerund **el gerundio;** see **gerund** & **gerundio** in the index.

get *v.* **obtener, recibir, sacar (qu);** get back *v.* **recobrar;** get up (oneself) *refl. v.* **levantarse**

gift **el regalo;** to give as a gift *v.* **regalar**

giggle *v.* **reírse sin motivo**

gimnasia *n.f.* gymnastics; **el gimnasio** gymnasium; **el traje de gimnasio** gym suit

giraffe **la jirafa**

girl **la muchacha, la chica**

give *v.* **dar;** give as a present *v.* **regalar;** give me **dame, deme (da, dé)** *imper.* of **dar**

glass (drinking) **el vaso**

glove **el guante**

go *v.* **ir;** go back (return) *v.* **regresar, volver (ue);** go down *v.* **bajar;** go in *v.* **entrar (en);** go out *v.* **salir (de);** go to bed *refl.v.* **acostarse (ue);** go up *v.* **subir a**

goal (sports) **el gol;** goalie **el guardameta (del equipo de fútbol)**

God **Dios**

gold **el oro**

good *adj.* **buen, bueno, -a, -os, -as;** good evening **buenas noches;** good morning **buenos días;** good night **buenas noches;** Good heavens! **¡Caramba!** See **buen, bueno** in the index.

good-bye **adiós;** to say good-bye to, take leave of *refl.v.* **despedirse (i) de**

good looking *adj.* **guapo, guapa**

gordo, -a, -os, -as *adj.* fat

Gosh darn it! **¡Caramba!**

gozar (c) de *v.* to enjoy; **el gozo** joy

gracias thank you, thanks; **gracias a** thanks to; **¡Muchísimas gracias!** Thank you very much! Thanks a lot! Many thanks! **darle (las) gracias a una persona por** to thank someone for; see the entries *absolute superlative* and **por** in the index.

gracioso, -a, -os, -as *adj.* gracious, charming

grade (mark in studies) **una nota**

Gran Bretaña *n.f.* Great Britain

gran, grande *adj.* great, big, large; see **gran, grande** in the index

grandfather, grandmother **el abuelo, la abuela**

grant *v.* **permitir**

grape **la uva**

grass **la hierba**

grato, -a, -os, -as *adj.* pleasing, pleasant, agreeable

gravemente *adv.* seriously; see the entry *adverbs* in the index.

great *adj.* **gran, grande;** see **gran, grande** in the index.

Great Britain **la Gran Bretaña**

greet *v.* **saludar;** Greetings! **¡Saludos!**

grid **la rejilla**

grief **el mal**

gritando *pres. part.* (**gerundio**) *of* **gritar** *v.* to shout, cry out, scream, shriek

group **el grupo**

gruñir *v.* to grumble, grunt, growl, creak

guante *n.m.* glove

guapo, -a, -os, -as *adj.* handsome, good looking, pretty

guardar *v.* to guard, keep; **el guardameta (del equipo de fútbol)** goalie, goal keeper; **el guardarropa** wardrobe, clothes closet; **guardarse de** *refl. v.* to

watch out for; **¡Guárdate de . . . !** *imper.* Watch out for . . . !

guerra *n.f.* war

guiñar el ojo *v.* to wink

gustar *v.* to please; **gustar a** to be pleasing to, to like; **No me gusta el café.** I don't like coffee. (Coffee is not pleasing to me.); **gustaría** *potencial* would (should) like, (would be pleasing to); **Me gustaría una taza de té.** I'd like a cup of tea (A cup of tea would be pleasing to me.); **gustar más** to prefer; see **gustar** in the index.

gusto *n.m.* taste, pleasure (synonyms: **el placer, la euforia, el júbilo, la satisfacción, la alegría**)

gym suit **el traje de gimnasio**

gymnasium **el gimnasio;** gymnastics **la gimnasia**

H

ha *pres. indic. of* **haber;** see **haber** in the index.

haber *v.* to have (used as an aux. v.; see **haber** in the index.) See also appendix.

había *imperf. indic. of* **haber; haber** + past part. **(participio)** of main v. gives you the *plup. indic.* of main v., *e.g.,* **había dado** had given; **había gastado** had spent; **había perdido** had lost; **se había perdido** had become lost, had gone astray, had gone the wrong way; **había recibido** had received; see **haber** in the index.

habíamos *imp. indic. of* **haber**

habitación *n.f.* room (where one lives)

habitar *v.* to inhabit, live (in), dwell, reside

hablando *pres. part.* (**gerundio**) *of* **hablar** *v.* to talk, speak; **hablará** *fut.,* **habló** *pret;* see **hablar** in the index.

habrá *fut. of* **haber;** there will be . . . ; see **haber** in the index.

hacer *v.* to do, make; **hace una hora** one hour ago; **hacerle una pregunta a una persona** to ask a person a question (to ask a question of someone); **hace veinte minutos que el médico está al lado de la señora Rodríguez.** The doctor has been at the (bed) side of Mrs. Rodríguez for twenty minutes; **hacer un gran servicio** to render (perform) a great service; see **hacer** in the index and the appendix.

hacía *imperf. indic. of* **hacer**

hacia *prep.* toward, to (in the direction of); **hacia él** toward him

haciendo *gerundio of* **hacer; La señora González está haciendoles preguntas a los alumnos de la clase.** Mrs. González is asking students questions in class; see **hacer** in the index.

haga, hagan *imper. & pres. sub. of* **hacer; Hágame el favor de . . .** Do me the favor of . . . (Please . . .); see **hacer** in the index and particular tenses and moods.

hair **el cabello;** haircut **un corte de pelo;** hairdresser **la peluquera, el peluquero;** hair styling salon **la peluquería**

half **la mitad**

hallar *v.* to find, come across; **hallarse** *refl.v.* to be found; **halle** *imper.* find; **La receta se halla . . .** The recipe is found . . . ; **hallado** *participio of* **hallar; hallé, halló** *pret.*

hallway **el pasillo**

ham **el jamón**

hambre *n.f.* **(el hambre)** hunger; **Tengo mucha hambre.** I'm very hungry; see **hambre** in the index.

hand **la mano;** hand over *v.* **entregar (gu)**

handsome *adj.* **hermoso, -a, -os, -as; guapo, -a, -os, -as**

happen *v.* **pasar, advenir**

happy *adj.* **contento, -a, -os, -as; feliz, felices**

hará, harán *fut. of* **hacer;** see **hacer** in the index.

has *pres. indic. of* **haber;** see **haber** in the index.

hasta *prep., adv.* up to, until; **hasta mañana** until tomorrow, see you tomorrow; **¡Hasta luego!** So long, see you later! **hasta que** *conj.* until

hat **el sombrero;** top hat **un sombrero de copa alta**

have *v.* **tener, haber (haber** is used as an aux. v.); to have a good time **divertirse (ie, i)** *refl.v.;* to have breakfast **tomar el desayuno;** to have lunch **almorzar (ue, c);** to have supper **cenar;** to have a lot of fun **divertirse mucho.**

hay *idiomatic v. form of* **haber** there is . . . , there are . . . ; see **hay** in the index.

haya *pres. sub. of* **haber; Cuando las haya encontrado . . .** When you have found them . . .

haz *imper. of* **hacer** *v.* to make, do; **Hazme caso.** Pay attention to me.

he *pron.* **él;** see the entry *pronouns* in the index.

he *pres. indic. of* **haber; haber** + past part. of main v. gives you the pres. perf. indic. of main v., *e.g.,* **he encontrado** I have found; **he gastado** I have squandered (spent); **he hecho** I have done, I have made; see the following entries in the index: **haber, hacer,** *participles.*

¡He aquí! Here is . . . ; Here it is . . . !

he who . . . **el que**

. . . (the one who . . .); see the following entries in the index: **el cual, el de, el que.**

head **la cabeza**

health **la salud**

hear *v.* **oír**

heart **el corazón**

hearth **el hogar**

Heavens! **¡Caramba!**

hecho *past part.* **(participio)** *of* **hacer; Tú has hecho . . .** You have done . . . ; **Tú no has hecho la lección.** You have not done the lesson; see **hacer** and *participles* in the index.

helado *n.m.* ice cream; **helar (ie)** *v.* to freeze

help *v.* **ayudar;** *as a n.,* **la ayuda**

hemos *pres. indic. of* **haber;** see **haber** in the index.

hen **la gallina;** cock, rooster **el gallo**

her *pron.* **ella** (as obj. of a prep.); *as dir. obj.,* **la;** *as poss. adj.* **su, sus;** see the entries *pronouns* and **su, sus** in the index.

here *adv.* **aquí;** Here is . . . **He aquí . . . ; Aquí tiene Ud. . . . ;** Here it is! **¡He aquí!**

herencia *n.f.* inheritance

hermana *n.f.* sister; **la hermanita** little sister; see the entry *diminutive endings -ito & -illo* in the index.

hermanito *n.m.* little brother; **hermano** *n.m.* brother

hermoso, -a, -os, -as *adj.* beautiful; **(contrario de hermoso: feo)**

hice *pret.,* **hiciera** *imp. sub. of* **hacer;** see **hacer** in the index.

hidden *adj.* **escondido, -a, -os, -as;** hide *v.* **esconder;** hide oneself *refl.v.* **esconderse**

hierba *n.f.* grass

hija *n.f.* daughter; **hija mía** (in direct address) my daughter; **hijo** *n.m.* son; **hijo mío** (in direct address)   my son; see the following entries in the index: **mío, mía, míos, mías, el mío, la mía.**

Hipócrates   Hippocrates (Ancient Greek physician)

hipócrita *n.m.f.* hypocrite

his *poss. adj.* **su, sus;** see the following entries in the index: *adjectives,* **su** and **sus.**

historia *n.f.* history, story

hit *v.* **golpear;** to hit against *v.* **dar contra**

hizo *pret. of* **hacer;** see **hacer** in the index.

hogar *n.m.* hearth, fireplace, home, residence

hoja *n.f.* leaf, sheet (of paper)

¡Hola! *interj.* Hey! Hi! Hello!

hold *v.* **tener;** see **tener** in the index.

hombre *n.m.* man; **todo un hombre**   all man, he-man

home   **el hogar;** in my home   **en mi casa**

hongo *n.m.* mushroom

honor *n.m.* honor

hop *v.* **saltar**

hope *v.* **esperar;** *as a n.,* **la esperanza;** hoping for   **en espera de**

hora *n.f.* hour, time; **¿Qué hora es?** What time is it?

horizontalmente *adv.* horizontally

horóscopo *n.m.* horoscope

horror *n.m.* horror, fright; **¡Qué horror!** Horrors! How awful! How terrible!

hot *adj.* **caliente; Hace calor.** It's warm, hot (weather)

house   **la casa**

how . . . ?   **¿Cómo . . . ?** See **¿cómo . . . ?** in the index.

how many . . . ? how much . . . ?   **¿Cuánto, -a, -os, -as . . . ?** See **cuanto, cuanta, cuantos, cuantas** in the index.

hoy *adv.* today

huevo *n.m.* egg; **un huevo pasado por agua**   soft boiled egg

hug   **el abrazo;** *as a v.* **abrazar (c)**

humo *n.m.* smoke

humorístico, -a, -os, -as *adj.* humorous

hundred *num.* **cien, ciento, cientos, cientas;** See these Spanish words and the entry *numbers* in the index.

hunger   **el hambre** *n.f.;* **Tengo mucha hambre.** I'm very hungry; see **tener** in the index.

hurl *v.* **echar**

husband   **el esposo, el marido**

hypocrite   **el (la) hipócrita**

I

I *pron.* **yo;** see the entry *pronouns* in the index.

iba *imperf. indic. of* **ir**

ice cream   **el helado; helar (ie)** *v.* to freeze

identificar (qu) *v.* to identify

if *conj.* **si;** see the entry *conjunctions* in the index; see also **si** *clauses* in the index.

iglesia *n.f.* church

igualmente *adv.* also, likewise, as well

ill *adj.* **enfermo, -a, -os, -as**

illuminate *v.* **alumbrar**

immediately *adv.* **inmediatamente, en seguida**

imperfecto *n.m. adj.* imperfect

importar *v.* to matter, be important; **No importa.** It doesn't matter.

in *prep.* **en;** in order (to)   **para;** in spite of   **a pesar de**

incertidumbre *n.f.* uncertainty

incesantemente *adv.* incessantly, without stopping

increíble *adj.* incredible, unbelievable

independencia *n.f.* independence

indeterminado *adj.* indefinite; **el artículo indeterminado**   indef. art.; see the entry *articles* in the index.

indicar (qu) *v.* to indicate, point out

indirect object   **complemento indirecto;** see the entry

attribute complement in the index.

infinitivo *n.m.* infinitive; see the entry *infinitives* in the index.

Inglaterra *n.f.* England

inglés *n.m.* English (language); *as an adj.,* **inglés, inglesa, ingleses, inglesas;** See the entries *name of language* and *nationality* in the index.

ingrato, -a, -os, -as *adj.* ungrateful

inhabit *v.* **habitar**

inheritance   **la herencia**

inmediatamente *adv.* immediately; see the entry *adverbs* in the index.

inquietar *v.* to worry

inquire *v.* **preguntar**

inscrita *adj.* inscribed, written

insistir *v.* to insist, persist

insolente *n.m.f., adj.* insolent, impertinent, "snippy"; **un insolente**   an insolent boy

inteligencia *n.f.* intelligence

inteligente *adj.* intelligent

interesante *adj.* interesting

intermission   **el entreacto**

interrumpe *pres. indic. of* **interrumpir** *v.* to interrupt

introduce *v.* **presentar**

introduction *n.f.* **introducción, presentación;** a letter of introduction   **una carta de presentación**

invierno *n.m.* winter

invitación *n.f.* invitation

invitar *v.* to invite

ir *v.* to go; see **ir** in the index and the appendix.

irse *refl.v.* to go away, leave

italics   **en letras cursivas**

izquierda *n.f.* left (as opposed to *right*)

J

jam   **la confitura**

jamón *n.m.* ham

jardín *n.m.* garden; **ej jardinero**   gardener

jeroglífico *n.m.* hieroglyph, rebus

jester   **el burlador**

jewel   **la alhaja, la joya**

jirafa *n.f.* giraffe
John **Juan**
join *v.* **unir**
Jorge George
joven *n., adj.* young; **jóvenes,** *pl.*
joy **la alegría, el gozo**
joya *n.f.* jewel, gem
Juana Jane, Jean, Jeanne; **Juanita** Jeannie
juega *pres. indic. of* **jugar (ue, gu)** *v.* to play
juego *n.m.* game; **juegos de manos** hand tricks
jugador, jugadora *n.m.f.* player
jugar (ue, gu) *v.* to play (a game or sport); **jugar al fútbol** to play soccer; **jugar al tenis** to play tennis; **jugar a los naipes** to play cards
jugo *n.m.* juice
juguete *n.m.* toy, plaything
julio *n.m.* July
jump *v.* **saltar**
junio *n.m.* June
juntar *v.* to join, connect
juntos, juntas *adj.* together
juramento *n.m.* oath

K

kangaroo **el canguro**
keep *v.* **guardar**; to stay in bed **guardar cama**
keep (a promise, a word) *v.* **cumplir**
key **la llave**
kid el **niño, la niña**
kill *v.* **matar**
kilómetro *n.m.* kilometer (about 0.62 mile)
kind (type, species) **la especie**
kiss *v.* **besar**; *as a n.,* el **beso**; to kiss your hand **besar la mano** (to express deep love, respect)
kitchen **la cocina**
kitten **el gatito**; see the entry *diminutive endings -ito & -illo* in the index.
knee **la rodilla**; kneeling **de rodillas**
knock *v.* **tocar (qu)**; to knock on the door **tocar a la puerta**

L

know *v.* **saber, conocer** (to be acquainted with); see **saber** and **conocer** in the index.

la *def. art. f.s.* the (**las,** *pl.*); *also dir. obj. pron.* her, you *f.,* it *f.;* **la de** that of, the one of; see *articles* and *pronouns* in the index.
lack *v.* **faltar**; *as a n.,* **la falta**; to be lacking *v.* **faltar**; see the entry **faltar** in the index.
lado *n.m.* side; **al lado de** at the side of; **al otro lado de la calle** on the other side of the street, across the street
ladrar *v.* to bark (dog)
lady **la dama**
lago *n.m.* lake
lama *n.m.* lama; *n.f.* mud, slime
lámpara *n.f.* lamp
land **la tierra**
language **la lengua**
lápiz *n.m.* pencil; **los lápices** *pl.*
large *adj.* **gran, grande**; see **gran, grande** in the index.
largo, -a, -os, -as *adj.* long
larguísimo, -a *adj.* very long; see the entry *absolute superlative* in the index.
las *def. art. f.pl.* the; *also dir. obj. pron.;* **las de** those of, the ones of; **Y las de mi marido.** And my husband's (and those of my husband); see *articles* and *pronouns* in the index; **las dos** the two, both
last *v.* **durar**; *as an adj.* **último, -a, -os, -as**; last night **anoche**; yesterday evening **ayer por la noche**; last year **el año pasado**; the last bid **la última oferta**
lástima *n.f.* pity; **¡Qué lástima!** What a pity!
late *adv.* **tarde**
later *adv.* **más tarde; luego**
laugh *v.* **reír(se)**; to laugh at **reírse de**

launch *v.* **botar**
lavar *v.* to wash (someone or something); **lavarse** *refl.v.* to wash oneself
le *obj. pron.;* see the entry *pronouns* in the index.
leaf **la hoja**
leap *v.* **saltar**
learn *v.* **aprender**; to learn to do something **aprender a** + inf.; to learn about **saber**
least *adv.* **menos**; at least **por lo menos**
leave *v.* **dejar** (to leave something or someone behind you); **partir, salir (de)**; see the entry *leave* in the index.
lección *n.f.* lesson; **las lecciones,** *pl.*
lectura *n.f.* reading (selection)
leche *n.f.* milk
leer (y) *v.* to read; **leerlo** to read it; **Voy a leerlo.** I'm going to read it.
left (as opposed to *right*) **la izquierda**
leg **la pierna**
legumbre *n.f.* vegetable
leí *pret. of* **leer (y)**
lejos *adv.* far
lemonade **la limonada**
lend *v.* **prestar**
lengua *n.f.* language
lentamente *adv.* slowly; see *adverbs* in the index.
les *obj. pron.;* see the entry *pronouns* in the index.
lesson **la lección; las lecciones,** *pl.*
let (go) *v.* **dejar**; see the entries **dejar** and *leave* in the index.
letra *n.f.* letter (of the alphabet); **en letras cursivas** in italics; **sopa de letras** alphabet soup
Let's . . . **Vamos a** + inf.; **Vamos a hablar** Let's talk; **Vamos a cantar** Let's sing; Let's begin **Vamos a comenzar;** Let's continue **Vamos a continuar;** Let's see **Vamos a ver (A ver);** Let's sit down **Vamos a sen-**

tarnos; Let's be serious! **¡Seamos serios!**

letter (of the alphabet) **la letra;** alphabet soup **la sopa de letras;** letter (that you write to someone) **la carta;** to mail (post) a letter **echar una carta al correo;** see the entry *letter writing* in the index.

levantar *v.* to raise (something or someone); **levantarse** *refl.v.* to raise oneself (to get up [oneself]); **Me levantaba . . .** I used to get up . . .

leyendo *pres. part.* **(gerundio)** of **leer (y)** *v.* to read; reading; **Pedro está leyendo.** Peter is reading.

leyera *imperf. sub.;* **leyó** *pret.* of **leer (y)**

libertad *n.f.* liberty

libra *n.f.* pound

library **la biblioteca**

librería *n.f.* bookstore

librero, librera *n.m.f.* bookseller

libro *n.m.* book

lie (falsehood, opposite of truth) **la mentira;** *v.* **mentir (ie, i)**

life **la vida**

light *v.* **alumbrar;** *as a n.,* **la luz; las luces,** *pl.*

like *v.* **gustar a; Me gusta la leche.** I like milk; see **gustar** in the index.

limonada *n.f.* lemonade

lindo, -a, -os, -as *adj.* pretty

line **la raya, la línea**

líquido n.m. liquid

listen (to) *v.* **escuchar; Escucho la música.** I'm listening to the music.

listo, -a, -os, -as *adj.* ready, prepared; clever

little (size) *adj.* **pequeño, -a, -os, -as;** little (not much in quantity) **poco**

live *v.* **vivir;** to reside, live (in), inhabit **habitar**

living room **la sala; el cuarto de estar**

lo *obj. pron. & neut. art.;* **lo mejor posible** the best possible; **lo que** what, which, that which; see the

entries **lo** and *pronouns* in the index.

lobby **el vestíbulo**

localidad *n.f.* seat, place (in a theater)

loco, -a, -os, -as *adj.* crazy; **estar loco** to be crazy; **volverse (ue) loco, -a** to go crazy; **La señora González dice:—¡Me vuelvo loca!** Mrs. González says:—I'm going crazy!

lomo *n.m.* back (of an animal)

long *adj.* **largo, -a, -os, -as** *adj.;* Long live . . . ! **¡Viva(n) . . . !**

Look! **¡Mira!** look (at) *v.* **mirar; ¡Miren mi programa!** Look at my program!

look for *v.* **buscar (qu); Busco mi libro.** I'm looking for my book; **Estoy buscando mi sombrero.** I'm looking for my hat; see **buscar** in the index.

los *def. art. m., pl. & dir. obj. pron.* the, them; see the entries *articles* and *pronouns* in the index.

lose *v.* **perder (ie);** to lose oneself *refl.v.* **perderse**

love *v.* **amar; Te amo, Juana.** I love you, Jean; *as a n.,* **el amor;** to be in love with **estar enamorado (enamorada) de**

luck **la fortuna; ¡Qué fortuna!** What luck!

luego *adv.* then, afterwards

lugar *n.m.* place; **en lugar de** in place of, instead of; **tener lugar** to take place; see **tener** in the index.

lunch *v.* **almorzar (ue, c);** *as a n.,* **el almuerzo**

lunes *n.m.* Monday; **el lunes** on Monday

luz *n.f.* light, daylight; **las luces,** *pl.*

LL

llamado *past part.* **(participio)** of **llamar** *v.* to call; **llamarse** *refl.v.* to call oneself, to call himself (herself), to be called, to be

named; **Me llamo Juan David.** My name is John David.

llave *n.f.* key

llegando *pres. part.* **(gerundio)** of **llegar (gu)** to arrive; **llegaron, llegué, llegó** *pret.;* **llegado** *participio*

llenar *v.* to fill; **lleno, -a, -os, -as** *adj.* full, filled

llevaba *imperf. indic.* of **llevar** *v.* to take (away), carry (away), transport, take (someone somewhere), wear; **llevarse** *refl.v.* to take long with oneself

llorar *v.* to weep, cry

llover (ue) *v.* to rain; **la lluvia** rain; **lloviendo** *pres. part.* **(gerundio); Está lloviendo.** It's raining·

M

macho *n.m., adj.* he-man, masculine, robust

madre *n.f.* mother; **la madre de Juana** Jane's mother; see the entry *possession with* **de** in the index.

madrugada *n.f.* dawn, daybreak; **de madrugada** at daybreak, at dawn

maestro, maestra *n.m.f.* teacher

magician **el mago**

magnificent *adj.* **magnífico, -a, -os, -as**

mail (post) a letter **echar una carta al correo;** see the entry *letter writing* in the index.

make *v.* **hacer;** to make a present of, to give as a gift *v.* **regalar;** see **hacer** in the index.

mal *n.m.* grief, evil, harm; *as an adv.,* poorly, badly; *as an adj.,* **mal, malo, -a, -os, -as** bad; see the entry **mal** in the index.

malgastar *v.* to spend foolishly, squander

mamá *n.f.* mom, mama

man **el hombre; Pedro es todo un hombre.** Peter is all man.

mandar *v.* to order, send,

command; **el man-do** command, order; see **mandar** in the index.

mano *n.f.* hand; **juegos de manos** hand tricks; **Deme la mano.** Give me your hand.

mantequilla *n.f.* butter

many *adj.* **mucho, -a, -os, -as;** so many **tanto, -a, -os, -as;** many people **mucha gente;** see the entries **mucho** and **tanto** in the index.

manzana *n.f.* apple

mañana *adv.* tomorrow; **hasta mañana** until tomorrow, see you tomorrow; *as a n.,* morning; **esta mañana** this morning; **todas las mañanas** every morning; **por la mañana** in the morning

mar *n.m. & f.* sea

maravilloso, -a, -os, -as *adj.* marvelous

marchar *v.* to march, walk, function, run (machine); **marcharse (a)** *refl.v.* to go away (to), leave (for)

María Mary

marido *n.m.* husband; synonym: **el esposo**

mark (grade) **la nota**

martes *n.m.* Tuesday; **el martes** on Tuesday

más adv. more; **el (la, los, las) más** the most; **más de** more than + a number; **más que** more than + no number; **sin más** without any more; **más tarde** later; **más que** more than; **más . . . que** more . . . than

matar *v.* to kill

match (sports), game **el partido**

mathematics **las matemáticas**

mayo *n.m.* May

mayor *adj.* older, bigger

mazo *n.m.* mallet

me *pron.* me, to me, myself; **Me gusta(n) . . .** I like . . . ; **Me gustaría(n) . . .** I would like . . . ; see *pronouns* and **gustar** in the index.

meal **la comida**

meaning **el significado;** meaningful *adj.* **significativo, -a, -os, -as**

meanwhile *adv.* **entretanto, mientras; mientras que** *conj.* as long as, while; **mientras tanto** meanwhile, (in the) meantime

meat **la carne**

mechón *n.m.* mesh, shock (of hair)

médico *n.m.* doctor

medio, media *adj.* half; **a las tres y media** at half past three; **media hora** (a) half (an) hour; **el medio** means, way, medium; **en medio de** in the middle of

Mediterráneo *n.m.* Mediterranean

mejor *adj.* better, best; **el (la) mejor, los (las) mejores** the best one(s); see **mejor/peor** in the index.

member **el miembro**

mend *v.* **reparar**

menor *adj.* younger

menos *adv.* less; **por lo menos** at least; **menos que** less than; **menos . . . que** less . . . than; see the entry **menos** and those that follow **menos** in the index.

mentir (ie, i) *v.* to lie, tell a lie

mentira *n.f.* lie, falsehood (opposite of truth)

merecer (zc) *v.* to merit, deserve

mes *n.m.* month

mesa *n.f.* table; **una mesita** little table; see the entry *diminutive endings -ito & -illo* in the index.

mexicano, -a, -os, -as *adj., n.* Mexican

mi *poss. adj.* my; see *possessive adjectives* and **mi, mis** in the index.

mí *pron.* me (used as obj. of a prep.); see the entry *pronouns* in the index.

middle **el medio;** in the middle of **en medio de**

miedo *n.m.* fear

miembro *n.m.* member

mientras (que) *conj.* while, meanwhile, as long as; see *conjunctions* in the index.

mil *num.* thousand; see the entries **mil** and *numbers* in the index.

milk **la leche**

mío; see this Spanish word and those that follow **mío** in the index.

¡Mira! *excl.* Look! **mirar** *v.* to look (at), watch; **mirando** *gerundio;* **Estoy mirando . . .** I'm looking (at) . . .

mis *poss. adj., pl.* my

mismo, -a, -os, -as *adj.* same

miss *v.* **faltar;** see **faltar** in the index.

misterioso, -a *adj.* mysterious

mitad *n.f.* half

modelo *n.m.* model

moderación *n.f.* moderation

moderno, -a, -os, -as *adj.* modern

modesto, -a, -os, -as *adj.* modest

modo *n.m.* manner, method, mode; **de todos modos** at any rate, anyhow

moho *n.m.* moss

moist *adj.* **mojado**

mom **la mamá**

moment **el momento, un rato, un instante**

Monday **el lunes;** on Monday **el lunes**

money **el dinero**

monstruoso, -a, -os, -as *adj.* monstrous

montaña *n.f.* mountain

month **el mes**

monument **el monumento**

morder (ue) *v.* to bite

more *adv.* **más;** more or less **más o menos;** see **más** in the index and those entries that follow **más;** see also **menos** in the index and those entries that follow **menos.**

moreno, morena *n.m.f. & adj.* dark, brunette

morir (ue, u) *v.* to die

morning la mañana; in the morning **por la mañana; todas las mañanas** every morning; *as an adv.,* tomorrow

mosca *n.f.* fly (insect)

moss **el moho**

mostrar (ue) *v.* to show; Be sure to read the introduction at the beginning of this vocabulary list.

mother **la madre**

motivo *n.m.* motive; **sin motivo** without a motive; **reírse sin motivo** to giggle

motorcycle **la motocicleta, la moto**

mountain **la montaña**

mouse **el ratón; los ratones,** *pl.*

movedizo, -a, -os, -as *adj.* moving, shifting

mover (ue) *v.* to move, stir

movies **el cine;** I'm going to the movies. **Voy al cine.**

much *adj., adv.;* **mucho, -a, -os, -as;** so much **tanto, -a, -os, -as;** much to do **mucho que hacer; muchas gracias** thank you very much; see **mucho** in the index and those entries that follow **mucho;** see also **tanto** in the index and those entries that follow **tanto.**

muchacha *n.f.* girl

muchacho *n.m.* boy

muchísimo *abs. superl.* of **mucho;** very much; see *absolute superlative* in the index.

muerde *pres. indic.* of **morder (ue)** *v.* to bite; see *stem-changing verbs* in the index.

muere *pres. indic.* of **morir (ue)** *v.* to die; see *stem-changing verbs* in the index.

muerte *n.f.* death

muerto *past part.* **(participio)** of **morir (ue)** *v.* to die; *as an adj.,* **muerto, -a, -os, -as** dead; see the entry *participles* in the index.

muestra *n.f.* sign

mueve *pres. indic.* of **mover (ue);** see *stem-changing verbs* in the index.

mujer *n.f.* woman; **las mujeres;** sinónimo: **la dama**

mumble *v.* **chistar**

mundo *n.m.* world; **todo el mundo** everybody; **el mundo entero** the whole world; see the entry **todo** in the index.

muñeca, muñeco *n.m.f.* doll, puppet; **un muñeco de nieve** snowman

murió *pret.* of **morir;** see *stem-changing verbs* in the index and read the introduction at the beginning of this vocabulary list.

mushroom **el hongo**

música *n.f.* music

must *v.* **deber;** see **deber** in the index.

mutter *v.* **chistar**

muy *adv.* very, much; see the entry **muy** in the index.

my *poss. adj.* **mi, mis;** my dear, my darling **querido mío, querida mía** (used in direct address, when speaking or writing to someone); see the following entries in the index: **mi, mis, mía, mío,** *possessive adjectives.*

mysterious *adj.* **misterioso, -a, -os, -as**

N

nacer (zc) *v.* to be born; see *orthographical changing verbs* in the index.

nada *indef. pron.* nothing, not anything; **de nada** you're welcome; **nada** requires **no** in front of the verb when **nada** is used as dir. obj.; does not require **no** in front of the verb when **nada** is in front of the verb; **No veo nada.** OR: **Nada veo.** I see nothing OR I don't see anything; see **nada** in the index.

nadar *v.* to swim

nadie *pron.* no one, nobody, not anyone, not anybody; see **nadie** in the index.

nail **el clavo;** fingernail **la uña**

name **el nombre; Mi nombre es José.** My name is Joseph; **Me llamo José.** My name is Joseph, *i.e.,* I call myself Joseph; to be named **llamarse** *refl.v.*

naranja *n.f.* orange (fruit)

nariz *n.f.* nose

naturalmente *adv.* naturally; see *adverbs* in the index.

náuseas *n.f.pl.* nausea; **sentir náuseas** *v.* to feel nausea

Navidad *n.f.* Christmas; **Feliz Navidad (Felices Navidades)** Merry Christmas

near *adv.* **cerca (de)**

neat *adj.* **neto**

necesario, -a, -os, -as *adj.* necessary

necesitar *v.* to need

neck **el cuello;** necktie **la corbata**

need *v.* **faltar, necesitar;** *as a n.,* **la necesidad;** see **faltar** in the index.

needle **la aguja**

negación *n.f.* negation, denial; see the entry *negation* in the index and the entries that begin with the word *negative.*

negro, -a, -os, -as *adj.* black

neighborhood **la vecindad**

nervioso, -a, -os, -as *adj.* nervous

net **la red**

neto *adj.* neat

nevando *pres. part.* **(gerundio)** of **nevar (ie)** *v.* to snow

never *adv.* **nunca**

new *adj.* **nuevo, -a, -os, -as**

New York **Nueva York**

newspaper **el periódico**

next *adj.* **próximo, -a, -os, -as;** the next time **la próxima vez;** next week **la semana que viene, la semana próxima**

ni *conj.* neither, nor; **ni siquiera** not even; **ni yo tampoco** me neither, nor I either

nice *adj.* **simpático, -a, -os, -as**

nieve *n.f.* snow; **un muñeco de nieve** snowman

night **la noche**; last night **anoche**; every night **todas las noches**

ninety *num.* **noventa**; see *numbers* in the index.

ningún, ninguno, -a, -os, -as *indef. pron., adj.;* see **ningún** in the index.

niña *n.f.* child (girl); **niñera** *n.f.* babysitter; **niño** *n.m.* child (boy); **Nosotros los niños . . .** We kids . . . ; **los niños, las niñas** children

¿No es verdad? Isn't it so? Isn't that right? Isn't it true?

no . . . más que nothing more than; see **más que** in the index.

¡No me diga! Don't tell me! You don't say!

nobody, no one *pron.* **nadie**; see **nadie** in the index.

noche *n.f.* night, evening; **todas las noches** every night, every evening; **por la noche** in the evening; **anoche** last night; **toda la noche** all night long

Noel el Papá Noel Santa Claus

noise **el ruido**

nombre *n.m.* name

none *indef. pron.* **ningún, ninguno**; see **ningún** in the index.

norteamericano, -a, -os, -as *adj. & n.* North American

North Pole **el Polo Norte**

nose **la nariz**

nosotros, nosotras *pron., m.f., pl.* we, us; **nosotros los niños . . .** we kids; see the entries *pronouns* and **nosotros los . . .** in the index.

nota *n.f.* mark, grade, note

note (short letter) **un billete, una nota, una esquela**; *as a v.,* **anotar**

notebook **el cuaderno**

nothing *indef. pron.* **nada**; nothing more than **no**

. . . más que; see **nada** in the index.

noticias *n.f., pl.* news

noun **el sustantivo**; see the entry *nouns* in the index.

nourish (feed) oneself *refl.v.* **alimentarse**

noventa *num.* ninety; see *numbers* in the index.

novia, novio *n.f.m.* sweetheart

novicio *n.m.* novice, beginner, apprentice

now *adv.* **ahora**; see *adverbs* in the index.

nueces *n.f.pl.* nuts, walnuts; **la nuez**

nuevo, -a, -os, -as *adj.* new; see *adjectives* in the index.

nunca *adv.* never; see *adverbs* in the index.

o

o *conj.* or

oath **el juramento**

obediente *adj.* obedient

obscuridad *n.f.* darkness

obstáculo *n.m.* obstacle

obtener *v.* to obtain; **obtenidas** obtained

ocasión *n.f.* occasion (time, opportunity); **en otra ocasión** some other time

ocupar *v.* to occupy

ochenta *num.* eighty; see *numbers* in the index.

ocho *num.* eight; **a las ocho y media** at 8:30; **a las ocho** at 8 o'clock; **a las ocho y cuarto** at 8:15

odd *adj.* **extraño, -a, -os, -as**; see *adjectives* in the index.

of *prep.* **de**; of course **por supuesto, ¡Claro!** of the **del, de la, de los, de las**; see the entry **de** in the index.

ofensivo, -a, -os, -as *adj.* offensive

oferta *n.f.* offer; **la última oferta** the last bid

offer *v.* **ofrecer (zc)**; *as a n.,* **la oferta**

office **la oficina**

oiga *pres. sub. & imp.,* **oigo** *pres. indic. of* **oír**

ojo *n.m.* eye; **guiñar el ojo** to wink

okay **de acuerdo**

old *adj.* **viejo, -a, -os, -as**; see *adjectives* in the index.

older, bigger *adj.* **mayor**

oler (hue) *v.* to smell; **oler a** to smell of

olfatear *v.* to smell

olor *n.m.* odor, smell, fragrance

olvidar (se) *v.* to forget; **No se olvide usted . . .** Don't forget . . .

omitir *v.* to omit

on *prep.* **en, sobre**; on (upon) entering **al entrar**; on (upon) seeing **al ver**; see the entries **al** and *prepositions* in the index.

once **una vez**

one *indef. art., adj.* **un, uno, una**; see the entry *articles* in the index.

one time **una vez**

only *adv.* **solamente, únicamente**; see *adverbs* in the index.

onward *adv.* **adelante**

open *v.* **abrir**; open, opened *as adj., & past part.* **(participio) abierto**

opinar *v.* to think, have an opinion

opposite *adj.* **contrario, -a, -os, -as**; **lo contrario** the opposite; see **lo** in the index.

or *conj.* **o, u**

oración *n.f.* sentence; *pl.,* **oraciones**

orange (fruit) **la naranja**

orar *v.* to pray

orden *n.m.* order; **en el orden** in (proper, correct) order

ordenar *v.* to arrange, put in proper order

ordinario, -a, -os, -as *adj.* ordinary

orientar *v.* to orient, instruct, explain

orilla *n.f.* shore, edge, brink, border

oro *n.m.* gold

os See the entry *pronouns* in the index.

osar *v.* to dare, venture

oso *n.m.* bear (animal)

otro, -a, -os, -as *adj.* other, another, others; **otra vez** again, once more; **en otra ocasión** some other time

ought (to) *v.* **deber**; see **deber** in the index.

outside *adv.* **afuera**

owe *v.* **deber**; see **deber** in the index.

oye *pres. indic.* of **oír**; **oyendo**, *gerundio* of **oír**; **oyera** *imperf. sub.* of **oír**

P

Pablo Paul

paciencia *n.f.* patience

package **el paquete**

padre *n.m.* father; **padre mío** my father (used in dir. address); **los padres** parents; see **mío** in the index.

pagar (gu) *v.* to pay (for)

página *n.f.* page (of a book)

pagué *pret.* of **pagar (gu)**

pail **el cubo, la cubeta**

paint *v.* **pintar**; paintbrush (artist's) **el pincel**

país *n.m.* country (nation); see **país** in the index.

pájaro *n.m.* bird; *sinónimo:* **ave** *n.f.*

palabra *n.f.* word

pálido, -a, -os, -as *adj.* pale

palm reader, palmist **la quiromántica, el quiromántico**

pan *n.m.* bread; **pan tostado** toast; **panadería** *n.f.* bakery

pane (window) **el cristal**

papá *n.m.* pop, papa, dad; **el Papá Noel** Santa Claus

paquete *n.m.* package, parcel

para *prep.* for, in order (to) + inf.; **para que** *conj.* in order that, so that; **para que** is a conj. that requires the sub. in the verb form in the following clause; see the entries *conjunctions*, **para,** and *subjunctive* in the index.

parada *n.f.* stop; **parada del**

autobús bus stop; **parada de taxis** taxi stand

parade **el desfile**

paragraph **el párrafo**

paraguas *n.m., s.pl.* umbrella; (*cf.* **para** + **aguas**)

parar *v.* to stop (someone or something); **pararse** *refl.v.* to stop (oneself); **una parada del autobús** a bus stop; **parada de taxis** (or **de coches**) taxi stand

parcel **el paquete**

pardon *v.* **perdonar; Perdóneme.** Pardon me; forgive me.

parecer (zc) *v.* to appear, seem

paréntesis *n.m.* parenthesis

parents **los padres**

párpado *n.m.* eyelid

párrafo *n.m.* paragraph

part **la parte; parte, parten** *pres. indic.* of **partir** *v.* to leave; **partes por todas partes** everywhere

participar *v.* to participate

partido *n.m.* game, match (sports)

partir *v.* to leave, depart, divide, split; **Vamos a partir.** Let's leave.

party **la fiesta, la tertulia**

pasado *past part.* (*participio*) of **pasar** *v.* to pass (by), happen, spend (time); **pasado, -a, -os, -as** *adj.* past; **un huevo pasado por agua** soft boiled egg

pasatiempo *n.m.* pastime, hobby

pasillo *n.m.* corridor, hallway

pass (by) *v.* **pasar**

pastel *n.m.* pastry; **pastelería** *n.f.* pastry shop

pata *n.f.* paw (of an animal); leg (of furniture)

patatas fritas *n.f., pl.* fried potatoes; also **papas fritas**

patience **la paciencia**

pay (for) *v.* **pagar (gu)**; pay one's compliments to *v.* **saludar;** to pay attention **prestar atención, hacer caso**

pedazo *n.m.* piece

pedestrian **el peatón**

pedir (i) *v.* to request, ask for; see **pedir** in the index.

Pedro Peter

pegado *participio* of **pegar** *v.* to stick, paste, cling

película *n.f.* film (movie); **el cine** movies; **Me gustaría ir al cine.** I would like to go to the movies.

peligro *n.m.* danger; *as an adj.,* **peligroso, -a, -os, -as** dangerous

pelo *n.m.* hair

peluquero, peluquera *n.m.f.* hairdresser, hair stylist; **peluquería** *n.f.* hairdressing salon

pen **la pluma**

pena *n.f.* grief, sorrow

pencil **el lápiz; los lápices,** *pl.;* pencil sharpener **el (los) sacapuntas**

penetrar *v.* to penetrate

pensar (ie) *v.* to think; **pensar en** to think of (about); **pensó** *pret.;* **pensar + inf.** to intend (to) + inf.; **pensar preparar** to intend (plan) to prepare

people **la gente;** many people **mucha gente**

peor See **peor/mejor** in the index.

pequeño, -a, -os, -as *adj.* little, small, short (size); see **pequeño** in the index.

perder (ie) *v.* to lose, to waste; **perdido,** *participio*

perdonar *v.* to pardon, forgive, excuse; **Perdóname (Perdóneme).** Pardon me.

perfil *n.m.* profile; **de perfil** side view

performance **la representación**

perhaps *adv.* **tal vez, acaso;** see *adverbs* in the index.

periódico *n.m.* newspaper

permit *v.* **permitir, dejar;** see **dejar** and **permitir** in the index.

pero *conj.* but; see *conjunctions* in the index.

persona *n.f.* person (**una persona** applies to a man or woman)

pertenecer (zc) *v.* to belong to

281

perro *n.m.* dog; **el perrito** little dog, doggie; see the entry *diminutive endings -ito & -illo* in the index.

pesar *v.* to weigh; **el pesar** sorrow, regret; **a pesar de** in spite of, despite

pescar (qu) *v.* to fish; **el pescado** fish (that you catch, cook, and eat); **el pez** fish (swimming in water), *pl.,* **los peces**

peseta *n.f.* peseta (monetary unit of Spain); **el peso** (one of several Latin American monetary units)

Peter **Pedro**

petición *n.f.* request

pez *n.m.* fish; see the entry **pescar (qu)** above in this list.

pharmacy **la farmacia**

piano *n.m.* **piano**

pick up *v.* **recoger (j)**

picture **el cuadro**

pide *imper.* of **pedir (i)** *v.* to ask for, request; **pidió** *pret.;* **Pídeselos a ella.** Ask her for them. **Pídeselos a él.** Ask him for them.

pie *n.m.* foot; **estar de pie** to stand, be standing

pie **el pastel, la tarta**

piece **el pedazo, la pieza**

piedra *n.f.* stone

pienso *pres. indic.* of **pensar (ie);** read the introduction at the beginning of this vocabulary list.

pierdo *pres. indic.* of **perder (ie);** read the introduction at the beginning of this vocabulary list!

pierna *n.f.* leg

pieza *n.f.* piece; play (theatrical); coin (of metal)

pig **el cerdo**

pincel *n.m.* artist's paintbrush

pinchar *v.* to puncture, prick

pintar *v.* to paint

pintor *n.m.,* **pintora** *n.f.* painter

pipa *n.f.* pipe

piscina *n.f.* swimming pool

pista *n.f.* track (race)

pitch *v.* **echar**

pity **una lástima**

pizarra *n.f.* chalkboard

place *v.* **colocar (qu), poner;** *as a n.,* **la localidad** (in a theater), **el lugar;** in place of **en lugar de;** to take place **tener lugar;** see **tener** in the index.

placer *n.m.* pleasure

plácido, -a, -os, -as *adj.* content, happy, placid

plato *n.m.* dish, plate

play *v.* **jugar (gu)** (a game or sport); **tañer** (play a stringed musical instrument); **tocar (qu)** (play a non-stringed musical instrument); *as a n.,* **la comedia** (theater), **la pieza** (theater)

playa *n.f.* beach, seashore

player (record) **el (los) tocadiscos;** *in sports,* **jugador, jugadora**

plaything **el juguete**

pleasant *adj.* **agradable; grato, -a, -os, -as; simpático, -a, -os, -as** please *v.* **agradar, complacer, dar gusto, placer;** please **por favor;** **Siéntese, por favor.** Sit down, please; to be pleasing to **gustar a;** see **gustar** in the index.

pleased *adj.* **contento, -a, -os, -as**

pleasure **el placer, el gusto**

plentiful *adj.* **abundante**

pluck (a stringed musical instrument) *v.* **tañer**

pluma *n.f.* pen

pobre *adj.* poor

pocket **el bolsillo**

poco, -a, -os, -as *adj., adv.* little (not much in quantity); **en pocos días** in a few days; see **poco** in the index.

poder (ue, u) *v.* to be able; **¿Podemos entrar?** May we come in? See **poder** in the index.

point out *v.* **indicar (qu), enseñar**

poison **el veneno**

polish *v.* **pulir**

Polo Norte *n.m.* North Pole

pollo *n.m.* chicken

pond **el estanque**

poner *v.* to put, place; **ponerse a + inf.** to begin + inf.; **ponerse** *refl.v.* to put on (clothing); **ponerse rojo** to blush (become, turn red)

ponga *pres. sub.,* **pongo** *pres. indic.* of **poner;** put

pool (swimming) **la piscina**

poor *adj.* **pobre, pobres**

pop **el papá**

por *prep.* for, by; **por favor** please; **por ejemplo** for example; **por lo general** in general, generally; **¿por qué . . . ?** why? **por la noche** in the evening; **por todas partes** everywhere; **por lo menos** at least; **por supuesto** of course; see **por** and **para** in the index.

pork **la carne de cerdo;** pig **el cerdo**

porque *conj.* because; see *conjunctions* in the index.

port **el puerto**

porvenir *n.m.* future

posar *v.* to perch; **posados** perched

posesivo, -a, -os, -as *adj.* possessive; see the entries *possession* and *possessive* in the index.

posible *adj.* possible

post (mail) a letter **echar una carta al correo**

postage stamp **un sello postal, un sello de correo;** also **estampilla**

postre *n.m.* dessert

potencial *n.m.* conditional (verb form in the conditional)

pound **la libra**

práctica *n.f.* practice; **practicar (qu)** *v.* to practice

prattle *v.* **charlar**

pray *v.* **orar, rezar, rogar**

precioso, -a, -os, -as *adj.* precious

preciso, -a, -os, -as *adj.* precise, accurate, exact; **Es preciso + inf.** It is necessary + inf. **Es preciso estudiar para aprender.** It is necessary to study in order to learn.

predilecto, -a, -os, -as *adj.* favorite

preferir (ie, i) *v.* to prefer

pregunta *n.f.* question; **preguntar** *v.* to ask, inquire, question

premio *n.m.* prize; **el primer premio** first prize

preocupes *imper. of* **preocupar** *v.* to preoccupy; **preocuparse** *refl.v.* to worry; **No te preocupes.** Don't worry.

preparación *n.f.* preparation

preparar *v.* to prepare; **prepararse** *refl.v.* to prepare oneself, get ready

preposición *n.f.* preposition; see *prepositions* in the index.

present **el presente;** present progressive **el presente progresivo** (verb tense); *as a n.,* gift **el regalo**

presentación *n.f.* presentation, introduction; **una carta de presentación** a letter of introduction

presentar *v.* to present, display, show, introduce

preserves (jam) **la compota**

prestar *v.* to lend; **prestar atención a** to pay attention to

pretty *adj.* **bonito, -a, -os, -as; lindo, -a, -os, -as, guapo, -a, -os, -as**

prick *v.* **pinchar**

priest **el cura;** also **el sacerdote, el padre**

primavera *n.f.* spring; see *seasons of the year* in the index.

primer, primero, -a, -os, -as *adj.* first; **el primer día** the first day; **el primer libro** the first book; **Es el primero de junio.** It's June 1st.; see **primer/primero** in the index.

primo, prima *n.m.f.* cousin

principiar *v.* to begin, start

principio *n.m.* beginning; **al**

principio at first, in (at) the beginning; **A buen fin no hay mal principio.** All's well that ends well.

prisa *n.f.* haste; **tener prisa** to be in a hurry; see **tener** in the index.

prize **el premio; el primer premio** first prize; see **primer/primero** in the index.

probar (ue) *v.* to test, try

problem **el problema**

proclaim *v.* **proclamar**

profesión *n.f.* profession

profesor, profesora *n.m.f.* professor, teacher

program **el programa**

prohibir *v.* to prohibit

prometí *pret. of* **prometer;** see *preterit* in the index.

promise *v.* **prometer;** *as a n.,* **la promesa;** to keep a promise **cumplir una promesa**

prompt *adj.* **pronto, -a, -os, -as; pronto** *is also an adv.,* quickly

promulgate *v.* **proclamar**

pronombre *n.m.* pronoun; **el pronombre relativo** relative pronoun; see the entry *pronouns* in the index.

pronounce *v.* **pronunciar;** to pronounce distinctly **articular;** see *pronunciation of Spanish sounds* in the index.

pronto *adv.* quickly, fast; *as adj.* prompt, quick, fast

pronunciación *n.f.* pronunciation; see *pronunciation of Spanish sounds* in the index.

propiedad *n.f.* property

proverb **el proverbio, el refrán (los refranes), el dicho;** see *proverbs* in the index.

próximo, -a, -os, -as *adj.* next; **la próxima vez** the next time; **la semana próxima** next week

prueba *n.f.* test; **probar (ue)** *v.* to test, try

pude *pret. of* **poder (ue)** *v.* to be able; see **poder** in the index; also read the in-

troduction at the beginning of this vocabulary list.

pueblo *n.m.* town, (people)

puede *pres. indic. of* **poder (ue); Puedes ir a verla.** You can go to see her; see **poder** in the index.

puerta *n.f.* door

puerto *n.m.* port

pues *adv.* well, then

pulir *v.* to polish

pull away *v.* **arrancar (qu)**

puncture *v.* **pinchar**

puntear *v.* to dot, mark a point, a dot

punto *n.m.* point, period; **en punto** on the dot, on the button; **Son las tres en punto.** It's exactly three o'clock. It's three o'clock sharp, on the dot, on the button.

pupil **el alumno, la alumna**

purchase *v.* **comprar**

purse **la bolsa**

pusieron *pret. of* **poner** *v.* to put, place; **ponerse** *refl.v.* to put on (clothing).

puso *pret. of* **poner**

put *v.* **colocar (qu), poner;** put on (clothing) **ponerse** *refl.v.*

Q

que *conj.* that; *as a rel. pron.* who, which, whom; *as an adj.,* what, which; **¡Qué almuerzo!** What a lunch! **¿Qué discos?** What records? **¡Qué discos!** What records! **¡Qué hombre!** What a man! **¡Qué clase!** What a class! **¡Qué lástima!** What a pity! What a shame! **¿Qué tal?** How are things? See the entries **qué** and **lo que** in the index.

quedar(se) *v.* to remain, stay; **¿Nos quedamos o partimos?** Shall we stay or leave? See **quedar/quedarse** in the index.

quédese *imper. of* **quedarse**

quemar *v.* to burn, fire; **quemado** *adj. & past part. (participio)*

querer (ie) *v.* to want, wish; **querer a** *v.* to like; see **querer** in the index.

querida mía, querido mío my dear (darling); see the entry **mío** and the entries that follow **mío** in the index.

querrá *fut.* of **querer; querría** *potencial of* **querer;** see **querer** in the index and read the introduction at the beginning of this vocabulary list.

question *v.* **preguntar;** *as a n.,* **la pregunta;** to ask a question **hacer una pregunta;** see **hacer** in the index.

Queta nickname for Henrietta, Harriet

quick *adj.* **pronto, -a, -os, -as;** quickly *adv.* **pronto;** see *adjectives* and *adverbs* in the index.

quien, quién *pron.* who, he (she) who

quiero *pres. indic. of* **querer;** see **querer** in the index.

química *n.f.* chemistry

quinta *ordinal num.* fifth; see *numbers* in the index.

quiromántica *n.f.* palmist, palm reader

quisiera *imperf. sub. of* **querer; Quisiera hablar.** I would (should) like to speak (talk); read the introduction at the beginning of this vocabulary list; see **quisiera** in the index.

quite *pres. sub. & imper. of* **quitar** *v.* to remove

R

rabbit **un conejo**

race *v.* **correr;** race track **la pista**

rain *v.* **llover (ue);** *as a n.,* **la lluvia**

raise (something or someone) *v.* **levantar;** raise (lift) oneself *refl.v.* **levantarse**

rama *n.f.* branch (of a tree)

rasgado, -a, -os, -as *adj.* torn

rato *n.m.* moment, short while, short time

ratón *n.m.* mouse; **los ratones**

raya *n.f.* line; **rayar** *v.* to scratch out, cross out; **Ráyelas.** Cross them out.

razón *n.f.* reason; **tener razón** to be right (as opposed to being wrong)

read *v.* **leer (y);** reading selection **la lectura**

ready *adj.* **listo, -a, -os, -as**

real *adj.* real, royal

really *adv.* **de veras, realmente, verdaderamente**

rebus **el jeroglífico**

recaer *v.* to fall over

receipt **el recibo;** to acknowledge receipt **acusar recibo**

receive *v.* **recibir**

receta *n.f.* recipe; prescription

recibido *past part.* **(participio)** *of* **recibir** *v.* to receive

recibo *n.m.* receipt, acknowledgment; **acusar recibo** to acknowledge receipt

recobrar *v.* to retrieve, get back, recover

recoger (j) *v.* to gather, collect, pick up, take, catch

recognize *v.* **reconocer (zc)**

recomienda *pres. indic. of* **recomendar** *v.* to recommend

record (that you play on a record player) **el disco;** record player **el (los) tocadiscos**

recover *v.* **recobrar**

red *n.f.* net

red *adj.* **rojo, -a, -os, -as**

redondo, -a, -os, -as *adj.* round; **la redonda** neighborhood; **a la redonda** round and round, roundabout, all around

reemplazar (c) *v.* to replace; **Reemplace Ud.** . . . Replace . . . , Substitute . . .

reflexivo, -a, -os, -as *adj.* reflexive; see the word *reflexive* in the index.

refrán *n.m.* proverb, refrain, saying; **los refranes;** see

refranes in the index.

refrigerador *n.m.* refrigerator

regalar *v.* to give as a present, to make a present of, to give as a gift; **el regalo** gift, present

regla *n.f.* rule

regresar *v.* to return, go (come) back, regress

reír(se) *v.* to laugh; **reír a carcajadas** to burst out laughing; **reírse sin motivo** to giggle

rejilla *n.f.* grid

rejoice *v.* **alegrarse (de)**

reloj *n.m.* watch, clock

rellenar *v.* to fill; **rellenado** filled

remain *v.* **quedar(se)**

remember *v.* **recordar (ue); acordarse (ue) de**

remitir *v.* to remit, forward, transmit

reparar *v.* to mend, repair; notice, observe

repaso *n.m.* review

repeat *v.* **repetir (i)**

repente *n.m.* impulse, sudden movement; **de repente** suddenly

repetí *pret.,* **repite** *pres. indic. of* **repetir (i)**

replace *v.* **reemplazar (c); Replace . . . Reemplace Ud.** . . .

reply *v.* **contestar, responder;** *as a n.,* **la respuesta, la contestación**

reponerse *refl.v.* to put itself back, restore itself

representación *n.f.* representation, show, performance; **las representaciones**

representar *v.* to represent

request (ask for) *v.* **pedir (i);** *as a n.,* **la petición**

require *v.* **exigir (j)**

reserva *n.f.* reserve, reservation

reside *v.* **habitar;** residence **el hogar**

respect *v.* **estimar;** *as a n.,* **el respecto**

responder *v.* to reply, respond, answer

responsable *adj.* responsible

respuesta *n.f.* reply, answer, response

rest *v.* **descansar;** see also **cansado** in this vocabulary list.

restaurante *n.m.* restaurant

restricción *n.f.* restriction

resultado *n.m.* result

retrieve *v.* **recobrar**

return (go back) *v.* **regresar, volver (ue);** to return (something to someone or some place) *v.* **devolver (ue); Voy a devolver este libro a la biblioteca.** I'm going to return this book to the library.

revelación *n.f.* revelation; **revelar** *v.* to reveal

revés *n.m.* reverse

review *v.* **repasar;** as a *n.*, el **repaso**

revoltijo *adj.* disordered, wild, crazy, twisted mass of hair style

revuelto, -a *adj.* disordered, wild crazy hair style

rezar *v.* to pray; *sinónimo:* **orar**

rice **el arroz**

rich, *adj.* **rico, -a, -os, -as**

riddle **una adivinanza**

ridículo, -a, -os, -as *adj.* ridiculous

ríe, ríen *pres. indic.,* **rieron** *pret. of* **reír(se)**

right (as opposed to *left*) **la derecha;** right (privilege) **el derecho;** to be right **tener razón**

río *n.m.* river; *also, pres. indic. of* **reír(se)**

roast beef **el rosbif**

rodilla *n.f.* knee; **de rodillas** kneeling

rogando praying; *pres. part. (gerundio) of* **rogar (ue)** *v.* to pray

rojo, -a, -os, -as *adj.* red; **ponerse rojo** to blush

Roma Rome

romper *v.* to break, shatter, tear; **roto** *past part.*

room **la habitación** (where one lives), **el cuarto;** bathroom **el cuarto de baño;** living room **la sala, el cuarto de estar**

ropa *n.f.* clothes, clothing

rosbif *n.m.* roast beef

roto *past part. of* **romper**

round *adj.* **redondo, -a, -os, -as**

row (of seats) **la fila**

rubbish **la basura**

rubio, rubia *n. & adj.* blond

ruego *pres. indic. of* **rogar (ue)**

ruido *n.m.* noise

rule **la regla**

run *v.* **correr;** run (machine) *v.* **marchar**

S

sábado *n.m.* Saturday; **el sábado pasado** last Saturday

sabelotodo *n.* **la señora Sabelotodo** Mrs. Know-it-all

saber *v.* to know (a fact), know how; see **saber** and **conocer** in the index.

saborear *v.* to taste, savor; **el sabor** taste, flavor; **sabroso, -a, -os, -as** *adj.* tasty, savory, delicious

sabremos *fut. of* **saber**

sacapuntas *n.m., s.pl.* pencil sharpener

sacar (qu) *v.* to take out (something), to get

sad *adj.* **triste**

sala *n.f.* room (large) living room; **la sala de clase** classroom; **la sala de ventas** sales room

salchicha *n.f.* sausage

salchichón *n.m.* sausage (thick, large); **los salchichones**

saldrá *fut. of* salir (de) *v.* to go out (of), leave (from)

sale *pres. indic. of* **salir (de)**

sale **una venta;** auction sale **una venta pública**

sales room **la sala de ventas**

saleslady **la vendedora;** salesman **el vendedor**

salga *imper.,* **salgo** *pres. indic. of* **salir**

salieron, salió *pret. of* **salir (de)** *v.* to leave (from), to go out (of) + dir. obj. noun or pron. **Pedro sale de casa.** Peter leaves the

house. Peter goes out of the house; see **salir (de)** in the index.

saltar *v.* to jump, leap, hop, spring

salud *n.f.* health

saludar *v.* to greet, pay one's compliments to, salute **¡Saludos!** Greetings!

same *adj.* **mismo, -a, -os, -as**

San Nicolás Saint Nicholas (Santa Claus)

sand **la arena**

sandwich **el bocadillo;** in some Latin American countries, **un sandwich**

sastre *n.m.* tailor

satisfecho, -a, -os, -as *adj.* content, satisfied; **satisfacer** *v.* to satisfy

Saturday **el sábado;** last Saturday **el sábado pasado**

sausage **la salchicha;** thick, large sausage **el salchichón**

savor (to taste) *v.* **saborear**

say *v.* **decir;** to say goodbye to *refl.v.* **despedirse (i) de;** a saying **un dicho, un proverbio, un refrán;** see the following entries in the index: **dicho,** *sayings in Spanish.*

scare away *v.* **espantar**

scene **la escena**

school **la escuela**

scream *v.* **gritar**

se See **se** in the index.

sé *pres. indic. of* **saber;** see **saber** in the index.

sea *imper. & pres. sub. of* **ser; ¡Sea usted razonable!** Be reasonable! **sea . . . sea . . .** whether . . . whether

sea **el (la) mar;** seashore **la playa**

¡Seamos serios! Let's be serious! **seamos** *imper. & pres. sub. of* **ser**

search *v.* **buscar (qu)**

seat **el asiento; la localidad** (in a theater)

secar (qu) *v.* to dry, wipe dry; **seco, seca** *adj.* dry

second *num.* **segundo;** see *numbers* in the index.

secreto *n.m.* secret

see *v.* **ver;** See you later! So long! **¡Hasta luego!**

seguir (i) *v.* to follow, continue

según according to; **según convenga** according to what is appropriate

seguramente *adv.* surely; see *adverbs* in the index.

seguro, -a, -os, -as *adj.* sure; **de seguro** surely

select *v.* **seleccionar, escoger (j)**

sell *v.* **vender**

sello (postal), sello de correo *n.m.* postage stamp

semana *n.f.* week; **la semana pasada** last week; **la semana que viene, la semana próxima** next week

sencillo, -a *adj.* simple

send *v.* **enviar (í);** to send for **enviar por**

sentado, -a *adj.* sitting down, seated

sentarse (ie) *refl.v.* to sit down; **se sentaron** *pret.;* **¡Siéntense Uds.!** Sit down!

sentence **la oración, las oraciones; la frase**

sentido *n.m.* meaning, sense; **sentimiento** *n.m.* sentiment, feeling

sentir (ie, i) *v.* to feel; **sentir náuseas** *v.* to feel nausea

señor *n.m.* gentleman, sir, Mr.

señora *n.f.* lady, woman, Mrs.

señoras y señores ladies and gentlemen

señores *n.m.pl.* Mr. and Mrs., gentlemen

señorita *n.f.* young lady, Miss

separar *v.* to separate, detach, sort, set apart

ser *v.* to be; see **ser** and **estar** in the index and the appendix.

será *fut.* of **ser**

serio, -a, -os, -as *adj.* serious

seriously *adv.* **gravemente;** see *adverbs* in the index.

serve *v.* **servir (i);** see **servir para** in the index.

servicio *n.m.* service; **hacer un gran servicio** to render (perform) a great service

serviste *pret.* of **servir (i);** see **servir para** in the index.

sesenta *num.* sixty; see *numbers* in the index.

set apart *v.* **separar**

setenta *num.* seventy; see *numbers* in the index.

several *adj.* **varios, -as**

Sevilla Seville

sexto, sexta *num.* sixth; see *numbers* in the index.

shampoo **el champú**

shape *v.* **formar**

sharpener (pencil) **el (los) sacapuntas**

shatter *v.* **romper;** *past part.,* **roto**

she *pron.* **ella;** see *pronouns* in the index.

shifting *adj.* **movedizo, -a, -os, -as**

shine *v.* **brillar;** The sun is shining. **Hace (Hay) sol**

ship **un barco, un buque**

shirt **la camisa**

shoe **el zapato;** shoeshop **la zapatería**

shore **la orilla, la costa, la playa**

short *adj.* **pequeño, -a, -os, -as** (persons); **corto, -a, -os, -as** (things)

short story **el cuento**

shout *v.* **gritar**

shovel **la pala**

show *v.* **enseñar, mostrar (ue), presentar;** *as a n.,* **el espectáculo, la representación** (theatrical)

shriek *v.* **gritar**

si *conj.* if; see *conjunctions* and **si** *clauses* in the index and the appendix.

sí *adv.* yes

sick *adj.* **enfermo, -a, -os, -as;** to be sick **estar enfermo**

sidewalk café **una terraza de café-restaurante**

sido *past part.* **(participio)** of **ser;** see **ser** and **estar** in the index and the appendix.

siembra *pres. indic.* of **sembrar (ie)** *v.* to sow, plant, scatter

siempre *adv.* always; see *adverbs* in the index.

siéntate (tú), siéntese (Ud.), siéntense (Uds.) *imper.* of **sentarse (ie)** Sit down; **siento** *pres. indic.* of **sentir (ie, i)** *v.* to feel; **Lo siento.** I'm sorry.

siesta *n.f.* siesta, nap, rest

significado *n.m.* meaning, significance

significativo, -a, -os, -as *adj.* meaningful

signo *n.m.* sign

sigo *pres. indic.* of **seguir (i)** *v.* to follow, continue

siguiente *adj.* following

sílaba *n.f.* syllable

silencio *n.m.* silence

silla *n.f.* chair

sillón *n.m.* armchair

silly thing **una tontería**

simpático, -a, -os, -as *adj.* pleasant, nice

simple *adj.* **sencillo**

sin *prep.* without; **sin cuidado** carelessly; **sin más por el momento** without any more for the moment; **sin embargo** nevertheless, all the same, just the same; see *prepositions* and **sin** in the index.

sinceramente *adv.* sincerely; see *adverbs* in the index; see also *letter writing* in the index.

sing *v.* **cantar;** singer **el (la) cantante**

sinónimo *n.m.* synonym

siquiera *conj.* although, even; **ni siquiera** not even; see *conjunctions* in the index.

sirvió *pret.* of **servir (i);** read the introduction at the beginning of this vocabulary list.

sister **la hermana;** little sister **la hermanita;** see *diminutive endings* -ito & -illo in the index.

sketch v. **describir, dibujar;** *as a n.,* **el dibujo**

skirt **la falda**

sky **el cielo**

sleep v. **dormir (ue, u); Está durmiendo.** He (She) is sleeping.

slim *adj.* **esbelto, -a, -os, -as;** see *adjectives* in the index.

slowly *adv.* **despacio, lentamente;** see *adverbs* in the index.

small *adj.* **pequeño, -a, -os, -as** (in size); **poco, -a, -os, -as** (in quantity); see *adjectives* in the index.

smash v. **aplastar**

smell v. **oler (hue), olfatear;** fragrance **el olor**

smile v. **sonreír (i)**

smoke v. **fumar;** *as a n.,* **el humo**

snack **el bocadillo**

snatch v. **arrancar (qu)**

snow v. **nevar (ie);** *as a n.,* **la nieve;** snowman **un muñeco de nieve**

so *adv.* **tan;** see *adverbs* in the index; see also **tan** in the index.

So long! See you later! **¡Hasta luego!**

so many, so much *adj.* **tanto, -a, -os, -as;** see **tanto** in the index.

so so *adv.* **así, así**

soberbio *adj.* superb

sobre *prep.* on, upon; see *prepositions* in the index.

soccer *n.m.* **fútbol;** soccer player **el (la) futbolista**

social gathering **la tertulia**

soft boiled egg **un huevo pasado por agua**

sol *n.m.* sun; **Hace sol (Hay sol).** It's sunny; **tomar el sol** to take a sun bath

solamente *adv.* only; see *adverbs* in the index.

sold *past part.* **(participio)** & *adj.* **vendido, -a, -os, -as; vender** v. to sell

soldado *n.m.* soldier

solely *adv.* **únicamente;** see *adverbs* in the index.

solo, -a, -os, -as *adj.* alone; only one; one single

solución *n.f.* solution

sombrero *n.m.* hat; **sombrero de copa alta** top hat

some *adj.* **algún, alguno, -a, -os, -as;** see **algún** in the index.

somebody, someone *pron.* **alguien;** see **alguien** in the index.

something *pron.* **algo;** see **algo** in the index.

sometimes *adv.* **algunas veces**

somos *pres. indic.* of **ser;** see **ser** in the index and the appendix.

son *pres. indic.* of **ser;** see **ser** in the index and the appendix.

son **el hijo**

sonar (ue) v. to ring, sound

song **la canción**

sonido *n.m.* sound

sonreír (i) v. to smile; **sonríe** *pres. indic.* of **sonreír**

sopa *n.f.* soup; **sopa de letras** alphabet soup

sorpresa *n.f.* surprise

sótano *n.m.* cellar

soul **el alma** *(f.);* **un alma bondadosa** a kind, helpful soul

sound **el sonido**

soup **la sopa;** alphabet soup **sopa de letras**

soy *pres. indic.* of **ser;** see **ser** in the index and the appendix.

Spain **España**

Spanish (language) **el español;** *as an adj.,* **español, española, españoles, españolas;** Spanish class **la clase de español;** see *name of language* and *nationality* in the index.

speak v. **hablar;** see **hablar** in the index.

special *adj.* **especial**

species **la especie**

spectator **el espectador, la espectadora**

speed **la velocidad**

spend (money) v. **gastar;** to spend foolishly **malgastar;** spend (time) v. **pasar**

spite of, in **a pesar de**

spoil v. **estropear**

sponge biscuit (cake) **el bizcocho**

sport **el deporte**

spring (leap, jump) v. **saltar;** spring (season of year) **la primavera**

squander v. **malgastar**

stadium **el estadio**

stairs, stairway **la escalera**

stamp (postage) **el sello postal, el sello de correo**

stand v. **estar de pie;** see **estar** in the index and the appendix.

start v. **empezar (ie; c), principiar, comenzar (ie; c) (a + inf.)**

state **el estado;** the United States **los Estados Unidos**

statue **la estatua**

stay v. **quedar(se);** see **quedar** in the index.

steak **el bistec**

stomach **el estómago;** stomach ache **un dolor de estómago**

stone **la piedra**

stop (someone or something) v. **parar;** bus stop **la parada del autobús**

store **la tienda**

storm **la tempestad**

story (literature) **el cuento, la historia**

strange *adj.* **extraño, -a, -os, -as**

straw **la paja**

street **la calle, la vía pública**

structure *n.f.* **estructura**

student **el (la) estudiante, el alumno, la alumna**

study v. **estudiar**

stupid *adj.* **tonto, -a, -os, -as;** stupid thing **una tontería**

su, sus *poss. adj.* his, her, your, their; see *possessive adj.,* **su, sus** in the index.

suave *adj.* suave, soft, smooth

subastador *n.m.* auctioneer

sube *pres. indic.* of **subir (a); ¿Por dónde se sube?** Which way do we get (go) upstairs? Which

287

way does one get (go) up-
stairs?

subir (a + dir. obj.) *v.* to get
in, get into, get on, go up

subject **el sujeto;** subject
(studied, courses of
study) **la asignatura**

subjuntivo *n.m.* subjunctive;
see *subjunctive* in the index.

substitute *v.* **sustituir (y)**

sucesivamente *adv.* suc-
cessively; **y así sucesivamente** and so on and so
forth

sucio, -a, -os, -as *adj.* dirty;
el más sucio de the dirt-
iest in; see **de** *(after a superlative)* in the index.

suddenly *adv.* **de repente,
de pronto;** all of a sudden **de repente;** see *adverbs* and **de** in the index.

suele *pres. indic. of* **soler
(ue)** *v.* to be accustomed
to, to be in the habit of

suena *pres. indic. of* **sonar
(ue)**

suffer *v.* **sufrir**

sufficient *adj.* **bastante**

sugar **el azúcar**

summer **el verano**

sumo *adj.* highest, greatest;
sinónimo; **supremo**

sun **el sol;** take a sun
bath **tomar el sol**

sunglasses **las gafas (contra el sol); gafas ne-
gras** dark eyeglasses;
also **gafas de sol**

superb *adj.* **soberbio**

superlativo *adj.* superlative;
see *superlative* in the index.

supersticioso, -a, -os, -as
adj. superstitious

supiste *pret. of* **saber**

suplicar (qu) *v.* to supplicate, implore, entreat

supper **la cena**

supremo, -a *adj.* supreme,
greatest; sinónimo: **sumo**

Sure! **¡Claro!** surely **de
seguro, seguramente**

surprise **la sorpresa**

sustantivo *n.m.* substantive
(noun); see *nouns* in the
index.

sustituyendo *pres. part.
(gerundio) of* **sustituir (y)**
v. to substitute

suyo suya See these
words in the index.

sweep *v.* **barrer**

sweets (candies) **los
dulces**

swim *v.* **nadar;** swimming
pool **la piscina;** swimming *n.* **la natación; Me
gusta la natación.** I like
swimming; see **gustar** in
the index.

syllable **la sílaba**

sympathy **la condolencia;**
a letter of sympathy **una
carta de condolencia;**
see *letter writing* in the index.

synonym **el sinónimo**

T

taberna *n.f.* tavern

table **la mesa;** little table **la mesita;** see *diminutive endings -ito & -illo* in
the index.

tailor **el sastre**

take *v.* **tomar;** take away **llevar;** take a trip **hacer un
viaje;** take a sun bath **tomar el sol;** take out
(something) **sacar (qu);**
take place **tener lugar**

tal *adj., adv.* such, as, so;
tal vez perhaps; **¿Qué
tal?** How are things? **tal
como** such as

talento *n.m.* talent

talk *v.* **hablar;** see **hablar** in
the index.

tall *adj.* **alto, -a, -os, -as**

también *adv.* also, too; see
adverbs in the index.

tampoco *adv.* neither, nor;
Ni yo tampoco. Me neither. Nor I, either.

tan . . . como as . . . as;
tan *adv.,* so; see **tan** and
*comparatives & superla-
tives* in the index.

tanto, -a, -os, -as *adj.* so
many, so much; see **tanto**
in the index.

tañer *v.* to pluck, play (a
stringed musical instru-
ment)

tarde *adv.* late; **más
tarde** later; *as a n.,* **la
tarde** afternoon

tarea *n.f.* homework

tarjeta *n.f.* card

taste *v.* **saborear;** *as a n.,* **el
gusto**

tasty *adj.* **sabroso, -a, -os,
-as**

tavern **la taberna**

te *refl., dir. & indir. obj. pron.*
you, to you; see *pronouns*
in the index.

tea **el té**

teach *v.* **enseñar**

teacher **el profesor, la
profesora, el maestro, la
maestra**

team **el equipo**

tear (rip, break) *v.* **romper**

teatro *n.m.* theater; **al teatro** at (to) the theater

telefonear *v.* to telephone

teléfono *n.m.* telephone; **llamar por teléfono** to telephone

televisión *n.f.* television;
television set **el televisor**

tell *v.* **decir**

tema *n.m.* theme, topic

temer *v.* to fear, dread

tempestad *n.f.* tempest,
storm

tenderly *adv.* **cariñosamente**

tendero *n.m.* shopkeeper

tendrá *fut. of* **tener** *v.* to
have, hold, possess; **tener
dolor de cabeza** to have
a headache; **tener
que** to have to; **tener
prisa** to be in a hurry;
tenga *imper. & pres. sub.
of* **tener; Tenga paciencia.** Have patience (Be pa-
tient)

tenis *n.m.* tennis

tent **la tienda**

Teodoro Theodore

tercer, tercero, tercera *ordinal num.* third; **el tercer
día, el tercer libro** the
third day, the third book;
see **tercer, tercero** in the
index.

terminado *participio of* **terminar** *v.* to end, terminate,
finish; **terminarse** *refl.v.* to

be all over, to be finished, to be ended (by itself); **Se terminó.** It's finished (all over).

ternera *n.f.* veal; **las chuletas de ternera** veal chops

terraza *n.f.* terrace; **una terraza de restaurante** sidewalk restaurant

tertulia *n.f.* party, social gathering

test **la prueba**

than See this word in the index.

thank you, thanks **gracias;** thank you very much **muchas gracias;** thanks to **gracias a**

that *neuter dem. adj.* **eso;** see **eso** in the index.

That's right! **¡Eso es!**

theater **el teatro**

their *poss. adj.* **su, sus;** see *possessive adj.,* **su, sus** in the index.

theme **el tema**

Theodore **Teodoro**

there *adv.* **allá;** see *adverbs* in the index.

there is . . . , there are . . . **Hay . . . ;** see **hay** in the index.

thing **la cosa**

think *v.* **pensar (ie); pensar en** to think of (about)

third *ordinal num.* **tercer, tercero, tercera; el tercer día, el tercer libro** the third day, the third book; see *numbers* in the index.

this See the entries *adjectives* and *pronouns* in the index.

thousand *num.* **mil;** see *numbers* in the index; see also **mil** in the index.

throw *v.* **echar;** throw away **botar**

ti *pron.* you *(as obj. of a prep.);* **para ti** for you; see *pronouns* in the index.

tía *n.f.* aunt

tie, necktie **la corbata**

tiempo *n.m.* weather, time; **a tiempo** on time

tienda *n.f.* tent, store

tiene *pres. indic. of* **tener**

tierra *n.f.* land

timbre *n.m.* tone; **tocar el timbre** to ring the bell. **Toca el timbre.** The bell rings; see **tocar** in the index.

time **la hora, el tiempo, la vez**

tímido, -a, -os, -as *adj.* timid

tío *n.m.* uncle

tipo *n.m.* type, kind

tired *adj.* **cansado, -a, -os, -as; estar cansado** to be tired

to *prep.* **a;** see **a** and *prepositions* in the index.

to her, to him, to you, to them, *etc. indir. obj. pronouns;* see *pronouns* in the index.

toasted bread **el pan tostado**

tocadiscos *n.m., s.pl.* record player

tocador *n.m.* dresser (for clothing)

tocar (qu) *v.* to touch, knock (on a door), to play (a musical instrument); **le toca a alguien** to be someone's turn; **Me toca a mí.** It's my turn; **¿A quién le toca?** Whose turn is it? **Toca el timbre.** The bell rings; see **tocar** in the index.

toda, -o, -os, -as, *adj.* all; **toda la fortuna** the whole fortune, all the fortune; **por todas partes** everywhere; **todo un hombre** all man, he-man; **todas las noches** every night, every evening; **de todos modos** at any rate, anyhow; **Todos tenemos gustos diferentes.** We all have different tastes; **todo el mundo** everybody; **todo el día** all day long, the whole day; **todos los días** every day; see **todo** in the index.

today *adv.* **hoy;** see *adverbs* in the index.

todo *pron.* all; **todos** everybody, all; see **todo** in the index.

together *adj.* **junto, -a, -os, -as**

tolerar *v.* to tolerate

tomar *v.* to take, have (a meal); **tomar el desayuno** to have breakfast; **tomar una decisión** to make a decision; **tomar el sol** to take a sun bath

tome *pres. sub. & imper. of* **tomar**

tomorrow *adv.* **mañana**

tontería *n.f.* stupid thing, foolish thing

tonto, -a, -os, -as *adj.* foolish, stupid

too *adv.* **también**

topic **el tema**

torn *adj.* **rasgado, -a, -os, -as**

toro *n.m.* bull

tortilla *n.f.* small cake; omelet; also a typical Mexican food

tortuga *n.f.* turtle

tostado *adj.* toasted

touch *v.* **tocar (qu);** see **tocar** in the index.

town **el pueblo**

toy **el juguete**

trabajar *v.* to work; **el trabajo** the work

track (race) **la pista**

traducción *n.f.* translation

traducir *v.* to translate; **al traducir** upon (on) translating; see **al** in the index.

traduzca *pres. sub. & imper. of* **traducir**

traer *v.* to bring; **traigo** *pres. indic. of* **traer; traeré** *fut.*

traffic (vehicles) **la circulación**

traje *n.m.* suit; **el traje de gimnasio** gym suit; **traje** *is also pret. of* **traer; trajera** *imp. sub. of* **traer**

tras *prep.* behind, after

tratar (de + obj.) to treat (of; a subject); **tratar de + inf.** to try + inf.

travel *v.* **viajar**

tree **el árbol**

trip **el viaje;** to take a trip **hacer un viaje;** see **hacer** in the index and the appendix.

triste *adj.* sad

truck **el camión**

truth **la verdad;** true **verdad, cierto**

tú *subj. pron., 2nd pers. s.* you; see *pronouns* in the index.

tu, tus *poss. adj.* your; see *adjectives* and **tu, tus** in the index.

Tuesday **el martes**

turtle **la tortuga**

tuve *pret. of* **tener**

tuyo, tuya, -os, -as *poss. pron.* yours; see **tuyo** in the index.

twenty *num.* **veinte;** see *numbers* in the index.

twice **dos veces**

two *num.* **dos;** two times **dos veces;** see *numbers* in the index.

type (kind, species) **la especie, el tipo, la clase**

U

u *conj.* or

Ud. (usted), Uds. (ustedes) *prons.* you; see *pronouns* in the index.

ugly *adj.* **feo, -a, -os, -as**

último, -a, -os, -as *adj.* last; **la última oferta** the last bid; contrario de último: **primero**

umbrella **el (los) paraguas;** *cf.* **para + aguas**

un, uno, una *indef. art.* a, an, one; see the following entries in the index: *articles (definite & indefinite), numbers,* **un, uno.**

una *imper. & pres. sub. of* **unir** *v.* to unite, join, match

unbelievable *adj.* **increíble**

uncle **el tío**

undergo *v.* **sufrir**

underneath *adv.* **debajo (de)**

understand *v.* **comprender**

ungrateful *adj.* **ingrato, -a, -os, -as**

únicamente *adv.* only, solely

único, única *adj.* only, solitary, single, alone

unir *v.* to connect, unite, join, bind, attach, match

United States **los Estados Unidos**

universidad *n.f.* university

until (up to) *adv.* **hasta;**

conj., **hasta que;** see *adverbs* and *conjunctions* in the index.

up (to go) *v.* **subir (a)**

upon *prep.* **sobre;** upon entering **al entrar;** upon seeing **al ver;** see **al** in the index.

usar *v.* to use, utilize, employ, wear; **usarse** *refl.v.* to be used

use *imper. & pres. sub. of* **usar**

útil, útiles *adj.* useful

utilize *v.* **utilizar, usar**

uva *n.f.* grape

V

va *pres. indic. of* **ir; se va** *pres. indic. of* **irse;** see **ir, irse** in the index.

vaca *n.f.* cow

vacaciones *n.f., pl.* vacation

vacío, -a, -os, -as *adj.* empty

valer *v.* to be worth

value *v.* **estimar**

vamos *pres. indic. of* **ir; Vamos a + inf.** Let's + verb; **Vamos a atacar . . .** Let's attack; **Vamos a buscar . . .** Let's search; **Vamos a comenzar . . .** Let's begin; **Vamos a comer . . .** Let's eat; **Vamos a continuar . . .** Let's continue; **Vamos a partir . . .** Let's leave; **Vamos a sentarnos . . .** Let's sit down; **Vamos a ver . . .** Let's see; **¿Vamos al cine?** Shall we go to the movies? **Vámonos** Let's leave; see **ir** in the index and appendix.

varios, varias *adj.* various, several

vas *pres. indic. of* **ir**

vaso *n.m.* drinking glass

ve, ven *v.forms of* **ir, venir, ver**

veal **la ternera;** veal chops **las chuletas de ternera**

veces *n.f., pl.* times; **una vez** once, one time; **dos veces** twice, two times

vecindad *n.f.* neighborhood, vicinity

vegetable **la legumbre**

veinte *num.* twenty; see *numbers* in the index.

velocidad *n.f.* speed, velocity; **en toda velocidad** at full speed

ven *v.form of* **ver** and **venir**

vende *pres. indic. of* **vender; se vende . . .** is sold; **se venden . . .** are sold

vendedor *n.m.* salesman

vendedora *n.f.* saleslady, saleswoman

vender *v.* to sell; **vendió** *pret.*

vendido *participio of* **vender**

vendrá *fut. of* **venir**

veneno *n.m.* poison

¡Vengan . . . ! *imper. of* **venir;** Come!

venir *v.* to come

venta *n.f.* sale; **una venta pública** auction sale

ventana *n.f.* window; **en la ventana** in (at) the window

venture *v.* **osar**

veo *pres. indic. of* **ver** *v.* to see; **¡Vamos a ver! (¡A ver!)** Let's see!

verá *fut. of* **ver**

verano *n.m.* summer

veras *n.f., pl.* reality, truth; **de veras** really, in truth

verás *fut. of* **ver**

verbo *n.m.* verb

verdad *n.f.* truth (true); **¿No es verdad?** Isn't it so? Isn't it true?

verdaderamente *adv.* truly, really; **verdadero** *adj.* real, true; see *adjectives* and *adverbs* in the index.

verticalmente *adv.* vertically

very *adv.* **muy;** *adj.* **mucho, -a, -os, -as;** very truly yours **atentamente;** thank you very much **muchas gracias;** see *adjectives, adverbs,* and *letter writing* in the index.

ves *pres. indic. of* **ver**

vestíbulo *n.m.* vestibule, entrance hallway, lobby

vestidos *n.m.* clothes, clothing

vestir (i) *v.* to dress (some-

290

one or something); **vestirse** *refl.v.* to dress oneself

¡Vete! *imper. of* **irse** *refl.v.* to go away; Go away! Shoo! Scat!

vex *v.* **enojar**

vez *n.f.* time; *pl.,* **veces; una vez** once, one time; **dos veces** twice, two times; **muchas veces** many times; **tal vez** perhaps; **la próxima vez** next time; **la primera vez** the first time

viajar *v.* to travel; **hacer un viaje** to take a trip

viceversa *n.m., adv.* vice versa

vicinity **la vecindad**

vida *n.f.* life

viejo, -a, -os, -as *adj.* old

viendo *gerundio of* **ver;** seeing

viene *pres. indic. of* **venir**

viento *n.m.* wind (air); **Hace viento.** It's windy.

vientre *n.m.* belly

viernes *n.m.* Friday

vieron *pret. of* **ver**

vigorosamente *adv.* vigorously

viniendo *pres. part.* (gerundio) *of* **venir**

vino *pret. of* **venir;** *as a n.,* wine

vio *pret. of* **ver**

violentamente *adv.* violently

visitar *v.* to visit

visitó *pret. of* **visitar**

viste *v. form of* **ver** and **vestir (i)**

visto *participio of* **ver**

¡Viva(n) . . . ! Long live . . . !

vive, vivo *pres. indic. of* **vivir** *v.* to live

vocabulario *n.m.* vocabulary

voice **la voz; en voz baja** in a low voice, softly; **en voz alta** in a loud voice, loudly

volando *pres. part.* (gerundio) *of* **volar (ue)** *v.* to fly

volver (ue) *v.* to go (come) back, return; **volverse** *refl.v.* to turn around, to become; **volverse loco** to go crazy **¡Me**

vuelvo loco (loca)! I'm going crazy! *also means* to turn sour (as in milk).

voy *pres. indic. of* **ir; Voy a leerlo.** I'm going to read it.

voz *n.f.* voice; **en voz baja** in a low voice, softly; **en voz alta** in a loud voice, loudly

vuelo *pres. indic. of* **volar (ue)**

vuelto *past part.* (participio) *of* **volver (ue)**

vuelvo *pres. indic. of* **volver (ue); Vuelva a poner . . .** Put back . . .

W

wait (for) *v.* **esperar;** waiting for **en espera de**

waiter **el camarero**

wake up (someone) *v.* **despertar (ie);** wake up (oneself) *refl.v.* **despertarse (ie)**

walk *v.* **andar, caminar, marchar;** *as a n.,* **el paseo;** to take a walk **dar un paseo**

walnut **la nuez;** *pl.,* **las nueces**

want *v.* **desear, querer (ie);** to be wanting *v.* **faltar;** see **faltar** and **querer** in the index.

war **la guerra**

wardrobe **el guardarropa**

warm *adj.* **caliente;** warmth **el calor;** It's warm today. **Hace calor hoy.**

wash (something or someone) *v.* **lavar;** wash oneself *refl.v.* **lavarse**

waste *v.* **gastar**

watch *v.* **mirar;** *as a n.,* **el reloj**

water **el agua,** *f.;* **agua fresca** fresh water

wave **la onda**

we *pron.* **nosotros, -as;** see *pronouns* in the index.

wear *v.* **llevar, usar;** wear out *v.* **gastar**

weather **el tiempo**

Wednesday **el miércoles**

week **la semana;** last week **la semana pa-**

sada; a week from . . . **de . . . en ocho días;** next week **la semana que viene, la semana próxima**

weekend **el fin de semana;** Have a nice weekend! **¡Pase Ud. un buen fin de semana!**

weep *v.* **llorar**

welcome *v.* **dar la bienvenida a;** you're welcome **no hay de qué, de nada**

well *adv.* **bien;** well then **pues;** see *adverbs* in the index.

wet *adj.* **mojado**

what, which, that which *adj., pron.* **que, qué, lo que, el cual,** *etc.*

What a (an) . . . ! See *what a . . . ! what an . . . !* in the index.

What time is it? **Qué hora es?**

when *adv.* **cuando**

where *adv.* **donde, ¿dónde?** where to? **¿adónde?** See **adondequiera, donde, dondequiera,** and *adverbs* in the index.

whether *conj.* **si;** whether . . . or **ya sea . . . o;** see *conjunctions* in the index.

while *adv.* **mientras;** *conj.* **mientras que;** after a little while **al poco rato;** see *adverbs* and *conjunctions* in the index.

white *adj.* **blanco, -a, -os,-as**

who *pron.* **que, quien, quienes, el cual, los cuales, el que**

whose is . . . ? whose are . . . ? See these entries in the index.

why *adv.* **¿por qué?**

wife **la esposa**

win *v.* **ganar**

wind (air) **el viento; Hace viento.** It's windy.

window **la ventana;** window pane **el cristal**

wine **el vino**

wink *v.* **guiñar el ojo**

winter **el invierno**

wipe dry *v.* **secar (qu)**

wish *v.* **desear, querer**

with *prep.* **con, de**

woman **la mujer**

word **la palabra**

work *v.* **trabajar;** *as a n.,* **el trabajo**

worry *v.* **inquietar, preocuparse**

worship *v.* **adorar**

worth (to be) *v.* **valer**

would like *cond.,* **querría** *cond. of* **querer;** I would like an ice cream. **Me gustaría un helado.**

Wow! **¡Ay!**

wrist watch **el reloj**

write *v.* **escribir;** *past part.* **(participio) escrito**

Y

y *conj.* and; see **e** and **y** in the index.

ya *adv.* already; **Ya sabemos que . . .** We already know that . . . ; **ya sea . . . o** whether . . . or

ya que *conj.* inasmuch as, since

year **el año;** last year **el año pasado**

yellow *adj.* **amarillo, -a, -os, -as**

yendo *pres. part.* **(gerundio)** *of* **ir**

yes *adv.* **sí;** yes, of course **¡Claro que sí!**

yesterday *adv.* **ayer;** yesterday afternoon **ayer por la tarde;** yesterday evening **ayer por la noche;** day before yesterday **anteayer**

yet *adv.* **todavía;** not yet **todavía no**

yo *pron.* I; see *pronouns* in the index.

you *pron.* **tú, Ud., vosotros, Uds.,** *etc.;* see *pronouns* in the index.

You don't say! **¡No me diga!**

young *adj.* **joven;** *pl.,* **jóvenes;** younger **menor**

your *poss. adj.,* **tu, tus, su, sus, el (la, los, las) de Ud.,** *etc.;* see *possessive adjectives* in the index.

yours *poss. pron.;* see *possessive pronouns* and *yours* in the index.

Z

zapatería *n.f.* shoe store

zapatero *n.m.* shoemaker

zapato *n.m.* shoe

Zodiaco *n.m.* Zodiac

Index